T0306278

THE ILLUSTRATED HISTORY OF THE

INCAS

THE ILLUSTRATED HISTORY OF THE INCAS

LEGENDS, MYTHS AND CULTURE OF THE ANCIENT NATIVE PEOPLES OF THE ANDES AND SOUTH AMERICA, WITH MORE THAN 500 PHOTOGRAPHS

DAVID M JONES

LORENZ BOOKS

CONTENTS

INTRODUCTION

When Francisco Pizarro and the Spanish conquistadors arrived in the Andes in 1532 they found a civilization of great sophistication and wealth. Well-planned cities with storehouses and complex ceremonial architecture, irrigated lands and an established system of agriculture, transport and communication routes, and an organized, hierarchical society were all signs of an intelligent and civilized people. Starting from the Cuzco Valley, the Incas had gradually expanded their power to form an empire, conquering and integrating land and settlements from the coastal plains inland to the rainforest. From its early roots it had developed from small farming villages to large cities with sophisticated forms of organization.

Below: A Middle Horizon bridge-spout effigy vessel from Tiwanaku with distinctive jaguar coat. Jaguars were revered by sierra cultures.

Yet despite these momentous achievements, the Incas' reign lasted less than 100 years. To understand how the Incas rose from around 40,000 people to form the largest empire in South America, we need to understand the land they lived in, their way of life, their conquests and spread of influence and, perhaps more than anything else, their religion and myths, for these lay behind so many aspects of Inca life and influenced everything from agriculture to temple building.

ANDEAN CIVILIZATION

South America comprises many dramatically different geological areas. From high Altiplanos to low coastal valleys, from lush, dense rainforest to dry, barren deserts, each landscape offers different rewards and challenges and shapes the lifestyles of its inhabitants. Such differences, and the geographical isolation of many settlements, led to different peoples in South America developing at different paces. At the same time, however, cultures in various large areas were aware of each other, and they developed links through trade, political alliance, conquest and the diffusion of ideas through direct or indirect contact.

Ancient South American cultures that can be described as 'civilizations' were confined to the Andes mountains and nearby western coastal valleys and deserts. Elsewhere, South American peoples did develop quite sophisticated societies and beliefs.

Above: Descending the Inca Trail from the Second Pass, the walker approaches the ridge-top ruins of the Sayaqmarka compound.

However, they did not build monumental ceremonial centres or cities, or develop technology of quite the same level of complexity as the Andean kingdoms and empires, and are therefore not defined as 'civilizations'.

This book concentrates on the 'Andean Area', where civilizations evolved in the sierras and adjacent foothills and coastal regions, north to south from the Colombian–Ecuadorian border to the northern half of Chile and east to west from the Amazonian Rainforest to the Pacific coast. City-states, kingdoms and empires evolved in this area, based on maize and potato agriculture and the herding of llamas, alpacas and vicuñas. The concentration of civilization in the Andean Area was due in part to the geography of the region. Within a relatively small area there is a range of contrasting landscapes, from Pacific ocean-bound coastal plains and deserts, to coastal and foothill valleys, to high mountain valleys and plateaux, to the eastern slopes running down to the edges of the rainforests and high pampas of Argentina.

A key factor in the development and endurance of these civilizations was access to and control of water, which became

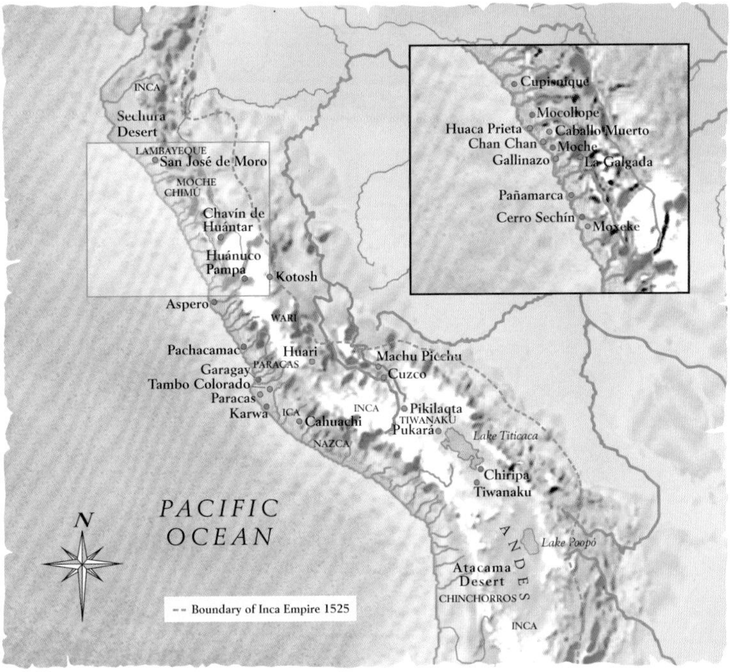

Above: General map of the Inca Empire and important sites, showing how the empire stretched the length of the Andes Mountains.

important not only functionally but also symbolically and religiously. Water was essential for agriculture, and people in naturally dry regions developed a sophisticated form of agriculture based on complex irrigation technologies, often combined with land terracing. As a result, a wide variety of crops was grown in both lowland and highland regions, which led to the development of trade between the two. The development of agriculture and trade led to different cultures specializing in different products – and not only essentials such as food but increasingly non-essential items such as ceramics and items with religious significance. As a result, these cultures developed into complex and orderly societies with sophisticated religious beliefs and structures. Thus empires are born.

SOURCES OF INFORMATION

Our knowledge of the Incas (and other South American peoples) comes from a variety of sources: from the Inca record-keepers themselves (both the *amautas* and the *quipucamayoqs*), from contemporary Spanish accounts and from archaeological investigations, both recent and in the past. All give us fascinating insights into a rich and colourful civilization with legendary rulers, a civil war, sacred places, mystical lines and images in the desert, imposing temples and evocative symbols, and a literal belief that the Incas will one day return to power.

Below: Reed fishing boats and huts on Lake Titicaca, between Peru and Bolivia. Such vessels and materials are still used today.

REMAINS OF EMPIRES

The buildings constructed by the cult of Chávin de Huántar in the Early Horizon, the Wari and Tiwanaku empires in the Middle Horizon and the Incas in the Late Horizon can be seen and marvelled at today, along with other remains from the Andean Area. Such remains help us to understand the architectural and engineering skills of the various peoples, their social organization, their main forms of occupation and trade, and their religions.

Chávin de Huántar was a pilgrimage centre, established *c.*900BC as a U-shaped centre (others include La Galgada and Sechín Alto, both built in the Preceramic Period). Its remains show a labyrinth of passages and galleries.

Other fantastic pre-Inca sites are the Gateway of the Sun at the Tiwanaku Akapana Temple; the Paracas Cavernas cemetery, known for its desiccated mummies; the Moche centre of Cerro Blanco, where two large ceremonial platforms – the Huacas del Sol and de la Luna – were built; and the Late Intermediate Period Chimú city of Chan Chan, which comprised a complex of compounds (*ciudadelas*) containing residences for the reigning king and earlier deceased kings.

Famous remains from the Incas themselves include the city of Cuzco, the 'navel of the world', rebuilt in the plan of a crouching puma, and site of the Coricancha Temple; Huánuco Pampa, a seat of provincial admininstration; and the dramatically sited hilltop sacred city of Machu Picchu, a massive landmark on the Inca Trail. In addition, Inca engineers constructed an impressive array of roads and bridges, as well as enabling land to be developed for farming through the construction of terraces and irrigation canals.

Above: Cotton-embroidered textile from the Early Horizon Paracas culture, with a figure reminiscent of the Chavín Staff Deity.

ANDEAN RELIGION

The legends and myths of the Andean peoples, together with the remains found by archaeologists, constitute a record of ancient Andean religious belief.

Religious beliefs and deities were intimately linked with the forces of nature. Ancient South American peoples felt compelled to explain the important things in their universe, beginning with where they came from and their place in the larger scheme of things. To do this they developed accounts of what they could see in the sky and in the surrounding landscape to help them understand which things were important, and how and why this was so. Thus, the Inca god Inti belonged to the life-giving force of the sun, and Lake Titicaca, the most sacred of waters, was seen as the origin of life.

The explanatory accounts of these concepts provided a framework for living and for understanding and relating to the mysteries of the world.

COMMON BELIEFS AND IMAGERY

There were long sequences of traditional development among Andean and western coastal peoples and cultures, helped by trading and social relationships between the two. Many deities were almost universal, although given different names by different cultures, but some were individual and distinct, belonging to particular peoples and civilizations.

Left: Gold hammered sheet-metal sun figure from Tiwanaku. The rayed head is reminiscent of the Gateway of the Sun.

Nevertheless, long-standing places of ritual pilgrimage linked areas and regions and persisted despite the rise and fall of kingdoms and empires. The site and oracle of coastal Pachacamac, for example, had such potency and precedence that even the Incas recognized and revered it, although they felt compelled to establish their imperial authority by building a temple to the sun god Inti in its shadow.

Common threads run through the mythologies of Andean Area civilization and its cultures. Today's modern division of religion and politics was unknown then, at a time when the entire basis of political power was derived from divine development and designation. In Inca society, and probably in Chimú and Moche and other cultures before them, rulers and priests were often one and the same. The Inca ruler himself was regarded as the living divine representative of Inti. Although each had specific roles, rulers and priests were intimately entwined in ruling and regulating every aspect of daily life. Ruler worship was carried beyond death through continuing ritual with the mummies of past Incas.

The landscape itself was considered sacred. Numerous natural features were regarded as semi-divine; ceremonial centres were constructed to represent myth; and ritual pathways were made across long distances, such as Nazca geoglyphic or Inca *ceque* routes.

There were many common religious elements among ancient Andean cultures, some of them almost universal, some more regional. In most regions, for example, there was a named creator god. During the later stages of Andean civilization – the Late Intermediate Period

Left: Nazca geoglyph forming a monkey in the desert of southern Peru. Such animals figure frequently in desert coastal cultures.

and Late Horizon – Viracocha, with many variations, was the creator god, especially among the sierra cultures and many coastal cultures. Along the central and southern Peruvian coast there was also a certain confusion and/or rivalry with the supreme god Pachacamac. Prototypes of the creator god Viracocha are apparent in the architectural and artistic imagery of earlier civilizations.

Religious imagery throughout the Andean Area was profoundly influenced from the earliest times by rainforest animals (jaguars, serpents and other reptiles, monkeys, birds) and included composite humanoid beings. In particular, both Andean civilizations and Amazonian cultures share a fascination with the power and influence of jaguars and other large felines, such as pumas. Among symbolic motifs that persisted through the different cultures of the Andean Area, in addition to the jaguar, were feline-human hybrids, staff deities (often with a composite feline face and human body), winged beings, and falcon- or other bird-headed warriors.

ANDEAN THEMES

Several common themes pervade Andean Area religion. As well as the creator Viracocha, almost all ritual had a calendrical organization. There was a calendar based on the movements of heavenly bodies, including solar solstices and equinoxes, lunar phases, the synodical cycle of Venus, the rising and setting of the Pleiades, the rotational inclinations of the Milky Way and the presence within the Milky Way of 'dark cloud constellations' (stellar voids). Consultation of auguries concerning these movements was considered vital at momentous times of the year, including planting, the harvest and the start of the ocean fishing season.

Sacrifice, both human and animal, and a variety of offerings were other common practices. A fifth, extremely important and ancient theme was the assignment of sacredness to special places, called *huacas*, which could be either natural or man-made. Most of them continued to be revered despite the rise and fall of political power. Another widespread trait was the use of hallucinogenic and other drugs, especially coca and the buds of several cacti, in rituals connected to war and sacrifice. Yet another common practice was ancestor reverence and worship, charged with its own special ritual and governed by the cyclical calendar. The mummified remains of ancestors were carefully kept in special buildings or chambers, or in caves, and brought out on ritual occasions.

It is this diversity, imaginative invention and richness of expression and depiction, as well as its 'alien' appeal – at least to Western readers – that makes the religion/mythology of Andean civilization so fascinating.

Below: Chinchorros mummies, c.5000BC, *in the Atacama Desert are the world's earliest known deliberate mummifications.*

DISCOVERING THE INCAS AND THEIR PAST

Unlike many other ancient civilizations worldwide, none of the Andean peoples invented an alphabet or any other form of writing. As a result, the first accounts of any ancient Andean culture or history were written by Spanish conquistadors, then later by 16th- and 17th-century Spanish chroniclers.

The conquistadors related what they observed on discovering the Incas, while later chroniclers recorded accounts of the empire, its people and culture. They used two sources of information for their records: *quipucamayoqs* and *amautas*. The first were people who devised the 'writing' system of knots known as *quipus*, which involved coloured cords tied into bundles with knots, while the second were court historians responsible for learning and relating details of their culture. Interpreting these accounts was not aided by the fact that many hundreds of languages and dialects existed at that time, although one language, Quechua, dominated.

During the 19th century, more was learned about Inca and pre-Inca civilizations from the studies and collections carried out by explorers and naturalists in the earliest excavations. Further additions to our knowledge come from the results and interpretations of 20th- and 21st-century archaeological discoveries, including that of the Inca sacred city of Machu Picchu.

Left: Shadows and light on the walls of the Sacsahuaman temple mimic the lighting on the sacred landscape that lies behind it.

THE SPANISH EXPLORATIONS

Europeans first discovered the New World ('Vinland') as early as AD986, although at that time they were unaware of the vastness of its lands. However, the settlement made there was all but forgotten by Europeans by the time Christopher Columbus and others began to explore across the Atlantic in the late 15th and early 16th centuries.

THE ARRIVAL OF THE SPANISH

After explorations from Hispaniola (modern Haiti and the Dominican Republic), during 1504–9, Spaniards established the first permanent occupation of Tierra Firme (the South American mainland) in Panama in 1509. From the isthmus, Francisco Pizarro and others explored and eventually conquered the vast Inca Empire of the Andes in 1533.

Their descriptions of the peoples and cultures they found formed the opinions of Europeans towards the new worlds they had 'discovered', and enhanced convictions already formed about the natives of the Caribbean islands. When Pizarro led his first expedition to Tierra Firme in 1524, the Aztec Empire had already been conquered by Hernán Cortés. (The reality that Columbus had not reached China but had found an unsuspected and unknown New World had become common knowledge.) Spaniards were sure that other vast empires and rich cities were there for the taking, and set out to conquer and exploit the wealth of these places for their own glory and enrichment.

With their belief that they were a superior race with a righteous duty to convert the 'heathens' they found to Christianity, to rule them and to exploit them, few Spaniards had any desire to engage with these civilizations.

Below: Atahualpa, the last Inca emperor, was engaged in a bitter civil war when Pizarro landed on the northern coast of the empire.

Above: Early 16th-century Spanish caravels were the type of ships used by the explorers and conquistadors.

A MAN WITH AMBITIONS

Pizarro made three expeditions: 1524–5, 1526–7 and 1531–3. In the first he only barely penetrated the coast of Colombia, but in the second he marched farther inland and sent his ship captain, Bartholomew Ruíz, down the coast. Pizarro met with a mixed reception but soon began to collect gold and silver objects, and to hear tales of vast cities and riches to the south. Ruíz brought back tales of many sightings of increasing population and civilization, and no apparent hostility or fear. Moreover, he encountered a balsa trading raft well out to sea laden with gold and silver objects, elaborate textiles and two traders from the Inca subject port of Tumbes, whom he brought to Pizarro along with the gold, silver and cloth. From these two men the Spaniards learned of fabulous Inca cities, palaces, llama flocks and endless stores of gold and silver objects.

Sufficient gold and silver was taken back to Spain to whet the appetite of the Spanish crown and to interest enough adventurers to raise funds to send a third expedition, this time into the Andes, with the purpose of conquest and conversion.

The Inca Empire discovered by Pizarro was at its greatest expansion, but had only recently itself conquered the kingdoms and peoples of the northern Andes and coasts of modern Ecuador and central Colombia. Nevertheless, Pizarro's chroniclers describe vast wealth in gold and silver objects, rich textiles, neatly laid-out cities and storehouses full of produce and other goods. There were masonry walls and fortresses of blocks so well fitted together that no mortar was needed, lands with irrigation systems and sophisticated agriculture and herds of 'sheep' (llamas). Balsa rafts traded up and down the coasts, while transport and communication were facilitated by a network of smooth roads and bridges along the coasts, across rivers and into the high mountains.

SMALLPOX AND CIVIL WAR

The Spaniards also found an empire in trouble, partly, although unknowingly, of their own doing. Ironically, smallpox, introduced into mainland America by the Spaniards in their conquest of the Aztecs, spread rapidly south from Mesoamerica, infecting the last conquering Sapa Inca (emperor), Huayna Capac (1493–1526), along with his heir apparent. As he became ill, Huayna Capac received reports from traders from the northern reaches of his empire of bearded strangers who sailed in strange ships. These reports coincided with a series of ill omens, and his priests prophesied evil and disaster when they witnessed the death of an eagle, which fell out of the sky after being mobbed by buzzards, during ceremonies in honour of the sun god Inti.

When Capac died, his son Huáscar seized the throne but was challenged by another son, Atahualpa, who commanded the Inca armies and marched from the northernmost province of Quito. The Inca court split into two supporting factions and civil war raged for six years. At the time of Pizarro's arrival at Tumbes on the coast of Quito province in 1532, Atahualpa's generals had only recently defeated Huáscar's army at the Inca capital, Cuzco, and captured his brother to secure the throne. The disruption caused by the civil war had weakened the Inca Empire's cohesion. As in Cortés' conquest of the Aztecs, Pizarro was able to exploit the ill omens prophesied by the Inca priesthood, which had created misgivings among the Incas.

Below: Francisco Pizarro and Diego de Almagro, his ambitious accomplice, as depicted by Guaman Poma de Ayala.

Above: Francisco Pizarro of Trujillo, of Estremadura, Spain (1475–1541), conqueror of the Incas.

CHRONICLERS AND INFORMANTS

From the earliest explorations of Tierra Firme, chroniclers among the conquistadors left descriptions of the peoples they encountered. Later, historians in the 16th and 17th centuries wrote accounts of the Inca Empire and its past and descriptions of Inca culture and other peoples. Even so, the lack of a written language among any of the Andean Area civilizations before the Spanish conquest necessitates that these descriptions of Inca history and religion be complemented with archaeological, artistic and architectural images and evidence, particularly for pre-Inca cultures.

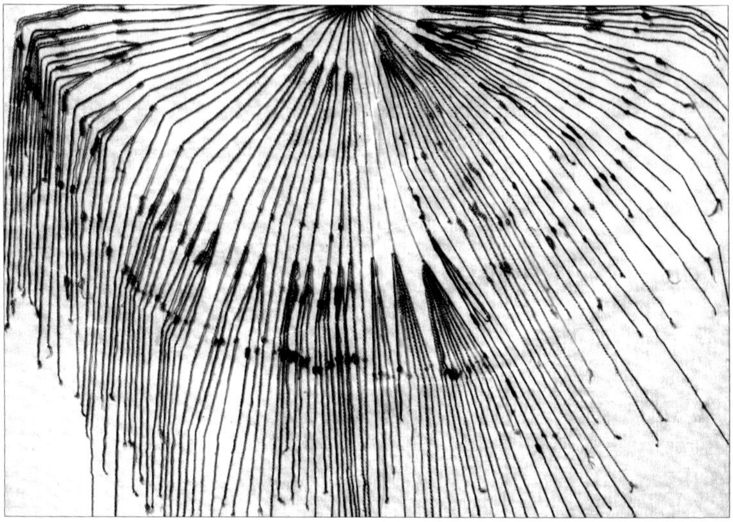

Above: The quipu, *a device of knotted and dyed cotton and wool string, was used by special court officials to keep records.*

KNOT HISTORIES

Although no Andean culture developed a writing system, the recording device known as the *quipu*, a system of tied bundles of string with distinctive knotting and dyed colours, served as an *aide-mémoire* to designated *quipucamayoqs* (literally 'knot makers'). Many of the first records of Inca culture transcribed by Spanish priests were based on the memories of *quipucamayoqs* and their recitals of Inca accounts and records, religious concepts and beliefs, and history.

Below: Felipe Guaman Poma de Ayala travelling in Peru. He chronicled the conquest of the Inca Empire and Inca life and culture.

For example, in the 1560s and 1570s the Spaniard Sarmiento de Gamboa, who was given the task of recording Inca history by the fourth Viceroy of Peru, Francisco de Toledo, claimed to have interviewed more than 100 *quipucamayoqs*, 42 of whom he actually names.

Colleagues of the *quipucamayoqs* were the *amautas* – officially appointed court philosophers and historians. They were responsible for memorizing, recounting, interpreting, reinterpreting, amplifying, reciting and passing on to successors the legends and history, family trees and special events of the Inca kings and queens. They therefore became another principal source of Inca history, legend, religious belief and social organization, and in this way were invaluable not only to the early Spanish chroniclers but also to colonial officials struggling to implement Spanish administration and to collect produce and taxes. The *amautas'* detailed knowledge of the Inca *ayllu* (kinship), *mitamaes* (redistributed peoples) and *mit'a* (labour service) helped the Spaniards to take advantage of and adapt a system of obligations that was already in place.

INTERPRETING SOURCES

There was a danger, however, of taking such sources too literally, and of having to cope with the problems of conflicting accounts. Spanish chroniclers' and Catholic priests' transcriptions of the descriptions of Inca history and culture by *quipucamayoqs* and *amautas* were fraught with opportunities for misinterpretation. Deliberately or accidentally omitting some facts, embellishing others, and amending and reinterpreting what they had been told meant events could be retold to suit a particular bias. The resulting conflicting versions could be used to argue a particular legal claim or to justify a particular Spanish action or exploitative practice.

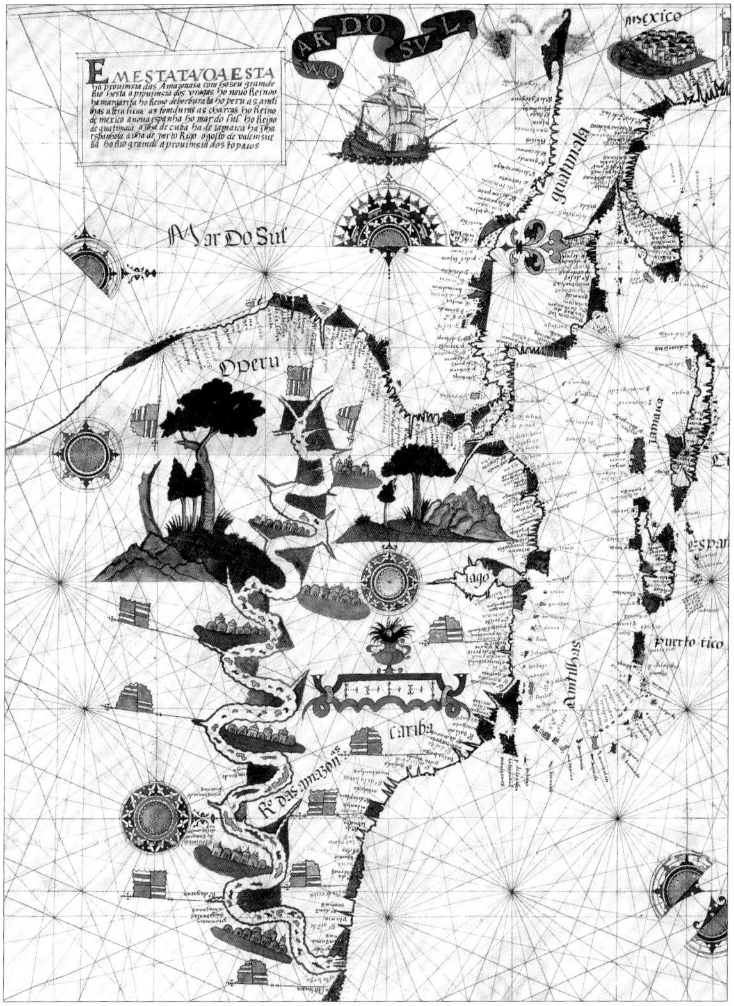

Above: An early navigational map of the Spanish possessions in the Caribbean, New Spain, northern Peru and the Amazon.

Nevertheless, the descriptions of Inca societies contained in these early records provide an invaluable source of information on Inca culture that can help make sense of archaeological evidence and vice versa.

SPANISH CHRONICLERS

About two dozen chroniclers' works provide information on the Incas and their contemporaries. Chief among them are the following writings. The mid-16th-century author Cieza de León's *Crónica del Peru* (1553 and 1554) contains much on Inca myth, while Juan de Betanzos' *Narrative of the Incas* (1557) recorded the subject from the point of view of the Inca nobility. Another record of Inca mythology is provided by Garcilasco de la Vega's (known as 'El Inca') *Comentarios Reales de los Incas* (1609–17), a comprehensive history of the Inca Empire.

The *Relación de los Quipucamayoqs* (written in Spain in 1608) comprises materials assembled to support the claims of a hopeful late pretender to the Inca throne, one Melchior Carlos Inca. He attempted to add depth and weight to his legitimacy by incorporating a version of the early foundation of Cuzco and the origin myth of the Incas, using as his source the manuscript of an inquest that had been held in 1542, the informants at which were four elderly *quipucamayoqs* who had served the Inca before the Spanish conquest.

Outside Cuzco, several sources provide accounts of myths from the regions of the empire. The exceptionally important Huarochirí manuscript, written in Quechua, *Dioses y Hombres de Huarochirí* (*c.*1610), records the myths of the central highlands of Peru. Two other sources relate accounts of the mythology of the peoples of the north Peruvian coast: Cabello de Balboa's *Miscelánea Antártica* (1586) and Antonio de la Calancha's *Crónica moralizada del Orden de San Augustinen el Perú* (1638).

THE CHRONICLERS

Accounts of mythology written by various Spanish-trained native Quechua-speaking authors include *Nueva Crónica y Buen Gobierno* by Felipe Guaman Poma de Ayala, written between 1583 and 1613, and *Relación de Antiguedades deste Reyno del Pirú*, which was written by Juan de Santacruz Yamqui Salcamaygua about 1613. Another set of documents, known as *idolatrías*, are records by Spanish priests and investigators who were attempting to stamp out idolatrous practices known to persist among the local populace under Spanish rule. These 17th-century documents are rich in information on local myth based on interrogations of local authorities, native curers and 'witches' and other local diviners.

Lastly, the Jesuit priest Bernabé de Cobo, drawing principally from earlier chronicles, compiled the most balanced and comprehensive synthesis of Inca history and religion, in his monumental 20-year work *Historia del Nuevo Mundo*, books 13 and 14 of which, in particular, deal with Inca religion and customs.

LANGUAGES, DRAWINGS AND *QUIPU*

Hundreds of languages and dialects were spoken by the peoples throughout the Inca Empire, a fact even enshrined in Inca creation history. However, with no written language, the Incas relied on fine-line engraving and knot tying to keep records. Both these methods of recording data, events and customs provide modern scholars with valuable information with which to interpret the artefacts and structures from archaeological excavations. A combination of these finds and the information provided by the fine-line drawing and *quipus* enables us to discern the vast workings of the Inca Empire, and even pre-Inca times, and gives a greater understanding of Inca and other Andean cultures' beliefs about the universe.

Above: An Early Intermediate Period Moche pot with a 'narrative' scene, here showing weavers using backstrap looms.

QUECHUA, AYMARA, MOCHICA

The principal language of the Incas was Quechua (known to them as *Runa Simi*). This language was used throughout the empire for its administration and economic functions. Aymará, generally thought by linguists to be older than Quechua, was spoken throughout the highland region around the basin of Lake Titicaca. Some scholars group the two languages together under the name Quechuamaran. In northern coastal Peru, Mochica was spoken, the language of the ancient Moche, their ancestors and descendants. Both Quechua and Aymará are widely spoken today in the Central Andes by some six million or more people. Mochica continued to be spoken in part of northern coastal Peru up to the beginning of the 20th century.

Below: An Inca quipucamayoq *depicted by Guaman Poma de Ayala in his* Nueva Crónica y Buen Gobierno, *c.1613.*

FINE-LINES IMAGES

Neither the Incas nor any of their Andean ancestors invented writing, and there are therefore no native historical records. However, fine-line drawings on pots reveal a great deal.

The graphic scenes they show provide records of a sort, depicting events. While such scenes are not specific historical events, many Moche fine-line drawings on ceramic vessels depict images representing commonly occurring episodes or practices in the culture. Such depictions provide invaluable information that contributes to the understanding of finds from archaeological excavations. For example, fine-line scenes of figures in burial rituals show deities, or priests-shamans in the roles of deities, which explains the presence of masks on the faces of the dead in Moche elite burials.

RECORDING WITH KNOTS

The *quipu* (or *khipu*; Quechua for 'knot') was a unique Inca Andean recording device. It comprised a central cord to which were attached numerous subsidiary cords or strings, like a fringe. The subsidiary cords were of different colours and they were tied into different sorts of knots with differing meanings. *Quipus* were mostly made of cotton cord, but llama wool was also sometimes used. About 700 *quipus* have been found.

ACCOUNTS OF MANY COLOURS

According to 16th- and 17th-century sources, prominent among which are the 16th-century conquistador and governor of Cuzco, Garcilaso de la Vega's *Comentarios Reales de los Incas* and the 17th-century *Historia et Rudimenta Linguae Piruanorum*, *quipus* had several uses.

Right: An Inca quipu, *which is unusually attached to a wooden rod. Specific* quipus *held records for individual cities.*

They were account 'books', in which the different colours, knots and sequences served as tallies of goods in Inca storehouses throughout the empire, or censuses of labour groups and sources; and they were mnemonic aids for recalling oral traditions – historical-literary events, including what modern scholars would call myth and legend.

The Incas used the decimal system in counting and knew positional mathematics. Knots in different positions on the same string and different types of knot were used to record thousands, hundreds and single units. The Incas were also aware of the concept of zero, duly represented by a cord without any knots. The key to reading such numerical *quipu* knots and positions was discovered in 1912 by Leland L. Locke. Analysing a *quipu* in the American Museum of Natural History, New York, he compared its knots and their positions to descriptions by Garcilaso de la Vega.

Additional meaning was recorded in the *quipu* through the use of colours and their sequences and combinations. Colours used included white, blue, yellow, red, black, green, grey, light brown and dark brown. Colours and their combinations represented types of goods or produce. For example, yellow could represent gold or maize corn.

SUBTLETIES OF MEANING

Further sophistication in meaning is represented by the orders of strings in series of the same colour. For example, in a counting of weapons stores, the most important ('noble') weapon was recorded at the left, and less noble weapons, in descending order, towards the right. The direction of the twisting of a cord itself added another layer of meaning: cords twisted to 'S' (clockwise) meant that the entire group referred to male categories or subject matter, while cords twisted to 'Z' (anti-clockwise) meant that the entire group referred to female categories or subject matter. Even individual knots can be made clockwise or anti-clockwise.

So-called 'literary' *quipus* incorporated textile ideograms (symbols used to represent whole words or concepts) among the strings. The same ideograms are found on Inca and pre-Inca textiles, pottery, sculpture and metalwork. The positions and numbers of knots below the ideograms indicate the syllables to be 'read'. The ideograms themselves relate to Inca (Andean) concepts of the universe, and to deities, man, animals and holy objects. An ideogram can also refer to a concept such as creation, the beginning of something, or to the elements and directions as represented by colours.

NAMING PLACES

The most recent breakthrough in *quipu* analysis has been made by Gary Urton and Carrie Brezine of Harvard University. Using a computer program designed to analyse the knot patterns in 21 *quipus* from a site in Puruchuco, an Inca administrative centre on the Peruvian coast, they discovered a recurring sequence of three figure-of-eight knots that appeared to represent a place name. The placement of this sequence at the start of these *quipus* represents the name for Puruchuco, and the patterns of colour combinations and string lengths appear to rank three levels of authority among them. Thus, wherever these *quipus* went, they could be identified with the Puruchuco administration and with Inca hierarchy, passing instructions down from high-level officials.

EXPLORERS AND ARCHAEOLOGISTS

The Spanish conquistadors peppered their chronicles with descriptions that gave glimpses of the Inca way of life. The accounts and histories of colonial officials and priests attempted to provide a complete record of Inca history, society and religion, even if biased consciously or unconsciously. In the 18th and 19th centuries, these publications began to be re-examined by European and American scholars. Excavations, crude for the most part, had begun to be undertaken in Europe and America by antiquarians curious to understand their own and other's pasts and eager to make collections of antiquities for museums.

Above: Alexander von Humboldt made the first attempts to collect Inca and pre-Inca antiquities and to understand their sequence.

TRAVELLERS' TALES

Although most such early 'archaeological' activity in the Americas took place in North America, some scholars and travellers began to realize that there were also ruins and remnants of ancient structures and artefacts throughout what had been the Inca Empire and elsewhere in South America. Paramount among these was Alexander von Humboldt (1769–1859).

Von Humboldt was the epitome of the late 18th/early 19th-century natural historian. As a gentleman traveller, scholar and popular lecturer, his travels were a combination of exploration, adventure and a pursuit of new knowledge, as he sought to uncover the continent's natural history, geography, geology and ancient history. In his two landmark publications – *Political Essay on the Kingdom of New Spain* (1811) and *Researches Concerning the Institutions and Monuments of the Ancient Inhabitants of America* (1814) – and in popular lectures he attempted to accumulate and record systematically as much data about the Americas as he could and to present it in a detailed but succinct manner. He attempted to remain unbiased in the way he recorded the data, trying to keep recorded fact and description separate from interpretation and speculation. Nevertheless, he was at

Below: Alexander von Humboldt travelled throughout South America gathering information for his treatise on the continent.

Right: Alphons Stübel at the Gateway of the Sun, Middle Horizon Tiwanaku. He published his notes with Max Uhle in 1892.

the same time a pioneer in his attempts to explain the presence of humans in the New World and their manner of coming and spreading throughout the two continents, as well as the apparent independent rise of sophisticated civilizations whose ruins were plain to see. His work and lectures brought international recognition to the antiquities of South America.

Following von Humboldt's example, and no doubt inspired by the explorations of John L. Stephens and Frederick Catherwood in Mesoamerica, books listing and describing sites and types of artefacts were published from the 1850s, and attempts were made to establish a historical framework for the bewildering amount of material that was being rediscovered about the ancient ruins of Peru and Bolivia especially. Frances de Castelnau published his *Expédition dans les Parties Centrales de l'Amérique du Sud, Troisième Partie: Antiquités des Incas et Autre peuples Anciens* in 1854; Johann Tschudi his five-volume *Reisen durch Süd Amerika* in 1869; Charles Wiener his *Pérou et Bolivie* in 1874; Ephraim G. Squier, echoing Stephens and Catherwood, his *Peru: Incidents of Travel and Exploration in the Land of the Incas* in 1877; and E. W. Middendorf his three-volume *Peru* in 1893–5, all primarily descriptive works.

Below: Ceramic kero *drinking vessels such as these were brought to private collectors and museums in the 18th and 19th centuries.*

DESCRIPTION AND EXCAVATION

Books and papers by Sir Clements Markham in 1856–1910, especially *A History of Peru* (1892) and *The Incas of Peru* (1910), were early attempts to synthesize and explain the data. A few scholars went one step further and actually undertook excavations: Alphons Stübel and Wilhelm Reiss excavated the Ancon cemetery on the Peruvian coast, an ancient burial place near Lima, and published their results in *The Necropolis of Ancón in Peru* (1880–7). Adolph Bandelier carried out excavations of Tiwanaku sites on islands in the Titicaca Basin, the results of which were published in 1910, and of Tiwanaku itself in 1911.

Bridging the development of archaeology between these early classifications and descriptions of Andean materials stands the all-important figure of Max Uhle (1856–1944), who was inspired by Alphons Stübel. In 1892 he collaborated with him to publish *Die Ruinenstaette von Tiahuanaco*, a study based on notes and photographs taken by Stübel at Tiwanaku. From 1892 to 1912, Uhle carried out regular fieldwork in Peru and Bolivia. Armed with a thorough knowledge of Inca and Tiwanaku pottery types, his excavations at Pachacamac on the Peruvian coast enabled him to establish the first breakthrough in the modern construction of the chronology of Andean ancient history. He knew Inca pottery to be 15th and 16th century in date; likewise he knew that Tiwanaku pottery was pre-Inca and completely unlike Inca ceramics. Therefore, he reasoned that the pottery he excavated at Pachacamac, because it was unlike Tiwanaku ware but was sometimes associated in layers with Inca ceramics at Pachacamac, must come between the two in date.

Uhle's work was the beginning of the assessment of series of styles of artefacts in combination with their relative position in the earth to build a chronology of the ancient cultures of the Andes. During the next 30 years he carried out other excavations, including work in Ecuador and northern Chile. He synthesized his own and others' work into a Peruvian area-wide chronology, the first for the Andean region, because he also linked his Ecuadorian and Chilean finds to the sequence. While many other scholars – European, North American and South American – worked throughout South America into the early 20th century, most of their work was limited to collecting, describing and classifying museum pieces.

MODERN INVESTIGATIONS

Modern methods in archaeology began in the 20th century. Alongside increasingly sophisticated reasoning to establish chronological sequences and relationships among artefacts and site structures, more careful methods of excavation and recording and numerous new scientific methods brought greater understanding – but also more questions. Archaeologists were no longer content just to describe, classify, date and display the past: they wanted to interpret and explain it too.

SEEKING ANSWERS TO QUESTIONS

Recording of stratigraphy (distinctive earth layers or associations between architectural features) enabled archaeologists to understand and interpret the relationships between artefacts, structures and other features. Archaeologists throughout the Americas began to direct their fieldwork towards finding evidence to answer special questions and understanding a much wider and deeper picture of ancient history. Investigations sought evidence on all aspects and classes of ancient society, not just on the elite and the exquisite.

In addition to excavations at the ruins of individual ancient cities, area surveys began to establish the extent of ancient remains, the relationships between them and the varying importance of different regions. Work focused on specific questions and historical problems: When did people first arrive in the Andes? When was the first pottery made? When did agriculture begin? How great was the influence of different cultures, kingdoms and empires?

Excavations yielded increasing amounts of metalwork and textiles and evidence of the artefacts and methods used to make them. Studies went beyond describing and classifying the art on ancient Andean pottery and stonework and explained the meaning of their depiction of scenes and religious events.

Above: The Black and White Portal at the Early Horizon temple at Chavín de Huántar. Early 20th-century archaeologists realized this was one of the first pre-Inca civilizations.

Below: Late 20th-century excavations near the Coricancha in modern Cuzco revealed Inca foundations and water channels.

MAKING DATES

During the first 60 years of the 20th century, Alfred L. Kroeber and John H. Rowe refined and expanded the timescale of Andean prehistory. On the basis of which materials were found and where they lay within the site's stratigraphy, Rowe defined a 'master sequence' of alternating Periods and Horizons that broadly defined the course of Andean ancient history. In the late 1940s the discovery of radiocarbon dating began to provide absolute dates for these cultural periods.

The first native Peruvian archaeologist, Julio C. Tello, began a life-long career excavating sites of the earliest periods of Andean civilization, notably Paracas cemetery on Peru's southern coast, Sechín Alto in northern Peru and Chavín de Huántar in the central Andes. He defined these remote periods when Andean civilization began and distinctive socio-economic and religious traits were established. In 1939, Tello and Kroeber established the Institute of Andean Research. Similarly, Luis E. Valcarcel, Tello's successor at the Lima Museo Nacional, promoted the rich interchange between different fields of study to clarify Inca and pre-Inca society.

INTERNATIONAL EXPEDITIONS

After World War Two, large-scale, long-running projects were undertaken throughout the Andes, addressing every period, from the earliest inhabitants to the Incas. Principal among these was the Virú Valley Project, begun in 1946 by Wendell C. Bennett, William D. Strong, James A. Ford, Clifford Evans, Gordon R. Willey, Junius Bird and Donald Collier.

In the 1960s and 1970s, Edward Lanning, Thomas Patterson and Michael Moseley worked on the central Peruvian coast. Thomas Lynch, Richard MacNeish and others clarified the Palaeoindian period. Seiichi Izumi and Toshihiko Sono of Tokyo University investigated Kotosh and other early ceramic ceremonial sites. Luis G. Lumbreras and Hernán Amat renewed the study of Chavín de Huántar, as did Richard L. Burger of the Peabody Museum. Donald Lathrap and his students worked in the eastern Andes and adjacent lowlands.

In the 1960s to 1980s, John Rowe, John Murra, Tom Zuidema, Gary Urton and many others renewed the study of the Incas, including excavations at Huánuco Pampa by Craig Morris and Donald Thompson. Large-scale projects were undertaken by Michael Moseley and Carol Mackay at Chan Chan, by William Isbell at Huari, by Christopher Donnan and Izumi Shimada in the Moche Valley and by Alan Kolata in the Tiwanaku Basin.

No summary of 20th-century Andean archaeology can ignore three of its most spectacular discoveries. In 1911 the young explorer Hiram Bingham rediscovered the Inca fortress and ceremonial precinct of Machu Picchu in the remote Urubamba Valley north of Cuzco, bringing it to world fame. In the 1980s, Walter Alva and Susana Meneses made astounding discoveries and excavations of fabulous, unlooted elite Moche tombs at Sipán in the Lambeyeque Valley of northern Peru. And in 1995 Johan Reinhard and Miguel Zárate discovered rich child burials high on Mt Ampato in the southern Andes, explaining the Inca ritual of *capacocha* sacrifice.

Above: Late 20th-century excavations by Walter Alva of the rare unlooted tomb of an Early Intermediate Period Moche lord at Sipán in the Lambayeque Valley, Peru.

Left: John H. Rowe recording findings at the Inca palace of Huyna Capac, at Quisphuanca, Peru.

RETURN TO SOURCES

Alongside 20th- and 21st-century excavations and analyses, archaeologists still return to the original texts: the chronicles and records of the conquistadors and colonial officials. However biased or conflicting these may sometimes be, they remain the only first-hand accounts of Inca society. Uhle knew that the ruins of Tiwanaku were pre-Inca because the Incas themselves told the Spaniards that the city lay in ruins when they subjugated the area. Similarly, when Morris and Thompson discovered 497 stone structures arranged in orderly rows along the hillside south of Huánuco Pamapa, the stacked pottery vessels of agricultural produce revealed these buildings to be none other than examples of Inca provincial storehouses in which, as described in the chronicles, they collected the wealth of the empire for redistribution.

In this way, the first Spanish accounts continue to help explain excavation finds and to provide a basis for interpreting aspects of pre-Inca civilization, whose material remains often demonstrate a link with Inca practices and social functions.

PART ONE

HISTORY

The vast continent of South America may form a more or less separate physical unit, but the ancient peoples who once lived there never formed a single culture. For this reason we cannot assess the continent as a whole but need to describe the people, culture, religion and mythology of each of many different groups.

Urban-based societies were confined to the Andes Mountains and nearby western coastal valleys and deserts. Cultures that built ceremonial centres, governed large areas and developed advanced metalwork, pottery, textiles and stone-carving technologies in present-day western Venezuela, Colombia, Peru, Bolivia, northern Chile and northwestern Argentina. In this book, this area is defined as the 'Andean Area'. Peoples elsewhere in South America developed sophisticated societies with complex religious beliefs, but they did not build monumental ceremonial centres or cities, develop technology of quite the same complexity or build kingdoms and empires.

The nature of the landscape itself provided stimuli for civilized societies to develop. Within a relatively small area the land ranges from Pacific coastal plains and deserts, with coastal valleys ascending east into the Andean foothills, to high mountain valleys and plateaux, then to the eastern Andean slopes descending to the high pampas and rainforests. A key factor in the development and endurance of these civilizations was water, which was important functionally as well as symbolically and religiously.

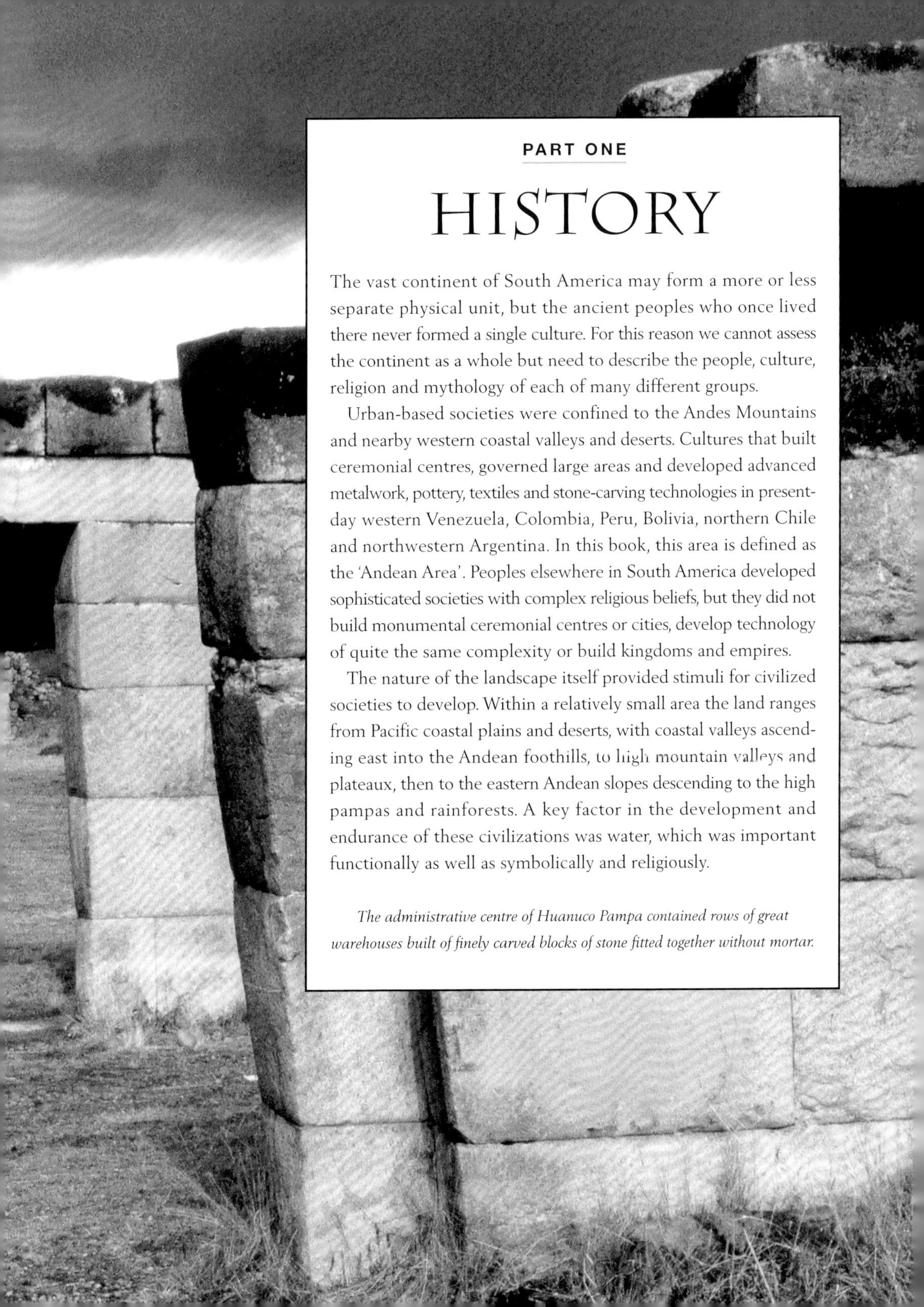

The administrative centre of Huanuco Pampa contained rows of great warehouses built of finely carved blocks of stone fitted together without mortar.

TIMELINE: THE INCAS AND THEIR ANCESTORS

CHRONOLOGY OF ANDEAN AREA CIVILIZATION

The chronology of the Andean Area is complex. Archaeologists have developed a scheme based on technological achievements and on changing political organization through time, from the first arrival of humans in the area (15,000–3500BC) to the conquest of the Inca Empire by Francisco Pizarro in 1532. The pace of technological development varied in different regions within the Andean Area, especially during early periods in its history. The development of lasting and strong contact between regions, however, spread both technology and ideas, and led to regions depending on each other to some degree. Sometimes this interdependence was due to large areas being under the control of one 'authority', while at other times the unifying link was religious or based on trade and technology.

Below: A wooden cup painted with an Inca warrior with shield and axe-spear.

The principal chronological scheme for the Andean Area comprises a sequence of eight time units: five Periods and three Horizons. Periods are defined as times when political unity across regions was less consolidated. Smaller areas were controlled by city-states, sometimes in loose groupings, perhaps sharing religious beliefs despite having different political organizations. The Horizons, by contrast, were times when much larger political units were formed. These units exercised political, economic and religious control over extended areas, usually including different types of terrain, rather than being confined to coastal valley groups or sierra city-states.

Different scholars give various dates for the beginnings and endings of the Periods and Horizons, and no two books on Andean civilization give exactly the same dates. The durations of Periods and Horizons also vary from one region to another within the Andean Area, and charts increase in complexity as authors divide the Andean Area into coastal, sierra and Altiplano regions, or even into north, central and southern coastal regions and north, central and southern highland regions. The dates given here are a compilation from several sources, thus avoiding any anomalies among specific sources.

Above: The sacred Intihuatana (Hitching Post of the Sun) at Machu Picchu.

CHRONOLOGICAL PERIOD	DATES	PRINCIPAL CULTURES
Lithic / Archaic Period	15,000–3500BC	spread of peoples into the Andean Area hunter-gatherer cultures
Preceramic / Formative Period (Cotton Preceramic)	3500–1800BC	early agriculture and first ceremonial centres
Initial Period	1800–750BC	U-shaped ceremonial centres, platform mounds and sunken courts
Early Horizon	750–200BC	Chavín, Paracas, Pukará (Yaya-Mama) cults
Early Intermediate Period	200BC–AD600	Moche, Nazca and Titicaca Basin confederacies
Middle Horizon	AD600–1000	Wari and Tiwanaku empires
Late Intermediate Period	AD1000–1400	Chimú and Inca empires
Late Horizon	AD1400–1532	Inca Empire and Spanish Conquest

LITHIC / ARCHAIC PERIOD (40,000–3500BC)

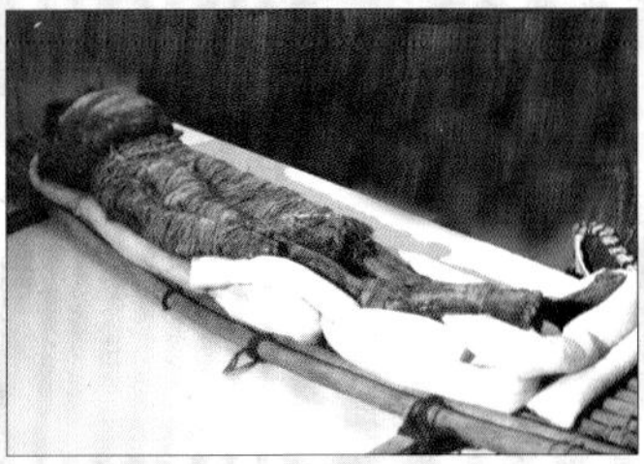

Above: This mummified body from the Chinchorros culture is 8,000 years old.

*c.*40,000 to *c.*20,000 years ago Ice-free corridors open up across the Bering Strait, but there is no evidence humans entered the New World until the late stages of this time period.

*c.*20,000BC Migrating hunter-gatherers, using stone-, bone-, wood- and shell-tool technologies, probably enter the New World from north-east Asia.

from *c.*15,000 years ago Palaeoindians migrate south and east to populate the Americas, reaching Monte Verde in southern Chile *c.*14,850 years ago.

*c.*8500–5000BC Hunter-gatherers occupy cave and rock shelter sites in the Andes (e.g. Pachamachay, Guitarrero, Tres Ventana and Toquepala caves). Evidence of tending of hemp-like fibre, medicinal plants, herbs and wild tubers.

*c.*5000BC First mummified burials in the Atacama Desert, Chinchorros culture.

Below: Mountains high in the Andes proved a challenge to early settlers.

PRECERAMIC / FORMATIVE PERIOD (3500–1800BC)

Above: Preceramic Period sculpture at the Temple of the Crossed Hands, Kotosh.

This period is sometimes also called the Cotton Preceramic.

*c.*3500–1800BC True plant domestication accomplished – cotton, squashes and gourds, beans, maize, potatoes, sweet potatoes, beans, chilli peppers. Llamas and other camelids herded on the Altiplano.

*c.*3000BC Coastal fishing villages such as Huaca Prieta flourish, using gourd containers but no ceramics, and produce early cotton textiles.

*c.*2800BC Early northern coastal civic-ceremonial centres begin at Aspero – Huaca de los Idolos and Huaca de los Sacrificios.

*c.*2400–2000BC Large, raised mound platforms are constructed at El Paraíso, La Galagada and Kotosh – Temple of the Crossed Hands. Spread of the Kotosh religious cult.

Below: Llamas and other camelids were first domesticated during this period.

INITIAL PERIOD (1800–750BC)

Above: View of the Colca Canyon shows terracing that began in this period.

Spread of pottery, irrigation agriculture, monumental architecture; religious processions and ritual decapitation begin.

from *c.*1800BC Sophisticated irrigation systems develop in coastal oases valleys, the highlands and Altiplano.

*c.*1800BC Construction at Moxeke includes colossal adobe heads.

*c.*1750BC Builders at La Florida bring the first pottery to this region.

*c.*1500BC Cerro Sechín flourishes.

*c.*1400–1200BC Sechín Alto becomes the largest U-shaped civic-ceremonial centre in the New World.

*c.*1300BC Construction of the five platform mounds at Cardál.

*c.*900BC U-shaped ceremonial complex at Chavín de Huántar begins.

Below: Garagay, central Peru, was a typical coastal U-shaped civic-ceremonial centre.

EARLY HORIZON (750–200BC)

Above: A stone severed head, with feline canines, from Chavín de Huántar.

Religious cults develop around Chavín de Huántar and Pukará. Decapitation, hallucinogenic drug use, spiritual transformation and ancestor worship become widespread.

from *c.*750BC The Old Temple at Chavín becomes established as a cult centre. Influence of the Lanzón deity and the Staff Deity spreads. The Paracas Peninsula serves as the necropolis site for several settlements, and the Oculate Being is shown on textiles and ceramics.

*c.*400–200BC The Old Temple at Chavín is enlarged to create the New Temple. The Chavín Cult spreads, especially at Kuntur Wasi and Karwa (Paracas).

*c.*400BC Rainfall fell in the Titicaca Basin. Pukará, northwest of the lake, is established, and becomes the centre of the Yaya-Mama cult.

*c.*200BC Chavín Cult influence waned.

Below: Vicuñas at Viscachani, now in Bolivia, were prized for their fine wool.

EARLY INTERMEDIATE PERIOD (200BC–AD600)

Above: The closely set stone blocks of the external walls of Sacsahuaman, Cusco.

The cohesion of Chavín disintegrates, and several regional chiefdoms develop in the coastal and mountain valleys.

from *c.*100BC Rise of the Nazca .

*c.*AD100 Burial of the Old Lord of Sipán in Lambayeque Valley.

*c.*AD100 to 500 The Nazca sacred ceremonial centre of Cahuachi flourishes.

*c.*1st century AD The Moche dynasty is founded in the northern coastal valleys.

*c.*AD250 Rise of oracle of Pachacamac.

*c.*AD300 Burial of the Lord of Sipán in Lambayeque Valley.

*c.*AD500 The Moche ceremonial platforms of the Huacas del Sol and de la Luna are the largest in the area.

*c.*AD700 Moche/Nazca power wanes.

Below: This giant Nazca desert geoglyph of the spider is visible from space.

MIDDLE HORIZON (AD600–1000)

Above: The Staff Deity depicted on the Gateway of the Sun at Tiwanaku.

Much of the Andean Area is unified in two empires: Tiwanaku in the south and Wari in the north. They share common beliefs around the creator god Viracocha.

*c.*AD300 Major construction of the central ceremonial plaza at Tiwanaku begins.

*c.*AD400–750 Major phases of building of elite residential quarters at Tiwanaku.

*c.*AD500 The rise of Huari, capital of the Wari Empire.

by *c.*AD600 Huari is a flourishing capital city and rival to Tiwanaku.

*c.*AD650 Pikillacta, the southernmost Wari city, is founded.

*c.*AD750–1000 Third major phase of palace building at Tiwanaku.

*c.*AD900–950 Burial of the Sicán Lords at Lambayeque.

Below: The reed boats on Lake Titicaca have been made for thousands of years.

LATE INTERMEDIATE PERIOD (AD1000–1400)

Above: The Late Intermediate Period Sicán Tucume pyramid, Lambayeque Valley.

An era of political break up is characterized by new city-states, including Lambayeque, Chimú and Pachacamac, the Colla and Lupaka kingdoms, and numerous city-states in the central and southern Andean valleys.

*c.*AD1000 Tiwannaku and Wari empires wane as regional political rivalry reasserts itself.

*c.*AD1000 Wari city-state is abandoned.

*c.*AD1000 Chan Chan, the Chimú capital, is founded in the Moche valley.

*c.*1100 The Incas under Manco Capac, migrate into the Cuzco Valley, found Cuzco and establish the Inca dynasty.

*c.*1250 City of Tiwanaku abandoned, perhaps because of changes in climate.

*c.*1300 Sinchi Roca becomes the first emperor to use the title Sapa Inca.

Below: The city of Cuzco was founded by Manco Capac, its legendary first ruler.

LATE HORIZON (AD1400–1532)

Above: The Inca hillside site of Winay Wayna overlooks the Urubamba River.

Above: Manco Capac, legendary founder of the Inca dynasty and 'son of the sun'.

In just over 130 years the Incas build a huge empire and establish an imperial cult centred on Inti, the sun god, whose representative on earth is the Sapa Inca.

*c.*1425 Viracocha begins the Inca conquest of the Cuzco Valley.

1438 Pachacuti Inca Yupanqui defeats the Chancas to dominate the Cuzco Valley.

1438–71 Pachacuti begins the rebuilding of Cuzco as the imperial capital to the plan of a crouching puma.

1471 Fall of the Kingdom of Chimú.

1471–93 Inca Tupac Yupanqui expands the empire west and south, doubling its size.

1493–1526 Huayna Capac consolidates the empire, building fortresses, road systems, storage redistribution and religious precincts throughout the provinces.

Below: The Spaniards built S Domingo on the foundations of the Inca Coricancha.

1526 Huayna Capac dies of smallpox without an agreed successor.

1526–32 Huayna Capac's son Huáscar seizes the throne but is challenged by his brother Atahualpa. A six-year civil war ends in the capture of Huáscar.

1530 Inca Empire at its greatest extent.

1532 Francisco Pizarro lands with a small army on the north coast and marches to meet Atahualpa at Cajamarca.

1532 Battle of Cajamarca and capture of Atahualpa, who is held for ransom.

1533 Atahualpa is executed.

1535 Francisco Pizarro founds Lima as his capital in Spanish Peru.

1541 Pizarro assassinated in his palace at Lima by Almagro and his associates.

Below: The sacred site of Machu Picchu was rediscovered by Hiram Bingham in 1911.

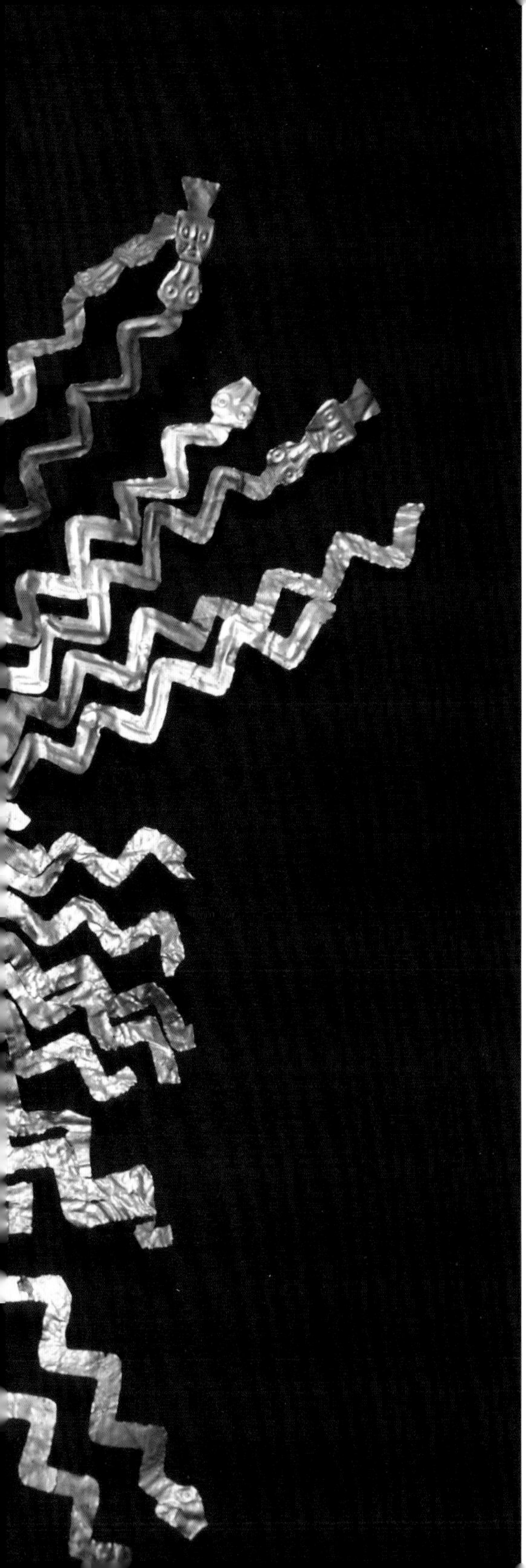

CHAPTER ONE

EMPIRE OF THE SUN

The Incas were a small group, or tribe, numbering perhaps 40,000 individuals or fewer in the Huantanay (Cuzco) Valley of modern central Peru. They were one group among many in the valley. Through conquest, first locally then beyond the valley, they built the largest empire that ever existed in the Americas. At its greatest extent, in AD1530, its northern border coincided roughly with the modern Ecuadorian–Colombian border, its southern extent stretched to modern central Chile, to the east it claimed regions into the lowlands bordering the Amazon Rainforest, and to the west it met the Pacific Ocean. Yet the Incas' rise to power lasted less than 100 years, and during the whole of this time they were engaged in wars of conquest or in the civil war at the end of this period.

Pachacuti Inca Yupanqui founded the imperial state of the Incas, and under his rule the Incas continued to dominate the Cuzco Valley. As the empire expanded, vast networks of roads were built to unite its far corners, coupled with impressive architectural and engineering feats that enabled planned towns and cities with great monuments to be built. Bridges were built and existing systems of terracing and irrigation expanded.

When the Spaniards under the leadership of Francisco Pizarro first arrived, the empire was still being expanded, but by the time of their third visit the empire was split by civil war. This war led eventually to the death of two rival sons of the Inca ruler, Huayna Capac, and the victory of Pizarro.

Left: The skilled metallurgists of the La Tolita culture were among many to depict the sun as a rayed golden mask.

LAND OF THE FOUR QUARTERS

The Incas called their world Tahuantinsuyu (or Tawantinsyu), literally meaning 'the land of the four united quarters'. Cuzco, the capital city, formed the focal point (although it was not the geographical centre) on which the four quarters were oriented and from which they emanated.

To the north-east of Cuzco was Antisuyu, the smallest quarter and the only one that did not border on the Pacific Ocean. To the north-west, stretching to the northernmost borders of the empire, was Chinchaysuyu. This quarter's northern extent had, in fact, only recently been extended into Quito province by the last conquering Sapa Inca, Huayna Capac (1493–1526), shortly before the arrival of the conquistador Francisco Pizarro in 1531. South and west of Cuzco was Cuntisuyu, second in size, and to the south-east was the largest of the four quarters, Collasuyu.

Below: Ephraim George Squier was the first to show a detailed plan of Inca Cuzco as a puma, its head formed by the fortress-temple of Sacsahuaman and its body and tail by the streets and water channels.

Above: The Huacaypata Plaza, Cuzco, now the Plaza de Armas, was the site of ritual celebrations at solstices and festivals.

UNEQUAL QUARTERS

The four quarters were not only unequal in size but in population. They also differed extensively in the types of terrain they encompassed. Together they comprised a vast territory stretching from modern Ecuador to central Chile, north to south, and from the Pacific coast to the eastern flank of the Andes mountain chain, west to east. The empire was inhabited by a great variety of peoples and languages, each with long traditions of local development, masterfully united and socially co-ordinated and manipulated by their Inca masters. The Incas recognized this diversity as the deliberate actions of the creator god Viracocha, who, having formed the second world and its human inhabitants out of clay, dispersed them after giving them the clothing, skills and languages of the different tribes and nations.

Mention of the partition of the empire into four quarters was, as such, virtually ignored in most of Inca history. One legend, however, recounted in Garcilaso de la Vega's early 17th-century work, *Commentarios Reales de los Incas*, describes the division as the work of an 'Un-named Man' who appeared at Tiwanaku after the destruction of a previous world by great floods. This near lack of explanation is especially curious given the emphasis in Inca legendary history on the progress of the state creation from Lake Titicaca – near the geographical centre of the empire – towards the north and west, into the Huantanay (Cuzco) Valley.

This progress in one direction makes sense for Antisuyu, Chinchaysuyu and Cuntisuyu, but not for Collasuyu, which lies almost entirely to the south of Lake Titicaca. One explanation might lie in the fact that the Incas recast the origin mythology of the peoples of Collasuyu in order to bolster their own claims of origin from the Titicaca Basin, thus legitimizing their right to rule the region. The Incas were aware of the remains of Tiwanaku to the south and west of the lake, and no doubt of the relics of other previous great cities of the region, and must have recognized them as the centres

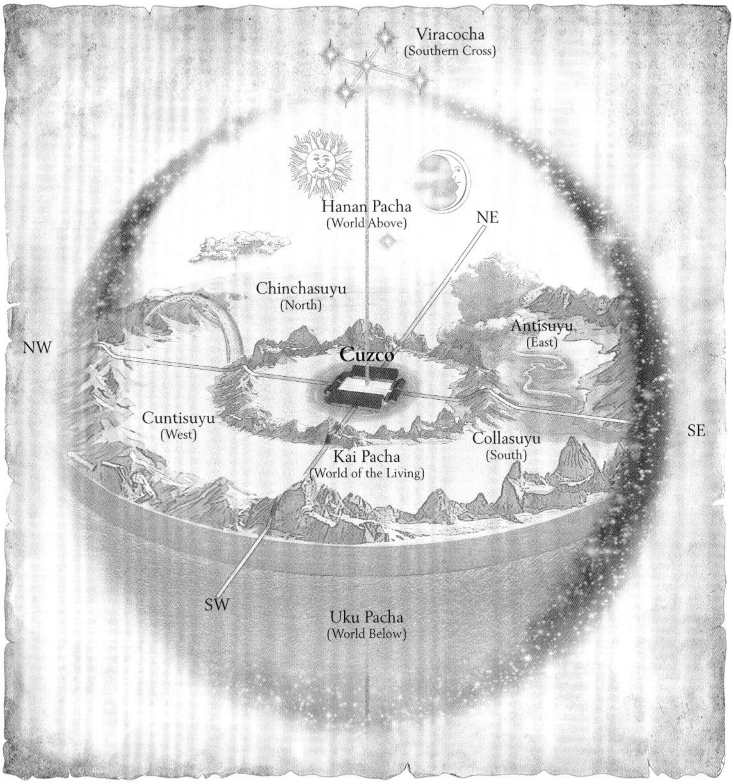

Right: A diagram of the land of the four quarters, based on a 1613 sketch by Juan de Santa Cruz Pachacuti Ymaqui Salcamaygua.

of former power bases. The Incas explained to the Spaniards that Tiwanaku lay in ruins when they invaded and conquered the Titicaca Basin.

THE FOUNDING OF CUZCO

The Incas regarded their capital at Cuzco as being at the centre of the world. Once again, Inca legendary history and heavenly associations formed the basis of their arrangments, for Cuzco equally reflected state and celestial organization. According to legend, Pachacuti Inca rebuilt the imperial city and the Coricancha (Sun Temple) in stone, being inspired by the ruined stone masonry of Tiwanaku. Indeed, archaeological excavations in the capital have shown that the Incas had no tradition of megalithic stone masonry before about AD1350–75, according to radiocarbon dating. The city was divided into upper (*hanan*) and lower (*hurin*) sections, respectively the quarters of the two social divisions of the populace believed to have been ordered by the first ruler, Manco Capac. Again according to legend, Pachacuti named the renewed city 'lion's body' (by which the Spanish chronicler meant a puma), and, from above, the plan of the city indeed resembles a crouching puma with a head and tail.

HIGHWAYS AND LINES

From the central plaza, Huacaypata, four great imperial highways and four sacred cosmic lines radiated to the four quarters. From the nearby Coricancha emanated 41 sacred *ceque* lines: sightings lines to the horizons and beyond. They were grouped into upper and lower sets and further divided into four quarters. The upper set was associated with Hanan Cuzco and with the quarters of Antisuyu (north-east) and Chinchasuyu (north-west), while the lower set was associated with Hurin Cuzco and with the quarters of Collasuyu (south-east) and Cuntisuyu (south-west). Together these highways, cosmic lines and *ceques* integrated the capital and the four quarters into the Inca state religion focused on Inti, the sun god, as a near equal to the creator Viracocha – perhaps another reason why they did not emphasize the history of the divisions.

Left: Inca surveyors linked the provinces of the entire empire with a masterly engineered road system.

ROADMAP OF THE STARS

A link with the heavens was further enhanced by the association of each of the four great highways along a route approximating (except when having to to go around hills and mountains) a north–south/east–west axis of Mayu (literally 'celestial river'), commonly known as the Milky Way. In the course of 24 hours, ancient Andeans observed that Mayu crosses its zenith in the sky, and in so doing forms two intersecting axes oriented north-east/south-west and south-east/north-west. Thus, the divisions of the sky provided a celestial grid against which their world of Tahuantinsuyu was projected.

CUZCO AND BEYOND

The Inca Empire stretched more than 4,200km (2,600 miles) from north to south and east to west across the Andes, from the Amazon rainforests and Argentine plains to the Pacific coast. Throughout this vast area lived a variety of peoples whose earlier cultural evolution united them locally and regionally, especially at an economic and religious level. This was exploited by the Incas, who imposed imperial rule and economic stability on the empire.

ALL ROADS LEAD TO CUZCO

Imperial Cuzco, the capital city, was considered to be the navel of the Inca world. From it and to it led all roads, both physically and spiritually. This network linked peoples and cultures as varied as fishing communities, such as the Uru in the Lake Titicaca Basin, and the Kingdom of Chimú on the Peruvian north coast, a state whose sophistication might have rivalled the Incas. The empire reached its greatest extent beyond the Cuzco Valley in less than 100 years of conquests.

Above: The vast Altiplano of Collasuyu, Bolivia, south of Cuzco, was added to the empire through the conquests of Sapa Inca Tupac Yupanqui (1471–93).

Below: Tambo Colorado, at the end of a major road running west, was one of many planned provincial administrative capitals.

SPREADING CIVILIZATION

A number of distinctive Inca cultural traits have been identified, which they spread to greater and lesser extents throughout the empire. These include: a corporate style of architecture, settlement planning, artefact styles, large-scale engineering works and terracing.

In the Cuzco area, most residential buildings (*kanchas*) were rectangular, single-room and single-storey affairs, arranged around courtyards. They were made of fieldstones or adobe bricks, gabled, with thatched roofs, and had doors, windows and internal niches usually of trapezoidal shape. A second basic form, the *kalanka*, was a rectangular hall used for several public functions. Structures for state purposes were mostly, but not always, made of finely cut and fitted stone. Most were in the capital and its immediate environs; fitted-stone architecture was rare in the provinces and restricted to special state buildings.

In settlement planning, the Incas practised a policy of relocating peoples away from their homelands for political and economic reasons. In such settlements, Inca engineers laid out *kancha* enclosures in blocks around Inca-style state administrative buildings where needed. Some provincial Inca settlements were established for specific purposes, perhaps one of the best known being Huánuco Pampa, an Inca imperial city about 675km (420 miles) north-west of Cuzco in the Chinchaysuyu quarter, which was established as a seat of provincial administration and also for the storage and redistribution of the products of the empire.

Above: Huánuco Pampa, a provincial administrative capital in Chinchasuyu, lay on the main northern trunk road up the spine of the empire, heading all the way to Quito.

In some provincial settlements, the Incas relied on local technology and adapted themselves to local political and social organization while retaining an over-arching control. In such cases any evidence of Inca presence, conquest and rule is found more in material culture, particularly pottery (but also textiles and metalwork), of distinctive Inca decorative design and techniques.

The vast majority of settlements were not Inca in origin and were, apart from the relocated populations in Inca-planned towns, left in their native styles and plans. Again, Huánuco Pampa provides an important example: the surrounding villages retained their local native character and Inca rule was exerted indirectly through local leaders.

Throughout the empire, Inca engineers were famous for their works. There were roads, bridges, agricultural terracing and accompanying systems of irrigation canals. Imperial highways linked Cuzco with the provincial capitals. Major imperial highways went north-west to Vilcashuaman, Huánuco Pampa, Cajamarca, Tumibamba and Quito and south-east to Chucuito, Paria, Tupiza, La Paya, Santiago and other cities. Westward-running highways branched off to major coastal cities – Tumbes, Pachacamac, Tambo Colorado, Nazca and others – and a parallel highway ran along the Peruvian coast as far as Atico. In many cases pre-existing roads were incorporated and it is often difficult to identify roads as specifically Inca-made unless there is also associated Inca architecture, or sometimes evidence of inhabitants. Similarly with bridges: it is often only the presence of stone foundations and Inca artefacts at river crossings that indicates where an Inca bridge stood.

Land terracing, especially throughout the Andes, was constructed to take advantage of every available opportunity to extend land for growing, especially maize. Again, it is not always possible to identify specifically Inca terracing from pre-Inca work without other associated Inca features, but it is certain that with the expansion of Inca domination the extent of terracing increased greatly.

KINSHIP AND TAXES

The Incas exploited and perhaps consolidated the economic and social arrangement called *ayllu*. This was a kinship charter based on actual or imagined descent between groups working the different environments between highlands and lowlands, especially farming and llama herding. Such a group of related people was an organization for both labour exchange and a common ownership of property, possessions and rights; it also established, monitored and regulated rules of social conduct, and solved social problems at various levels. In other words, it incorporated rights and responsibilities.

The Incas employed a state tax system of agricultural produce divided into three categories; land was divided accordingly to support each category. The first was for the support of the gods – in practical terms it went to the priests, other religious functionaries and shrine attendants. The second went to the emperor, to support the imperial household and into storage for redistribution in times of need. The third was for the communities themselves; it was collected, stored and distributed annually by local officials.

In addition to taxation there was a labour tax, or obligation, called *mit'a*. This was an annual draft of able-bodied males to undertake public work.

Although both *ayllu* and *mit'a* were established in pre-Inca times throughout much of the Andes, the Incas exploited and used them more extensively.

BUILDING AN EMPIRE

The Inca Empire began and ended in conflict. Its downfall was hastened by the Spanish invasion, yet, when the Spaniards arrived, the Incas were themselves engaged in civil war.

THE CUZCO VALLEY

The founding of the empire is obscured in elaborate legend and myth invented by the Incas. It began with a legendary figure and first ruler, Manco Capac, leader of the *ayars*, the legendary ancestors, and founder of the Inca dynasty. The founding involved mystical birth from the earth, the designation of Inca superiority and their destiny to rule.

There were four brothers, of whom Manco was senior, and four sisters/wives – providing consistency with the division of the empire into four quarters. It was Manco who ordered the division of the people into the *hurin* and *hanan* – the upper and the lower – and who formed 'the allies' into ten lineage groups: the ten *ayllus* of commoners at Cuzco to complement the ten royal *ayllus* of his and his brothers' descendants. After migration from Lake Titicaca and many adventures, Manco, his sister/wife, and other sisters, and their son Sinchi Roca arrived in the Valley of Cuzco, where Manco organized the building of the city. Sinchi Roca duly inherited the throne and allegedly commanded the people of the valley to cultivate potatoes. He was followed by his son Lloque Yupanqui. We have no idea how long these rulers reigned, or if there were more than are named.

Archaeology provides only hints of the development of Inca power in the Cuzco Valley. We know little of what lies buried beneath modern Cuzco, and almost nothing of what lies beneath the 16th-century Inca city. It has been occupied continuously since Inca times, if not before, and many Inca structures were themselves used as foundations for Spanish colonial and later structures.

Above: Manco Capac allegedly founded Inca Cuzco and ruled in the 12th century, in the Late Intermediate Period.

DEVELOPING POWER

Ceramic styles show us that the Incas were probably a local tribe, one of several in the valley, and that Cuzco began to emerge as a regional centre in the Late Intermediate Period from the early 13th century. No individual buildings, or any distinctive architectural style, can be identified with the Incas or with a specific Inca ruler until the reign of Pachacuti Inca Yupanqui (1438–71). We do not know whether the Incas ruled Cuzco from this early time, coexisted with their neighbours or actually lived elsewhere.

What is certain, however, is that they began to dominate the valley from at least about the beginning of the 15th century. A sort of defined style began to emerge in the late 14th and early 15th centuries and was strengthened by Pachacuti Inca Yupanqui. It was he who began the formation of the Inca imperial state; and the Late Horizon, which began *c.*1400, is defined by the beginning of his hegemony.

The intervening rulers between Lloque Yupanqui and Pachacuti are a mere name list: Mayta Capac, Capac Yupanqui, Inca

Left: Puca Pukara fort near Cuzco was used in wars against the neighbouring peoples in the Cuzco Valley and adjacent valleys.

Above: Pachacuti Inca Yupanqui expanded the Inca Empire with conquests into Cuntisuyu, Chinchasuyu and Collasuyu.

Roca, Yahuar Huacac, Viracocha Inca and Inca Urco. We have little knowledge of their achievements other than that they inherited rulership of the Cuzco Valley, and continued to dominate their neighbours and strengthen their power within the valley. Mayta Capac defeated a local tribe called the Alcavicças, who were apparently dissatisfied with the Inca overlordship in the valley.

WAR AGAINST THE CHANCAS

Only Viracohca Inca and Urco emerge from legend as real people. During troubled times, undoubtedly the war with the Chancas (another valley tribe), Viracocha claimed that the god Viracocha came to him in a dream, calmed his fears and inspired him to rule. However, he and his son and named heir, Urco, fled Cuzco with much of the populace when the Chancas advanced on the city. Urco enjoyed the shortest reign – less than a year in 1438 – if he actually reigned at all.

Below: The tiered wall of Sacsahuaman, which forms the north-west quarter (Chinchasuyu) of Inca Cuzco.

His brother, Yupanqui, was more steadfast and stayed to defend the city. He too claimed divine inspiration, in an earlier incident giving him a vision of the future. In official Inca history, Yupanqui rallied his companions and repulsed the first two attacks. He called upon the gods for help and the very stones in the field allegedly became Inca warriors. The Chancas were defeated and, taking the name Pachacuti Inca ('Earth-shaker King'), he assumed the throne.

TO THE LIMITS OF THE EMPIRE

The date of 1438, which comes from the chronicler Miguel Cabello de Valboa, marked Pachacuti's defeat of the Chancas and his succession to the throne. He subdued the Cuzco Valley and declared all Quechua-speakers there to be honorary Inca citizens. He began Inca imperial aspirations by conquering the Lupaqa, Colla and other city-states to the south-east around Lake Titicaca. Then he turned his armies over to his son and chosen heir, Tupac Inca Yupanqui, to continue campaigning, while he returned to Cuzco and devoted his energies to consolidating the power of the Incas.

Pachacuti is credited with developing Inca statecraft and with organizing the institutions and systems that were the hallmarks of Inca rule: national taxation and labour levies, roadways and an imperial communication network, and extensive warehousing of food and other commodities for redistribution throughout the empire. He also established the official Inca state religion based on worship of Inti – the sun – and commissioned much building in the city, including the temple-fortress of Sacsahuaman, which was dedicated to the worship of Inti.

Tupac (1471–93) extended the empire to its greatest extent with conquests to the north and south, especially of the powerful Chimú Kingdom on the north coast, defeating King Minchançaman. His successor, Huayna Capac (1493–1526), campaigned throughout the empire, largely consolidating earlier gains. He had recently subjugated the kingdom of Quito when he died suddenly of smallpox. In the turmoil that followed, two of his sons, half-brothers by different wives, claimed the succession: Huáscar, governor of Cuzco, and Atahualpa, who controlled the army in the north.

CIVIL WAR

Spanish sources leave some doubt as to whether Huayna Capac, the twelfth Inca ruler, had actually named his successor when he died suddenly. Some sources say there was an heir apparent, a young son Ninancuyuchi, others that Huayna Capac favoured his son Huáscar, or that he secretly hoped that another son, Atahualpa, would use his control of the army to supplant Huáscar. Still other sources indicate that he had planned to divide the empire among several sons, or even that the empire was so far extended that it was effectively dividing itself in 1526.

Needless to say, the various factions that still existed at the time of the Spanish conquest recited to Spanish chroniclers the versions of events and descendants that suited them. Nevertheless, upon Huayna Capac's death, the Spaniards had just arrived off the northern coast of the empire and the Incas plunged into a bloody civil war that itself threatened the demise of the empire and all it stood for.

Below: Soldiers of Atahualpa's army lead his brother Huáscar into captivity after his defeat at the Battle of Huánuco Pampa.

Above: An Inca soldier painted on a wooden kero *drinking vessel, wearing traditional battle dress – a tunic and feather headdress.*

ONE THRONE: THREE HEIRS?

Huayna Capac had campaigned in the north of the empire for ten years. He had gone north, originally to quell a rebellion in Quito province, taking with him his sons Ninancuyuchi and Atahualpa. In Cuzco he left four governors, one of whom was Huáscar, another of his sons by his many wives. When an epidemic of smallpox broke out in the north and Huayna Capac contracted it, he anointed in formal ceremony his son Ninancuyuchi as his heir. But Ninancuyuchi also died of smallpox, and this situation left a dilemma and a plethora of possible claimants to the throne.

Huáscar seized the throne in Cuzco but was contested by Atahualpa, his younger half-brother. Atahualpa had been involved in the campaign against and subjugation of the Quito region in the far north of the empire. At his father's death he was left in command of the Inca armies of the north. At the death of Huayna Capac and Ninancuyuchi, he at first seemed to accept Huáscar's rise to power and ordered new palaces to be built for Huáscar in the northern city of Tumipampa. The local chief, Ullco Colla, however, resented Atahualpa and spread rumours of a plot against Huáscar. In the ensuing intrigue, Atahualpa and Huáscar became enemies and the former marched to confront his brother. The Inca court split into two supporting factions and civil war raged for six years.

BATTLE BETWEEN BROTHERS

Huáscar declared Atahualpa to be *auca* – a treasonous enemy of the state. He sent the army he commanded in Cuzco to attack Atahualpa and capture him in Quito.

Below: The imposing tiered walls of Sacsahuaman imply its use as a fortress as well as its main purpose as a temple to Inti.

But in a major battle Huáscar's forces were utterly defeated, and Atahualpa continued a relentless march south.

Huáscar sent larger armies against him. There were running battles and Huascar's forces were defeated but without conclusive results. Rivalry even broke out among Huáscar's generals. Huáscar sent even greater forces against Atahualpa, who again defeated them, until finally, in 1532, Huáscar himself marched with an army against him. Atahualpa's experience in the northern campaigns finally proved decisive, and this time Huáscar was taken prisoner. The final battle took place at Huánuco Pampa, north-west of Cuzco.

Atahualpa, whose forces were flushed with their victories, relied on speed. His generals marched immediately against Huáscar before further reinforcements could arrive from Cuzco. Given what had already transpired, Atahualpa offered no peace negotiations. The battle apparently lasted most of the day until Huáscar's troops broke and Huáscar was forced to flee with his immediate retinue of about 1,000 retainers and troops. Atahualpa's forces soon overtook him, however, seized Huáscar and put the remainder of his followers to death.

Above: Dressed in distinctive tunics and armed with axe-headed spears and shields, Inca armies subdued the empire.

ROYAL SACRILEGE

The ruthlessness of this prolonged war continued when Atahualpa marched on and captured Cuzco. He feigned a plan to return Huáscar to the throne as Sapa Inca and declared a day for the event. He commanded the attendance of the nobles and leaders of the empire, the provincial governors and chief administrators, many of whom were related to Huáscar, indeed to Atahualpa as well. Together they comprised the *panaca*, descendants of the royal household.

The provinces of the empire had been divided since the civil war had begun. Many cities had simply continued life as usual, while others in the most remote or recently conquered reaches of the empire rebelled or simply ignored Inca rule for the time being, awaiting the outcome of events. Now that Atahualpa was victorious, and apparently in control, however, they were being called upon to declare their loyalty.

Once everyone was gathered in Cuzco, Atahualpa had them all slain, so effectively ending further resistance by destroying the *panaca's* very existence.

Yet Atahualpa went further still in his aim to eliminate the royal family: he ordered the burning of the mummy of Tupac Yupanqui, the tenth Sapa Inca and ancestor of the *panaca*.

CONQUEST OF THE EMPIRE

Even before Francisco Pizarro (1475–1541) began his Andean explorations, an entire empire, that of the Aztecs, had been conquered in Mesoamerica by his countryman Hernán Cortés.

PIZARRO'S RETURN

A veteran of an expedition to Panama in 1509, Pizarro was eager to emulate Cortés. After two voyages from Panama to the South American mainland, he had returned with enough knowledge of the coast, stories of rich cities inland and to the south, and examples of gold and silver objects and textiles to convince him another civilization of great wealth lay to the south.

In 1526, had he attempted on his second expedition to invade the fringe of the Inca Empire, he would surely have been defeated. The empire was at its height under Sapa Inca Huayna Capac (1493–1526), with provincial garrisons and a strong army able to move quickly from centre to province along an efficient road system. In 1531, however, an attack and pillaging of the coastal, provincial port of Tumbes by the inhabitants of Puná Island went unavenged, for Capac's successor, Huáscar, was otherwise engaged.

Below: The walls and defensive gateway of the fortress city of Rumicolca, about 35km (21 miles) southeast of Cuzco.

Pizarro visited Tumbes in 1526. When he returned in 1532, he still had the two native interpreters from the town, whom he had taken with him to Spain to raise royal permission and funds for his third expedition. Now the Inca Empire was in a state of turmoil. Huáscar's army had recently been defeated by his half-brother, Atahualpa, Huáscar had been captured, and Atahualpa had seized the throne.

IMPERIAL OMENS

Even before this civil war, Huayna Capac told his sons that Inti, the sun god, had informed him that his reign was the last of the twelve Sapas. Inca rule would end with the arrival of powerful strangers, whom he believed to be the foreigners recently reported arriving by sea on the north coast. Their coming was foretold by ill omens: during ceremonies honouring Inti, an eagle was mobbed and killed by buzzards and the priests prophesied disaster; and one night the new moon had three halos – one red, one black, one smoky.

Above: Francisco Pizarro, who was born illegitimate in Trujillo, Estremadura, turned from swineherd into soldier of fortune.

The priests said the red ring foretold war between the Sapa's descendants, the black ring the demise of Inti and the smoke the vanishing of the empire. These were weaknesses that Pizarro could exploit.

Huayna Capac ordered his sons to obey the strangers, for they were in every way superior. Written after the fact, the Spanish-Inca historian Garcilaso de la Vega's account appears to be a combination of political expediency and rationalization for the collapse of the empire, which the Incas believed to be perfect. In reality, weaknesses in the Inca hierarchy, civil war, the size of the empire and the shear audacity of Pizarro better explain the subsequent events.

THE MARCH TO CAJAMARCA

The arrival of reinforcements from Panama brought Pizarro's grand army to 260 men (198 foot soldiers and 62 cavalry). Tumbes had supported Huáscar in the civil war, providing a ready-made ally. Leaving a garrison in Tumbes, Pizarro marched inland with his best troops.

Left: A fanciful depiction of Atahualpa before his capture by Pizarro. Inca soldiers did not march and fight naked.

To win more allies, he adopted a pacific approach. He forbade looting, and encouraged his Dominican friars to convert the heathens; but opposition, where met, was put down brutally – opposing provincial chiefs were burned as examples. His campaign became a crusade.

Atahualpa marched his army – reportedly 40–50,000 warriors – nearly 1,600km (1,000 miles) to Cajamarca to await Pizarro, who was himself travelling on a litter. With 110 foot soldiers and 67 cavalrymen, Pizarro camped near Tambo Grande and sent his lieutenant, Hernando de Soto, to reconnoitre. De Soto returned with an Inca official bearing gifts and an invitation to Cajamarca. Pizarro accepted the gifts, sent the official back with gifts of his own and a message that he represented the most powerful emperor in the world, offering service against the Sapa's enemies, and continued his slow march south and east towards the 4,000m (13,000ft) pass to Cajamarca.

Atahualpa sent a gift of ten llamas. The messenger gave an account of the war with Huáscar, and Pizarro allegedly delivered a speech declaring peaceful intentions, but was prepared for war if challenged. Another day's march involved being greeted by an Inca official with *chicha* (maize liquor) in gold cups – he was to lead the Spaniards to Cajamarca.

An allied chief whom Pizarro had sent to Atahualpa returned. He attacked Atahualpa's official, calling him a liar, and claimed that the Sapa had refused to receive him. He said that Cajamarca was deserted and Atahualpa had deployed his army on the plain ready for war. Atahualpa's ambassador retorted that Cajamarca had been vacated to make it ready for Pizarro – that it was the Sapa's custom to camp with this army on campaign (meaning the civil war). These exchanges must have left Pizarro more confused than ever.

Finally Pizarro, his men suffering from altitude sickness and exhaustion, climbed the hills into Cajamarca Valley. At any time Atahualpa could have destroyed him, yet he did nothing.

ETIQUETTE OBSERVED

Pizarro marched into Cajamarca's main courtyard on 15 November 1532, passing the vastly larger Inca army, his men arranged in three divisions to make the most of his comparatively meagre force. No envoy awaited or arrived. De Soto and 20 cavalrymen, then Hernando Pizarro with another 20, were sent to seek Atahualpa, who waited for them at his quarters, together with his court and some 400 warriors.

The Spaniards had to push their way through the Inca ranks. Accounts of the exchange vary: de Soto impressed the Incas with a display of horsemanship, then invited Atahualpa to the Spanish camp. Hernando arrived. Atahualpa declared that he was fasting and would visit on the next day. He claimed that one of his chiefs had killed three Spaniards and a horse back on the march. Hernando denied that any Inca could overcome a Spaniard. Atahualpa complained that one of his provincial chiefs had disobeyed him and Hernando bragged that ten horsemen could put down the revolt. *Chicha* was brought in large gold vessels. Etiquette was served; macho was displayed. It was left at that.

Below: Hernando Pizarro and Hernando de Soto were sent by Francisco Pizarro as envoys to Atahualpa at Cajamarca.

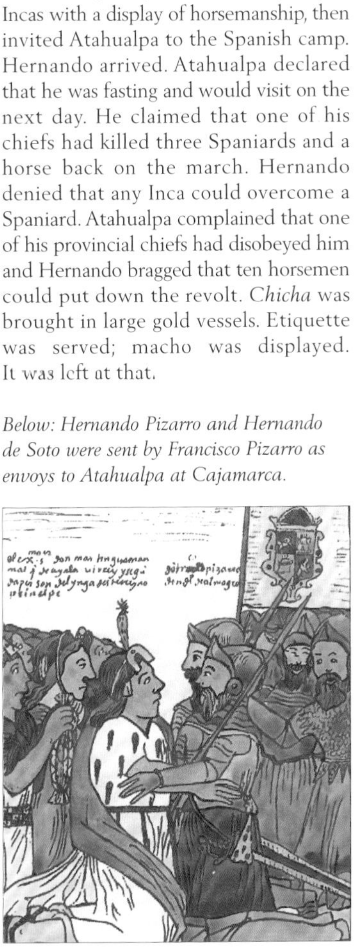

CAPTURE AND REGICIDE

Atahualpa arrived at the Spanish camp late on 16 November. There had been debate among his advisers and he had decided to visit with an armed entourage. Inca warriors lined the route and surrounding grasslands. Atahualpa, carried by his chiefs on a litter adorned with gold and silver plates, was preceded by elite warriors in colourful chequered livery, singing, dancing and sweeping the roadway before him. Atahualpa himself was bedecked with gold and turquoise jewellery, and the entire retinue displayed his wealth and majesty.

The journey was less than 6km (4 miles), yet Atahualpa hesitated, sent a messenger that he would come the next day, then changed his mind and resumed progress, now with only 6,000 unarmed followers. Atahualpa's indecision revealed a lack of human confidence despite his obsession with displaying his dignity and status as a living god. He simply could not understand the nature of the men he was dealing with.

SLAUGHTER AND CAPTURE

Entering the empty courtyard, Atahualpa was greeted by Pizarro's friar, Valverde, brandishing a Bible and a crucifix. He delivered a discourse on Christianity. Historians will forever remain unsure of the ensuing events. Despite the message having to pass through an interpreter, it seems clear that Atahualpa understood what was being demanded of him: renunciation of everything he believed in, of his entire world. Allegedly, Valverde handed him the Bible; allegedly he threw it down, pointing at the sun and declaring 'My God still lives.'

Valverde retrieved the Bible and retreated. Pizarro gave the signal to attack: a cannon was fired into the crowd, followed by arquebuses (long-barrelled guns); then his men charged. Atahualpa's chiefs fought with bare hands to save their emperor, and were butchered in the attempt. A wall collapsed in the frenzy of retreating natives. Those trapped in the courtyard were slaughtered until night fell and Atahualpa was taken captive. Thus treachery was accomplished. It must have seemed to Pizarro that this was the only way to succeed against clearly overwhelming odds. The chronicler Zárete records that the whole plot had been discussed and decided the night before. Pizarro had indeed emulated Cortés by taking the emperor hostage.

Left: In early meetings with Atahualpa's noble ambassadors, Francisco Pizarro and Hernando De Soto professed peace.

GREED AND BETRAYAL

The passivity of Atahualpa's people and army is astounding. They simply melted away, leaving their possessions in camp. The Spaniards looted Cajamarca and the chiefs' tents, seized the army's llama herds and raped the women abandoned in the royal baths.

The remainder of the story is equally sordid. Realizing Pizarro's lust for gold and silver, Atahualpa offered to fill the 5.5 by 7m (18 by 23ft) room in which he was held, as high as he could reach, with gold. Pizarro demanded that, in addition, the adjoining smaller room be filled twice with silver. Atahualpa agreed to these demands, asked for two months, and ordered the collection of gold and silver objects from all over the empire.

Above: Having captured Atahualpa at Cajamarca, Pizarro imprisoned him in a palace room while a ransom was negotiated.

At Atahualpa's request, three Spaniards, including de Soto, were sent to Cuzco to hasten the collections. They found the captive Huáscar, who offered to treble his half-brother's ransom. Learning this, Atahualpa gave secret orders for Huáscar to be murdered.

In January 1533, Hernando was sent on an expedition to Pachacamac. In April, Diego de Almagro and reinforcements arrived from Panama. Pizarro bided his time, while his soldiers grew restless – they had come for conquest and spoils.

There remained the problem of Atahualpa. Despite incomplete fulfilment of his agreement, Pizarro absolved him of further obligation, but still held him – 'for security'. He was now an encumbrance; Pizarro wanted power and Atahualpa, now only a rallying point for native rebellion, stood in his way. De Almagro and his men wanted action and plunder. Rumours of native insurrection, the 'demands' of his

men and the Spanish Inquisition provided Pizarro with justification for a 'trial'. He and de Almagro were the judges. Atahualpa was accused of usurpation of the Inca throne and the murder of Huáscar the true heir, of inciting insurrection, of distributing gold and silver that should have been used to fulfil his ransom agreement and of adultery – as Sapas had numerous wives – and idolatry. He was convicted and condemned to be burned at the stake.

THE END OF INCA RULE

The final shameless act in these procedures followed. Twelve captains called the affair a travesty of justice, but were persuaded of its political expediency. When Atahualpa realized that he was to be burned, he agreed to be baptized a Christian for the favour of strangulation, for if he were burned, in Inca belief he would be condemned in afterlife, unable to be mummified and to continue to participate in life.

Right: Despite this image, Atahualpa was strangled to death, after becoming a Christian to avoid being burned at the stake.

Pizarro finally marched to Cuzco and established Spanish government – a year after the events in Cajamarca. Alleged plans for insurrection by Challcuchima, one of Atahualpa's own generals, 'justified' his execution. A puppet Sapa, Manco, another of Huayna Capac's sons, was crowned. The last of Atahualpa's generals, Quizquiz, was defeated and fled to Quito, where he was killed by his own men.

The first years of Spanish rule were fraught with embittered rivalry between Pizarro, de Almagro and others. Pizarro enjoyed power for a mere eight years before being assassinated by rivals.

Below: The alleged 'ransom room' in Inca Cajamarca in which Atahualpa was imprisoned after being captured.

CHAPTER TWO

THE LAND

The continent of South America has a geography of extremes. Its mountains are some of the highest in the world – up to 7,000m (23,000ft); its deserts are some of the driest; its rainforests some of the wettest and densest; and its western offshore seas – the Humboldt Current – teem with some of the most abundant fisheries. Climates range from damp, steaming jungles to cold, dry deserts, and from cool, high plains to lofty, oxygen-rare summits. Rainfall can range from near zero to as much as 8,000mm (315in) a year.

Within this continent lies the Andean Area, which includes the two Cordilleras of the Andes, bordering the Amazon Rainforest on one side and the Atacama and other deserts on the other. Here humans have had to adapt to life at high altitudes. South of the Cordillera lies the Altiplano, where much of the area's farming is carried out. Here potatoes and other root crops were grown, and large herds of llamas kept for their wool. To the west lie coastal valleys and oases within the desert, where a variety of crops were grown.

East of the Andes is another world. The eastern mountain flanks descend more gradually through forested slopes, known as *montaña*, to the low, hot tropical forests, known as the selva. Here human settlement was more dispersed, yet products of the rainforest remained prominent in Andean and western coastal cultures throughout history.

Despite such extremes and a land of independent settlements, the Incas did not live in isolation: rather trade and social contact linked the settlements in both highlands and lowlands.

Left: The Callejon de Huaylas in north-central Peru epitomizes the sweeping slopes and high sierra valleys of the Andes.

PEAKS AND MOUNTAIN VALLEYS

The Andean Cordillera has been shaped in two distinct ways: by the movement of tectonic plates and by the weather.

FORMATION OF THE ANDES

Nearly two million years ago, the westward-moving South American continental plate met the eastward-moving Nazca ocean plate along the Pacific coast, moving at up to 15cm (6in) a year. The ocean plate, which has a heavier stone composition, was pushed beneath the lighter and less dense continental plate. Friction and drag where the two plates met caused folding, which created the Andean mountain chain. Where the ocean plate melted from the friction, the sedimentary rocks cracked, hurling molten rocks to the surface as volcanoes.

Below: Llamas, alpacas and vicuñas helped Andean civilizations to develop and survive in the Altiplano and high mountains.

Along their widest stretch, the spine of the Andes comprises two parallel ridges. On the east, the higher Cordillera Blanca borders the Amazon Rainforest. On the west, the Cordillera Negra fronts the Atacama Desert. South of this broad range the ridges diverge to flank, east and west, the broad Altiplano; to the north the mountains split into several ridges running parallel to the main ranges, and are cross-cut by shorter ridges to frame numerous sierra basins and valleys known as *puna*.

EFFECTS OF THE WEATHER

The distant Atlantic Ocean is the source of most of South America's precipitation. Westward-moving rain and snow meet the high Andes and fall on the eastern escarpments. West of the Andes, which lies in the rain shadow, a more arid Pacific weather pattern predominates. The Andes become drier as they become higher, and the Altiplano around the drainage of the Lake Titicaca basin forms a huge region of uninterrupted agricultural flatlands. Ninety per cent of Andean drainage runs east, ultimately to the Atlantic. Ten per cent drains into the Pacific, in numerous short, east–west-running river valleys from the western Andean flank.

Above: In the challenging terrain of the sierra valleys and basins, rivers provided the vital water needed for agriculture.

The Andes also deflect prevailing ocean winds to blow north, causing the Pacific to flow northwards along the coast. Upwelling water from the deep tectonic trench brings cold, nutrient-rich and therefore seafood-rich currents, but also chills the air, so causing sparse rainfall.

A CHALLENGING ENVIRONMENT

The mountainous and highland regions of the Andes provide one of the most challenging environments on earth to their inhabitants. High mountain ecosystems are characteristically of low productivity, yet the majority of people in the central Andes live above 2,500m (8,200ft). Such altitudes comprise steep-sided valleys and basins, rugged terrains and a generally fragile landscape. Limited flat agricultural land, poor soils and a short growing season make production difficult. In addition, low oxygen levels, infrequent rainfall, high winds, high solar radiation and prevailing cold temperatures make survival tenuous.

Above: Mt Ausangate, in the central Peruvian Cordillera, was a typical abode of apu *spirits: sacred deities who inhabited the peaks.*

ADAPTING TO ALTITUDE

The high altitude causes stress on all life forms, and in humans, in particular, it decreases blood oxygen saturation by up to 30 per cent, which means breathing can be difficult for the unaccustomed. Andean peoples' bodies have, of course, become adapted to these conditions, with large chest cavities and lung capacity. Their cellular metabolism has modified to sustain higher red blood cell numbers. Nevertheless, strenuous work demands more energy to sustain the raised breathing, circulation and metabolic rates needed to maintain body temperature. As a result, highland peoples need to eat more to maintain a high basic metabolic rate, yet ironically they live in an environment where it is difficult to produce and obtain the necessary food for this diet.

The peopling of the Andes was thus a slow process, with generations at one altitude gradually becoming adapted to life at that level before their descendants could move into the next, higher zone, where the adaptive process took place again. Europeans, for the most part from comparatively lowland environments, have still been adapting through the generations since colonization began.

Unfortunately, we have no records of how lowland South Americans fared or coped with the high altitudes. Comparisons of the skeletons from lowland and highland burials, however, show that the two populations were more related within than between their respective groups.

POTATOES AND LLAMAS

In these highlands, agriculture consisted of a combination of root crops and herding. Because there are relatively few sizeable valleys – the valleys around Cuzco being exceptions – the steep slopes of valley and basin sides had to be adapted to provide flat areas for cultivation. Considerable labour and expertise were devoted to building millions of hillside terraces (*andenes*) and networks of irrigation canals.

The staple highland crop was the potato. Beans, squashes, peppers and peanuts were also important food crops. Maize can be grown at altitudes of up to 3,300m (11,000ft), but is at great risk from frost and hail at such heights.

The only domesticated animals were camelids (llamas, alpacas and vicuñas), dogs, guinea pigs and ducks. Llamas were herded in great flocks and provided the only pack animals for transport. They were also used for their wool (as were alpacas), meat and medicine. Dogs were raised as hunting companions and for food. Guinea pigs and ducks were raised for food, and also eggs in the case of the latter.

Below: Geographic map of the Andean Area, showing coastal plains, the Andes and the eastern rainforest.

ABUNDANT PLAINS – THE ALTIPLANO

The vast Altiplano (high plain) south of the central Peruvian Andes is formed where the principal Cordillera Blanca and Cordillera Negra diverge. Centred towards Lake Titicaca at the present Peruvian–Bolivian border, it lies at nearly 4,000m (13,000ft) above sea level. It forms a long trough, 800km (500 miles) north-west to south-east and drains north to south through a chain of lakes from Lake Azangaro in Peru through Titicaca to Lake Poopó in Bolivia. It is the largest expanse of agricultural flatlands in the Andean Area. The depth (up to 200m/650ft) and expanse (8,600 sq km/3,320 sq miles) of Lake Titicaca provides, as do the other lakes, a moderating influence on local temperatures.

In much of this region there was less need for labour-intensive terracing. Instead, pre-Hispanic peoples developed several methods for intensifying agricultural production. Rivers were tapped by canals dug to channel their waters into the fields and to regulate ground water levels. In addition, check dams were constructed to collect and store run-off water, and aqueducts and dikes were made to divert and distribute it among the fields to water the crops.

Above: The sparser, bleaker high plains of the southern Altiplano provide little scope for agriculture, but they were widely used for llama herding.

Below: The high plains of the southern Andean plateaux are punctuated by volcanic cones, such as El Misti, believed to be the homes of gods whose destructive powers were feared.

CLAIMING THE LAND

During periods of high precipitation, the large region of low land, relatively speaking, around Lake Titicaca and the other lakes was reclaimed for agriculture by creating long, wide, ridged fields of mounded soils. They were separated by channels of slow-moving water, which provided protection from frost by releasing overnight the heat they had absorbed from the sun during the day. Nevertheless, to help maintain dense population levels, the steep slopes of the surrounding hills were also terraced to provide extra agricultural fields.

In drought years, when the lake level could drop by as much as 12m (39ft), some 50,000ha (124,000 acres) of formerly

Above: Alpacas were a species closely related to the llama. They provided a finer grade of wool than the llama.

cultivated land were left without the usual water channels and were simply abandoned temporarily.

As in the *puna*, the principal crops of the Altiplano were root vegetables. There were multiple varieties of potato, various tubers, legumes and grains such as quinoa domesticated from regional native species. In addition, the lakes, and especially Titicaca, provided a rich variety of aquatic resources. The deep, cold waters of the lakes supported abundant fish stocks, which had been exploited from early times. Migrating waterfowl (ducks and flamingos) provided plenty of seasonal meat and eggs. The shallow lakeshores harboured edible reeds – also used for roof thatching, clothing and for making fishing boats, and various water plants provided animal forage and were gathered as fodder for domesticated llama herds and guinea pigs.

GREAT HERDS OF LLAMAS

The llama and alpaca were both cornerstones of the Altiplano economy. Great herds of them were especially kept in the southern and northern Altiplano to sustain a pastoral way of life. From being the hunting grounds of the earliest inhabitants, these grasslands became the focus of llama and alpaca domestication from as early as 5000BC. Throughout the Andean Area they were bred carefully for multiple purposes. The primary reason was for their wool, providing woven textiles for clothing, hats, bags and slings, as well as for exchange with lowland settlements for their produce. Textiles were also used to fulfil social taxation obligations.

As well as wool, several by-products were also of value. Llama meat and fat were important sources of protein and energy. Their bones were made into many tools, from scrapers, knives, needles and awls to musical instruments. The hides were made into clothing and other articles. Their dung was used as fuel and provided a source of fertilizer to re-enrich fields left fallow between growing seasons. Whole llamas were frequently sacrificed in religious ceremonies, and figured prominently in Andean cosmology. Finally, they were the pick-up trucks of pre-Hispanic Andeans, used to transport commodities over long distances.

Below: Vicuñas were prized for their fine wool and have adapted to high altitudes, where drought and freezing nights are the rule.

Above: Llamas were valuable, sure-footed pack animals for transporting goods between highlands and lowlands.

LIFE AT THE EDGE

Beyond the Altiplano lake basins, and especially towards the southern extreme of the great trough that forms the Altiplano, the landscape becomes increasingly arid. It would have been unsuitable for agriculture, or even llama herding, except in various isolated areas where a tenuous growing season could have been exploited with careful irrigation.

WESTERN DESERTS AND COASTAL VALLEYS

The western descent to the coastal strip of the Andean Area was an important and rich area of isolated cultural oases, at least in earliest pre-Hispanic times.

The region's climate is controlled by the Humboldt Current, which brings cold water northwards along the coast and creates cool, arid conditions inland. While the coastal air remains humid, causing coastal fog, temperature inversion (whereby air decreases in temperature less quickly than usual as it climbs) over the land inhibits rainfall and creates deserts inland – chiefly the Sechura in the north and the Atacama in the south of the Andean Area.

There is more arable land in the northern coastal valleys than in the southern coastal area. From north to south. there are three climate zones: semi-tropical in the north, sub-tropical in the middle and sub-tropical to desert in the south. The principal pre-Hispanic products of the coastal valleys and desert oases were maize, beans, squashes, peanuts, manioc, avocado and other semi-tropical fruits, and cotton.

Above: Eroding salt deposits of ancient raised shorelines are seen here at San Pedro de Atacama in Chile, the driest desert environment in the world.

Left: Off-shore islands, such as Ballesta Island, Peru, were valuable sources of guano, used as fertilizer and a valuable trade item.

IRRIGATION SYSTEMS

Along the Pacific watershed of the coastal strip virtually all desert farming and 85 per cent of sierra–coastal valley agriculture is reliant on run-off irrigation. More than 60 short rivers, rising in the steep western Andean slopes, descend through rugged then quickly levelling terrain to the Pacific Ocean. Tapping them for their water involved elaborate, labour-intensive projects to dig canals and channels to bring water from distant rivers to terraced fields. The very nature and sophistication of such works encouraged different regions to work together to establish and maintain them.

In the southern region of the coastal strip large expanses of desert provided a different challenge. Here people needed to bring water from the nearby sierra and from more widely spaced rivers. The Nazca and other rivers in this region flow on the surface in the upper valleys only; down-valley they disappear into subterranean channels. In response to this condition, and perhaps enhanced in times of drought, the peoples of the area built elaborate underground irrigation systems of aqueducts to bring water from the underground rivers and to gather the water table through an arrangement of trenches and tunnels into catchment cisterns that could be tapped when needed.

Above: Vast deserts along the coasts of Peru and northern Chile contained scores of river valleys, providing oases for early agriculture.

HARVESTING THE SEA

In addition to agriculture, especially in the northern valleys (and largely independently from the southern desert valley agricultural societies), coastal cultures exploited the extremely rich maritime resources of the Pacific. Molluscs and crustaceans were collected on the foreshore; large and small fish were taken in nets and by hook (anchovies and sardines were harvested throughout the year and seasonally, respectively); sea mammals were hunted with harpoons; and sea birds were regularly taken. Offshore islands, havens for vast seabird colonies, provided a regular source of guano for fertilizing the fields. Even edible kelp leaves were collected as a food source.

One commodity sought from farther north was the bivalve *Spondylus princeps* – the spiny or thorny oyster. Native in the coastal waters from Ecuador north to Baja California, it was exploited by coastal peoples from as early as 3000BC. Its collection is not easy, because its habitat is 18–50m (60–160ft) deep. Nevertheless, divers regularly collected it, and throughout pre-Hispanic times it provided a rich source of coastal and inland trade to both the north and south. It was sought as a ritual object and provides evidence of long-distance trade and contact between different cultures.

OASES CULTURES

In times of drought, oases cultures were stretched severely and it required, besides their religious beliefs, fortitude and ingenuity to sustain their cultural ways. Each river supplying an oasis valley, desert oasis or western sierra basin was otherwise isolated. Such isolation enabled several nearly self-governing populations to arise and maintain their independence. At the same time, however, there was a need for contact and the trading of goods from one region to another. Such links between desert oases, and indeed valleys, were spiritual and military enterprises whose strengths waxed and waned throughout Andean Area history.

Left: Ancient peoples of the desert coastlands relied on the rich harvest of the sea, and traded exotic shells with highland cultures.

THE *MONTAÑA* AND EASTERN RAINFORESTS

The geography of the eastern flank of the Altiplano and Cordillera provides a complete contrast to the western Cordillera. Here there are high, bleak plateaux called the *montaña* or Ceja de Selva, where the terrain and vegetation make agriculture difficult and careful terracing and water management are necessary. Llama herding is widespread here. Starting at about 4,000m (13,000ft) above sea level, the *montañas*, known as cloud forests, drop towards the east until they merge with true tropical forest. Rainfall averages 2,000–4,000mm (80–160in) a year.

RAINFOREST PRODUCTS

In addition to llama products, the hard and soft woods of the slopes provided the only major source of timber and wood for everyday and religious objects in the Andean Area. Agriculture on the middle slopes included maize, beans, squash, peanuts, peppers and cotton, all of which were transported by llama caravans specially commissioned by the rulers and elite of the Altiplano.

Most importantly, the *montaña* was the source of coca *(Erythroxylon coca)*, used for both practical and spiritual purposes. The alkaloid compounds derived from the dried leaves of the coca plant or shrub provided (and continue to provide today) stimulation to relieve the fatigue of strenuous labour at high altitudes. It was also a ritual commodity of symbolic and real importance from very early times. Its importance and limited availability also encouraged political arrangements and even wars over its control. The true tropical rainforest lies mostly outside the Andean Area. Here precipitation can be in excess of 8,000mm (315in) per year, and it flows into rivers destined for the Atlantic Ocean. However, both the eastern *montaña* descending from the Altiplano and the north-eastern slopes from the northern Andes meet the Amazon Rainforest.

Above: The dense rainforests of Antisuyu were the source of many products, including hallucinogenic mushrooms.

Below: The stealth and power of the jaguar was revered by Andean peoples. It was a common 'form' for shape-changing shamans.

This closeness of *montaña* and rainforest encouraged cultural links, trade for rainforest products and a reverence for its creatures. The red, blue and yellow feathers of rainforest parrots, kingfishers and macaws were coveted by highland peoples. Harpy eagle feathers were also sought, and the bird's predatory nature admired. Cayman and serpent representations featured in much highland art and religious iconography, starting with the Chavín culture. Gold collected in placer mines, hallucinogenic plants (especially mushrooms and tobacco), resinous woods and various tropical fruits and medicinal plants all made their way to Andean cities. Jaguar pelts and monkeys were sought as both were revered animals whose cunning, courage, fierceness and cleverness was to be emulated.

THE LIMITS OF CIVILIZATION

The eastern boundaries of the Inca Empire extended to the edges of the Amazon. To the Incas this was the land of the Antisuyu quarter and the eastern edge of Collasuyu quarter, the place where civilization ended and savagery began. It was Inca Roca, the sixth Inca ruler, who defeated the Chunchos of Antisuyu only by adopting their savage tropical forest methods of fighting – he 'became' a jaguar and wore a green cloak. Viracocha, the eighth Sapa Inca, established the boundary between civilized highlands and savage Antisuyu when he destroyed the town of Calca 'with a fireball', 'propelling' it to the other side of the River Vilcanota. Manco Capac, the founding Inca – who was defined in legend as carrying maize, the highland, civilized crop – defeated the Hualla Indians in the Cuzco Valley. They were described as growers of rainforest crops such as peppers and coca.

The Incas made several attempts to conquer parts of the rainforest, but the environment proved too alien. Once within the forest, Inca generals lacked familiar points of reference on a visible horizon and their disorientated armies thrashed about in the dense, unfamiliar terrain. Pachacuti Inca Yupanqui, Tupac Yupanqui and Huayna Capac all sent campaigns into the jungles, and all were defeated. Despite this, bowmen from the *montaña* and tropical forest borders were recruited into the Inca army.

Above: Exotic rainforest birds provided the colourful feathers for ritual capes, tunics and headdresses made by skilled craftsmen.

A PLACE APART

To the Inca, the rainforest was *hurin*, feminine and subservient, despite their failure to conquer any of it or coerce any of its inhabitants into taxable submission. Ollantaytambo and Machu Picchu in Antisuyu defined the edge of Inca civilization, and one of their purposes in their border positions was to attempt to control coca production.

The trading relationship between highland cultures and tropical forest peoples was mostly one-way: from the tropical forest to the highlands. Although trade, both in commodities and ideas, was brisk at the borders, no serious attempts were made by highland peoples to colonize the rainforest or to establish large trading settlements at the borders. The rainforests remained in this passive role throughout pre-Hispanic history, providing precious raw materials, imagery and inspiration, but otherwise remaining a separate world.

Left: Winding rivers in the rainforest were home to the cayman, the South American crocodile, which inspired religious images.

LAND OF EXTREMES

The Andean Cordillera occupied by the Incas and their predecessors is an area of extremes, both environmental and ecological. They include the full global range of geographic landscapes and seascapes, from dense rainforests to teaming oceans. The Cordillera's inhabitants would have had to cope with fundamental contrasts in terrain, soil, water resources, sea, weather and temperature, depending on where they settled. Characteristically, though frustratingly for farmers, where there is adequate level land for cultivation there is often little water, and vice versa. Equally, seasonal and cyclical weather patterns mean that periods of regular rainfall, producing fertile growing conditions, are interspersed with periods of drought sometimes lasting years, decades or even centuries.

IRREGULAR RAINFALL

The mountainous landscape of the Cordillera means that rainfall is irregularly distributed. It is seasonal, starting about late October and November, climaxing between December and March and virtually disappearing from June to September. This annual cycle is decidedly irregular, however, swinging between values above and below the median, which occurs only about once every four years. This irregularity introduces another paradox in Andean survival. Rainfall for higher-altitude agriculture, where farmers devised methods to make more cultivatable land available, but where there is less water, generally fluctuates less. Yet run-off agriculture, which is generally more productive, is possible mostly where the rainfall fluctuates the most.

Highland farming is most successful when rainfall is heavy enough to cause sufficient run-off for crop production. (The run-off is stored in a structure of suitable size and construction and used to water the land during dry periods.) But arid mountain soils absorb fixed amounts of moisture, and so run-off occurs only when this absorption level is exceeded. Rainfall exceeding this capacity generally occurs only between about 3,900m (12,800ft) and 4,900m (16,100ft). Above about 5,000m (16,400ft) most available water is locked-up in glaciers and ice fields. Therefore, severe fluctuations in rainfall in this crucial altitudinal zone have a severe effect on the amount of run-off water available down-slope in the most important agricultural basins and valleys. This unbalanced relationship between rainfall and run-off also explains the dramatic variation of the rivers of the Pacific coastal valleys.

Above: The Incas conquered the parched, desiccated surface of the Atacama and other western coastal deserts.

STRESSFUL CONDITIONS

The effects of living at high altitude and coping with low blood oxygen saturation made life stressful for early Andeans. They needed to eat more than lowlanders to maintain their metabolic rate, yet changeable weather patterns and scarce foodstuffs made life precarious. Supporting and sustaining civilization in highland regions was thus measurably more costly in many ways than it was in lowland areas.

Alongside the daily stresses of living, earth movements and weather cycles caused problems. Tectonic activity, both small and large scale, brings disastrous consequences. Relentless tectonic creep exacerbates erosional patterns and affects canals and water collection methods by altering slopes, damaging canals and affecting their performance.

Left: The lush, well-watered Amazonian rainforest proved to be too alien and disorientating to the Inca armies.

Sudden disaster also came from earthquakes and volcanoes. Shifts from the plates that formed the Andes brought an earthquake of magnitude 7 or greater on the Richter Scale about once a decade. The immediate effects and consequent landslides caused fatalities as well as damage to buildings, canals and other structures. Volcanic activity persisted throughout ancient times, and into the present, especially in the northern Andean Area in Ecuador, southern Colombia and the Vicanota region of southern Peru.

Unable to explain these events scientifically, peoples of the Andes developed their own spiritual explanations involving cosmic battles and angry gods. Even into modern times they believed in mountain gods. When Mount Huaynaputina in southern Peru erupted in AD1600, the power of the explosion blew the entire crown of the mountain away, leaving a huge crater. Natives believed the event to be a rebellion of the ancient deities against the victory of the Christian gods.

Below: The sierra valleys were well watered but challenging. Raised fields and terracing maximized the amount of level ground for crops.

THE DREADED EL NIÑO

The phenomenon known as El Niño disrupted even what could be regarded as the 'regular' rainfall cycles described above, introducing perennial episodes of hostsile weather conditions. El Niños occur about every four to ten years. They are caused by the warming of the eastern tropical Pacific, changing atmospheric conditions, and altering weather cycles in the far and central Pacific. The conditions also act to magnify the effects of changes in solar radiation. Usually lasting about 18 months, El Niños generate torrential storms accompanied by cataclysmic floods along the western coasts. Simultaneously, because the weather patterns have been reversed, the mountains and Altiplano become subject to prolonged periods of drought.

Above: The high sierra provided abundant water for mountain valleys and oases, as well as mountain gods and burial places.

Along the desert western coasts, tonnes of debris deposited by earthquake-induced landslides, having lain loose for years, are flushed into the sea in the floods. Ground into fine sands by wave action, it is redeposited along the beaches. Strong offshore winds then collect it into huge dunes that can choke the life out of cities and settlements far inland.

Even longer-term droughts and wet periods affected Cordillera civilization. Evidence from glacier ice shows a substantial increase in atmospheric dust caused by drought between *c.*2200 and 1900BC; other extended droughts occurred in 900–800BC, 400–200BC, AD1–300, 562–95 and 1100–1450. Wetter periods occurred in AD400–500, 900–100 and 1500–1700.

LIVING WITHIN THE LANDSCAPE

Andean cultures faced great challenges, many of which were presented by the landscape around them. With its high mountains, dense rainforests and arid deserts, much of the Andean Area was not suitable for habitation, but, even so, communities developed wherever they could.

ESTABLISHING LINKS

Most early Andean communities developed in isolated situations in the western coastal valleys, the desert oases and the basins that lay between the mountains. Surrounding terrain made such settlements, by their very nature, independent and self-sufficient for the essentials of life.

Despite their isolation, however, such communities began to make contact with peoples in other regions and from other cultures. This may have been instigated as much by curiosity as by a desire to foster trade in order to supplement limited foodstuffs and other goods. As these links became established, social contact and trade took place across long distances. Inca civilization, as the empire was expanded, developed and exploited long-established patterns of long-distance trade.

Below: Maize was grown on the north coast of South America and throughout the Andean Area at 2,000–3,000m (6,600–9,800ft).

Above: This burial mantle displays a religious motif of mountain pumas or rainforest jaguars, from whose tails dangle trophy heads.

CONTRADICTORY CONDITIONS

Successful agriculture in the Cordillera and the development of civilization relied upon adequate sunshine, favourable temperatures, fertile soil, arable land and sufficient water – and also on the presence/availability of domesticated plants and animals.

In the *punas*, where agricultural settlements were carefully managed, the ruggedness and steepness of the land, along with poor weather conditions, increase with altitude, making the lower slopes the obvious places to develop. Yet in times of drought, mountain precipitation and soil moisture shift up-slope by 100–400m (320–1,300ft) above normal distribution, leaving these lower slopes arid. Claiming and maintaining drought-tolerant ground for agricultural purposes required massive investments in materials and labour to check the erosion of thin mountain soils on steep slopes and to direct water to fields and terraces, and considerable will and co-operation to accomplish it.

The dramatically different environmental conditions between highlands and lowlands described earlier in this chapter

clearly reinforced the economic and cultural differences among the mountain, maritime-oasis, and *montaña* and rainforest peoples.

Each region in the Andean Area had strengths and weaknesses to encourage, challenge or inhibit its inhabitants. During periods of regional settlements, these varying strengths encouraged cultural variety. Yet, at the same time, the most important river valleys were centres for the spread of cultural developments that unified different regions. Prominent examples include the Chavín culture from its mountain valley, the Moche people in the Lambayeque and adjacent northern coastal valleys, the Nazca culture from its southern coastal desert oasis, the Wari and Tiwanaku 'empires', respectively in the high Cordillera and the Altiplano, and the Incas from their central Andean mountain valley.

Sierra basins and east–west-running river valleys of the western coast form self-sufficient oases for settlements. Steep mountain gorges, high passes and dry deserts make access between regions difficult and inhibit contact between their inhabitants, separating and segregating rather than uniting them. Vast amounts of effort would have been needed to incorporate large areas into states and kingdoms, as occurred throughout Andean prehistory.

Below: The potato provided a staple of the Andean diet. It was cultivated at elevations of 2,000 to nearly 4,000m (6,600–13,100ft).

The periods of drought described above affected farming reliant on run-off water much more than agriculture reliant on direct rainfall. This was because arid, absorbent mountain soils better retained the moisture available. Alternating wetter periods brought greater benefit to run-off agriculture and coastal irrigation schemes because of the reversals of the 'normal' distributions of weather patterns and precipitation.

REDISTRIBUTION OF ASSETS

Cultivation reliant on run-off water normally provides higher yields than rainfall farming. Thus, the vast plains of the Altiplano were exploited with raised fields, and the western coastal valley and desert oases with re-channelled water from the rivers. Both areas developed joint labour schemes to build the necessary structures. Such methods secured more arable land at high altitudes than in the lowlands, but, frustratingly, only about 20 per cent of Andean cultivated crops grow well above 3,000m (9,800ft), while 90 per cent grow best below 1,000m (3,300ft), so there is a limit on how much production increases.

Above: The transport of goods by llama caravans enabled trading between lowland and highland regions to take place.

These differences in the distribution of productive land, crops and resources led to the development of relations between regions to the point that they were dependent upon each other. Raw materials and products were exchanged through trade from very early times, but also through conquest and coercion. During periods of unity, not only were produce and rare commodities traded between coast and mountain, and between mountain and *montaña* and rainforest, but also the ruling elite actually redistributed groups of people to moderate the effects of adverse seasonal weather patterns. These practices are well documented for the Inca, and archaeological evidence from earlier cultures, kingdoms and empires indicates that such practices were developed much earlier.

The redistribution of both goods and labour enabled rulers to maintain control by making sure that everyone under their rule had sufficient resources to live on. To such an end, the Incas used llama caravans to take produce and manufactured goods between highlands and lowlands. Potatoes, maize, peanuts, chilli peppers, coca leaves and much else were transported in woollen and cotton sacks in llama caravans.

CHAPTER THREE

SACRED LANDSCAPES, SACRED SKIES

The ancient Andean cultures revered every aspect of their environment: the landscape and seascape, and the very skies above them. Unable to explain their universe scientifically, ancient Andeans, like other ancient peoples, explained their surroundings with reconstruction stories that were rooted in their view of the world.

The Milky Way, known as Mayu, was thought to be *the* celestial river, and thus the source of all moisture – a vital part of Andean life. Mayu also had important influences on daily life, and the Incas formed links between the stars in the sky and myths. They also formed a view of a cyclical world.

Nature was considered a living, breathing being. It was something to engage with rather than to conquer, to co-operate with rather than to dominate. The landscape and skies were animate and charged with interactive, reciprocal forces.

There were many sacred places called *huacas* within the Andean Area. Most *huacas* were natural places, but others were man-made or were human modifications of natural work. Mountain tops, known as *apus*, were also venerated, although volcanoes and earthquakes were more feared for their destructive powers – the anger of the gods.

Further elements of mystery are added to the Andean landscape by Nazca lines, forming natural figures and shapes in the desert, and *ceque* lines – sacred pathways radiating from Cuzco.

Left: Mt Illimani, in the Cordillera Real, and other peaks were believed to be the source of water and the homes of the gods.

PLACES OF WORSHIP

To the Incas, and no doubt to their Andean Area ancestors, their entire surroundings were sacred. Throughout the landscape, special places that had been revered for generation after generation, and where offerings were made or special rituals performed, were known as *huacas*. As well as the powerful central deities of the Inca pantheon, whose presences were manifested in individual temples in the Coricancha in Cuzco, Andean peoples recognized a host of lesser nature gods, spirits and oracles that existed throughout the land. *Huacas* were places where such lesser figures could also be revered and, if necessary, placated.

INCA *HUACAS*

Huacas were hallowed places where significant mythological events had taken place and/or where offerings were made to local deities. It is thought that all Andean cultures had *huacas* that were special to them, and thus most *huacas* were of ancient origin. The majority were natural features of the landscape, such as mountaintops (*apus*), caves, springs and especially stones or boulders, but they could also be man-made objects, or natural objects or landscape features modified by human workmanship. An Inca *huaca* could also be a location along a sacred *ceque* line (a sacred route), such as the pillars erected on the western horizon above Cuzco for viewing the sunset from the Capac Usnu for special astronomical observations.

In and around Cuzco there were more than 300 *huacas*. Other Inca sacred places were concentrated wherever there was an association with a ruler. For example, Huayna Capac, the twelfth Sapa Inca, undertook a special pilgrimage to visit the favourite places of his father, Tupac Yupanqui, in Cajamarca, as did Atahualpa those of Huayna Capac in the northern provinces before marching against his brother Huáscar. Ironically, it was in Cajamarca that Atahualpa met defeat at the hands of Pizarro.

Ceque lines themselves, by their very nature as sacred or ritual pathways, were also *huacas*, and, equally, they incorporated *huacas* as points along the sacred routes they provided.

Below: The sacred Intihuatana (Hitching Post of the Sun) at Machu Picchu typifies natural outcrops carved as sacred huacas.

Above: The outcrop of Qenqo, north of Cuzco, was one of the Inca's most sacred huacas. *It resembles a seated puma.*

ANCESTRAL *HUACAS*

Royal and elite mausoleums, where the mummified remains of ancestors were kept, were also regarded as *huacas*. Spanish colonial sources identify many Inca royal *huacas*; and Chan Chan, the capital of the rulers of Chimú, surrounded their royal mausoleum compounds. These records reveal what appear to be the two basic classifications of such man-made *huacas*: the *huacas adatorios* – the sanctuaries and temples where gods and goddesses were worshipped; and the *huacas sepulturas* – the burial places of the most important members of the deceased.

A characteristic *huaca* is the collection of stones known as the Pururaucas around Cuzco. These were revered as the re-petrified ancient stones that had allegedly risen up and become Inca warriors to help Pachacuti Inca Yupanqui defend Cuzco against the Chancas in the early 15th century. Other examples include Qenqo, just north of Cuzco, where one large

Above: Stone cairns on mountain passes were a special type of huaca *called an* apacheta. *They were thought to hold local deities' spirits.*

upright boulder was left untouched, presumably because its silhouette resembled that of a seated puma, and the sacred shrines and statues of Viracocha at Cacha and Urcos. In some cases a *huaca* was a combination of the natural and the miraculous. Once again the stones of Pururaucas are a prime example. Another is the stone of the ancestor brother Ayar Uchu atop Huanacauri Mountain, which is believed to be the petrified body of that ancestor. Yet another example is Pariacaca, which/who seems to have been simultaneously a mountain and a mobile deity or culture hero.

PROVINCIAL *HUACAS*

The movements and final resting places of important rulers strengthened attachments to the natural symbolism of *huacas* as ancestral or 'parental'. The hill called Huanacauri above Cuzco, for example, was regarded as the father of three of the founding Inca ancestors, each turned to stone as a prominent rock or crag. Other Andean peoples regarded the local mountains as being 'like parents' who gave birth to the local community. Indeed, such beliefs are enshrined in the story of the creation of peoples by the god Viracocha, who assigned each people their region as a sacred act.

Most tribes, 'nations' and towns undoubtedly had a particular place that was recognized as their group's *huaca*. Equally, most kinship groups, the *ayllus*, also had their own *huacas*. It was believed that the spirit of the *huaca* exerted a special influence over the lives and destinies of the members of the group. *Huacas* continue to be recognized by local peoples in the Andes today in a mixture of pre-Christian and Catholic belief.

LINKS FROM PAST TO PRESENT

Reverence at *huacas* and the following of *ceque* lines represented a strengthening of the past, a reassurance of the present and an insuring of the future. Indeed, the myth-history attached to Inca sacred places infused the very landscape.

The stories attached to individual *huacas* have survived mostly in fragments. Many are recoverable, however, from traditions transcribed in the longer narratives of Inca history. Although the sacred *huaca* system is well known in and around Cuzco, there is less surviving direct evidence of other local shrines; but much may still be discovered through further research.

Below: All rivers and lakes were held sacred by ancient Andeans because water was universally recognized as the source of life.

SACRED WATERS

Water was vital to the Incas and their predecessors, and as such was revered almost as a god. They believed the cosmos itself to include a celestial ocean upon which the Earth floated.

Above: Lake Titicaca came to be regarded by ancient Andeans as the birthplace of the world, sun and moon and the human race.

CELESTIAL RIVER

The Milky Way, Mayu, was *the* celestial river, counterpart to all earthly rivers and the source of all moisture. Water from the sea was collected into Mayu, flowed into and across the sky and was released as rain and snow on the mountains to fill the streams, rivers and lakes, flow into the sea, and form as dew, frost, mist and fog on the land and over the ocean. From small runnels developed the mountain streams and rivers that watered the landscape. Humans then exercised the utmost ingenuity to make the most of the collection of water and use it to water crops.

Inca records transcribed in the Spanish sources describe how Andean farmers followed Mayu's movements carefully, for the solstices of the Milky Way coincide with the beginnings of the wet and dry seasons. Weather patterns, however, were periodically disrupted by El Niño events, causing long periods of drought in areas where regular seasonal rain had made the land fertile. Such times were very difficult for people in the western sierra, valley and desert oases, mountain basins and the Altiplano.

Such careful observation and the invention of an explanation of the seasonal associations demonstrates the seamless link in the pre-Hispanic Andean mind between the practical necessity of water and the sacred origin of it. In addition to its strictly practical uses, water played an important role in religious ritual. Andean peoples reliant on rainwater for their agricultural survival made offerings to the natural forces through the deities that controlled them. By 'feeding' the gods in this way, they created a reciprocal obligation, which, it was hoped, would secure a reliable supply of water.

Below: The River Urubamba was a major source of irrigation in the central Andes and one of the most sacred rivers.

HIDDEN WATERS

This sacred and practical association began with the earliest Andean civilizations. In religious ceremonial centres, water clearly played an important part and was used to complement ritual. U-shaped temples were oriented towards mountain sources of water. At Chavín de Huántar, an intriguing aspect of the galleries and passages within its temples is the apparent acoustic use of water within its hidden interior. The system of conduits to the chambers could literally be made to roar when water was flushed rapidly through the drains and the sound vented around the chambers. What this sounded like and what feelings it evoked in the hearts and minds of worshippers in the courtyards outside can only be imagined.

In the Early Intermediate Period, the Nazca culture inhabiting the dry desert landscape of the southern Peruvian coast naturally found the capture, collection and use of water paramount to their survival. One of the functions of their geoglyphs was the promotion and maintenance of communication with distant mountain deities who controlled the flow of water. For geological reasons, the Nazca River (and others in this drainage system) disappears into subterranean channels at mid-valley. The site of the ceremonial centre of Cahuachi in the mid-Nazca River drainage area appears to have been deliberately placed between the two zones of surface water flow. Residential settlements up and down the valley apparently used Cahuachi as their sacred gathering place for worship. Underground cisterns connected by aqueducts and reached by stone-cobbled spiral paths formed a system of water supply and control.

Below: The sacredness of water was encapsulated in channels and fountains in Inca cities, as here at Machu Picchu.

Above: The zigzag water channel cut into the natural outcrop at Qenqo branches, then rejoins. It was used for ritual libations.

THE PUMA'S TAIL

Given the earlier Andean preoccupation with the importance of water, it is no coincidence that one-third of the sacred *ceque* pathways around Cuzco led to or were otherwise oriented by the major springs and other sources of water in the region. When Pachacuti Inca Yupanqui rebuilt Cuzco after securing Inca supremacy in the valley, the Huatanay and Tullumayu rivers were partly re-routed to conform to the new plan of the city – that of a crouching puma. At the south-east end of the city, where the two rivers converge, the triangular patch of land thus created forms the puma's tail.

SACRED TITICACA

The sacredness of water in pre-Hispanic Andean civilization is most fundamentally shown in the singular reverence for Lake Titicaca as the place of origin. The focus of the Tiwanaku Empire in the Early Intermediate Period and Middle Horizon, Titicaca was regarded as the legendary place of the origin of the cosmos. Peoples throughout the Andes created myths and legendary historical links to establish their origin at Titicaca/Tiwanaku.

MOUNTAINS OF THE GODS

In a land dominated by dramatic landscapes, it was inevitable that mountains and their features and characteristics became the focus of awe and were imbued with divine powers. Mountains were regarded as the dwelling places of the gods or even as the gods themselves. They were associated with weather patterns and recognized as the ultimate source of water.

SACRED MOUNTAIN LOCATIONS

Among the mountains there were several special types of *huacas*. A stone or stones regarded as the petrified ancestor of a people or *ayllu* was known as a *huanca*. Especially prominent or large boulders in the landscape, which were believed to incorporate the essence of an ancestor of one or more local kinship groups, were typical examples of *huancas*. Such *huancas* were (and still are) to be found in town centres or placed upright in the middle of a field. As the physical manifestation or representation of an ancestor, they were thought to act as a guard on the interests of the local community.

The *apacheta* comprised a pile of stones at the top of a mountain pass or at a crossroads. *Apachetas* were believed to hold the spirits of local deities, and travellers would seek the favour of these gods by leaving offerings of coca leaves (*Erythroxylon coca*, the source of cocaine) or clothing, or by adding a stone to the heap before continuing their journeys. In a practical way, such features also no doubt acted as way-markers for travellers unsure of the route ahead.

With virtually every mountainscape dominated by volcanic peaks, they were only too evident as sources of mysterious power. Such special *huacas* were venerated as *apu* (literally 'lord') and were believed to have a direct influence on animal and crop fertility for those who lived in their vicinity. Sacred pilgrimages to such mountaintops to seek the favour of the spirit of the *apu* were a regular feature of Andean traditional religion – a long-standing practice that continues to the present day.

Below: The primeval Moche mountain god, also associated with the creator god Ai Apaec, is depicted at the Huaca de la Luna.

Above: The Late Intermediate Period Sicán Tucume pyramid in the Lambayeque Valley mimicked the shape of a mountain.

THE PRIMEVAL MOUNTAIN GOD

The concept of a god of the mountains was one of the most ancient aspects of Andean civilization. In one of his earlier manifestations, as the mountain god of the Moche, he was recognized as both a creator and sky god, but was believed to have played only a remote part in human affairs. He thus remained nameless but was represented frequently on Moche pottery and textiles with feline features. The depiction of images of fanged beings on Chavín pottery of much earlier date might have been his prototype, and thus the concept of a divine mountain power was spread far and wide.

The obvious association of mountains and the weather was reflected in the close association of the mountain god and Ai Apaec, sky god or perhaps son. The mountain god's throne was usually placed on a mountaintop, beneath which his manifestation as Ai Apaec was more active in association with terrestrial affairs. Moche military conquest and/or ritual combat was partly undertaken for the purpose of taking prisoners for sacrifice to these deities. According to some authorities, Ai Apaec was also the principal god of the Chimú of the Late Intermediate Period, derived from the Moche culture. Others argue that Ai Apaec simply means 'to make', and was therefore an invisible creator comparable to later Inca Viracocha.

Above: Volcanoes were recognized as the homes of the gods, whose anger with humans was also shown by destructive earthquakes.

VOLCANOES AND EARTHQUAKES

Volcanic eruptions, although not frequent occurrences, were seen as the wrath of the gods, not necessarily as punishment for wrong-doing in a retributional sense, but rather simply as demonstrations of how much the fate of humankind was in the hands of the gods. Earthquakes were even more prominent in this role and were perhaps equal in importance only to water and the sun in influencing Andean civilization.

Earthquakes disrupted the very framework of civilization, wreaking great physical damage and affecting the fabric of society and its organization. Reliance on water and its careful redirection and distribution from mountains to agricultural terraces paradoxically left the dependants knowingly vulnerable to the destruction of the terraces by the very deities who provided the water and who dwelled at its source.

Cyclopean architecture and the close-fitting blocks of Inca architecture also reflect the influence of earthquakes. Built to withstand seismic shocks, Inca architecture is often more stable than the Spanish colonial and later structures that replaced it or were built on Inca foundations. Perhaps even the fact that so many *huacas* are stones was influenced by earthquakes: such natural formations, as part of the landscape often not destroyed in earthquakes, may have been perceived to be one of the immutable elements of cosmic structure.

A principal god of earthquakes was Pachacamac, synonymous with and worshipped at one of the most ancient sites of Andean civilization. The site and the god rivalled the Island of the Sun in Lake Titicaca for supremacy as the most sacred location of the Andean Area. Pachacamac was the Earth-shaker – even the most minor tremor was a reminder of his presence and power. In recognition and reverence, Pachacuti Inca Yupanqui assumed the name of Earth-shaker after his defeat of the Chancas and domination of the Cuzco Valley.

THE INFLUENCE OF MOUNTAINS

The divinity of mountains also influenced the architecture of ancient Andean civilizations. From earliest times, U-shaped temple structures were oriented to the mountains, perhaps opening their arms to the divine powers and pleading for the water they provided. Pyramidal temple structures seemed to mimic in miniature the mountains around them, and yet themselves still dwarfed the humans who built them, seemingly reminding them of their powerlessness in the hands of the gods. The fabric of many pyramidal mounds, which were built of millions of adobe (mud) bricks, is the result of the mixing and moulding together of both earth and water – the two fundamental mountain elements.

The sacredness of mountains and their power over the survival of civilization remained a feature throughout Inca times. Llibiac, a god of thunder and lightning, was the principal deity of the Llacuaz Ayllu of Cajatambo – showing the continuity of belief and its interconnection with Andean social organization.

A final and rather poignant reminder of mountain-top sacredness is the use of remote mountain peaks as the place of child sacrifice in Inca times. In recent years the discovery of the freeze-dried mummies of some of these sacrifices has provided some of the most spectacular and informative evidence of pre-Hispanic religious practices.

Below: Mt Ausangate in the Cordillera Central was the personification of the apu *sacred mountain spirit.*

LINES IN THE DESERT

The coastal desert *pampa* of southern Peru was the home of the Nazca culture, which flourished from about 200BC to AD500. All aspects of Nazca culture were dominated by ritual. Perhaps the most dramatic evidence of this was the making of lines and images in the desert in the form of geoglyphs. Many people have investigated the lines and their meaning over decades, including Paul Kosok, Maria Reiche and Anthony Aveni.

Other line figures were made in the Pacific coastal valleys from Lambayeque to northern Chile.

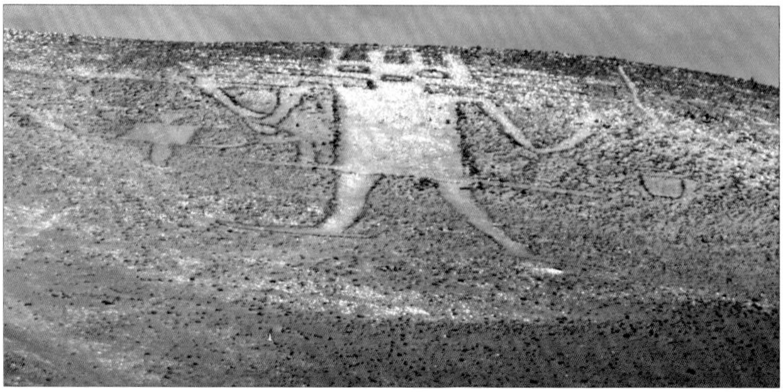

Above: The Giant of Atacama at Cerro Unitas, northern Chile, is the world's largest hill figure at 86m (280ft) high.

SHAPES IN THE DESERT

The Nazca desert lines are the most famous examples of pre-Inca sacred routes. The lines, which can be best seen and most appreciated from the air, were made by scraping the patinated desert surface gravel and stones to one side to reveal the lighter coloured, unpatinated under-surface. The lines are formed by the combination of light sand and aligned gravel and stones. The region's natural aridity has helped to preserve them.

More than 640 sq km (425 sq miles) of the desert are covered with these lines, figures and shapes. They comprise recognizable figures, geometrical shapes and seemingly random lines and cleared areas. Recognizable figures are of animals revered in the Nazca religious concept of the world – spiders, monkeys and birds – plus flowers and human-like supernatural figures. Some lines run perfectly straight for great distances across the desert. Others spiral, or converge on a single point. Altogether there are some 1,300km (800 miles) of such lines.

Below: The sacred route at Cantalloc on the Nazca Desert plain of southern Peru typifies a geometric geoglyph in its spiral pathway.

FIGURES AND PATTERNS

There are two principal types or groups. Figures on low slopes or hillsides seem to be placed such that they are obvious to travellers on the plains below, even though seen obliquely. Patterns of lines, both straight and curving, form 'enclosed' or designated areas, geometric shapes and large cleared patches.

Sets of lines form geometric patterns, and clusters of straight lines converge on common nodes, or, conversely, radiate from 'ray centres' on hills. In his researches, the archaeo-astronomer Anthony Aveni has identified and mapped 62 such nodes and radiations. Some of the lines lead to irrigated oases, or link sites, such as the line between the settlement of Ventilla and the ritual centre of Cahuachi. Individual straight lines of various widths are more than 20km (12½ miles) long. One famous set of lines, which forms a huge arrow of 490m (roughly 1,600ft), pointing towards the Pacific Ocean, is thought to be a symbol to invoke rain.

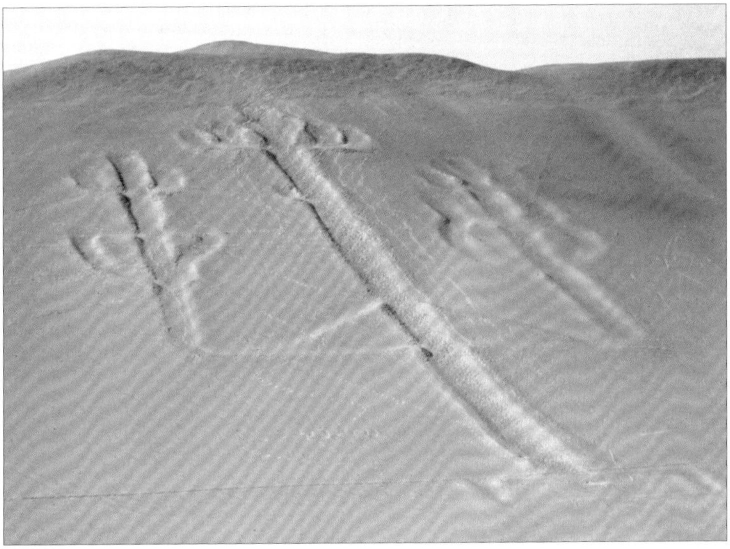

Each animal or plant figure comprises a single continuous line, with different beginning and ending points. The line never crosses itself. There is a hummingbird, a duckling, a spider, a killer whale, a monkey, a llama, several plants and human-like beings, as well as trapezoids and triangles of cleared areas, zigzags and spirals. Altogether there are some 300 such figures, and, combined with the lines, about 3.6 million sq m (10.8 million sq ft) of *pampa* floor have been scraped away to create them.

MYSTERIOUS LINES?

The Nazca figures are difficult to conceive, and certainly impossible to see as whole figures from the ground, except obliquely. Their presence has prompted a variety of speculation regarding their meaning, and argument has raged for more than 60 years over the meanings of these and other geoglyphs. Proposals range from their having been made by beings from outer space – for which there is categorically no evidence – to their use for astronomical observation – which seems plausible but has not yet been conclusively demonstrated.

There is no evidence that the lines were made by anyone other than the Nazca themselves. Although we will never know the exact meaning of each line or figure, they are clearly ritual lines, shapes and figures that reflect Nazca religious concepts. Their similarity to patterns on pottery and textiles, associations with Nazca burials and mummification, and with Nazca settlements and water sources reflects Nazca cosmology.

Below: The great hummingbird geoglyph on the Nazca Desert plain represents a messenger from the gods.

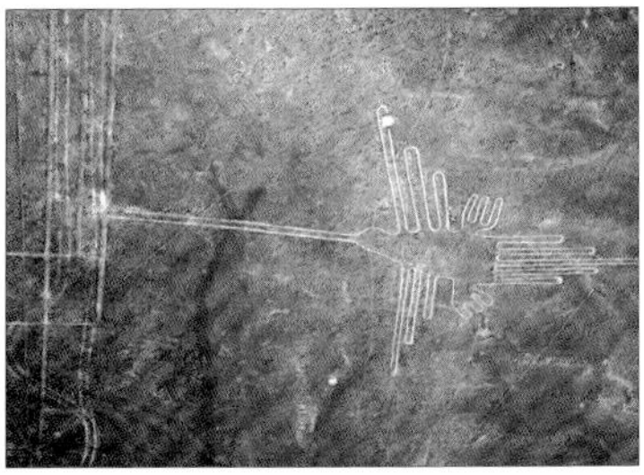

Creating the lines was a simple matter of proportional geometry. There is no difficulty in tracing an envisioned figure in the sand, and then translating the shape into a giant figure on the ground: only multiplication and proportional ratios are necessary to replicate a drawing using strings and pegs to trace and pace out the positions of the lines and patterns. Straight lines that cross the desert are easily produced by aiming at fixed positions on the horizon. Practical experiments to make neo-Nazca lines have proved the ease with which they can be created and the relatively small number of people and time needed to do so.

WHAT WERE THEY USED FOR?

The most plausible, and indeed obvious, explanation of the meaning of the Nazca lines is linked to the landscape, climate and accompanying features of Nazca settlement and material culture. The lines were associated with the Nazcas' necessary preoccupation with water and the fertility of their crops, together with the worship of mountains – the ultimate source of irrigation waters – and a pantheon of deities or supernatural beings who were believed to be responsible for bringing or withholding the rains.

Above: The geoglyph at Paracas, southern Peru, might have been a symbol of desert fertility and an orienteering aid to fishermen.

Some lines may be related to astronomical observations – especially the positions of the sun through the year – that reflect times for planting and harvesting. Geometric patterns are ritual pathways, created and owned by groups within Nazca social organization for ceremonial processions. Ceremony, praying to the gods for the elements of life itself, is part of the 'mystery' of the lines. The axes of most lines run parallel to watercourses. Other lines are just as clearly the paths between settlements and the ceremonial centres themselves.

The number of lines, and their creation over a period of 700–800 years, overmarking each other in great profusion, shows that they were not conceived as a grand overall plan. The lines and figures appear to have been made by and for small groups – perhaps even individuals. Some may have been created for a single ceremony; others were used repeatedly. 'Solid' cleared areas might have been for congregations, while figures probably formed ritual pathways to be walked by people for specific ritual purposes.

CEQUE PATHWAYS

The *ceque* system of sacred routes was a uniquely Inca theoretical and practical concept interwoven with myth, astronomical observation, architectural alignment, and the social and geographical divisions of the empire. Sacred routes, however, were vital parts of pre-Inca cultures as well, and in this light the Inca *ceque* lines can be seen as integral with a long tradition of systems of sacred routes and pathways dating from pre-Hispanic Andean culture.

Ceques were straight, sacred 'lines' radiating from the Coricancha sacred precinct in Cuzco. Each line linked numerous *huacas* along its length. There were 41 such lines uniting 328 *huacas* and survey points within and around Cuzco. It is perhaps significant that the 328 *huacas* and stations correspond to the number of days in the 12 sidereal lunar months (328/12 = the 27.3-day period of the rotation of the moon around the Earth–moon centre of mass). They were grouped according to 'upper' (*hanan*) and 'lower' (*hurin*) Cuzco and thus to the four quarters of the empire. Although theoretically straight, for practical purposes *ceques* sometimes had to obey the restrictions of the actual terrain through which they ran.

MULTIPLE PURPOSES

Points along the lines also served to regulate land holdings, water distribution, labour divisions, and ritual and ceremonial activities. *Ceques* were used as processional routes followed by *capacocha* (sacrificial individuals) at the beginnings of their journeys to the place of sacrifice. Combinations of *ceques* and their associated *huacas* distinguished the different *panaca* kin-group land-holdings within Inca society.

Above: Inca roads followed valley routes between cities, crossing mountain passes and river gorges using grass-fibre bridges.

For example, sunset on 26 April and the observation of the setting of the Pleiades on or about 15 April were made from the same place in the Capac Usnu plaza in central Cuzco. The settings were viewed between two stone pillars, together regarded as a *huaca*, which had been erected on the skyline west of the city. Farther on, beyond the horizon, another *huaca* was the spring named Catachillay, another name for the Pleiades.

The movements of Mayu, the Milky Way, were linked to the *ceque* system by a division separating the four quarters along the intercardinal (between-the-compass-points) axis of Mayu, and the southernmost point of Mayu's movement in the night sky.

The 16th-century Spanish chronicler Juan de Betanzos describes the sixth *ceque* of Antisuyu quarter, on which lay the sixth *huaca*, as 'the house of the puma'. Here the mummified body of the wife of the emperor Pachacuti Inca Yupanqui was kept, to whom child sacrifices were offered.

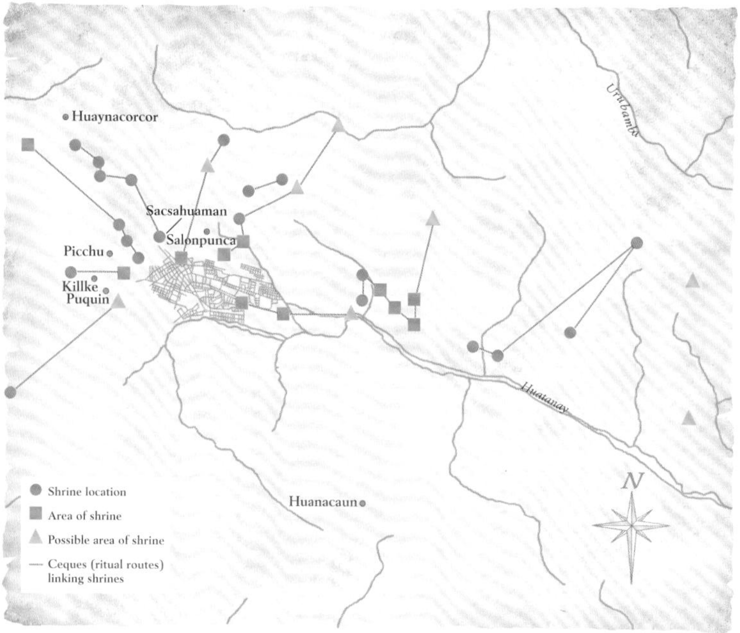

Below: Map showing the ceque *system of sacred or ritual routes linking the shrines and their locations.*

CEQUES AND SOCIAL STRUCTURE

Once again it was the vital importance of water in Andean life that formed an important part in the creation and use of the *ceque* ritual routes. The four *suyus* (quarters) of the Inca Empire, represented in the four divisions of Cuzco, were demarcated by the organization of the flow of water through the city. In turn, the radiating *ceque* lines organized the kinship *ayllu* groups into a hierarchy of positions either up or down river. This hierarchy itself reflected the nature of Inca society, in which different *ceque* lines were associated with the different bloodlines, particularly with the royal *panacas*, each of which was the origin of one of the primary descendants of the Inca ruler.

Thus, each *ceque* was created by and held information about irrigation, the Inca calendar and religious worship. Each *ceque* and its functions were maintained and tended by the appropriate kinship group and social rank – aristocratic, mixed-blood or common – in a rotational system as the *ceque* lines were marked off around the horizon surrounding Cuzco.

In his *Historia del Nuevo Mundo*, Bernabé de Cobo describes the eighth *ceque* in the Chinchaysuyu (north-west quadrant). At its seventh *huaca*, a hill called Sucanca, a channel brought water from Chinchero. Two towers erected on the hill marked the position of the rising sun on the day when maize planting had to begin. Consequently, sacrifices at the *huaca* were directed to the sun, soliciting him to appear and shine through the towers at the appropriate time.

The system of *ceque* lines also regulated the Inca organization of annual labour, especially seasonal labour to do with agriculture and the maintenance of irrigation systems. Once a year, in the central plaza of upper (*hurin*) Cuzco, a ritual ploughing took place. Chosen representatives from 40 families selected from the four quarters dug up as if for planting a designated portion of the plaza field. Such a system of shared civic responsibilities and duties in prearranged patterns and rituals, and at determined times through the seasons of the year, appear to be a culmination of such systematic practices in pre-Inca cultures.

Left: The modern Inca Trail near Intipunku, Peru, follows the route of an ancient Inca road from Cuzco.

Above: The modern Plaza de Armas, Cuzco, was the ancient Huacaypata Plaza, centre of the Inca capital.

WHERE ARE THEY NOW?

The Dutch anthropologist Tom Zuidema devoted more than 40 years to the study of *ceques* and the sources of their organization and meaning. The *ceque* routes are described in considerable detail in Cobo's chronicle and other Inca colonial sources. However, the structures, such as towers at *huacas*, have long since been dismantled.

In the late 1970s Zuidema and archaeo-astronomer Anthony Aveni devoted four seasons of fieldwork to careful interpretations of the chronicles and surveyed the likely routes of *ceques* and locations of the *huacas* in Cobo's descriptions, using their knowledge of the terrain and landscape around Cuzco. Their efforts proved the validity of the system. In addition to mapping the locations of numerous *huacas*, they located three original places where astronomical *huacas* were used for measurements. One was a pair of towers to mark sunset at the June solstice, situated on a hill called Lacco, north of Cuzco. The second, another pair of towers, marked the December solstice from the Coricancha. The third was four pillars on Cerro Picchu, in western Cuzco, marking planting time; sighted from the *ushnu* stone in the Coricancha, they were used to track the sun on its mid-August passage through its lowest point.

RELIGION AND TRADE

The agricultural staples of Andean civilization were maize corn, the potato and various squashes and legumes. Pastoralism – llama herding – in upland regions and the exploitation of rich marine fauna were practised. In the Andean Area, variety and diversity of crops decreases with altitude. Consequently, people in upland regions were characteristically both farmers and herders because the combination of activities was more productive than either was singly.

In contrast, in lowland areas ancient Andeans tended to be specialists, engaging primarily in agriculture in the coastal desert valleys or in marine fishing. Here, by contrast to the uplands, the pursuit of one activity or the other as a full-time occupation was more productive than practising a combination of the two. In tropical forest areas, people needed to combine several sources of living – farming small cleared forest plots, hunting and fishing the rivers.

Above: From the most ancient times, the peoples of valleys and basins used terracing and irrigation channels to maximize land use.

EARLY TRADE

Yet, even from the earliest times, although the bulk of the population was engaged in producing food through agriculture or marine fishing, there was contact between different regions for the exchange of the products of different areas. These contrasting activity zones, spaced across the land but with very different farming activities at varying altitudes, required different solutions to the problems of supply and demand, and fostered the classic highland–lowland reciprocal trade of the Andean Area.

In upland regions, communities of farmers tended to be self-sufficient in producing their own essentials through a combination of hill farming and herding. In the lowland valleys and marine fishing areas, however, communities of specialists bartered for each other's produce. The variety of activities for making a living and the practice of exchange between regions naturally led to the movement of people and ideas, as well as of goods, between areas.

The physical nature of water preservation, its distribution in elaborate irrigation systems, the making of raised fields and extensive hill terracing have been described elsewhere. Maximum exploitation was made of physical resources and modifications of the natural landscape to increase production, presumably partly as the solution to rising population. Yet soon, living at mere subsistence level would not be enough for most people.

Left: The importance of maize to northern coastal oasis valley cultures is shown in this Early Intermediate Period effigy vessel of maize cobs.

Above: Inca farmers harvesting a potato crop, depicted by Guaman Poma de Ayala in his Nueva Crónica y Buen Gobierno, *c.1613.*

GROWTH IN RELIGION

Natural processes were in control of the seasons and thus of the water supply and of agricultural success or failure. Ancient Andeans modified their landscape as much as they could to alleviate the seeming unpredictability of nature. However, lacking scientific explanations for the seasons, their direct observations led to the creation of supernatural explanations, or in other words, religion.

They also began to understand the connections between seasonal changes and recurring natural occurrences in their different regions, for example that drought on the coasts corresponded with greater rainfall in the mountains. All Andeans lived under the same sky, and their observations of the heavens also enabled them to invent explanations for the world around them and to exchange these explanations with each other.

Having moved beyond existing at mere survival level, Andean peoples now related their day-to-day experiences to cosmological ideas that explained them. To appease and solicit the gods who controlled human fate, significant numbers of people in society were devoted to the production of objects that produced no immediate physical subsistence, but did aid spiritual well-being. By the time of the Late Intermediate Period and Late Horizon urban civilizations of the Chimú and the Inca, large numbers of specialist craftspeople were state-sponsored producers of non-essential goods (non-essential only in the sense of not being necessary for survival, but nevertheless considered essential for the well-being of society).

Potters, metallurgists, textile and feather workers were employed by the state to make huge amounts of specialized objects solely for burial and royal tombs. In addition, priests and dedicated royal historians and record-keepers were employed to continue and sustain state religion and history. Furthermore, regional administrators were required to regulate the collection, storage and redistribution of produce to ensure that all citizens of the state had enough to live on, and to support those not actually engaged in agriculture, herding, marine fishing or trading.

TRADE IN RITUAL OBJECTS

For each community to practise its religious beliefs, it needed the objects and images that it perceived to be significant. Finding these items, however, often meant looking outside the settlements, thus expanding trading relationships that had hitherto dealt purely with essential goods.

As urban and ritual sites became more complex and relationships between settlements more elaborate, the exchange of both types of goods grew more organized and sophisticated. The images on pottery, textiles and architecture, and the artefacts found in archaeological sites and burials in the earliest settlements and ritual centres in uplands, lowlands and tropical forests show that each sought the produce and exotic materials of the other.

Marine products such as the thorny oyster, shark teeth, stingray spines and shells were important ritual objects that became essential in ceremony in both upland and lowland religious centres. Likewise, mountain deities, ocean gods and sky gods were considered the explanations or the controllers of human fate. The attributes of tropical animals – particularly jaguars, serpents and monkeys – were revered among mountain and forest dwellers alike. Hallucinogenic products such as mushrooms, coca and cactus buds, essential in shamanism and religious ritual, were traded over great distances.

With trade, direct or indirect, came ideas. Although regions of Andean society worshipped special local deities, there soon developed a core of features that can be called pan-Andean religious concepts.

Below: Coastal valley peoples' reliance on the sea is represented by this Moche stirrup-spout vessel of a fisherman and his totora *craft.*

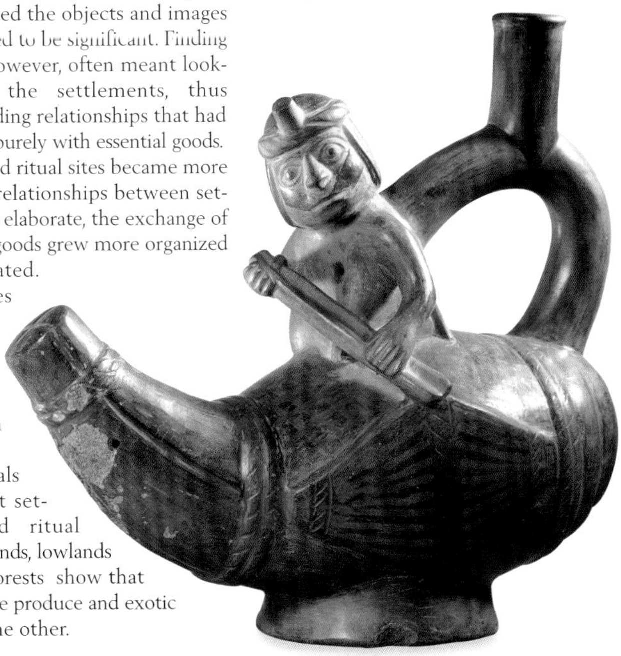

COSMOS AND GALAXY

Throughout the world, agricultural societies and others living close to the elements recognized the relationships between the seasons and the cycle of their farming, herding and fishing activities. They also learned to make connections between the movements of the stars and planets and the sequence of their yearly tasks. Ancient Andeans were no exception in this.

We know most about the cosmological beliefs of the Incas in particular because they were partially recorded and preserved by Spanish priests and administrators. General themes through the evolution of Andean civilization show that it is unlikely that Inca beliefs were unique to them, except in certain details. Rather, it seems more likely that Inca cosmology represents, generally, the product of beliefs common throughout the Andean Area. The unusual and specific features of the Andean environment, such as the dramatic mountains, led to responses and explanations that fitted the ancient Andeans' own view of life.

WORLDS ABOVE AND BELOW

Andean cosmology saw the universe as a series of layers. The terrestrial layer – Kai Pacha or Hurin Pacha, the Lower World – is punctuated and represented in numerous sacred places and phenomena called *huacas*, as described earlier. Nature was thought of as a dynamic, living being, composed of interactive forces and perceived in dual and reciprocal form: everything was part male and part female, dark and light, hot and cold, positive and negative. Deep reverence was held for Pacha Mama, the earth mother, and for Viracocha, the creator god (also known by various other names).

Below the terrestrial layer was an inner-terrestrial sphere, Uku Pacha, the World Below, while above was the outer, celestial sphere, Hanan Pacha, the World Above. The underlying primeval belief envisaged a remote past when giant beings and superhumans 'emerged' from the earth to battle for its domination. A great flood then engulfed the world, sweeping away these beings and transforming them into the landscape. Thus, they became the mountains and plains, the rivers and valleys, the oceans and rocky shores.

The first humans ascended from Uku Pacha in various versions, coming from caves, from the earth itself and from springs and other earth cavities. Directed by the sky god or creator god, different people chose their homes and occupations in life according to the god's directions. The world before humans became a text of sacred places from the earliest times, representing the story of time and the changing landscape, from super beings to the present human beings. In this way, all life represented a continuous cycle and nourished the reverence for people's

Above: The Torréon temple at Machu Picchu was used as an astronomical observatory for sightings of the night sky.

Left: The Milky Way, known to the Incas as Mayu, the celestial river. Here seen with a meteorite streak running through it.

ancestors, who were perceived as beings in another state but still interactive with the present.

CYCLICAL WORLD

These cosmological beliefs fostered a relationship with the earth that strove to work with it rather than to master it. Knowing that elemental forces were beyond their control, and to some extent unpredictable, ancient Andeans believed that there were always balancing forces to maintain the equilibrium over time, and sought the permission of the gods to use the landscape and enjoy its largesse. In this universe, human beings were only one part, and they were considered of less importance than the plants, animals, landscape and celestial bodies who personified the deities.

It was believed that the gods were all-powerful, and could instantly bring about the end of humankind if not worshipped and appeased. Humans could not survive if the sun suddenly ceased to shine, or if the rains stopped for ever.

The world was believed to have evolved and to operate in cycles known as *pachacuti* (literally a 'revolution': from Quechua *cuti*, 'turning over', and *pacha*, 'time and space'). The annual seasons, the revolutions of the stars and planets in the sky, and human life itself were all cyclical, and so incorporated both time and space. The Incas thought of themselves as the final creation in a succession of creations, destructions and re-creations of the world and its inhabitants by the gods in an effort to create the most perfect form of beings to honour them.

Above: The Intihuatana (Hitching Post of the Sun), at Qenqo, north of Cuzco, was formed by natural outcrop pillars.

THE INCA CALENDAR

Most prominent and observable in Hanan Pacha was Mayu, the Milky Way, the celestial river. Mayu's movements across the night sky were observed keenly by the Incas and their predecessors. Observation of Mayu was the starting point for correlations between the calendar and the natural changes of earthly conditions and seasons. This Andean concept of Mayu as the starting point is in marked contrast to the calculations of most other cultures, which proceed from observations of the movements of the closest single celestial bodies – the sun and the moon. By contrast, their observations of the Milky Way are of a vast galactic rotation.

DIVIDED UNIVERSE

The Incas also partitioned the universe horizontally according to the points of the compass, forming an imaginary cross corresponding to the axis of the Milky Way, which lies between the compass points. This is Mayu's southernmost point of movement in the night sky as it crosses its highest point through a 24-hour period. A vertical axis passed through Hanan Pacha, Hurin Pacha and Uku Pacha, intersecting the centre of the quartered cross and holding the cosmos together as an interacting organic whole.

HEAVENLY CONSTELLATIONS

Observation of the Milky Way as the starting point for formulating a calendar and as the axis of the universe provided an all-encompassing scheme by the Incas to chart the correlations between the positions of the stars and changes on Earth, and to organize daily, seasonal and annual labour and ritual on this basis. The movements of all the celestial bodies were used by the Incas to regulate and predict zoological and botanical cycles, both wild and domestic, and to organize the care of their crops and llama flocks. Theses celestial beings were held responsible for procreation on Earth.

DIVISIONS OF MAYU

The plane of the Milky Way's rotation inclines noticeably from that of the Earth by 26–30 degrees. Mayu's movements follow a sequence that rocks it slowly through the course of the year such that during half the year it tilts from right to left and then changes during the other half of the year to tilt from left to right. When Mayu's movements are plotted from the southern hemisphere, the broad band of the 'river' forms another tripartite division, this time of the sky into three sections: above, below, and Mayu.

These divisions of the sky provided a celestial grid against which all other astronomical observations could be plotted, including not only the obvious luminated planets, stars and constellations but also immense stellar voids, or 'dark cloud' constellations. The Incas devoted considerable effort to tracking and calculating the paths of celestial bodies and constellations. Careful records were kept of the first appearances (heliacal risings) and last settings (heliacal settings) of stars and planets.

DARK MATTERS

Most of the named constellations and prominent individual stars are within or very close to the axial plane of the Milky Way. In Andean astronomy, individual stars or constellations were named as architectural structures or as agricultural implements. Seemingly in contradiction, Andean so-called 'constellations' are the dark spaces, the interstellar dark matter, between the stars.

Above: An Inca astrologer as depicted in Guaman Poma de Ayalaís Nueva Crónica y Buen Gobierno, c.*1613, complete with sighting stick and* quipu *records.*

To the Incas, these voids were named animal constellations: an adult llama, a baby llama, a fox, a condor, a vulture, a falcon, a tinamou (a partridge-like bird), a toad and a serpent. The luminary bodies included Collca (literally 'the granary'), which is the Pleiades; Orqoi-Cilay (literally 'the multicoloured llama'), another star group, and Chaska-Qoylor (literally 'the shaggy star'), which is also known as Venus or the morning 'star'.

CONSTELLATIONS AND MYTHS

Practical observations and applications were interwoven with myth. For example, the toad constellation, although he creeps across the night sky, always wins the nocturnal race against the tinamou, for the tinamou, or *yutu*, is slow and stupid and flies around aimlessly when stirred.

Left: The dark spaces between the stars represented various constellations to the Incas, including the condor and the fox.

Right: The Horca del Inca, Bolivia, is one of many ridge-line sets of stone pillars for astronomical sightings.

The solstices of Mayu coincide with the Andean wet and dry seasons, and thus the celestial river was used to predict seasonal water cycles. Yacana, the 'dark cloud' llama disappears at midnight, when it was believed to have descended to Earth to drink water and thus prevent flooding. In contrast, black llamas were starved during October, in the dry season, in order to make them weep, seen as a supplication to the gods for rain.

Collca, the Pleiades, disappears from the night sky in mid-April, at the beginning of harvest. It reappears in the sky in early June, after the harvest has been gathered, and is thus associated throughout the Andes with these activities and called 'The Storehouse'.

One *ceque* route from Cuzco also associates myth with the Pleiades. A female coronation gift made from a provincial chief to Huáscar was Cori Qoyllur, 'Golden Star'. She proceeded along the *ceque*, stopping at *huacas* on the route for banquets and to make sacrificial offerings to the gods. The *ceque* itself is aligned with the disappearance of the Pleiades in mid-April. Another *huaca* marks the sun's lowest point on 18 August, the beginning of maize-sowing. Cori Qoyllur thus represents wives who walk the *ceque* at night and are transformed into *huaca* stones. Cori Qoyllur was herself turned to stone as a *huaca*, marking the point where the Pleiades disappear, and she is held responsible for fecundity in the Inca universe.

CELESTIAL MOVEMENTS

The movements of the sun were used to calculate the two most important ritual dates in the year – the winter and summer solstices, Capac Raymi and Inti Raymi. In like manner, the first appearance of the Pleiades just before sunrise was correlated with the regular sidereal lunar months (the 27.3-day period of the rotation of the moon around the Earth– moon centre of mass), beginning on 8–9 June and ending on 3–4 May. In Ayrihua (the month of April), as this lunar-plotted year ended, there were ceremonies in Cuzco honouring the royal insignia, and a pure white llama was dressed in a red tunic and fed coca (*Erythroxylon coca*) and *chicha* (maize beer) to symbolize the first llama to appear on Earth after the great flood that destroyed the previous world.

AXIS OF THE MILKY WAY

Mayu's movements were reflected in the organization of the Inca Empire into its four quarters, and also regulated the routes of the four principal highways emanating from Cuzco to these quarters. For, except for a certain necessity to respect the physical demands of the landscape, these routes approximated the axis of the Milky Way, which lies between the compass points. Mayu's axes were also associated with sacred *ceque* ritual alignments, at least one of which correlated to the southernmost point in the Milky Way's movements.

CHAPTER FOUR

EARLY SETTLERS TO EMPIRE BUILDERS

The sweep of human history in the New World started at least 15,000 years ago, when humans migrated into the New World from the Old World, though the exact timing and detail of how long this journey took are obscured in the distant past.

During the Lithic, or Archaic, Period, humans began to live a more sedentary lifestyle. As with early human culture in the Old World, the existence and nature of the beliefs of these earliest South Americans can only be deduced from the very few facts available, combined with speculation.

In the earliest settlements, South Americans developed a more stable source of food in the beginnings of domestication of both plants and animals. Hunting and gathering and the exploitation of sea resources were never abandoned, however.

Later, the development of ceramics and, later still, metallurgy brought greater and greater divisions of labour within Andean societies, and consequently greater complexity. Sophisticated architecture, including U-shaped complexes, and masonry and adobe building techniques also developed.

Social hierarchies, elitism and rulership evolved alongside technological advances, as did religious belief and the explanation of human existence. In the absence of written records, archaeologists and historians seeking to understand the nature of the earliest Andean societies can only project what they know of later societies into the past.

Left: A marching, club-wielding warrior of the procession carved on stone monoliths at Cerro Sechín.

THE FIRST ARRIVALS

The story of the human colonization of the North and South American continents began at least 15,000 years ago. The earliest dating for human occupation comes from Monte Verde, southern Chile – about 14,850 years ago. Following herds of migratory land animals, and possibly sea animals as well, intrepid colonizers, the Palaeo-Indians, crossed the Bering Strait when world climatic change created a land bridge there at the end of the last great glacial period.

The new continent was occupied by an abundance of fauna and flora, most of which had evolved indigenously, independent of Old World animals and plants, for millions of years. Some of the large game animals or their immediate ancestors, such as the Columbian mammoth, or American mastodon, had probably migrated from Asia during earlier breaks, known as interstadials, in world glacial periods long before the human migration, when climatic fluctuations had opened and closed earlier Bering land bridges.

The Lithic culture of this period persisted for about 10,000 years, to about 5,000 years ago, when post-Ice Age (Pleistocene) sea levels became stable at about where they are today. During this time definitive changes occurred in climate and environment: glaciers retreated from huge sheets of ice to mountain isolation; global ocean levels rose by about 100m (330ft); ecological zones shifted as climate changed and animals, plants and humans migrated to higher altitudes; meteorological patterns and marine currents shifted. The results were the climatic and environmental conditions of the present.

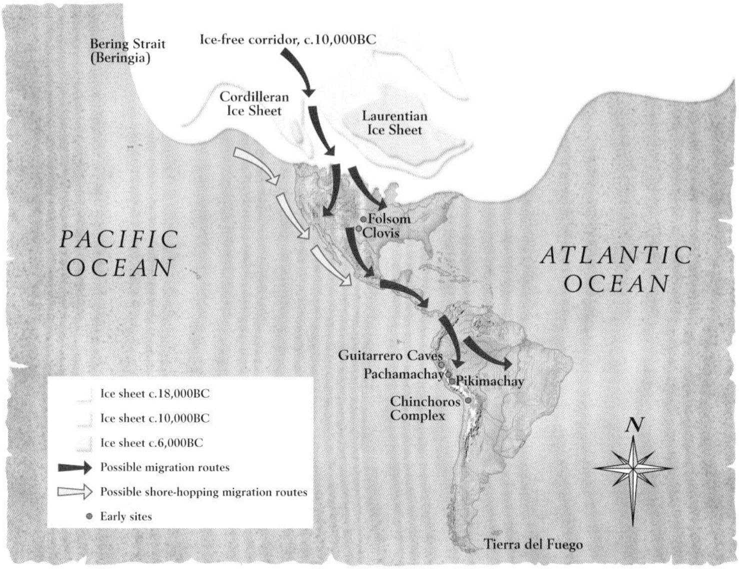

Above: Map of the early settlements of South America showing possible migration routes and the shrinking of the ice sheet.

Below: Migrants used stemmed chert spear points with the atl-atl *(spear thrower).*

MIGRATION ROUTES

Evidence for the very earliest human occupants in North America is sparse. Only the records for the later millennia of the Lithic Period are more abundant. Several claims for much earlier human occupation, from several sites in South America – for example Pikimachay Cave, Peru, 20,000 years ago – are not universally accepted. Nevertheless, the long journey from northernmost North America into and throughout South America must have taken place over many generations, indicating that migration probably began significantly earlier than the earliest dates for occupation in Chile.

The geologically traced pattern of glaciation in North America reveals an ice-free corridor between the great glacial sheets of Canada, through mid-continent, at this migration period. It has long been assumed that this was the most logical route into the interior. It has also been argued that an equally viable route would have been along the western coasts. Any evidence for coastal migration, if it exists, lies beneath the present ocean. Nevertheless, radiocarbon dates from Peruvian and Chilean coastal sites prove that occupation along the shoreline began at least 11,500 years ago, from the time when evidence for occupation in the New World in general is more abundant. Another recent theory suggests that a smaller and earlier migration possibly

Above: Large, fluted spear points, such as this chert Palaeo-Indian Folsom point, were used to hunt big game.

came from Europe across the ice floes of the North Atlantic into north-eastern North America. This argument is based on conclusions about similarities between the Solutrian lithic culture of south-western France, which flourished about 22,000 to 16,500 years ago, and the Clovis stone point tradition of North America, though this theory is rigorously disputed.

PALAEO-INDIAN SITES

The pace of migration is impossible to calculate and can be based only on a set of assumptions and speculations about population numbers, available game and other living resources, and the need to continue moving south. Thus, the precise time of the beginning and the exact nature of the migration cannot be known.

The evidence of molecular biology and DNA in contemporary Native Americans proves descent from three or four biologically distinct populations. There were, therefore, several incidents of original migration by different groups into North America. The biology and blood-group evidence shows that descendants from only one of these groups crossed the Isthmus of Panama into South America.

The earliest confirmed, substantially occupied Palaeo-Indian site is Monte Verde, Chile. Here were found round sling stones, grooved stones for use in a bolas, and chipped stone artefacts, including long projectile points, scrapers mounted on wooden handles and possibly a drill. Other wooden finds include a lance, digging sticks and mortars. Dwelling remains were of pole-and-animal-skin-framed huts, joined at their sides and forming two rows. Separate was an isolated, open-sided, wishbone-shaped structure with a small platform at the back. Its packed sand and gravel floor had remains of burnt medicinal plants and chewed leaves, and around the structure were hearths, medicinal plants and mastodon bones.

Other Palaeo-Indian sites with several traditions of fluted projectile-point shapes, including harpoon points for maritime hunting, have been found; they generally date from about 11,500 years ago and later.

PLANTS AND BELIEFS

The earliest-known domesticated plants come from this early period, from Guitarrero Cave, northern Peru. Although fibre plants dominated the findings, specimens of domesticated beans and chilli peppers were found, both *not* native to the region and thus cultivated there.

Representations of the earliest Andean beliefs are partly actual and partly speculative. There are suggestions of some form of shamanism and perhaps a belief in a multi-layered world with the Earth layered between celestial and inner spheres. The remains at Monte Verde show special use of plants and animal bones at a specialized structure, supporting shamanism. Concrete evidence of belief in an afterlife, or at least the honouring of selected deceased, comes from fishing settlements at Chinchorros and La Paloma on the central Peruvian coast. From the former come the earliest mummified remains in Andean culture (*c.*5000BC). From the latter come the first bodies buried in an articulated, decorated state.

Below: The coastal peoples of the Chinchorros culture (c.6000–1600BC) mummified chosen individuals after death.

DEVELOPING COMMUNITIES

The Lithic Period did not end abruptly. An increasingly sedentary lifestyle developed towards the end of the period in some areas of South America, while in others a hunter-gatherer economy continued to form most or a significant part of people's lifestyles. In the Andean Area, village life became more important as an adaptation to developments in climate and habitat in the post-Ice Age environment. Sedentism, or the shift of people from living in non-permanent settlements to permanent settlements, was not at first accompanied by the development of pot-making in Andean South America, and so archaeologists call the period the Preceramic, or Formative, Period, or sometimes the Cotton Preceramic.

EARLY DOMESTICATION

Recognition of the usefulness of particular plants and animals fostered the special observation of these species and gradual greater attendance to their care and proliferation. The process of domestication was an evolutionary one, helped wittingly by humans but with practical rather than specific scientific understanding. In the archaeological record, the end result is recognizable only when genetic changes render the plants and animals biologically distinguishable from their wild progenitors. Thus, the beginning of the process cannot be pinpointed in time.

The results, however, show anatomical changes that are unmistakable. Equally, the regular cultivation of species in areas outside their normal wild distributions shows human mastery over their use. The earliest known domesticated plants date to about 10,000 years ago in the Andean Area, from Guitarrero Cave in northern Peru. Fibre plants dominate most assemblages of Lithic Period sites. Numerous wild hemp-like plants were used to make a wide range of artefacts, from tools and clothing to bedding. Many other kinds of plant were apparently of medicinal importance – and perhaps also of religious importance.

At Guitarrero Cave, locally native tubers, rhizomes, fruits, chillies and beans were found; from Tres Ventanas Cave, central Peru, at an altitude of 3,900m (12,800ft), also come tubers – ulluco and the potato; and from several cave deposits in the Ayacucho region come gourds.

THE FIRST CIVILIZATION?

As sedentary lifestyles increased from the time of these earliest domesticated plants to about 5,000 years ago, communities derived greater proportions of their nutrition from this source, alongside intensive tending and gathering of wild food sources. Andean Preceramic communities cultivated mostly self-watering regions, relying on rainfall and river run-off, and developed agro-pastoralism with llama herding. Coastal peoples pursued lifestyles exploiting the rich marine resources and cultivated cotton in seasonally watered valley bottoms. Such diversity was the beginning of the highland–lowland (or coastal) division.

The variety of environments within the Andean Area, both in different regions and at different heights, discouraged integration between communities, although it was forged within them. Nevetheless, the products of different regions were sought after and traded over long distances with increasing regularity, and with this trade the exchange of ideas was inevitable.

There is little evidence for powerful regional political leadership, but there *is* evidence of integrated communal effort in the form of the first monumental architecture between about 3000 and 2000BC. Inter-regional contact and trade also began the long Andean tradition of textile use – cotton cultivated in the lowlands and llama wool from herding in the highlands continued the earlier Andean Area focus on fibre technology, including the earliest weaving.

ARCHITECTURE AND TEXTILES

Increasing reliance on cultivation drew sierra populations to lower altitudes, into well-watered highland valleys and basins. Shared religious beliefs, manifested in architecture and on textiles, is known as

Left: The Preceramic Period adobe mud sculpture at the Temple of the Crossed Hands, at Kotosh (c.3000BC).

the Kotosh Religious Tradition in the highlands, after Kotosh, a site in highland central Peru at about 2,000m (6,600ft). Farther north, La Galgada was another highland valley community. Along the western coast more than a score of early sites are known, including Huaca Prieta, Salinas de Chao, Aspero and El Paraíso in north-central coastal Peru. Here architectural traditions called Supe, Aspero and El Paraíso developed.

The architecture at these sites varies in detail. For example, Supe Tradition communal structures are smaller and are associated with domestic buildings and artefacts, indicating they were constructed by their local communities. The much larger structures at sites of other traditions indicate more regional communal efforts, as centres for several communities. What is common, however, is the beginning of Andean central worship and a long generic tradition of ceremonial mounds and sunken courts or plazas. Both oval and rectangular examples of sunken plazas are known. The two elements were made adjacent to each other and, in general, the plazas were smaller in area than the adjacent mounds.

Below: Cotton, domesticated by at least 3000BC in the northern Peruvian coastal valleys, was a valuable commodity to trade.

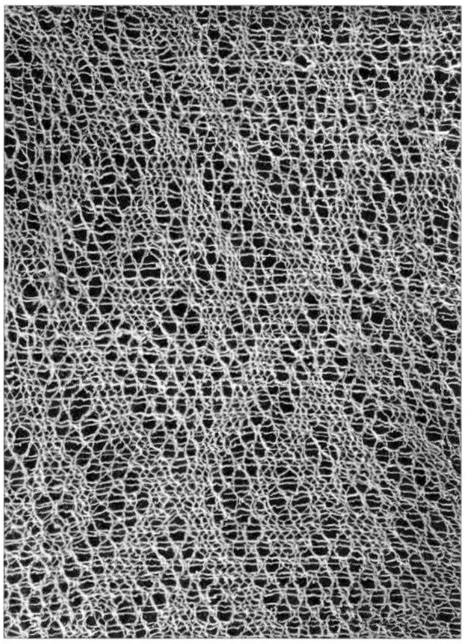

Above: Cotton was typically woven into open-work fabrics, such as this Chancay textile from the Late Intermediate Period.

These combined civic-ceremonial constructions are the earliest manifestations of Andean universal belief. They show both vertical and horizontal divisions of space for ceremonial purposes, and the special making and use of such space for communal worship drawing several communities together.

Alongside these architectural developments, textile design and decoration began to predominate among other media, such as stone, bone, shell, gourds, wood and basketry. Cotton was twined with spaced wefts and exposed warps; looping, knotting and simple weaving were also developed. The geometric nature of lattice-like fabric lent itself to angular decoration in different colours and to symmetry. Stripes, diamonds, squares and chevrons were used individually, in patterns, and to depict humanlike beings and animals that were important locally in an economic sense and universally as revered beings. Crabs, fish, raptors and serpents predominate.

Although the specifics of belief systems of such an early period can only be surmised, such detailed imagery, through its universality and repetition, reveals underlying religious belief. Coastal animals and motifs were copied in the highland traditions and vice versa. It seems that religion was, even at this early period, at the foundations of Andean civilization.

NEW AGRICULTURE AND ARCHITECTURE

The environmental diversity within the Andean Area meant that communities had to adapt in varying ways to suit conditions. The increasingly sedentary lifestyles of ancient Andeans reveals their increasing ability to manipulate the environment to increase domesticated production. However, progress was uneven. The wild progenitors of the classic cultigens that provided the bulk of carbohydrate and protein nutrition of ancient Andeans – maize, potatoes, beans and squashes – were native to different altitudes and regions, as were llamas and the other camelid species.

Following the Preceramic Period, the pre-eminent technological developments were pottery and irrigation agriculture. Archaeologists call it the Initial Period.

FARMING AND CERAMICS

In South America, pottery-making was discovered outside the Andean Area. The earliest ceramics were made in coastal Ecuador by the end of the 6th millennium BC, and the well-watered tropical areas of Colombia and Ecuador were the first areas where the 'civilization-defining' combination of intensive agriculture and pot-making became the predominant lifestyle by about 3000BC. The spread of intensive farming and ceramics followed a path of least resistance, from low self-watered environments to higher self-watered regions, to the more arid high Andes and western coasts.

By about 1800BC the combination was well established in northern and central highland Peru and in the fertile valleys of the north-central coast; by 1600BC, communities in the Titicaca Basin in the southern Andes were making pottery; and another few hundred years later ceramics had diffused to the dry coasts of southern Peru and northern Chile. In Altiplano regions, however, agriculture was combined with llama herding, while in coastal valleys agriculture was teamed with fishing.

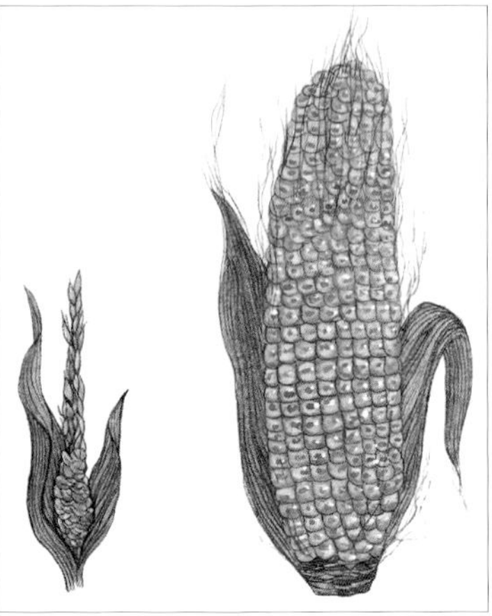

Above: From its diminutive wild ancestor, maize (Zea mays) spread into the Andean Area from Mesoamerica.

PAN-ANDEAN FOUNDATIONS

The increased security of grown food and rich sea resources, together with plentiful supplies of cotton and wool, made increases in population inevitable. With the ability to irrigate and terrace the valleys and basins and thereby increase the yields and available land for agriculture, new areas could be opened. The practice of exchange of coastal and highland products continued the flow of contact among otherwise independent regions and communities. At the same time, the architectural and religious practices begun in Preceramic days continued.

The intensified concern with stable agriculture deepened the reverence for 'mother earth', setting the stage for the veneration of Pacha Mama (as she was known to the Inca). The need to regulate agricultural, herding and fishing activities throughout the year encouraged careful observation of heavenly bodies, the stars

Left: The people of Garagay decorated their ceremonial centres with sculpted and painted adobe walls.

Above: Garagay in the Rimac-Chillon Valley, central Peru, was a typical coastal U-shaped civic-ceremonial centre in the Initial Period.

and constellations, and of Mayu (the Milky Way) as a whole. These two facets were the fundamental elements of ancient Andean religion. The strengthening and consolidation of these foundations in the Initial Period secured their prevalence throughout the remainder of Andean ancient history.

U-SHAPED COMPLEXES

The Preceramic Period tradition of monumental architecture continued. It was a great age of civic-ceremonial construction. Hundreds of sites are known but relatively few have been excavated extensively.

Ceremonial mounds and platforms were built up using soil-filled mesh bags for interior bulk and adobe brick exteriors. Clearing the silt that built up in irrigation canals provided an abundance of suitable fine clays for bricks to build bigger and more elaborate structures. Sunken courts became larger, presumably to accommodate growing congregations. Subterranean temple complexes became more extensive and façades were decorated with relief sculpture and painted in bright colours.

The Paraíso Tradition that started in the Preceramic Period developed the enduring form of civic-ceremonial architecture in the northern Andean Area – the U-shaped complex. Regional details varied, as ever, but the classic elements were the same everywhere. A large central platform-mound formed the base of the U. In front of it, flanking a large central plaza, were two lower, elongated platforms. Variations included rectangular or circular sunken courts, wings extending from the central platform, walled vestibules and multiple temples on the platforms.

The builders of ancient ceremonial complexes seemed consciously to vie with one another in ostentation and display. Visual impact was important. Themes for enduring Andean architectural religious advertisement are exemplified by Cerro Sechín, where at least 27 megalithic slabs were erected along the front of the temple mound, carved in low relief. They depict dead individuals, many of them dismembered, and individual heads in a gruesome afterlife procession. At Garagay and Moxeke, human–animal transformation is depicted in adobe friezes of insects with human heads, fanged heads in spider webs, humans with fangs and condor features. At Huaca de los Reyes there is an adobe head sculpture with a fanged mouth.

The largest U-shaped complexes were in the coastal valleys: Sechín Alto, Sechín Bajo, Cerro Sechín, Huaca de los Reyes, El Paraíso, Cardal, Garagay, La Florida and Moxeke-Pampa de los Llamas. A prominent highland example is La Galgada.

In the Titicaca Basin, a separate architectural tradition began at Chiripa, featuring a large mound with a central sunken court at the top surrounded by rectangular temples.

EXPANSION HALTED

Communal practices of civic-ceremonial construction begun in Preceramic times increased with the communal activities of canal building and shared land use. The intensification of farming, herding and fishing, expansion into new areas and increased growth to support a great labour force were self-propelling processes. Their only limitations were the availability of land and the unpredictabililty of climate.

And so it was. For beginning about 900BC, towards the end of the Initial Period, the pattern of El Niño and related climatic events brought severe drought that prevailed for centuries.

ORACLE AND SHRINE: CHAVÍN DE HUÁNTAR

Generalized themes permeated Andean cultures during the Initial Period. Although the valleys, mountain basins and coastal oases were largely independent, each was dominated by one or a few civic-ceremonial centres, and religion was developing across communities as a unifying theme. This process culminated in the first great period of region-wide unification: the Early Horizon.

DROUGHT AND DISASTER

The prolonged drought that began and defined the end of the Initial Period was a phenomenon not previously experienced by Andean farmers. Disaster ensued as crops failed year upon year. The new irrigation systems could not cope, and the extra land brought into cultivation as village farming became more efficient and sophisticated was useless when drought prevented farmers from watering it.

Before they abandoned many of the sites, the ancient builders of the U-shaped civic-ceremonial complexes must have devoted considerable time in pondering why the gods had forsaken them.

Below: The mysterious Lanzón Stone was erected in the dark oracular chamber within the Old Temple at Chavín de Huántar.

Above: Sharp-toothed images of stylized caymans were a common symbolic Chavín motif in stone carvings on walls.

A UNIFYING CENTRE

The regularity and the quantity of rainfall began to increase again from about 800BC. By now, northern sierra and coastal Andean communities that had weathered the drought through several generations were very subdued. However, religious themes that had begun in the Initial Period did not disappear; instead they re-emerged within two extensive regional spheres of influence – the northern and southern Andean Area – under the newly encouraging conditions.

The more widespread unifying sphere was centred in the northern Andean Area at Chavín de Huántar, sited on the eastern slopes of the Cordillera Blanca in the Mosna Valley, more than 3,000m (9,800ft) above sea level.

Chavín de Huántar was established about 900BC or shortly after, at the beginning of the drought, as a new U-shaped civic-ceremonial centre joining La Galgada as an extension of the U-shaped Tradition that had developed in the coastal valleys. It went through several phases of development, initially mainly confined within its immediate valley as it persisted through the drought years. Chavín de Huántar appears to have been deliberately and strategically located in the Andes roughly midway between the coast to the west and the tropical lowlands to the east. From its position it controlled several passes running between mountains. In a time of scarcity, but with an entrenched tradition of inter-regional exchange, such a strategic position must have given Chavín special status and importance among declining civic-ceremonial sites. Its location appears to cater to both the mountain deities, believed to control the weather and rainfall, and the coastal deities, where the revered Pacha Mama (earth mother) of valleys that were once productive was apparently now forsaking her people.

As climatic conditions and agricultural production improved, Chavín's artistic influence began to spread. With its distinctive symbolic art, it became the source and focus of a pan-Andean religion. Principal themes focused on feline and serpentine attributes, on fish and other aquatic animals, on human-like raptors, and on a pervasive Staff Deity. These images appeared on the architecture of Chavín de Huántar itself, and on Chavín

Below: Tenoned, stone severed heads, with feline canines, were typical wall 'decorations' at Chavín de Huántar.

Above: The façade of the New Temple at Chavín de Huántar, which incorporated and enlarged the Old Temple from c.500BC.

ceramics, textiles and metalwork. The spread of Chavín symbolic art went hand-in-hand with its equally crucial role in the spreading of emerging technology.

BIRTH OF A CULT

Chavín was not the largest ceremonial centre of the Early Horizon, but it was certainly one of the most elaborate. It does not seem to have been a centre of political power or unity, except perhaps within its valley, but it was a unifying centre for religions. Although not truly urban in layout and proportions, it must have accommodated a resident population of priests, officials, artisans, servants and pilgrims to support and serve the cult. Its deliberate establishment at the beginning of the drought period and persistence through it must have made it seem a particularly blessed ceremonial centre to ancient Andeans. It therefore became the focus of pilgrimage for peoples throughout the northern Andes.

The centre of the site was a classic U-shaped complex, which went through several phases of temple development, both inside and out. Within its base ceremonial platform, called the Castillo, was a multi-galleried temple. The original (Old) temple housed the cult object of the Lanzón, an obelisk-like, lance-shaped stone carved with human, feline and serpent attributes and the snarling mouth of the Chavín supreme deity. The gallery holding it has an upper oracular chamber.

The New Temple, which combined and enlarged the Old, was entered through an elaborate doorway: the Black and White Portal. Its two columns – dark (male) and light (female) – were carved with human-like raptor figures. The New Temple housed the cult figure known as the Raimundi Stela, an elaborately carved slab depicting the Staff Deity.

In the courtyard outside the temple complex stood the Tello Obelisk, a huge stone carved with two jungle caymans, and other animal and plant symbols.

The temple galleries included an elaborate system of water channels. When water was flushed through the system, accompanying acoustic properties literally made the temple roar.

Chavín's importance lasted for some 700 years, into the 3rd century BC. The power of its cult continued to spread through a second period of drought, roughly 400–200BC, the persistence of which perhaps precipitated its eventual decline.

STAFF DEITY AND TROPHY HEADS

One of the most prominent Chavín deities was the Staff Deity. This was a figure with feline, raptor and serpentine attributes, holding a staff in each hand with outstretched arms on either side of the body. Sometimes the staves were serpents. The Staff Deity could be male or female, identifiable by distinctive characteristics.

Another distinctive Chavín Cult theme was the trophy head. Appearing on all media, these were disembodied human heads, often with feline or serpentine attributes, thought to portray shamanistic transformation.

Below: The dual-columned stone Black and White Portal of the New Temple at Chavín de Huántar.

SOUTHERN CULTS: PARACAS AND PUKARÁ

Environmental decline occurred in the southern Andean Area, along the coast and in the Altiplano in the late Initial Period. In the Peruvian southern coastal desert, the natural aridity, exacerbated by drought in the inland mountains, presented a considerable challenge to the ingenuity of the coastal fishing village inhabitants. In the Titicaca Basin, the lake level fell dramatically and fields were abandoned all along the southern shores, as farmers could no longer raise crops or feed animals there.

PARACAS MUMMY BURIALS

The Paracas Peninsula was the site of a necropolis of elite burials. Apart from the Chinchorros mummy burials in northern Chile, the Paracas desiccated mummies are the earliest in the Andean Area, beginning a long tradition of mummification in Andean civilization. The elaborately wrapped, multilayered burial bundles demonstrate a preoccupation with the continued life, or participation in the present, of physically deceased important individuals. The richest ceramic and textile products, and exotic goods from afar, were saved for the burials; indeed, some goods were produced specifically for this purpose. Their existence begins the equally long Andean tradition of ancestor worship.

While the peninsula is the site of the Cavernas cemetery, the inhabitants who created it lived in the adjacent area inland around Cerro Colorado, where some 54ha (137 acres) of scattered domestic architecture has been found. The economy was based on local fishing.

The cemetery was a specially dedicated site. The dead were placed in their mummy bundles into large subterranean crypts, which were either bell-shaped pits or masonry-lined rectangular mausoleums. These were used through several generations, and the individuals appear to be kin. As the numbers of burials appear to exceed the requirements of the immediate adjacent settlements, it is thought that the necropolis was also a pilgrimage or cult centre serving communities through a wider region.

Above: The flying Oculate Being of the Paracas and Nazca southern coastal cultures, depicted on a woollen burial shroud.

The stages for the preparation for these burials were inland in the Chincha Valley. These comprised low rectangular mounds aligned at the front and back of a high-walled central court, sunk to near ground level, such as the one found at Huaca Soto. The court walls are so thick that the complex is reminiscent of a single mound with a sunken summit courtyard. Huaca Soto comprised two interior courts, plus a thick-walled frontal entry court. The whole structure was 70m (230ft) by 200m (650ft) and stood 15m (49) high.

IMPORTANCE OF PUKARÁ

In the Altiplano around Lake Titicaca, emphasis on mother earth (Pacha Mama) and father sky (Yama Mama) continued as people remained close to the land and struggled to cope with drought. The importance of the regional centre at Chiripa waned and the site was eventually left to decline. The replacement for Chiripa as the focus of religion became the ceremonial centre of Pukará, some 75km (47 miles) north-west of the lake. Pukará arose around 400BC and exerted its influence over the Titicaca Basin for four centuries.

Unlike U-shaped complexes, Pukará comprised monumental masonry-clad structures terraced against the hillside. The principal terrace had a monumental staircase and was topped by a rectangular sunken court with one-room buildings around three sides, reminiscent of the Chiripa complex.

The hallmark of Pukará cult symbolic art was the depiction of *yaya* (male) and *mama* (female) figures on opposite sides of slab monoliths erected at Pukará and other sites. Other Pukará stone carving, pottery and textiles displayed ubiquitous Andean images, including felines, serpents, lizards and fish.

Like the Chavín Cult, Pukará art images featured disembodied human heads. Some of these were trophy heads accompanying realistically depicted humans; others accompanied supernatural beings with feline or serpentine attributes, as in the Chavín Cult, and are thought to represent shamans in transformational states. Many Pukará temple sites were rebuilt and used over several centuries. The assemblages of structures around Pukará sunken courts show considerable variety.

Above: Nested geometric patterns in the Pukará culture included the multi-stepped 'Andean Cross'.

In this way, Paracas, Pukará and Chavín styles, although distinct, show themselves to have a pan-Andean combination of features, including, especially, the Chavín emphasis on feline, serpentine and raptor attributes. The combination of cotton textiles and the importation of alpaca and llama wool for use by Paracas weavers shows another highland influence.

THE OCULATE BEING

One supernatural being or deity that stands out as distinctly Paracas, and which carries on in the succeeding Nazca civilization, is known as the Oculate Being. Depicted on textiles, the being was portrayed horizontally – as if flying upside-down – as if looking down on humankind, and crouching. His/her frontal face has characteristic large, circular, staring eyes, and long, streaming appendages originate from various parts of the body and end in trophy heads or small figures.

Below: Early Horizon Paracas mummified bodies were buried in multiple layers of cloth, the richness of which reflected their status.

PARACAS AND PUKARÁ LINKS

There are generic artistic links between the Paracas and Pukará art styles and symbols used. Both styles feature monochrome and polychrome pottery with multicoloured motifs framed with incised lines. Some of the earliest phase styles, especially at Paracas, are attributed to Chavín influence because they represent a change from the local pottery that preceded it. There is an emphasis on non-human faces adorned with fangs and feline whiskers, especially on pottery. As Paracas pottery developed, it showed a more naturalistic style akin to Pukará ceramics. Local coastal subjects such as falcons, swallows, owls and foxes later predominated. The images and patterns painted on Paracas pottery were also used in their textiles.

Below: The bodies of Paracas mummies were tightly constricted into compact bundles and held by cords.

NAZCA CONFEDERACY AND MOCHE STATE

Cult foci such as Chavín, Paracas and Pukará represent distinct local political entities that were united between their regions predominantly by religion. The following Early Intermediate Period saw the break up of Chavín's religious unity, but also the rise of at least one regional state political unity.

COASTAL POWER BASES

As in the Early Horizon, there were two principal regional bases: one north, one south – both coast-based. Centres between mountains and on the Altiplano persisted, but by about 200BC Chavín de Huántar had begun to wane and its importance as a pilgrimage centre was languishing. The construction of new monumental architecture became restrained in central and northern Peruvian valleys that lay between mountains. The decline of Chavín influence is attributed to it lacking the political attributes necessary to maintain long-term stability.

Below: Exposed Nazca group burial in the southern coastal desert. Tombs were often reopened to insert new mummy bundles.

Above: Nazca woven and dyed woollen tunic, exemplifying the exchange of highland llama wool for coastal craftsmanship.

In the Titicaca Basin, Pukará was eclipsed by its contemporary and power inheritor, Tiwanaku. The real political ascendancy of Tiwanaku in the southern Altiplano, however, was yet to dominate the region, although the monumental architecture that was to become its hallmark had begun.

A NEW CULT CENTRE

Nazca civilization flourished in the southern Peruvian coast and adjacent inland valleys from *c.*100BC to *c.*AD700. It continued the Andean tradition of religious cult practices by remaining a focus of regional worship and pilgrimage.

The dominance of daily life by ritual was emphasized across the desert floor by the Nazca geoglyphs, whose nature and importance in ritual have been described earlier. Perhaps like the Paracas necropolis, the sheer number of lines and ritual pathways, and the apparent short-term use of many of them, meant that they served a much wider community than just the settlements immediately nearest them.

THE NAZCA CONFEDERACY

Two of the most important Nazca settlements were Cahuachi and Ventilla, the first a ritual 'city', the second an urban 'capital'. Ventilla, the largest Nazca site recorded, covered at least 200ha (495 acres) with terraced housing, walled courts and mounds. It was linked to its ceremonial and ritual counterpart by a Nazca line across the desert.

Through the centuries, increasing drought in the highlands to the east caused growing aridity in the coastal plains. Such was the pressure for water that the Nazca invented an ingenious system of underground aqueducts and galleries to collect and channel underground waters around Cahuachi to minimize evaporation and to provide water in the dry season.

On pottery and textiles the Nazca continued to develop themes begun by people in the Paracas culture. Preoccupied

Above: The strong facial features on this Moche effigy-jar indicate it may have been a portrait of a real person, who seems to be male.

with and motivated by religious symbolic art and ceremonial ritual, they used mythical beings and deities to decorate effigy vessels and cloth with serpent beings, monkeys and other animals, and trophy heads. A cult practice collected caches of trepanned, severed trophy skulls of sacrificial victims in Nazca cemeteries.

Nazca settlements appear to be in part a continuation of Paracas, since Paracas layers are found beneath some Nazca settlements. The cooperative nature of Nazca culture for control of water and for making geoglyphs shows strong ties with other regions but no centralized political power. It was more like a confederate state of independent but highly interacting cities.

THE MOCHE STATE

In the northern Peruvian coastal valleys, the roughly contemporary Moche created the Andean Area's first true state. Here a Moche elite embarked on military domination of the northern valleys between the Sechura Desert and the Casma Valley. They ruled from their capital at Cerro Blanco in the Moche Valley, where by AD450 two huge pyramidal structures of adobe bricks had become the focus of political and religious power. The Huaca del Sol was a four-tiered, cross-shaped platform with a ramp on the north side; the Huaca de la Luna, at the foot of Cerro Blanco, was a three-tiered structure with walls that were richly decorated by friezes depicting mythological scenes and deities. The two ceremonial platforms sat within a sprawling metropolis, which at its maximum size occupied about 3 sq km (740 acres).

Roughly 100 years later, a sand sheet choked the canal system and stifled agriculture, causing abandonment. The focus of Moche politics and religion shifted north to the Lambayeque Valley, to the sites of Pampa Grande and Sipán. The rise of the Wari State, to the south-east out of the Andes, also appears to have been an influence.

The large city of Pampa Grande covered some 6 sq km (1,485 acres) and flourished for about 150 years. Its most imposing structure, Huaca Fortaleza, had a similar function to Huaca del Sol and was the focus of the elite residents of the city. Like Cerro Blanco, Pampa Grande was abandoned abruptly, owing to a combination of agricultural disaster caused by an El Niño weather event and the continued expansion of the Wari State. Internal unrest may also have been a factor.

Left: A pattern of crabs sculpted in adobe mud on a wall frieze at the Huaca de la Luna, Moche, shows its coastal heritage.

Above: In all Pacific coastal cultures, seafood formed an important part of the local cuisine, such as this crayfish on a Nazca pot.

A DERIVED CULT

Moche imagery became a potent religion, with distinctive art symbols and a pantheon of gods much derived from the Chavín Cult. It was characterized by humans and humanized animal figures, serpents, frogs, birds (owls in particular) and sea animals (crabs and fishes), and by standardized groups and ceremonial scenes, including a coca ritual recognizable by distinctive clothing and ritual combat.

Murals, friezes and decorative designs on pottery depict the capture and sacrifice of 'enemies', drinks offered by subordinates to lords and gods, and persons passing through the night sky in moon-shaped boats. Richly furnished burials at Sipán, which are some of the few unlooted tombs of the Andes, reflect scenes that confirm the images on walls, ceramics, textiles and metalwork excavated from other Moche sites.

Although the names of the Moche deities ae not known, the later Chimú Ai Apaec and Si (sky/creator god and moon goddess) may have derived from Moche deities. Especially prominent on ceramics and textiles is the ritual depiction and rich ceremony of the Decapitator God. A Moche mountain god has been identified in an oft-depicted feline-featured being.

MOUNTAIN EMPIRES: WARI AND TIWANAKU

In the Middle Horizon, ancient Andeans began to consolidate large areas of land into political states for the first time. Politics and religion became a corporate whole in official state cults that were imposed with military and economic conquest. Local religious deities were assimilated, easing the imposition of official state religion.

Two dominating empires arose: Wari in the north and Tiwanaku in the south. Despite political and military rivalry, both cultures shared a use of religious iconography and symbols, which arose as a result of their collection and consolidation of the local deities, cults and similarities in religious imagery in the regions they conquered.

Below: Sculptured stone severed heads are tenoned into the walls of the Kalasasaya sunken court at Tiwanku.

DOMINATING THE HIGHLANDS

The city of Huari, which had been established in the preceding Early Intermediate Period, began rapid expansion within the central Andean Huamanga and Huanta basins from about AD600. For the next 200 years its armies conquered and dominated the highlands and coastal valleys of central and northern Peru almost to the present Ecuadorian border.

The capital city occupied a plateau among mountains, 2,800m (9,200ft) above sea level. As a civic, residential and religious centre, it grew rapidly to cover more than 300ha (740 acres), with peripheral residential suburbs occupying a further 250ha (620 acres). Alongside military expansion, the Wari spread a religious hegemony characterized by a distinctive use of symbolic art, much of which shows continuity with ancient Chavín traditions, which survived the political fragmentation of the Early Intermediate Period. Shortly before AD800, however, a political crisis caused building within the capital to abate rapidly and cease. At the same time, Pachacamac, a political centre and religious shrine on the central Peruvian coast that had flourished as a cult centre since the later Early Intermediate Period, and which had only recently been occupied by the Wari, began to reassert itself and possibly even to rival Wari power. Wari expansion ended abruptly, and the capital was abandoned by AD800.

DOMINATING THE ALTIPLANO

The Tiwanaku power base emanated from the Titicaca Basin of southern Peru–northern Bolivia, at 3,850m (12,600ft) above sea level. Like Huari, the city was founded in the Early Intermediate Period and became the capital of a unified state established through conquest and economic domination. In its heyday it occupied 4.5 sq km (1,100 acres).

The earliest major constructions at the site were begun by AD200, and by AD500 Tiwanaku was the capital of a considerable empire within and beyond the Titicaca Basin, stretching east and west to the Bolivian lowlands, west and northwest to the Peruvian coast, and south into northern Chile. Its cultural and religious influence extended even farther. Its chief rival to the north was the Wari Empire, and the two empires 'met' at the La Raya pass south of Cuzco, which became a sort of buffer zone between them. Curiously, the prosperity of Tiwanaku endured for roughly a millennium, fortuitously matching the 1,000-year periods of ages in Andean cosmology.

Tiwanaku's core comprised ceremonial-religious-civic structures, including monumental buildings, gateways and stone sculptures exhibiting religious motifs and gods whose depiction shows obvious affinities to Chavín images.

This core, aligned east–west, was confined within a moat and was surrounded by residential compounds built of adobe bricks.

Tiwanku belief was a culmination of the religious antecedents that appear to have united the peoples of the Titicaca Basin from as early as 1000BC. Ceremonial architecture at Chiripa and Pukará, for example, heralds that at Tiwanku.

The location of the city appears to have been chosen deliberately both for its position in the midst of fertile land and for the perceived sacredness of the landscape. The surrounding natural features constituted every element regarded as sacred within Andean Area religion: the sacred waters of Lake Titicaca to the west, the snow-capped peaks of the sacred mountains to the east, and in the middle of the lake the sacred Island of the Sun and Island of the Moon.

Above: The ruins of Pikillaqta, the largest and southernmost Middle Horizon Wari highland city, which guarded the border between the Wari and Tiwanaku empires.

Left: The so-called 'monk' monolith at Tiwanaku. Such large stone statues were believed by the Incas to represent a former race of giants from an earlier age.

A SHARED RELIGION

Much of the religious and mythological imagery of Wari and Tiwanaku was virtually identical and originated in much earlier times. Derivation from Chavín demonstrates the continuity of pan-Andean religious belief. Despite the two capitals' obvious military opposition, scholars have entertained the possibility that religious missionaries from one city visited the other. It might have been that the priests were willing to set politics aside and let religious beliefs transcend such matters.

Shared religious imagery included in particular the Staff Deity image, winged beings in profile (sometimes with falcon and condor heads) and severed trophy heads. Winged beings appear both accompanying the Staff Deity and independently, and seem to be running, floating, flying or kneeling. The frontal Staff Deity, with mask-like face, radiating head rays (sometimes ending in serpent heads), and dressed in tunic, belt and kilt, appears on pottery and architecture and might have been the prototype for the creator god Viracocha.

Despite this apparent religious unity, the focus of the religious imagery at Huari differed from that at Tiwanaku. At Huari it was applied primarily to portable objects, particularly to ceramics; at Tiwanaku it was applied to monumental stone architecture, but rarely appeared on pottery. Thus, while Wari ceramics spread the word far and wide, Tiwanaku imagery was more confined to standing monuments in the capital and a few other sites. Similarly, religious ceremony at Huari appears to have been more private and confined to smaller groups, judging by its architecture, while at Tiwanaku it seems to have been more public and to have taken place inside large compounds designed for the purpose. Tiwanaku's bold pyramidal platforms and huge sunken courts contrast starkly with the repetitious, incremental, unit-like constructions at Huari.

KINGDOMS AND SHRINES

The Late Intermediate Period is defined by the break-up of the Wari and Tiwanaku empires. Once again political fragmentation prevailed in the Andean Area while, as in earlier periods, a certain pan-Andean religious unity persisted.

BREAK-UP AND RIVALRY

In the Altiplano, the Tiwanaku state succumbed to a multitude of smaller city-states collectively known as the Aymara Kingdoms: Colla, Lupaka, Cana, Canchi, Umasuyo and Pacaje. Rivalry was stirred up, and this was perpetuated by repeated droughts from about AD1100 through the next 400 years as El Niño weather events and consequent adverse environmental conditions affected Lake Titicaca's water level and the productivity of the surrounding land.

In the central and northern sierra the first glimmerings of what would become the Inca culture began to manifest themselves in distinctive art styles in the Cuzco Valley. People in these regions abandoned many of the cities and towns in the valleys and moved to higher, moister locations, and towards the wetter eastern Cordillera. Competing centres protected the resources of their immediate areas: Pikillaqta (a southern Wari survival), Chokepukio (Wari's nearest inheritor), and clusters of settlements of ethnic groups known as Lucre, Killke, Wanka (whose capital was Wari Wanka) and Campa, and the Gran Pajaten city in Chachapoyas. Petty rivalry and temporary alliances were typical.

Along the central and southern Andean Area coasts the periods of drought affecting the highlands were even more severe. It was precarious enough in such desert coasts, but stress increased when irrigation systems failed as run-off from the mountains was further reduced. Mountain cities, by contrast, were able to survive on rainfall agriculture. The stress and decline of coastal centres incited local rivalry and the establishment of numerous small polities fighting for survival: Chiribaya, Ica and Chancay.

Below: The great ramp to the summit of the temple to Pachacamc and one of its numerous surrounding courts.

THE KINGDOM OF CHIMÚ

Two of the most prominent centres that stand out and perhaps typify this period were Chimú – or the Kingdom of Chimú – and Pachacamac. As in the Early Intermediate Period, these centres of power were coast-based.

Above: For this Chimú wooden and mother-of-pearl jaguar figurine, a Pacific shell was used to create the coat of a rainforest animal living thousands of kilometres (miles) away.

The Chimú were the inheritors of Early Intermediate Period Moche power in the Moche and Lambayeque valleys. Duplicating the Moche pattern, the Chimú conquered to north and south, invading and subduing the northern Peruvian coastal valleys from the sea. Through later Inca records, historians of Chimú encounter legends of early kings of Chimú and the earlier dynasty founded by the legendary ruler Naymlap and ending with the disastrous reign of Fempellec.

The Kingdom of Chimú was the largest Andean Area state up to its time. At its height it controlled two-thirds of all irrigated land on the desert coasts, while elsewhere states were more localized.

Some scholars believe that the term 'Kingdoms' of Chimú is more appropriate, as the nature of the valley politics indicates that there may have been dual or multiple rulership among them. Inca records gleaned by the Spanish conquistadors describe two dynasties: Taycanamu at Chan Chan in the Moche Valley and Naymlap in the Lambayeque Valley. In the latter, it is tempting to equate the rich burials of the Sicán Lords with the descendants of Naymlap.

CHAN CHAN OF THE CHIMÚ

The fantastic site of Chan Chan, capital of the Taycanamu rulers, was founded around AD1000. It comprised a massive complex of individual compounds covering an area of 6 sq km (1,480 acres), around which domestic and workshop suburbs spread to cover 20 sq km (4,940 acres) in total. Each walled compound (known as a *ciudadela*) of the central core was rectangular in plan, its long axis oriented north–south, and made of thick walls up to 9m (29½ft) high of poured adobe mud. Most had only one entrance, on the north side, guarded by painted wooden human figures set in niches on either side. Each court contained the residences of the reigning Chimú king, his retainers and officials. Around other courtyards within the compounds were store rooms, U-shaped structures called *audiencias*, and burial platforms. Adjacent wings contained rooms for service and maintenance retainers, as well as walled-in wells.

From the historical records we know the names of at least three Chimú deities: the creator god Ai Apaec, the moon goddess Si and the sea god Ni. Chimú religious imagery merges Moche and Wari styles, and continues the long Chavín traditions of fanged beings, jaguars and serpentine images.

Below: The Tschudi complex: even the walls of smaller enclosures within the ciudadelas *of the Chimú capital at Chan Chan were carefully moulded with geometric decoration.*

Above: The great temple-platform at Pachacamac – a huge pyramid of adobe bricks that grew to the size of a hill.

THE CULT OF PACHACAMAC

The site of Pachacamac on the central Peruvian coast was established in the Early Intermediate Period. In the wake of Chavín decline, it rose to prominence as a cult and pilgrimage site in the later half of the period, from about AD250. It was at this time that the first phases of the pyramid-platform to the sun and adjoining Temple to Pachacamac were built and presumably when the cult statues were installed. The name itself, in Quechua, means 'earth-maker'.

As a centre of local political power in the Middle Horizon, Pachacamac succumbed to Wari conquest, but as a religious cult centre it weathered the period of subjugation to persist as a cult and pilgrimage centre for more than 1,000 years through the Late Intermediate Period into Inca times. As a creator god, Pachacamac was the only serious rival to Viracocha, supreme god of the Inca, for that title.

CONQUEST AND EMPIRE: THE INCAS

Above: Map showing extent of the Inca Empire and the Four Quarters from the time of the legendary founder Manco Capac to the rule of Huayna Capac in the 16th century.

The final chronological period of ancient Andean Area history is the Late Horizon, which began about AD1400. It is marked by the rise of the Inca and their domination of the Andean Area, forming the largest empire ever known in the New World. Inca hegemony lasted a mere 132 years, however, until it met its match in cunning and military guile in the person of Francisco Pizarro.

EARLY BEGINNINGS

Inca beginnings were in the early Late Intermediate Period. During the political fragmentation of that period, the Inca were one of several local tribes or ethnic groups competing for survival within the Cuzco region and among numerous city-states scattered throughout the sierra. From the founding of the Inca ruling dynasty by the legendary Manco Capac in the mid-13th century, the Inca began to conquer the sierra and coastal regions and to unify them into a state in which central control was paramount. As with earlier Andean states, military conquest brought economic regulation and compulsory state religion. Both impositions on the losing parties were made more palatable through long-surviving traditional pan-Andean religious concepts, and by the incorporation of local deities, cults and religious practices into existing versions and the inclusion of local rulers in Inca government.

Below: A carved wooden face on a post from the Inca coastal regions, c.1400.

Manco Capac and his successors first defeated local rivals within the Cuzco Valley. The threat of their arch-enemy, the Chancas, nearly ended this early progress when they marched on Cuzco in 1438. The crushing of the Chancas by Pachacuti Inca Yupanqui, steeped in legend and the source of some of the most sacred *huaca* sites around the city, secured Inca domination of their immediate territory.

It was from this date that the Incas began their rapid expansion throughout the Andean Area. The date highlights the fact that the empire endured less than 100 years as the pre-eminent power in Andean America.

DOUBLING THE EMPIRE

Pachacuti ruled until 1471. His first campaigns subdued the city-states of the central Andes north to Huánuco and south to the northern and western shores of Lake Titicaca. The biggest prize of all was the conquest of the Kingdom of Chimú, which occurred in 1470–1. Together with his son and principal heir, Tupac Yupanqui (The Unforgettable One), Pachacuti doubled the size of the Inca Empire in less than ten years, incorporating Chimú and beyond into what is now Ecuador.

Above: Inca warriors attacking a fortress during their many campaigns of conquest, shown in Nueva Crónica y Buen Gobierno.

Upon his succession, Tupac Yupanqui more than doubled the size of the empire again, in 22 years of long and ruthless campaigns – to the coast west of Cuzco and to the farthest southern reaches, into modern Chile and Argentina. Upon his death, the throne was briefly disputed. Once secured by Huayna Capac, one of Tupac's sons, his reign (1493–1525) was occupied principally with campaigns to fill in corners in the northern provinces, mainly in the eastern Andean foothills and selva, with consolidation of Pachacuti's and Tupac's conquests, and with putting down local rebellions. Huayna Capac's attempts to conquer the selva had limited success.

KEYS TO SUCCESS

The success of Inca rapid expansion and domination lies in what had been established and entrenched in Andean political, social and economic structures before then. The Middle Horizon Wari and Tiwanaku empires, the former including the Cuzco region, had consolidated (as did the Late Intermediate Period Chimú) principles of centralized political control, organized through a network of administrative centres, roads and rapid communication. The practice of labour tax used levies of workers to co-ordinate labour distribution; it was an annual obligation to the central government. Such structures enabled the gathering, storage and redistribution of goods and the exchange of commodities between highland and lowland regions, ensuring the prosperity of all.

The Incas reconstituted these systems where their remnants remained and imported them into regions where they had not formerly existed. They maintained political power through the control of resources and the practice of resettling large groups of people around the provinces, and by using existing local chiefs to administer their command and removing to Cuzco the sons of local rulers, to hold hostage.

The nature of pan-Andean religious belief reinforced the Inca's 'right to rule' through the incorporation of local deities and icons into the state religion. At the same time it imposed the official state cult of Inti – the sun – personified by the Sapa Inca himself. In addition to hostages, the Incas took regional sacred objects to the capital; and craftsmen from the provinces were removed to Cuzco to construct buildings and produce imperial goods for the royal household.

Right: On this Moche pot, two warriors probably engage in ritual combat while one of them holds a decapitated head.

ELEMENTS OF COLLAPSE

Perhaps inevitably, strains and tensions within such a vast and diverse empire brought successional rivalry. It had happened when Tupac died, and when Huayna Capac died, a bitter civil war broke out between his two sons Huáscar and Atahualpa. This was the situation in which Francisco Pizarro arrived on his third visit, in 1532.

Manipulating this disruption, Pizarro was able to bring the empire to its knees with a few hundred Spaniards. He exploited resentment in the recently conquered provinces to gain native allies, he played one royal faction against the other in the dispute over succession and used the assassination of one brother, Huáscar, by the other, Atahualpa, to imprison the latter and demand a huge ransom that bankrupted the empire. By such methods the Spaniards kept the Incas off balance. As the empire's cohesion crumbled, the alliances, social organization and economic structure of the empire were reconfigured to suit Spanish greed and rule. Feeble revolts attempting to reinstate Inca power were quickly crushed by increasing Spanish might in the new colony.

CHAPTER FIVE

THEMES AND PEOPLES

The earliest sites of human habitation in the Andean Area date to about 11,500 years ago. It has been biologically demonstrated that the inhabitants of the New World descend from three or four distinct populations and several incidents of migration into North America, but that migrants into the South American continent all descend from only one of these groups.

The diverse landscape and regional variety of the Andean Area encouraged technological, social and economic innovation. As the hunter-gatherer lifestyle of the earliest Lithic Period evolved into an era of farming and permanent settlement, people adapted differently to the challenges provided by the coastal and mountain environments, and many different cultures developed throughout the Andes from the late Initial Period onwards.

Different languages also developed, and linguists have identified major language groups within this area. Indeed, throughout South America they estimate as many as 2,000 languages were once spoken, though only about 600 have been attested.

Recognition of the existence of different peoples among ancient Andeans is revealed in their many stories of the origins of humankind. In one story, the creator god Viracocha shaped men and women from clay then painted them in different colours, wearing different styles of clothing, and gave them their languages, cultural practices, songs, arts and crafts, and the knowledge of agriculture to distinguish between the different tribes and nations.

Left: The eastern façade and entrance to the Temple of the Cult of Chavín, the first great ancient Andean pilgrimage centre.

CIVIC-CEREMONIAL CENTRES

Two principal themes characterized pre-Hispanic Andean civilization: a general unity through shared religious beliefs across the Andean Area, and a settlement pattern of independent yet linked communities. From the earliest farming villages, through the construction of monumental civic-ceremonial centres of increasing complexity, to the establishment and growth of cities, universal patterns developed in cross-regional trade, shared methods of craftsmanship and organized political and social systems of labour. This was for growing crops and for the production of pottery, textiles, metalwork and other artefacts. With detailed variation, these universal patterns gave developmental impetus to the process and progress of Andean civilization.

ARCHITECTURAL 'TRADITIONS'

Different 'traditions' of civic-ceremonial architecture developed in tropical, desert coastal and sierra settings. Within varied lifestyles, regional cultures centralized religious belief and integrated labour to build special places for communal worship. These special places held sacred objects that represented the gods, and some places became sites of pilgrimage serving large regions. Eventually, a select few became the most important pilgrimage centres, some of them enduring for long periods.

In the forested north (now in Ecuador), Valdivia Tradition settlements were characterized by central oval or circular plazas, with domed oval communal structures surrounded by houses. Sometimes the communal buildings were on top of low earthen mounds. One type, known as a 'charnel house', was for mortuary ritual, to prepare corpses for burial elsewhere; a second type, called a 'fiesta house', was for feasting and drinking.

In the coastal valleys of northern and central Peru the establishment of civic-ceremonial centres became a mainstay of Andean civilization from about 2850BC. Known as the Supe-Aspero Tradition and the El Paraíso Tradition, they take their names from the 17-mound centres in the Río Supe Valley and the site of Aspero, and from El Paraíso. Both traditions featured raised mounds that provided flat, open spaces on top for congregational ritual and to support complex multi-chambered structures. Ceremony seems to have emphasized public-oriented activity, the flat top providing a stage for the ritual to be viewed by a large congregation assembled in front of the mound. Within this cohesive theme there was considerable variation in the sizes and shapes of coastal platforms and in the building complexes on top. Ceremony involved burnt offerings, but the locations and contexts of these varied.

REGIONAL CENTRES

The extensive platforms at Salinas de Chao, Los Morteros and Piedra Parada lack surrounding domestic remains, indicating that they were built as venues for communal ritual by the peoples of surrounding settlements. The extensive 17-mound complex of the Supe Valley also suggests regional worship, and perhaps influence beyond. If true, the extended 'site' was the earliest in a long Andean tradition of pilgrimage sites. In contrast, at Río Seco, Bandurria, Culebras, Huaynuna and Huaca Prieta the modest sizes of the ceremonial structures

Left: Desert coastal oases valleys, where water was precious, developed ritual centres alongside sophisticated irrigation systems.

Right: Reconstruction of the circular sunken court and the terraced platforms built against the hill slope at Salinas de Chao.

and associated domestic buildings and refuse indicates that they were built by and largely for their local communities.

Many chambers in the complexes on top of Supe-Aspero platforms included rectangular niches, possibly for sacred objects. At Caral, the ceremonial complex includes an element of exclusion where it enclosed a large walled plaza with a 'fire altar' in one corner; another chamber housed a sacred obelisk. At Huaynuna, Piedra Parada and Caral there is evidence of contact with sierra ritual in the construction of oval ceremonial chambers and sunken courtyards. Room complexes of later building phases at some sites feature bilateral symmetry.

ASPERO

The largest of the Supe sites, Aspero, comprises an extensive mound complex: six major flat platforms and 11 lower (1–2m/3–6½ft) mounds surrounded by 15ha (37 acres) of public and domestic remains. The larger mounds rise up to 4m (12ft) above the valley floor, or 10m (32ft) where banked against the side or top of a hill. Two of these, Huaca de los Idolos and Huaca de los Sacrificios, produced radiocarbon dates as early as 3055 and 2850BC respectively. Both platforms underwent several phases of covering and later enlargement.

The free-standing platform at Huaca de los Sacrificios included an elite, textile-wrapped ritual infant burial, apparently accompanied by an adult sacrifice, showing that social hierarchy had clearly become established. At Huaca de los Idolos, one ritual chamber on top of the platform included a buried cache of 13 or more deliberately broken clay figurines.

EL PARAISO

The largest Preceramic Period stone-built civic-ceremonial centre was El Paraíso. Radiocarbon dates of 2000BC and later indicate that its civic-ceremonial complex represents a transitional stage from the Preceramic traditions and the Initial Period U-shaped complexes described earlier. It comprised two long parallel raised platforms (250 x 50m/820 x 140ft) forming the sides of a U framing a 7ha (17 acre) plaza. The base of the U comprises several smaller ruins rather than a central platform. Other masonry complexes were built near by as El Paraíso expanded. Evidence of fire ritual and an absence of domestic debris around the ceremonial complexes indicate that El Paraíso was built as a ritual centre for people living throughout a larger region.

Right: A figurine of unbaked clay, which was deliberately broken and buried at Huaca de los Idolos. The fragmentary figure is shown in the first two drawings; the drawing on the right shows a projected reconstruction.

COMMUNAL RITUAL: KOTOSH

Farming community peoples in the mountain valleys of central and northern Peru also cultivated communal ritual by building large communal structures. While the environment of isolated valleys was conducive to social division and variation between valleys, the development of similar corporate constructions demonstrates social union and amalgamation, reveals contact among valleys and reveals underlying common religious belief here as well. To build such structures required political control and the mobilization of communal labour. The buildings must also have served civic and administrative purposes.

THE KOTOSH TRADITION

Ritual and special-purpose architecture in the sierra is known as the Kotosh Tradition, after the type-site, Kotosh, situated at about 2,000m (6,600ft) above sea level, in a region of temperate climate and limited seasonal rainfall in the eastern Andes. Its location typifies lower sierra village settlement and offered access to the natural resources of both higher and lower ecological zones. The early Kotosh economy was mainly hunting and gathering – there are many chipped stone tools and debris, and charred seeds, but at first no evidence of cultivated plants. Anatomical changes on the animal bones found at Kotosh show that guinea pigs and llamas were domesticated, or at least kept and herded. Deer bones show that hunting remained an important source of meat.

Like coastal architectural traditions, Kotosh sites featured platform mounds. These mounds, however, were more standardized in shape and size, and served as platforms for structures of a more excluding nature. A characteristic of the Kotosh tradition was the raising of a large twin ceremonial mound complex, indicating the early establishment of social division into two kin-related groups.

Excavations at Kotosh reveal long periods of use, perhaps through generations, comprising ten superimposed constructions. Early mounds were built by people who made no pottery, and the later mounds were made by their pottery-making Initial Period and Early Horizon descendants.

A second Kotosh form was the sunken court or plaza (*plazas hundidas*). Every platform mound and plaza was a place of protocol and designed behaviour. People participated in the construction of these non-subsistence buildings and in prescribed ritual activity, presumably led by religious specialists.

The contemporary site of La Galgada, in the central sierra north of Kotosh, demonstrates similar characteristics. At about 1,100m (3,600ft) above sea level and located roughly equidistantly between the Pacific coast and the semi-tropical eastern selva, it too exploited both zones for ornamental products. La Galgada burials

Above: As a staple of life, maize and other crops exemplified Pacha Mama (Mother Earth), from which all life sprang.

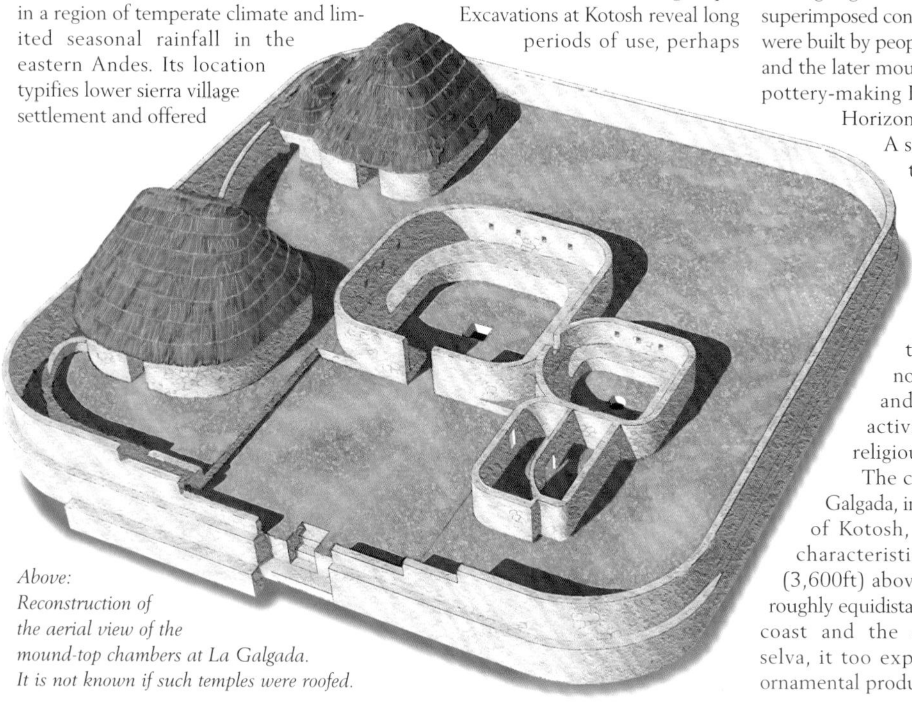

Above: Reconstruction of the aerial view of the mound-top chambers at La Galgada. It is not known if such temples were roofed.

contain shell beads and discs from the coast and Amazonian tropical bird feathers from the east. The La Galgada economy was demonstrably based on farming. There are remains of domesticated beans, squashes, fruits, chilli peppers, gourds, cotton and a single maize cob. Remains of ancient irrigation canals are consistent with the necessity of irrigation to grow these plants.

POSITIVE AND NEGATIVE SPACES

Platforms and sunken courts organize space in two distinct ways. Platforms are positive structures – exterior and elevated. They divide space vertically and support hierarchical buildings for special purposes. The mounds themselves, and more especially their buildings, hide ritual from the general populace and render them exclusive to specialists. Sunken courts, on the other hand, constitute negative space – interior and secluded. Their walls restrict space and confine activities within them. At most sites both platforms and sunken courts were built, though at a few sites only a sunken court was built.

SOCIAL DIVISIONS

The ceremonial constructions at La Galgada, as at Kotosh, comprise twin mounds surrounded by dwellings, again indicating a two-part social division. Each mound has a main central platform and subsidiary buildings. Each comprises a series of superimposed mounds and buildings, and the larger platform produced radiocarbon dates ranging between 2200 and 1200BC.

Both Kotosh and La Galgada were clearly sites of regional importance. The presence of exotic commodities at both sites implies the beginnings of exchange between coast and sierra and between sierra and tropics – a tradition so characteristic of later Andean civilization. Their inhabitants had succeeded in achieving an economy and lifestyle that afforded them the time to marshal their labour for the purely non-subsistence activity of special architecture, religiously focused sites and special burials. These constructions, to their builders' minds, were vital to the continuity of their existence and were the earliest such sites in an Andean tradition of meeting such existential or religious needs in this way.

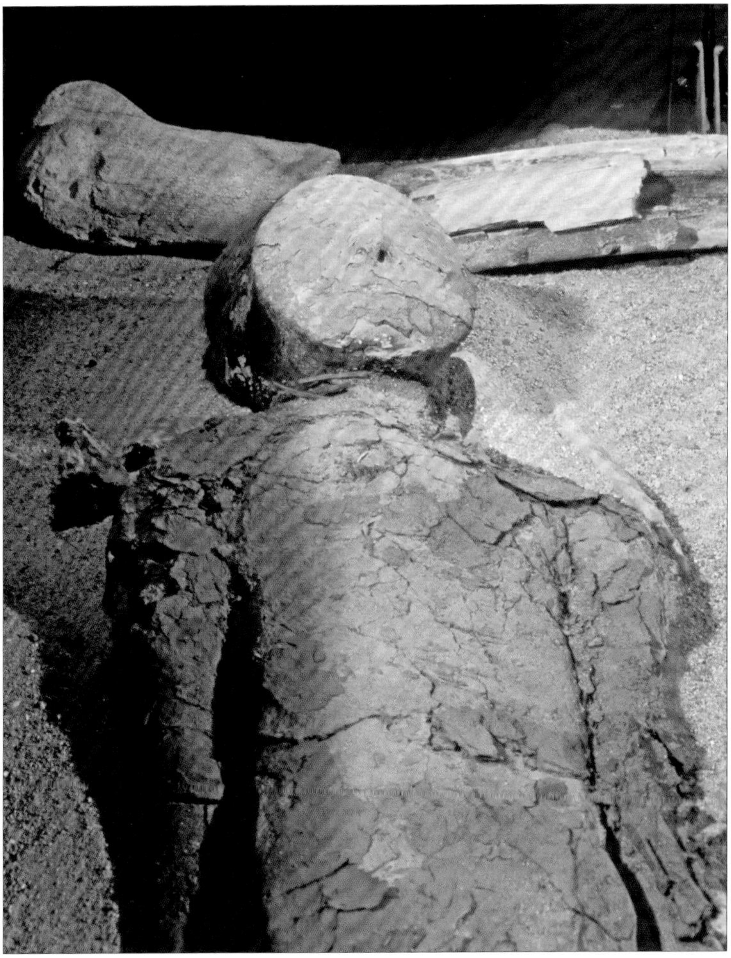

Above: The ritual honouring of important ancestors began perhaps with mummification among the Chinchorros of northern Chile.

THE CHINCHORROS

Much farther south of the coastal and sierra traditions, sites on the desert coast of Peru and northern Chile reveal a singular economy based on the riches of the sea. Chemical analysis of the bones of the inhabitants of the culture shows a diet of 90 per cent marine foods. So rich were the marine resources that large towns could be supported with little or no farming of edible cultigens. Coastal floodplain plants were gathered and later cultivated for fuel, clothing fibre, shelter, water craft, nets, fishing line and floats, basketry and other tools for marine exploitation.

Chinchorros domestic structures include burials of the earliest mummified bodies, preserved with salt and reed-mat wrappings, presaging the Andean traditions of both mummification and burial among the living to keep the deceased as part of the present.

EXCHANGE OF GOODS AND IDEAS

The architectural traditions of Kotosh, Supe-Aspero and El Paraíso reveal the beginnings of an exchange that became characteristically Andean. It involved the interchange of both commodities and religious ideas within and between geographical zones: among respective regions at similar heights (horizontal exchange) and between highland and lowland communities, such as sierra and coast and sierra and selva (vertical exchange).

Above: *Highland staples, particularly the potato, also became lowland staples through trade between the two areas.*

DISTRIBUTION AND EXCHANGE

The exchange of goods became a necessity in Andean civilization for the trading and obtaining of either key products that could not be grown in one zone or another or exotic materials that were native to one zone or another.

Adaptation within Andean civilization was shaped by the distribution of natural resources and by the limits within which various domesticated plants and animals could be grown, reared and herded. For example, food staples such as maize can be grown at altitudes up to about 3,000m (9,800ft), but are at risk from frost and hail; crops frequently fail. Maize domestication and cultivation thus spread from coast to highlands. In contrast, the potato, originally a highland crop, was eventually cultivated throughout a range from nearly sea level to 3,800m (12,500ft). A similar division into zones applies to growing cotton and herding llamas and alpacas for meat and wool. Tropical fruits and lowland products such as peanuts, avocados, manioc, chillies and squashes were redistributed among zones through trade as they became part of Andean Area culture.

In coastal desert oases, resources were similar despite the long coastline. The same is true of vast tropical lowlands. Environmental similarities are reinforced by limited annual temperature fluctuation. These factors contribute to exchange within and between valleys or selva regions. At increasing elevation, however, seasonal variation increases and growing periods shorten. In highland areas, zones of cultivation are compressed and stacked within the environment. Highland peoples consequently practise greater vertical movement within these zones to pursue cultivation in basins and valleys and herding in the Altiplano. These factors contribute to exchange between communities at different altitudes within the highlands and also between highlands and lowlands.

Left: *Exotic objects, such as this Pacific spiny or thorny oyster, were traded from the far northern coasts to the highlands.*

AVAILABILITY AND DEMAND

It is frequently the case in the Andean Area that where abundant flatlands (potentially useful for crop-growing) occur, there is less rainfall, a threat of drought and a need to irrigate. In contrast,

Above: The decorations on many Moche pots depict scenes of daily life. Here a fisherman sets out in a balsa boat.

highland zones have greater rainfall and are less affected by drought, but flat lands suitable for agriculture are more restricted and there is a need to increase growing space by terracing. For these different reasons both zones required the input of organized labour as populations increased. However, fewer than 20 per cent of major Andean cultivated plants grow above 3,000m (9,800ft), while 90 per cent thrive best below 1,000m (3,300ft). This inversion of available land and crop diversity created a perennial strain on supply and demand, and it is this tension that underlays exchange between peoples at different elevations in ancient Andean civilization.

MOVEMENT OF PEOPLE

Exchange was not only of goods but also of peoples, adapting to different land zones to exploit cultivation possibilities. Andean highland peoples regularly exploited irrigated farmlands for maize, cotton, peppers, gourds and squashes in a lowland zone, in middle-zone potato lands and in Altiplano herding pastures. Furthermore, evidence in Inca times shows that the peoples in these zones were kin-related groups with a regularized system of obligations and duties to the whole group.

Among coastal valley and plain cultures the sea provided a natural highway for the movement of goods and peoples up and down the coast. The Moche kingdom, for example, was a seafaring nation that pursued conquest from one valley to another by sea invasion.

As regions came under the control of larger political entities, the redistribution of products required greater regulation and intricate administration. To maintain economic balance, both products and labour needed control and regulation. Later imperial cultures, and ultimately the Incas, practised active transportation of peoples within the empire and colonization of regions to obtain materials from distant areas or exotic locations.

RITUAL GOODS AND IDEAS

To maintain religious integrity and appease the gods, and so secure the well-being of humans, rulers needed to obtain exotic raw materials considered essential for ritual. Thus, tropical products such as tobacco, coca and forest mushrooms required not only secured sources but also organization and security in transport. The use of cotton and llama wool textiles at coastal and highland sites, and of coastal shells (including *Spondylus princeps* – the spiny or thorny oyster from Ecuador and farther north) in highland ceremonial contexts confirms the early beginnings of both horizontal and vertical exchange. As weaving became an entrenched part of Andean cultural expression and part of state control, the redistribution of cotton and wool became heavily regulated in Inca times and was no doubt equally regulated in earlier kingdoms.

The exchange of exotic products across such distant regions implies the exchange of ideas associated with the items and their suppliers. The nature of both highland and coastal ceremonial architecture from the earliest Preceramic times shows recognition of mountain, earth and sea gods throughout Andean cultures, and the association of them in ritual structures.

Below: From ancient times, coastal valley oases probably consisted of numerous small growing fields sharing an irrigation system.

CONFLICT AND CO-OPERATION

Coastal El Paraíso was the first example of the U-shaped ceremonial complex that became the hallmark of Initial Period civic-ceremonial architecture. This period showed both the start of a widespread similarity in civic-ceremonial construction and signs of conflict between political units. These are manifestations of the two alternating themes of political cohesion and fragmentation in Andean civilization.

The combination of platform mounds and sunken courts in the late Preceramic Period at Kotosh, La Galgada and coastal sites may have constituted a Kotosh Religious Tradition, perhaps the first widespread Andean 'religion'. Scholars speculate that to agricultural people the sunken court was the focus for veneration of the Pacha Mama (Mother Earth), or even for the ritual re-enactment of creation or birth in a descent into the court and re-emergence from it. Where both structures were built, the sunken court was situated before the ascending staircase of the platform, its own staircase aligned to it. This combination – the elevated and the subterranean – suggests rituals that proceeded from a descent into Mother Earth followed by an ascent into the sky to the father Apu (or vice versa perhaps).

Above: When peoples gather to trade their produce, ideas are also exchanged and bonds developed between different regions.

FARMING AND RITUAL

In the early centuries of the third millennium BC, climatic improvement and increased rainfall fostered the spread of intensive agriculture throughout the Andean Area. Intensive agriculture with irrigation works at coastal sites was added to maritime exploitation.

Agriculture and pastoralism spread into the higher sierra and Altiplano, including the Titicaca Basin. Increasing population and agricultural production, and the exploitation of new lands, brought economic prosperity. Easier living created time for increased sophistication of political structure and for concern with religious concepts.

Left: Conflict between city-states is evident from at least the Initial Period in stone sculptures of warriors, as at Cerro Sechín.

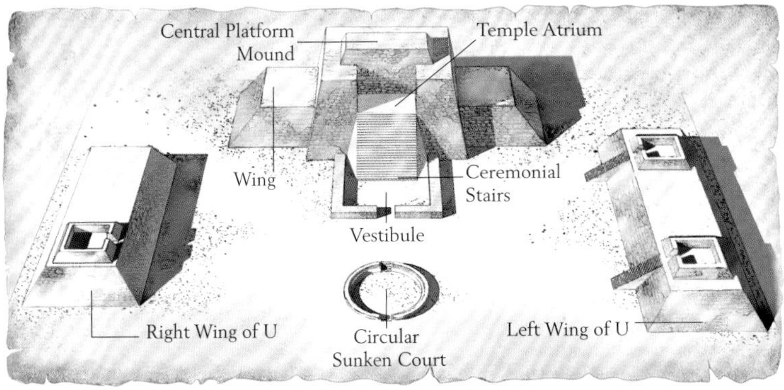

Above: A U-shaped temple showing the large central platform mound flanked by left and right wings and a circular sunken court.

Intensive agriculture, manifested by irrigation works and concern for rain and run-off water, may have fostered increased veneration of Mother Earth, Pacha Mama, and of mountain deities represented by Apu. Increased concern with the Milky Way (Mayu) accompanied the need to track the movements of stars and planets for agricultural scheduling.

These concerns brought an unprecedented spate of civic-ceremonial complex-building throughout the Andean Area. As in the Preceramic Period, Initial Period coastal complexes were small and local and also vast, presumably to serve a wide region. There were scores of complexes throughout the valleys. New phases of building at Kotosh, La Galgada and El Paraíso created U-shaped complexes at the last two sites about 1900 and 2000BC respectively. Sunken courts changed from circular to rectangular.

The largest Initial Period civic-ceremonial complex was at Sechín Alto in the coastal Casma Valley. Begun around 1400BC, the huge platform forming the base of its U-shaped complex was 300m (980ft) long and 250m (820ft) wide and still stands 40m (130ft) above the plain. Platforms forming the arms of the U flank a succession of plazas, including two circular sunken courts, in an area 400m (1,300ft) wide by 1,100m (3,600ft) long. Surrounding this complex was 10.5 sq km (2,600 acres) of buildings and smaller platforms. Other classic coastal U-shaped centres included Huaca de los Reyes, Cardal, La Florida, San Jacinto and Garagay.

SIGNS OF CONFLICT

Accompanying this unity in architectural form were signs of conflict between the political units associated with different civic-ceremonial centres, or perhaps between valleys. Cladding their ceremonial mounds with hand-made mud bricks, the builders of different sites vied with each other to decorate them with enormous adobe friezes, often painting them in rich colours. Two smaller, yet imposing, sites exemplify theses developments, both in the Sechín–Casma Valley.

Cerro Sechín was a multi-roomed sanctuary adorned with adobe friezes painted with felines and fish. About 1200BC, this complex was filled to make a large rectangular platform surrounded by a facing of incised megaliths. Two processions of armed warriors carry axe-like clubs and march from the sides around the front of the building to converge on the main entrance. On either side of the entrance, monoliths depict fluttering banners.

A few kilometres (miles) away, Llamas-Moxeke is dominated by two huge rectangular platforms about 1km (½ mile) apart and equidistant from a square court. The Moxeke platform, 25m (82ft) high and 165m (540ft) on each side, had a façade decorated with huge niches framing high-relief friezes painted red, blue, white and black. Figures depicted include two human faces, two richly dressed individuals and a person with his back turned out and arms bound behind him as if a prisoner.

The coastal flowering lasted until about 900BC, from which time a period of drought took severe effect and almost all coastal ceremonial complexes were abandoned within a century or two. Sierra ceremonial complexes faired better, many remaining functional into the last few centuries BC, into the Early Horizon. The rise of a new highland U-shaped ceremonial centre, Chavín de Huántar, hailed the beginning of an ecumenical Andean religion that was widespread and enduring.

Right: Co-operation within and between cities enabled people to build and maintain extensive field terraces and irrigation systems.

RELIGIOUS COHESION

The common use of platforms, U-shaped complexes and the association of sunken courts suggests religious ecumenicalism, and use both for ritual and civic functions – even that the two activities were functionally intertwined. A Kotosh Religious Tradition has earlier been suggested.

In the succeeding Early Horizon, while coastal centres remained modest after centuries of drought began to abate, one sierra centre arose that without question became a cult and pilgrimage centre. It was the 'cathedral' of Andean religion and included all the classic features that had been developed in earlier periods in coastal and sierra traditions. This was Chavín de Huántar.

THE RISE OF CHAVÍN DE HUÁNTAR

From about 900BC, as coastal ceremonial centres were abandoned, Chavín de Huántar rose to prominence. It was not urban in size or layout and lacked a surrounding domestic district. Instead it comprised a modest complex to accommodate a small population of priests, officials, artisans, servants and pilgrims to support and serve its cult. Its influence stretched throughout the central and northern Andes, and west and east to the coast and tropical lowlands. Further, it played a crucial role in the dissemination of technology. Its central location appears to have established and perpetuated its importance.

At its largest, the Chavín de Huántar ceremonial centre covered about 42ha (104 acres), with 2,000–3,000 inhabitants. The Old Temple framed a circular sunken courtyard. Scores of sculpted heads project from its four-storey stone walls. The temple interior comprises a labyrinth of interconnecting narrow passages and chambers, the southern wing of which was later doubled in size as the site flourished, and is known as the New Temple, although both temples were used simultaneously after the expansion.

MONOLITHIC SCULPTURE

In one interior gallery stands the stone idol called the Lanzón (after its lance-like shape) or Great Image, probably the earliest pan-Andean oracle: a carved granite monolith 4.5m (15ft) high. The Lanzón faces east and portrays a humanoid form, but overall depicts a monster visage. Its right hand is raised and its left lowered by its side; its feet and hands end in claws. Its mouth is thick-lipped, drawn in a hideous snarl and punctuated by long, outward-curving canines. Its eyebrows and hair end in serpent heads; its earlobes hang heavy with pendants. It wears a tunic and headdress, both of which are decorated with feline heads. Its notched top protrudes through the ceiling into an upper gallery in which priests probably sat in secrecy, projecting their voices as that of the god.

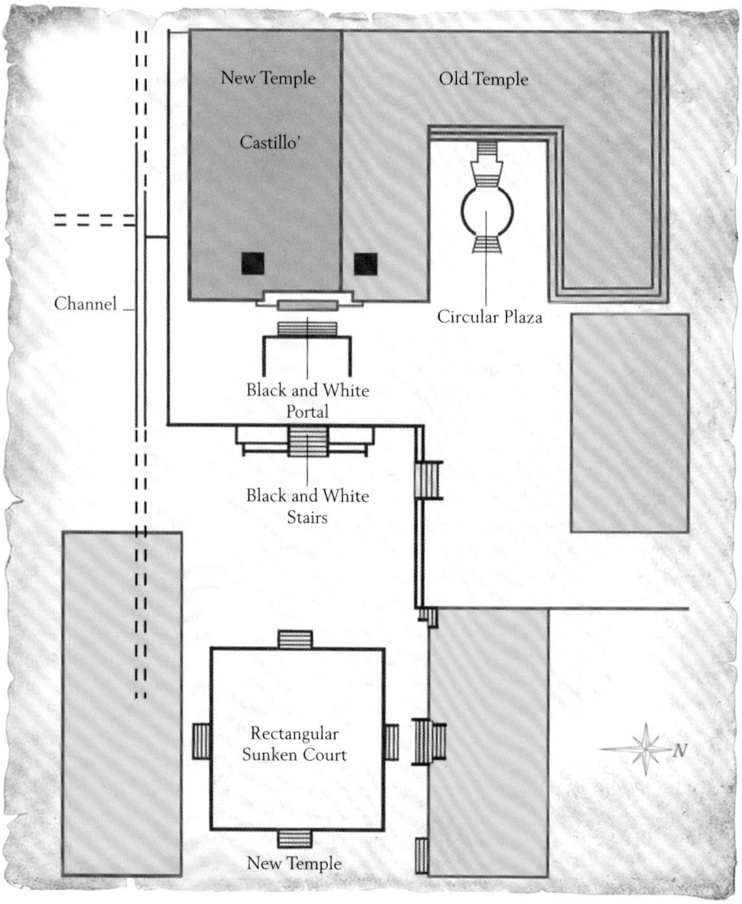

Left: Plan of Chavín de Huántar, one of the most elaborate ceremonial centres of its period, with its U-shaped temples.

Above: *The ray-encircled Staff Deity is the central figure on the Gateway of the Sun in the Kalasasaya enclosure at Tiwanaku.*

CULT CENTRE

That Chavín de Huántar was the site of a cult seems indisputable. In a gallery next to the sunken plaza, excavators found 800 broken ceramic vessels decorated in styles from cultures as far apart as the northern coast to the central highlands. Scattered among bowls and containers were llama, deer, guinea pig and fish bones – thought to have been either offerings or a store of ritual trappings for ceremonies.

Chavín iconography drew its inspiration from both the natural world – animals, plants and aquatic life – and a variety of ecological zones – the ocean, coast, the mountains and tropical lowlands. The Tello Obelisk is a low-relief carved granite monolith 2.5m (8ft) high, in the shape of a supernatural cayman. Notched at the top like the Lanzón, it probably also stood upright in a gallery or courtyard. Additional carvings on and around the cayman depict plants and animals, including peanuts and manioc from the tropical lowlands and *Strombus* and *Spondylus* shells of species native to the Ecuadorian coast, attesting to the wide influence of the Chavín Cult. Other carvings depict jaguars, serpents, and harpy or crested eagles.

As the cult's fame spread and the site was enlarged, ceramic styles and other exotic foods, plants and animals continued to inspire its artistic imagery. Evidence from the domestic buildings shows the development of social hierarchy in the unequal distribution of goods and of craft specialization. The cult supported artisans applying its symbolism to portable artefacts and spreading it through exchange, thereby expanding and entrenching the cult.

With the expansion of the south wing of the temple, the imagery became more elaborate. The relief of a new supreme deity was erected in the patio of the New Temple. Like the Lanzón, this is a humanoid figure with a fanged mouth, multiple bracelets, anklets and ear pendants. It holds a *Strombus* shell in its right hand and a *Spondylus* shell in its left hand.

THE STAFF DEITY

Another huge carved stone slab, the Raimondi Stela (2m/6½ft long), depicts a deity who in some ways epitomizes the cult: the Staff God/Goddess. Ubiquitous in Chavín iconography, this figure was portrayed with male or female attributes. The full-frontal, standing figure is a composite of animal and human characteristics. Like those of other Chavín deities, the hands and feet of this figure end in claws, the mouth displays huge curved fangs and the ears are bedecked with ornaments. The arms are outstretched and clutch staffs in one form or another, themselves elaborately festooned with spikes and plume-like decorations.

The exact significance and meaning of the Staff Deity is unknown. That he/she was a powerful deity is attested by the application of the image all over Chavín de Huántar on stones and walls, and throughout the central Andes and coast on portable objects, including ceramics and textiles. The potency of the Staff Deity is likewise demonstrated by the fact that the imagery of a frontal, staff-bearing deity endured from the Early Horizon until Inca times. Given this exceptional importance, it seems certain that the Staff Deity was a supernatural being with a distinct 'personality', possibly a primeval creator god.

Left: *The Raimondi Stela at Chavín de Huántar is the ultimate representation of the Staff Deity. It can be read either way up.*

PEOPLES OF THE EMPIRE

Spanish administrative and judicial archives contain chronicles and records of the Inca conquest of numerous ethnic groups, chiefdoms and political units called *señorios*. From these sources we have a veritable roster of the peoples of the empire.

RIVALS OF THE INCAS

Guaman Poma de Ayala's history refers to the chiefdom of the Ayarmacas, one of the many politico-ethnic divisions of the Acamama region around Cuzco. As the first powerful Inca rivals, the Ayarmacas played an instrumental role in the founding of Cuzco. Poma de Ayala identifies 'some first Incas' called Tocay Capac and Pinahua Capac, whom other sources call 'kings', or identify as generic titles for the rulers of two allied chiefdoms – Ayarmaca and Pinahua – comprising 18 towns south of Cuzco.

Prolonged Ayarmaca campaigns against the Incas of Cuzco resulted in stalemate. However, as the Incas subdued other neighbours and expanded within the valley, the Ayarmaca lords were relegated to the status of local chiefs within the Inca hierarchy. As the Incas wrestled for control, their new arch-rivals became the Chancas, whose defeat in 1438 was a defining point in the rise of the Inca state, and the traditional date for the beginning of the empire, along with Pachacuti Inca Yupanqui's ascent to the throne.

PEOPLES OF THE INCA EMPIRE

Pachacuti turned his attention to the Altiplano chiefdoms. His predecessor Viracocha had formed an alliance with the Lupaqas of Chucuito against the Hatun Colla, but

Above: Huayna Capac, 12th of the Inca dynasty and the last great conquering emperor, ruled from 1493 until 1526.

Below: One of the greatest Inca conquests involved capturing the Chimú fortresses, such as that of coastal Paramonga.

Above: The centre of the empire was Cuzco, here seen from the fortress-temple of Sacsahuaman overlooking the city.

success against the Chancas changed Pachacuti's perspective on domination. The Collas were utterly defeated in battle, and the peace scene frequently depicted on *kero* drinking vessels shows the Collas wearing especially tall headdresses, emphasizing the cultural variety and distinction between ethnic groups. At the victory celebration in Cuzco, Pachacuti ordered the beheading of the Colla leaders, warning others who might resist.

The effect was immediate and the remaining Altiplano lords accepted Inca overlordship without further resistance. This Cuntisuyu quarter formed the core of the empire, incorporating the chiefdoms of the Soras, Lucanas, Andahuaylas, Canas, Canchis, Paucarcollas, Pacajes and Azángaros, and exposing the western coastal *señorio* of Collao.

The Chinchas of Collao submitted peacefully at the intimidating approach of Inca armies led by Tupac Yupanqui. Pachacuti and Tupac next expanded north, creating Chinchaysuyu quarter, valley chiefdoms falling one after another: the Guarco and Lunahuaná chiefdoms in the central Andes; the Collec *señorio*, including the Chuquitanta, Carabayllo, Zapan, Macas, Guaraui, Guancayo and Quivi chiefdoms; and the Ychsma *señorio*.

Below: In less than 100 years, the Incas subdued peoples from Ecuador to Chile and from the Pacific to the Amazon Rainforest.

THE KINGDOM OF THE CHIMÚ

The Inca armies marched on the vast, ancient northern Kingdom of Chimú. Garcilasco de la Vega's *Comentarios Reales de los Incas* describes the confrontation:

The brave Chimú [Minchançaman], his arrogance and pride now tamed, appeared before the prince [Tupac Inca Yupanqui] with as much submission and humility, and grovelled on the ground before him, worshipping him and repeating the same request [for pardon] as he had made through his ambassadors. The prince received him affectionately in order to relieve [his] grief … [and] bade two of the captains raise him from the ground. After hearing him, [Tupac] told him that all that was past was forgiven. … The Inca had not come to deprive him of his estates and authority, but to improve his idolatrous religion, his laws, and his customs.

Unlike the treatment of Colla leaders, Tupac set a new precedent, incorporating new states and recognizing their integrity under Inca overlordship. Perhaps the size and importance of Chimú prompted special treatment.

Farther north, the coastal chiefdoms of the Quito, Cañaris, Huancavilcas, Manta and Puná were conquered; then the Huarochirí, Yauyos, and the *señorio* of Guzmango. These northern chiefdoms fell so rapidly that there was hardly time for incorporation and consolidation; archaeology and the chronicles, however, attest to the rapid imposition of Inca rule, installation of local elites as provincial governors and collection of tax produce into large centres for redistribution.

OUTSIDERS AND REBELS

The Incas also recognized peoples beyond imperial borders, against whom their campaigns were less successful. The chronicles of Tupac Yupanqui's incursions into the selva of Antisuyu quarter mention the Opataris, Manosuyu, Mañaris, Yanaximes, Chunchos and Paititi.

Many chiefdoms accepted diminution of their authority reluctantly. Tupac's son Huayna Capac campaigned against the Chiriguanas of Collasuyu quarter, and, in the far north, the Chachapoyas of Chinchaysuyu, the Caranquis, Otavalos, Cayambis, Cochasquis and Pifos, all of whom had rebelled. The Huanca of Chinchaysuyu allied themselves to Pizarro in a final bid to throw off Inca domination.

The Incas strove for political unity by utilizing local rulers and incorporating them into the Inca hierarchy, giving local elites and subjects a sense of belonging. Nevertheless, local independence had lasted for generations, so there was considerable resentment of Inca impositions, particularly among more far-flung peoples. This potential instability, especially at the death of Huayna Capac in 1526, played into Spanish hands.

CHAPTER SIX

POWER AND WARFARE

By the end of the Initial Period, civilization in the Andean Area had established an underlying unity in religious concepts and some basic civic-ceremonial architectural forms, culminating in the cohesion in the Chavín Cult in the Early Horizon. Subsequent periods continued the alternation of less-unified periods and more politically unified horizons, although in every period there were some kingdoms or empires.

Patterns established in earlier periods continued to focus on three areas: the central and northern Peruvian coastal valleys, the central and southern Peruvian/Bolivian sierras and Altiplano, and the southern Peruvian and northern Chilean coastal deserts. Within each of these areas powerful social hierarchies developed and elite individuals ruled alongside a specialized priesthood or state shamans. Elite individuals were buried elaborately in rich tombs, sumptuously adorned and often accompanied by sacrificial victims. State cults of the dead flourished, establishing the principle of a continuously revolving cycle of life and death and the perpetuation of the dead in the living world.

The principles of state control over ordinary citizens became stronger and more elaborate, culminating in one of the two greatest empires ever established in the Americas: the Inca Empire. The chronicles and histories preserved by Spanish priests and administrators, together with archaeological discoveries, make it possible to gain a detailed picture of the way of life and beliefs of the Incas.

Left: This painted Chimú textile depicts a shaman in a trance, surrounded by snarling felines, serpents and birds.

THE NAZCA CONFEDERACY

Early Horizon Chavín was not a state religion. It brought religious unity throughout the central and northern Peruvian Andes and coast, but it was not a centralized state.

The number and variation in size and architecture of civic-ceremonial centres, and the large domestic populations of many, indicate both local rule and social organization. Specialist artisans spread and perpetuated the cult by making large quantities of portable objects adorned with Chavín symbolic art, constantly reminding the inhabitants of the towns and cities of their over-arching religion. Chavín de Huántar remained the premier pilgrimage centre, and constant trade among coastal and mountain valleys re-enforced shared beliefs.

Contemporary with later Chavín was the Paracas culture on the southern Peruvian coast. Like Chavín, Paracas was not a centralized state. The most famous Paracas feature – its Cavernas cemetery of richly adorned, carefully mummified burials – was a distinct locale serving, but physically separated from, the living town of Cerro Colorado. Close spiritual association between Paracas living and dead, demonstrated by the lavish treatment of the latter by the former, shows a cult-like relationship between religion and a loose socio-political organization. With some early Chavín influence, Paracas religion soon developed its own character, which was particularly represented by a prominent figure known as the Oculate Being.

Below: Nazca effigy jar suggesting a severed head. Ritual decapitation, widespread in Andean civilization, was a Nazca speciality.

Above: Nazca burials include collections of trophy heads and were often wrapped in textiles fringed with pictures of woven heads.

NAZCA CITY-STATES

In the same desert coastal area as the Nazca were the Early Intermediate Period inheritors of the Paracas legacy, *c.*100BC–AD700. As with Paracas, no strong central Nazca political unity prevailed; rather there was a loose confederation of city-states in the river valleys. Ventilla, the largest Nazca site known, covered at least 200ha (495 acres) with terraced housing, walled courts and small mounds, and is thought to have been a Nazca 'capital' of one such city-state.

Ventilla was linked to its ritual counterpart, Cahuachi, by a line or 'road' across the desert. Cahuachi comprised a profusion of ceremonial kin-group mounds and associated plazas scattered over 150ha (370 acres). The mounds were built of adobe bricks modifying the tops of about 40 natural hills in mid-valley. The largest mound, known as the Great Temple, was a 30m (98ft) high modified hillock comprising six or seven terraces with adobe-brick retaining walls.

Cahuachi's location was chosen deliberately at mid-valley where, for geological reasons, the Nazca River disappears underground and re-emerges down-valley. Increasing drought in the sierra to the east intensified desert aridity and pressure for water conservation. The Ventillana-Cahuachi people constructed an elaborate system of subterranean channels to direct water into cisterns, which were reached by spiral ramps on terraces faced with river cobbles, and from which water could be drawn for irrigation.

Left: A Nazca warrior or masked shaman with spear and atl-atl *(spear thrower), in a stance reminiscent of the Chavín Staff Deity.*

A CITY FOR RITUAL

Cahuachi was a sacred 'city', where the citizens performed religious ceremonies and where the dead were prepared and then buried. The burials and artefacts associated with the mounds show that the entire site was a pilgrimage centre and ritual burial ground of family plots, each kin-group constructing its own mound. The focus was on ancestor worship and a pantheon of gods now nameless.

Some burials were of elite or favoured dead, while others appear to be sacrificial victims. Honoured burials were mummified and accompanied by exquisitely decorated, multicoloured woven burial coats and pottery, and sometimes by animal sacrifices. Others – men, women or children – had excrement inserted in the mouth, the skull perforated and threaded on a cord, the eyes blocked, the mouth pinned by cactus spines or the tongue removed and placed in a pouch. The meanings of such ritual practices are unknown, but the relationship between Ventilla and Cahuachi resembles and perpetuates the affiliation between the living and dead at Cerro Colorado and Cavernas.

NAZCA CRAFTS

Nazca textiles and pottery continued many Paracas traditions. They were adorned with images of the gods: half-human, half-animal – felines with long, ratcheted tails, spiders with human faces, birds, monkeys and lizards. Fringes on some textiles display rows of dangling heads or mummified skulls with staring eyes, or lines of figures wearing short tunics, dancing above round-eyed deities who seem to be flying, continuing the Oculate Being tradition.

Caches of severed and trepanned skulls and dangling heads on textiles represent a Nazca trophy-head cult of sacrificial victims. Like the severed heads so prominent at Chavín de Huántar and other northern sierra and coastal sites, they demonstrate the strength of severed-head symbolism in ancient Andean religion.

RITUAL PATHWAYS

Ritual dominance of daily life was further emphasized across the desert floor by geoglyphs – the famous Nazca lines. Desert figures and patterns, resembling those on Nazca ceramics and textiles, began to be made as early as the settlements at Cahuachi, Ventilla and other sites, but increased in number and complexity as Cahuachi was abandoned. Hundreds of geometric patterns, clusters of straight lines and recognizable figures frequently cross, but individual patterns or figures are each made of a single, continuous line. Animal and other figures each comprise a single line with different beginning and end points.

Nazca geoglyphs were ritual pathways, walked for reasons no longer fully understood, but which presumably involved religious cycles. Each figure or pattern appears to have been made by and for a small group – or perhaps even an individual – each for a separate, but jointly agreed purpose and small group's use. Experiments have shown that a few people can make a geoglyph in a short time. Their number and interference with each other indicates that geoglyph-making endured over a long time period, and that individual patterns may have been for short or even a single use.

Increasing aridity of the region and disastrous earthquakes appear to have caused the Nazca to abandon Ventilla, Cahuachi and other sites. At the same time, an increase in the number and elaboration of geoglyphs seems to indicate increasing ritual, perhaps asking the gods for help.

Below: In the Nazca desert, water was channelled from underground rivers to subterranean cisterns with terraced entrances.

THE MOCHE STATE

In contrast to the loose confederacy of the Nazca, the Early Intermediate Period in the northern Peruvian coastal valleys saw the emergence of Moche state-builders.

Above: This fierce, grimacing, half-human, half-jaguar face is that of the Moche Decapitator God at the Huaca de la Luna.

THE FIRST TRUE STATE

Moche is arguably the first true ancient Andean state or kingdom. For about the first 600 years AD it dominated the northern coastal valleys from the Piura Valley in the north to the Harmey Valley in the south. The Lambayeque and Moche valleys are roughly in the middle of the area, a few valleys apart.

The Moche state comprised two neighbouring spheres, northern and southern, in which two related languages were spoken: Muchic from the Lambayeque Valley northwards and Quingan in the south.

Of an energetic military temperament, Moche rulers established a powerful kingdom over several hundred years through conquest and domination of the valleys north and south of the southern sphere 'capital' at Moche in the valley of the same name. From the 4th century, Moche rulers mounted campaigns from valley to valley by sea, and many Moche pots depict narrative battle scenes of armies and pairs of warriors. A developing strong social hierarchy was reflected in burial practices.

Below: The invading warrior on this Moche stirrup-spout vessel stands on a fanged-beast-prowed boat.

Quingan speakers remained dominant, and Moche was the capital city for several hundred years.

HUACAS DEL SOL AND DE LA LUNA

The focuses of political and religious power in the capital were the two huge pyramidal structures known as the Huaca del Sol and the Huaca de la Luna, which reached their full sizes around AD450. Each required a massive amount of labour and was built of millions of hand-made adobe bricks. Distinctive marks on the bricks record the different labour gangs who built the platforms. The sudden appearance of similar platforms in the valleys indicates Moche conquest of the local populations.

Huaca del Sol, the seat of the Moche dynasty, comprised a four-tiered platform in the plan of a huge, stubby-armed cross of unequal parts. Its 40m (130ft) high summit was reached by a north-side ramp. Just 500m (1,640ft) away stood the Huaca de la Luna at the foot of Cerro Blanco. La Luna was a three-tiered structure whose walls were richly decorated with friezes depicting mythological scenes and deities. The area between the two platforms, occupied by dwellings and workshops, is believed to have been the elite residential area of the city. Around this core a sprawling urban setting covered as much as 3 sq km (740 acres).

NEW CAPITALS

In the 6th century Moche power shifted north and the new 'capitals' became Sipán and, later, Pampa Grande, both in the Lambayeque Valley. Moche the capital was eventually eclipsed altogether when climatic change brought drought and the formation of a huge sand sheet that clogged the city's canal system, stifling agriculture and causing the inhabitants to emigrate. Some of Moche's inhabitants were

Above: Huaca del Sol at Moche was the largest solid, adobe-brick pyramid platform ever built in the New World.

probably responsible for the settlement of Galindo farther up the valley. Early encroachment on Moche territory by the nascent Wari state from the south-east might also have played a role in the northern power shift.

The late phase of Moche culture (Moche V) blends into the Middle Horizon, in which the Wari Empire dominated across the northern Andean Area. Nevertheless, this final, 150-year flowering of Moche culture is reflected in the rich ruler burials at Sipán, some of the few unlooted tombs of pre-Hispanic Andean civilization. They contain sumptuous burials, richly furnished with the exquisite ceramics, metalwork and textiles of Moche state artisans. These artefacts depicted scenes or represent themes similar to those on the walls, ceramics, textiles and metalwork found at Moche and other sites.

MOCHE RELIGION

Like Chavín, Moche imagery represented a potent religion, with distinctive symbols and a pantheon, albeit much derived from Chavín. It was characterized by humans and humanlike animal figures, serpents and frogs, birds (owls in particular) and sea animals (crabs and fish), and also by standardized groups and ceremonial scenes, including a coca ritual recognizable by distinctive clothing and ritual combat. Murals, friezes and vignettes on pottery depict the capture and sacrifice of 'enemies' being led with ropes around their necks, the drink offerings by subordinates to lords and gods, and persons passing through the night sky in moon-shaped boats.

Such narrative scenes offer scholars some of the earliest 'historical' sources to corroborate archaeological interpretation. Some of the characters depicted have been discovered in elite burials, being represented by their regalia. For the first time, pre-Hispanic Andean personages, if not known individuals, can be recognized.

No Moche deities are known by name. However, when the Moche state declined, the inheritors of their legacy, the Chimú, worshipped Ai Apaec, a sky/creator god, and Si, the moon goddess. They may represent religious continuity from Moche times, and were perhaps represented on the murals of the Huaca del Sol and Huaca de la Luna pyramids. The coastal region also revered a mountain god, represented by images of a feline-featured being on Moche ceramics and textiles, and on wall friezes. Even more prominent were fanged deities and a deity known as the Decapitator God, who appears frequently in the rich ceremony and ritual depicted on pots and textiles. Later Moche imagery shows a mingling with Wari style, and subtle changes in the depiction of eyes and headdress ornaments suggest the beginnings of the influence of Chimú imagery.

Left: A helmeted, kneeling Moche warrior or shaman, painted for combat, with a socketed hand, perhaps to hold a spear or war club.

THE EMPIRE OF TIWANAKU

At the same time as Chavín influence was waning in the northern sierra and coast, the peoples of the Titicaca Basin shifted their own religious fervour from the early ceremonial complex at Chiripa to several sites north of the lake. The principal site was Pukará, and the religious tradition is known as Yaya-Mama. The imagery of Yaya-Mama included universal Andean subjects – felines, serpents, lizards, birds and fish, and severed heads – but was focused especially on stone monoliths with carved male (*yaya*) and female (*mama*) figures on opposite sides.

Above: The great semi-subterranean court of the Kalasasaya Temple, Tiwanaku, was one of the main ceremonial courts of the capital.

TIWANAKU CITY

In the 1st–2nd centuries AD, however, the focus of the Titicaca Basin's political power and religious influence shifted south of the lake again as the city of Tiwanaku grew.

Below: The great Gateway of the Sun at Tiwanaku depicts a central Sun God or Staff Deity, flanked by rows of running 'angels'.

At 3,850m (12,600ft) above sea level, Tiwanaku expanded between AD200 and 500 to cover 4.5 sq km (1,100 acres) as the capital of a considerable empire within and beyond the Titicaca Basin, stretching east and west to the Bolivian lowlands, west and north-west to the Peruvian coast, and south into northern Chile. Its cultural and religious influence extended even farther, but its north-western frontiers were established where it met its chief Middle Horizon rival, the Wari Empire, at the La Raya pass south of Cuzco and in the upper reaches of the Moquegua drainage area west of Titicaca.

The core of the city formed a ceremonial-religious-civic centre, including several monumental buildings, gateways, and stone sculptures exhibiting religious motifs and gods, whose artistic symbols show particular affinities to those of Chavín, and whose influence shows the continuity of ancient religious beliefs. The civic centre was aligned east–west, confined within a moat, and surrounded by residential compounds of adobe bricks.

Tiwanaku religion was a culmination of beliefs that united the peoples of the Titicaca Basin from the Initial Period through civic-ceremonial complexes at Chiripa and Pukará. Surrounding the capital were the natural features long regarded as sacred: the waters of Lake Titicaca to the west and the snow-capped mountain peaks to the east. Tiwanaku was located in the midst of fertile land, enhanced by a sophisticated system of dikes, canals, causeways and aquaducts to irrigate crops.

The ceremonial centre was planned on a grid pattern and its structures oriented on the points of the compass. The moat around the religious precinct segregated it from the residential sections of the city, making it an artificial island, a representation of the sacred Islands of the Sun and Moon in the lake.

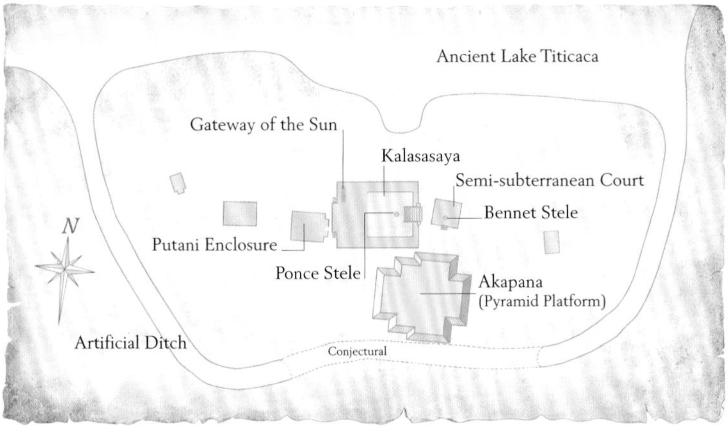

Left: Site map of Tiwanaku showing the Gateway of the Sun, the Akapana Temple, the Kalasasaya and other monuments.

A TRULY IMPERIAL CAPITAL

Construction of the major elements had begun by AD300. Stone temples, sunken courts, gateways and architraves were carved with religious imagery. Some of the buildings were probably residential palaces, but the gateways and gargantuan monumental sculptures were the focuses of public open spaces meant for civic participation in ritual and ceremony. Traces of gold pins within the stone blocks and remains of paint show that the sculptures were decorated and/or clothed in textiles.

The core of the artificial island was the Akapana Temple, a mound raised 17m (56ft) high in seven sandstone-clad tiers. Lake Titicaca and Mt Illimani are visible from the summit. Roughly T-shaped, a quadrate cruciform sunken court of andesite and sandstone slabs occupies the 50 sq m (540 sq ft) summit. Staircases climb the east and west terraces, and two staircases enter the court near rooms that might once have been priests' quarters. Subterranean stone channels drained water from the sunken court to the Tiwanaku River.

South-east of Akapana, the Pumapunku Temple T-shaped mound comprised three sandstone-slab-covered tiers, rising 5m (16ft) high and covering 150 sq m (1,615 sq ft). Its sunken summit courtyard has carved stone doorways and lintels and might have been the original location of the Gateway of the Sun.

Right: The monumental stairway of the Kalasasaya sunken court leads through a dressed-stone portal framing the Ponce Stela.

North of Akapana is the Semi-Subterranean Temple, a sunken court 28.5 x 26m (94 x 85ft), entered by a staircase on its south side. Its interior walls are adorned with carved stone heads, and at its centre stand several carved stone stelae, originally including the 'Bennett Stela' (now in La Paz). Standing 7.3m (24ft) high, it portrays a richly dressed human thought to be one of Tiwanaku's rulers or the divine ruler. He/she holds a *kero* beaker and a staff-like object, perhaps a snuff tablet.

KALASASAYA

The Kalasasaya – north of Akapana, west of the Semi-Subterranean Temple – is a low-lying rectangular platform 130 x 120m (427 x 394ft). It forms a large ceremonial precinct for public ritual, with walls made up of sandstone pillars alternating with smaller ashlar blocks. Its stairway is carved from stones set between two gigantic stone pillars.

The famous Gateway of the Sun stands at its north-west corner. It appears to comprise two monolithic stone slabs supporting a third, carved, slab across their tops, but is in fact a single huge andesite block. The crossing top face is completely carved: the central figure portrays the 'Gateway God' – a humanlike figure standing on a stepped platform resembling the tiered mounds of the sacred precinct itself. Holding staffs with its outstretched arms, it bears an obvious resemblance to the Chavín Staff Deity. It is flanked by three rows of winged figures in profile.

Within the Kalasasaya stands the giant stone Ponce Stela, 3.5m (11ft 6in) tall and visible from within the Semi-Subterranean Temple framed by the main gateway. Like the Bennett Stela, it portrays a ruler or deity, richly clothed/carved and holding a *kero* beaker and staff/snuff tablet.

Tiwanaku endured until about AD1000, waning between 900 and 1000 as climatic change brought repercussions throughout the Andean Area.

THE WARI EMPIRE

Huari was the capital city of the Wari Empire and the northern rival of Tiwanaku. Together the two empires represent the political cohesion that united the Middle Horizon for more than 500 years.

BIRTH OF AN IMPERIAL STATE

Wari dominated the central Andes and coastal valleys, and expanded into the regions of the north almost to the Ecuadorian border. One of its northernmost outposts was the city of Cajamarca in northern Peru; its southernmost was Pikillaqta near Cuzco. It met Tiwanaku expansion at the Pass of La Raya, south of Cuzco, and openly confronted Tiwanaku in the upper reaches of the Moquegua drainage area west of Titicaca, where it established a colony on the defensive summit of Cerro Baúl. This region, split between Tiwanaku in the north-west and Wari in the south-east, constituted a buffer zone between the two empires.

Below: The need for the hilltop fortress of Carangas is an example of the tense rivalry between the Wari and Tiwanaku empires.

From humble beginnings in the 3rd century AD, major constructions at Huari from the 5th century reflect the city's growing power. Its main period of imperial expansion lasted from about AD600 to 800.

The capital occupied the plateau of a mountain valley at about 2,800m (9,180ft) above sea level between the Huamanga and Huanta basins. Serving as a civic, residential and religious centre, it grew rapidly to cover more than 100ha (247 acres), then 200ha (495 acres), then 300ha (740 acres), with an additional periphery of residential suburbs occupying a further 250ha (620 acres). Its population has been variously estimated at 10,000–35,000 inhabitants.

From about 600 the Wari state spread a dominant religion, characterized by a distinctive symbolic art, through military expansion in much the same way that its coastal rival, the Moche, had expanded earlier in the northern coastal region.

Shortly before 800 there appears to have been a political crisis that caused building within the capital to slacken and cease. Simultaneously, the political centre and religious shrine of Pachacamac, on the central Peruvian coast, began to reassert itself and possibly even to rival Wari power. Pachacamac had flourished since later Early Intermediate Period times and had only recently been occupied by the Wari. Similarly, in its north-west provinces, the rising local power of the Sicán lords of the Lambayeque Valley challenged Wari overlordship in the late 7th century. Wari expansion ended abruptly and the capital was abandoned by AD800.

Above: The city of Huari was gradually expanded through regular additions of angular walled precincts and dressed-stone sectors.

RUINS OF THE CAPITAL

The architecture of the site of Huari, although megalithic, has not survived well. Some of it approximates the grandeur of the ceremonial architecture at Tiwanaku, although more crudely. Numerous walls remain as high as

Above: The rigidly planned border fortress of Pikillaqta, the southernmost Wari town, included an extensive defensive wall.

6–12m (20–40ft). There were several rectangular compounds, and some buildings had projecting walls that supported multiple storeys.

In contrast to Tiwanaku, however, Huari's rapid expansion appears to have occurred at random, without the deliberate and preconceived planning of its competitor. The huge enclosure of Cheqo Wasi (or Huasi) included dressed stone-slab chambers. Two important temple complexes were Vegachayoq Moqo and Moraduchayoq, the latter a semi-subterranean compound resembling the one at Tiwanaku. In keeping with the comparatively frenetic pace of Huari's development, the Moraduchayoq Temple was dismantled around AD650.

SHARED RELIGION

Wari and Tiwanaku's political ambitions and military aims made them political rivals, yet they also shared symbolic religious imagery and mythology.

Much of the religious and mythological art imagery of Tiwanaku and Wari was virtually identical, which demonstrates religious continuity from the Early Horizon through the Early Intermediate Period. Despite military opposition, scholars entertain the possibility that religious missionaries from one city visited the other. It might have been that the priests were willing to set politics aside and let religious beliefs transcend such matters.

Continuity and similarities of religious symbols used in art include, in particular, the Staff Deity image, but also winged and running falcon- and condor-headed creatures – often wielding clubs – and severed trophy heads. It is reasoned that similarities in imagery show similarities in religious and cosmological belief. It seems that the gods of Chavín endured as the Staff Deity of Tiwanaku and Wari, and were responsible for human origins and for the fertility of crops and flocks. Winged beings appear both accompanying the Staff Deity and independently, and were depicted running, floating, flying or kneeling. The Staff Deity – with mask-like face, radiating head rays (sometimes ending in serpent heads), and tunic, belt and kilt – appears on pottery and architecture and might have been the prototype for the creator god Viracocha.

Despite such apparent religious unity, the focus of religious imagery in Wari differed from that in Tiwanaku. In Wari it was applied primarily to portable objects, particularly to ceramics; in Tiwanaku, however, it was concentrated on monumental stone architecture, and appeared less frequently on pottery or textiles. Thus, while Wari ceramics and textiles spread the word far and wide, Tiawanaku imagery was more confined to standing monuments at the capital and a few other sites. The ceremonial core at Tiwanaku was designed and developed as a preconceived plan, and was therefore one of public ceremony and, apparently, participation. The Wari capital of Huari, by contrast, appears to have developed more haphazardly, and religious structures were smaller and more private, implying that they were the focus of ritual of a more personal and intimate nature.

RIVALS OR ALLIES?

Given these similarities and differences, the exact nature of the relationship between the two kingdoms or empires remains enigmatic. The two empires seemed to keep each other at arms' length, but they may have exchanged political and religious ambassadors to each other's capital city. Nevertheless, it is clear that religious concepts and imagery prevailed through the politically fragmented Early Intermediate Period as well as within the more unified imperial Middle Horizon.

Below: Although political rivals, Wari and Tiwanaku shared a religion, here represented by a kero *drinking cup with a serpentine motif*

THE KINGDOM OF CHIMÚ

Adverse climate change and early Wari incursions in the early Middle Horizon pushed late Moche power north to the Lambayeque Valley. A new capital was established at Pampa Grande, which endured for about 150 years. Moche religious belief also changed, dropping much of the old pantheon and focusing on maritime imagery – a precursor to the Chimú symbols that followed in the Late Intermediate Period.

PAMPA GRANDE

This new capital covered some 6 sq km (1,485 acres). Its most imposing structure, Huaca Fortaleza, appears to have served a function similar to the Huaca del Sol at Moche. Rising 38m (125ft) above the valley floor, its summit was reached by a 290m (950ft) ramp. At the top, columns supported the roofs of a complex of rooms, one containing a mural showing feline beings. Huaca Fortaleza was probably the elite sector of the city, with lower-class residences spread around it.

Like Moche, Pampa Grande was abandoned abruptly, owing to agricultural disaster caused by an El Niño weather event and the continued expansion of the Wari Empire from the south. Fierce internal unrest may also have occurred, for archaeological evidence has revealed intense destructive fires in the centre of the city, so hot that adobe mud bricks of the Huaca Fortaleza were fired.

Below: The founders of the Chimú dynasty arrived from the sea, as demonstrated by this Chimú stirrup-spouted burnished pot.

THE SICÁN LORDS

The inheritors of the late Moche flourishing in the Lambayeque Valley were the Sicán Lords. For centuries overshadowed by the power of the Wari Empire, they emerged as a local power and made rich burials from the 9th to the 14th centuries at Batán Grande as Wari power waned.

The Sicán Lords were one of many local resurgences repulsing Wari and Tiwanaku power.

Above: Detail of a painted cotton Chimú textile of a shaman or chieftain flanked by two felines and wielding an axe.

After Pampa Grande and Batán Grande, northern coastal power shifted again, back south to the Moche Valley, where the rise of the Kingdom of Chimú (or Chimor) eclipsed Sicán power.

THE RISE OF THE CHIMÚ

The Chimú established their capital across the Moche River at Chan Chan, in the shadows of Moche Huacas del Sol and de la Luna.

Chimú was the largest Andean Area empire before the Incas. Over 400 years, Chimú lords subdued the northern coastal and inland valleys, eventually controlling two-thirds of the irrigated land along the desert coast. With Chimú begin obscure historical accounts, although these are filtered through Inca interpretations.

The Chimú came from outside the valley and their history seems to hark back to a legendary conqueror called Naymlap, possibly the Moche king who invaded the Lambayeque Valley. Naymlap's eldest son, Cium, established a dynasty of 12 rulers, each of whom kept the green stone statue-idol of Yampallec set up by Naymlap. The final ruler, Fempellec, wanted to remove the

idol but was thwarted by 'the devil', and the priests, who abducted Fempellec, threw him into the ocean and ended the dynasty.

Two sources describe the foundation of Chimú by a conqueror from the sea (possibly from Lambayeque), variously called Chimu Capac or Taycanamu. A dynasty of 12 rulers might correspond to the Chimú compounds at Chan Chan, although the Chimú king list recorded by the Incas names only ten kings.

CITY OF THE LIVING AND DEAD

Chan Chan was founded about AD1000 and was conquered by Inca Tupac Yupanqui in the 1470s. Its core was an inner city of the living and the dead, a complex of individual compounds (called *ciudadelas*) covering 6 sq km (1,480 acres). Surrounding residential and industrial suburbs covered another 14 sq km (3,460 acres). There are ten compounds (although different interpreters propose between nine and twelve). Nine compounds have a truncated pyramid in the south-east corner, entered from above through a court to a suite of cells and a larger room thought to have housed the mummified body of a king.

Below: A wooden figure with a mud-plaster face mask. This would have stood in a niche at the entrance to a ciudadela *compound.*

Each *ciudadela*, a rectangle oriented north–south, comprised a miniature city enclosed within thick poured-adobe mud walls up to 9m (30ft) high, most with a single, northern entrance. Niches on either side of the entrances held painted wooden human figures as guards. Established as the court of the ruler, each *ciudadela* formed the residence of the reigning king, his officials and retainers, and became a sealed city of the dead after his death. Inner walls divided the compounds into courtyards surrounded by houses, storerooms, U-shaped structures (*audiencias*) and walled-in wells. Resident retainers perpetuated a cult of each deceased king. Along the south walls of the compounds ramps led up to burial platforms for each royal family.

The U-shaped structures appear to reflect recognition of and reverence for ancient U-shaped ceremonial complexes of the area. Burials were placed in and near them and their shape may represent a 'cosmic niche'. Association with store rooms suggests that they were also for redistribution, part of a tightly controlled system for the collection and distribution of wealth, foods and commodities among the nobility and general populace, according to social rank.

Above: The core of the Chimú capital at Chan Chan comprised ciudadela *compounds, each devoted to the cult of a deceased king.*

Five monumental adobe mounds at Chan Chan might have been temple platforms, although they have been so damaged by treasure seekers that it is not possible to be sure of their function. One platform, however, contained more than 200 bodies, including young women who might have been sacrificed to accompany a Chimú king into the afterlife.

Generally, Chimú imagery found at Chan Chan and elsewhere was a merging of Moche and Wari styles. Chimú ritual architecture reveals Wari influence in fanged deities, jaguars, jaguar-humans and serpents alongside marine imagery. The *ciudadela* walls were carved with repetitious friezes of geometric patterns, images of birds and marine animals, and of the double-headed rainbow-serpent being, the last apparently associated with Si, the moon goddess, one of the few Chimú deities that we know by name. Ai Apaec was the sky/creator god who was very ancient to this region, and Ni, the sea god, reflects northern coastal marine importance.

THE INCA EMPIRE

The Inca Empire was the largest political unity ever created in the New World. It was as large and powerful as many contemporary states in Europe.

DESTINED TO RULE

The foundation of the empire, or the early stages of the Inca state, is steeped in the legendary journey of a band of brothers and sisters. Modern scholars regard the tale as a mythical hero-legend, especially in its mystical implications of underground journeys and re-emergence from the earth. The archaeological and historical evidence shows that the Incas arose in the Cuzco Valley as one among many local 'tribes' or nations – town- or city-states – all of which were of long-standing native origin.

The arrival of influential individuals from outside, however, may have some basis in fact as a group of assertive individuals who were able to persuade the Incas of their rulership abilities and legitimacy, and to lead them on a path towards domination of their rivals in the valley. Once the Incas had overcome their neighbours, their rulers embarked on a dedicated programme of conquest beyond the valley. From Pachacuti Inca Yupanqui, who overcame the Incas' principal rivals, the Chancas, in 1438, the conquest of vast territories in all directions from Cuzco was what drove the empire.

The Incas believed in their destiny, and therefore in their right, to rule. They considered themselves to be the pinnacle of cyclical development in the world – politically, religiously and socially. They and their systems were not the culmination of, but the final solution to a predetermined course of history that would end sometime in the future by the empire's descent into chaos and by the beginning of, or more accurately, the 'turning over', of the cycle and the start of a new 'Sun' or age.

Below: Map of Cuzco with an inset map showing how the city plan was in the shape of a crouching puma.

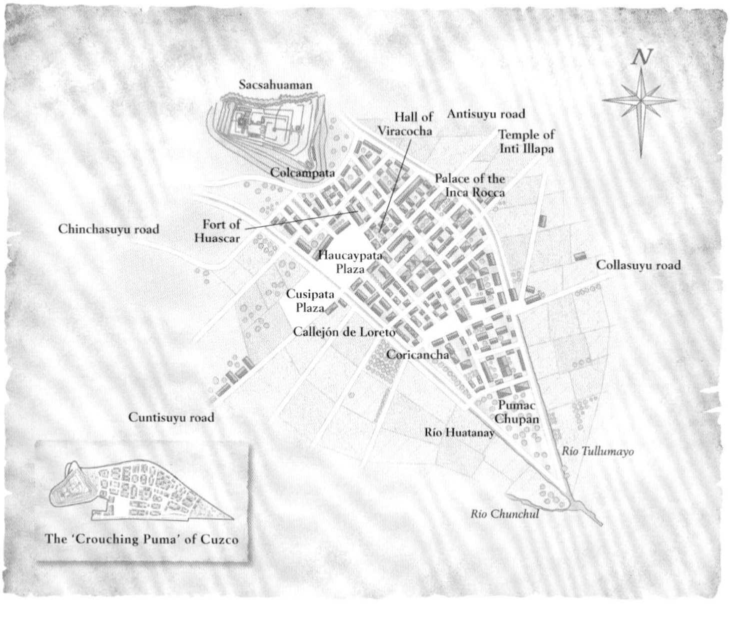

Above: In addition to the axe-spear, a favourite Inca weapon was the stone- or iron-headed war club.

RECORDING HISTORY

The Incas recorded their history orally and through the use of bundles of knotted string called *quipus*. State history was kept by imperial officials called *amautas* (court historians) and *quipucamayoqs* (knot-makers). Using *quipus* as an *aide-mémoire*, they were responsible for keeping the state histories alive through detailed oral history and regular recital. They kept, and on official state occasions reminded the populace of, the official history of the foundation and growth of Cuzco and of the Inca conquests. The early history was grounded in the story of the founder brother-sister pairs and their legendary journey, and of the exploits of early leaders and state heroes. The *amautas* also memorized and recited the royal genealogy, a formidable task, as Inca rulers had several wives and many children, and the royal household grew to include hundreds of members.

As the empire was expanded through conquest, the *amautas* were tasked with adding to the official history of the state, and with reconciling the events and situation 'on the ground' with Inca concepts and their perception of the cycle. To do this, much of their new subjects'

Above: The circular tower and surrounding walls of Sacsahuaman at Cuzco may represent the sun as the central temple to Inti.

myths, legends, histories, dynastic ties and religious tenets were recast and/or incorporated into the Inca story, as if they had been part of the history in the first place. This official version was particularly important in the establishment of Inti the sun as the supreme being and object of official state worship, which had to be construed in such a manner that it was acceptable to conquered peoples who harboured their own local deities, most of whom were long-standing and entrenched.

Paralleling the obscurity of the early stages of the Inca version of history, the archaeological record leaves scholars with little evidence of pre-Inca Cuzco. The capital has been continuously occupied since Inca times, especially since being substantially rebuilt by Pachacuti Inca Yupanqui and his successors through the 15th and early 16th centuries. As a result, many Inca structures form the foundations for Spanish Colonial and later buildings, and therefore it is not known what lies beneath. No recognizably distinct Inca architectural style can be identified with any of the pre-Pachacuti Inca emperors. It is not certain if the earliest Inca rulers ruled from Cuzco, co-existed with other local rulers or even lived in Cuzco.

SUBJUGATION PROBLEMS

Inca subjugation was through armed conquest, but such was the success and perceived inevitability of Inca rule that many tribes gave them little resistance. Nevertheless, resentment among peoples at the extremes of the empire led to frequent truculence, even open revolt, and peoples beyond the imperial borders raided into the fringes, sometimes with local collusion.

Tribes of the eastern tropical forests were the only group that successfully resisted conquest. The Incas, a mountain people, were psychologically attuned to distance vistas and lines of sight, and to a landscape of rugged variation. In attempting conquest into the rainforests flanking the eastern Cordillera, therefore, they were simply out of their element. Their commanders were lost; their points of reference were lost. They were up against an illusive foe that fought not *en masse* in open warfare but by stealth from protected cover. Yet the Incas admired tropical forest warriors and used their bowmen in the imperial army. Similarly, animals of the rainforest, especially the jaguar, were revered for their power, strength and cunning.

Below: A kero or painted wooden drinking cup showing an Inca warrior in a feather headdress and holding a spear.

POLITICS OF EMPIRE

The Inca Empire was divided into four unequal quarters, radiating from Cuzco. The quarters were known as *suyus* and formed Tahuantinsuyu – the 'four united parts' or 'four parts together'. The word itself is recorded only in later Spanish colonial sources, and it is not known if the Incas actually used the word themselves in this context. The term might have been first used around 1570 by Titu Cusi Yupanqui, the leader in Vilcabamba of an Inca revolt against Spanish rule. Alternatively, use of the term might have been an inflation of a more restricted use for the organization of the *ceque* shrines around Cuzco, first located by the Spanish magistrate Polo de Ondegardo.

Antisuyu, the smallest part, comprised the eastern Andean slopes and tropical forests north-east of Cuzco; Collasuyu, the largest part, stretched south-east from Cuzco, comprising southern Peru, the Titicaca Basin, western Bolivia, north-western Argentina and northern Chile; Chinchasuyu comprised the north-west region of western Peru and Ecuador; and Cuntisuyu comprised south-western Peru to the coast. The common point of the four *suyus* was the Coricancha Temple, the most sacred precinct in Cuzco. From this point radiated real and sighted sacred lines and routes known as *ceques*.

Above: A collca *(storehouse) built in traditional Inca vernacular style at Ollantatamba in the Urubamba Valley.*

Below: Inca accountants keep records on a quipu *of the collection of produce into storehouses for distribution among subject peoples.*

INCA STATE ORGANIZATION

The Inca state was rooted in the past, following a long line of political and social arrangements that had developed in the Andean Area from early times. Much of Inca state organization owed a debt to the Middle Horizon and Late Intermediate Period empires of the Wari, Tiwanaku and Chimú.

The foundation of Inca strength, and often the basis of others' capitulation, was the ancient Andean practice of the formalized exchange of goods and ideas between highlands and lowlands – between mountain and coast, Altiplano and desert. The Wari and Tiwanaki states had established regional administrative centres, formalized systems of exchange, roads and way-stations, and a sponsored state cult. In the farther-flung regions of the Inca Empire, administrative centres often had to be created from scratch if nothing lingered there from earlier times.

KEEPING CONTROL

The Inca appointed provincial governors (*tocoyrikoqs*) over conquered nations and city-states. Local chiefs (*curakas*) were incorporated into the system by being retained alongside the *tocoyrikoqs*, and together the pair administered the regional *mit'a*, or labour tax. Inca state tax was of three types: agricultural, *mit'a* and a textile tax. Agricultural taxes were extracted from the produce of *ayllu* kinship-owned land, imperial land and general communal land regulated by the *curakas*; it involved the labour of men and women. The *mit'a* tax was extracted only from able-bodied men. The textile tax was paid mainly as cloth woven by women, but also included fibre cordage and rope made by men.

Inca state control was maintained in a number of ways. In addition to military force, they practised various forms of removal and hostage holding.

One form was the deliberate transfer of whole or portions of populations within the empire. Known as *mitamaqs*, the practice was used to exercise demographic and social control, and to sustain an even economy. Local *curakas* were removed with their people. By shifting large groups of people around within the empire, the Incas could redistribute labour and the commodities grown and produced by different groups and mix peoples' ideas of geographic identity and religious/mythological concepts. One prominent example was Inca Tupac Yupanqui's relocation of thousands of individuals from several ethnic groups to the Cochabamba Valley (Bolivia) in Collasuyu, where the Inca wanted to increase coca production.

Relocating loyal peoples to frontier provinces helped to secure the imperial borders against hostile outsiders. Conversely, relocating rebellious groups served to break up and disperse potential seditious peoples within the empire. An example was the relocation of the Cañari people of Chinchasuyu, after defeating them in battle, to the Yucay Valley near Cuzco. The Cañari became such loyal servants that the Inca granted them the status of Incas-by-privilege. The practice undoubtedly had a significant impact in creating a state religion, and the result authorized the Incas to rule as a chosen people, whose semi-divine ruler was sanctioned by the creator god Viracocha.

Above: Communications in the empire were maintained by a system of trunk roads from Cuzco and linking roads to provincial towns.

FRAGILE EMPIRE

Rapid expansion of the Inca Empire in the 15th century brought together a multitude of local ethnic groups, large and small city-states and regional political confederations, and many languages, customs and local religious practices. The rapidity and incompleteness of expansion, as well as the disruption caused by the Spaniards, who first arrived in 1502, probably undermined state stability and contributed to a lack of cohesion. The variety of ethnic groups contributed to local loyalty, and Inca political practices were designed more for securing state revenue and begrudging state loyalty by one form of coercion or another than for genuine national unity. Even the Inca practice of relocation kept people within their ethnic units rather than integrating nationalities.

SOCIAL ORGANIZATION

The general populace of the empire was known as the *hatun-runa* ('great populace'), the bulk of which were farmers or herders. Within the empire, however, the people were subdivided into units by age, occupation and kinship groups.

INCA SOCIAL UNITS

The Inca administration organized the empire into a hierarchy of units comprising up to 10,000 individuals. The smallest unit was ten individuals, which was overseen by a foreman. Ten such units were overseen by a 'chief of 100'. A regular census was taken and monitored, and any necessary reorganization carried out accordingly.

The populace was classified into a number of age groups according to the types of work each was expected to do. For example, many males, especially single males, between the ages of 25 and 50 were expected to serve in the army. Others were expected to work the land, including work on imperial lands to fulfil the labour tax. Census records were kept on *quipus* by special officials who were known as *runaquipu-camayoc* ('people-*quipu*-specialists').

Family lineages or kinship groups were organized into *ayllus*. An *ayllu* comprised the group of related individuals, their property, and a social charter of recognized mutual and collective obligation among the members.

Below: On the Altiplano *of Collasuyu the Incas used raised and irrigated fields to feed the growing population of the empire.*

THE SAPA INCA AND *PANACAS*

The Inca ruler was known as Sapa Inca – 'sole' or 'unique' Inca. Each Sapa Inca was regarded as the direct descendant of the founder-brother Manco Capac, and simultaneously the manifestation of the sun – Inti – on Earth. His presence brought light and warmth to make the world habitable. Such belief perpetuated the early Andean melding of politics and religion: the Sapa Inca was not only the supreme ruler, but also the supreme god on Earth, presented in human manifestation.

The ruling Sapa Inca had many wives, one of whom was his principal wife. Maternal descent was of equal, if not dominant, importance in Inca succession to the throne. The royal household comprised several *ayllus*, called *panacas*. Each *panaca* was divided into two halves – termed *hanan* (upper) and *hurin* (lower). A principal responsibility of the *panaca* was the care of the mummy of the deceased Sapa Inca. Thus, in theory, a new *panaca* was formed at the death of each emperor. Within the Cuzco Valley, peoples conquered in the early expansion of the empire were given special benefits and called 'Incas-by-privilege'.

Above: Inca potato and quinoa planting, depicted by Guaman Poma de Ayala in his Nueva Crónica y Buen Gobierno, *c.1613.*

SECURING GOODS AND LOYALTY

Each *ayllu* owed *mit'a* service to the royal household, and the produce of their labour belonged to the state or, ultimately, to the Sapa Inca. *Mit'a* labour could take the form of working royal agricultural lands, tending royal llama flocks or producing quotas of goods such as ceramics, metalwork or textiles in state installations. It could even involve working as keepers and clerks in the *collcas* (royal warehouses) into which the produce provided by *mit'a* labour was collected.

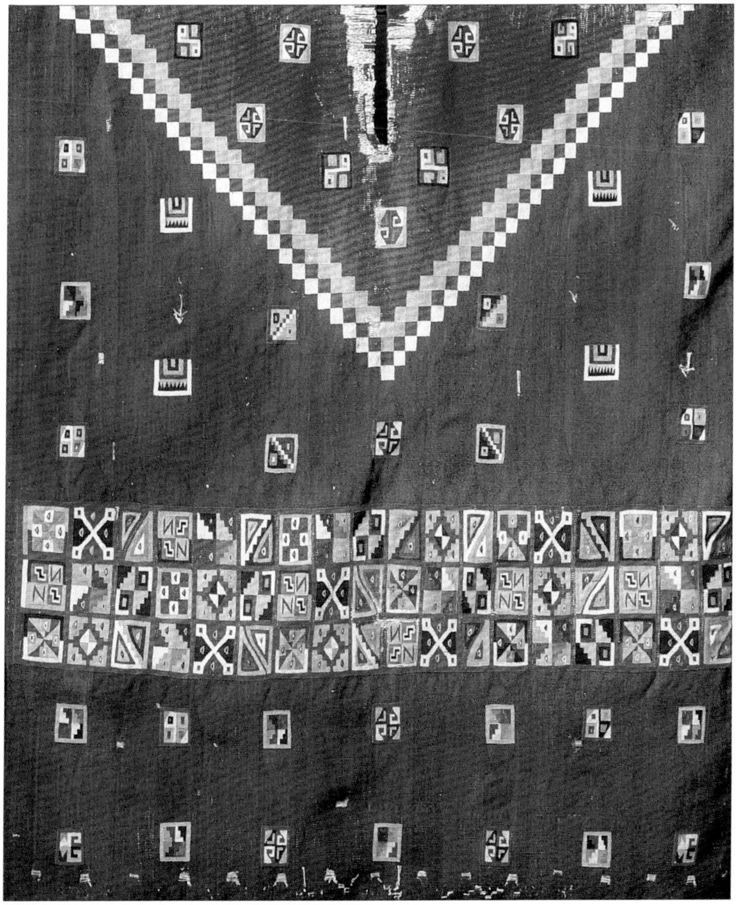

Above: The production of exquisite textiles for the rulers and nobles, and for the army, was an Inca state-sponsored industry.

Collca storehouses were distributed throughout the provinces. In them were stored agricultural produce, especially maize, and industrial products – surpluses of food, ceramics and other manufactured goods, and textiles for redistribution. In return for organizing and providing *mit'a* labour, the *curakas* received payment in luxury items from the Sapa Inca: fine textiles, metalwork and *chicha*, the beer made from fermented maize. It has been suggested that one reason behind continued Inca expansion was the need to secure more *mit'a* labour to meet the state's pact with the *curakas*, clearly a system that perpetuated itself.

The Sapa Inca's court also included selected retainers known as *yanacona*. These individuals were given various positions within the empire, including appointments at local-level governorships, whose loyalty to court could be relied on because they had no direct ties to the native population.

Members of the local elite, or the sons and daughters thereof, were taken to Cuzco as hostages. They were treated well, but were nonetheless held under house arrest. Likewise, the sacred objects of conquered peoples were removed to Cuzco to be held for safe-keeping as a means of ensuring loyalty – a practice used by the Wari and the Tiwanaku and continued by the Incas. Another practice was to train the sons of local chiefs to fill positions in the lower ranks of Inca bureaucracy, thus encouraging through them the loyalty of subject peoples. So impressed were the Incas with the Chimú that they took their lords back to Cuzco along with an entourage of their best gold- and silversmiths.

CHOSEN WOMEN

Another detached group within Inca society comprised the *acllas* (literally 'to choose'): 'chosen women' picked to serve in the state cults, particularly those of the sun and of the moon. Usually chosen when they were prepubescent girls so that they could be trained for the position, *acllas* also often became secondary wives and were used in imperial marriage alliances. *Acllas* were housed in special buildings called *acllahuasi*. The principal one was in Cuzco, but *acllahuasi* were also located in many provincial administrative centres. The fact that these chosen women were removed permanently from their homelands at an early age meant that they became so incorporated into the Inca system that they retained little attachment to their provincial roots and were therefore loyal to the empire.

Below: This Inca storehouse is within walled compounds among terraced fields, making maximum use of available growing surfaces.

PART TWO

MYTH AND RELIGION

The peoples of the ancient Andean civilizations regarded their entire surroundings as sacred. Maintaining a balanced relationship with the landscape, seascape and skyscape was considered essential to their well-being in the land of the living. Shamans were responsible for maintaining a dialogue with the past and, theoretically, with things to come in an endless cycle of history. Sacred powers were everywhere, and were both revered and feared. Ritual offerings, sacrifices and the maintenance of a link between the living and the dead were a necessary part of everyday life. Although we call it 'myth' today, Andean peoples' beliefs and their perception of the universe was their religion.

This part of the book concentrates on the deities and their stories as recorded mostly by Spanish chroniclers and by native record-keepers who were converted by Spanish priests. Although there were elements of regionalism, many deities were universally accepted throughout the Andean Area, sometimes under different names. Ancient Andean beliefs tended to be widespread, both at a given time and through time. The narrative of Andean belief in a cyclical history even incorporated their eventual defeat by outsiders, but continues today in the belief that time will turn again, reversing their defeat in perpetual revolution.

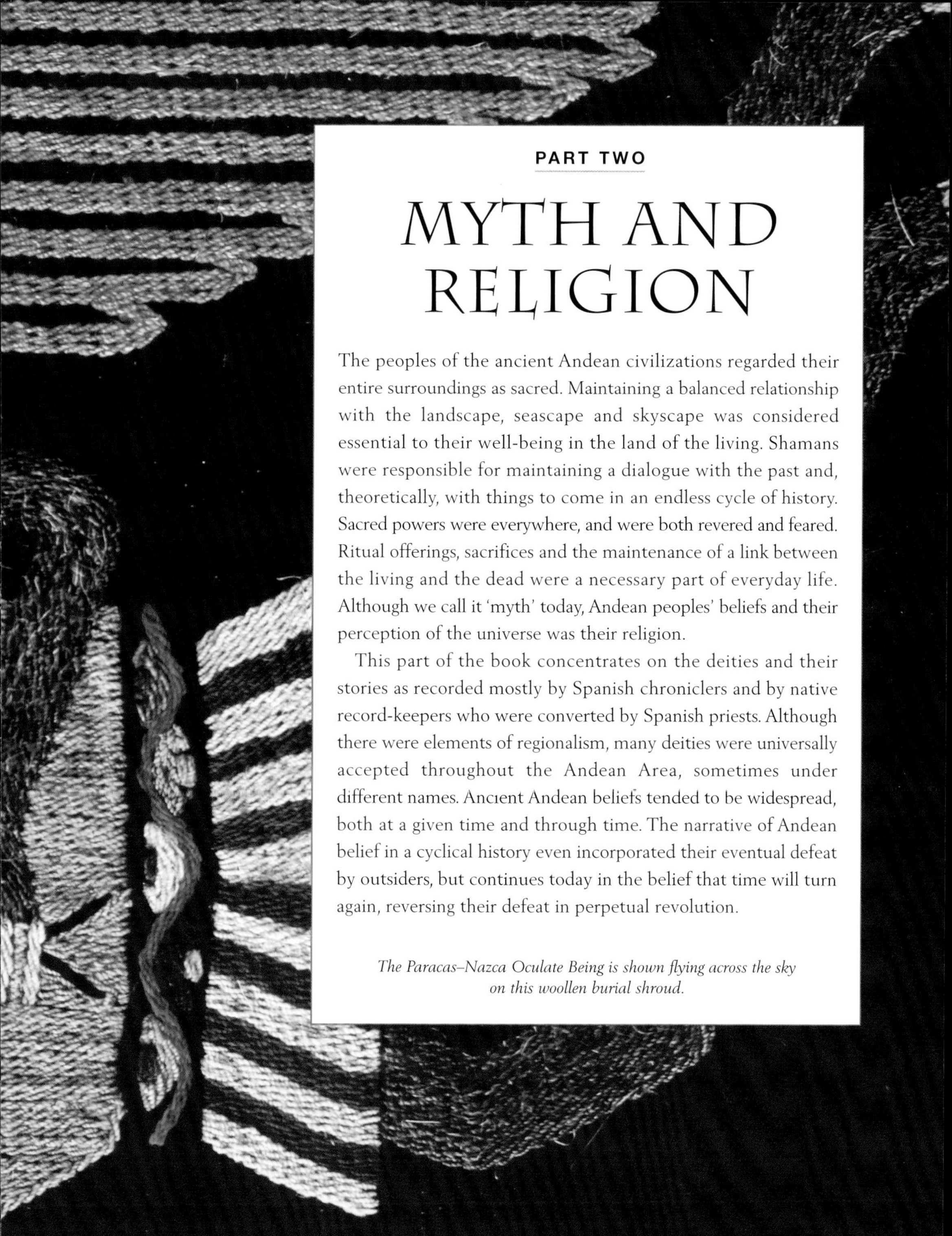

The Paracas–Nazca Oculate Being is shown flying across the sky on this woollen burial shroud.

CHAPTER SEVEN

A PANTHEON OF GODS

Sanctity permeated the ancient Andean world. Sacred powers were everywhere, in all living things. Survival in this world, the land of the living, was dependent not only on producing enough to eat, but also on revering the gods and appeasing them through rituals, sacrifices and offerings. At the same time, there was a fatalism in the belief in the great cycle of being, of life and death, which gave rise to the reverence of ancestors.

The peoples of the Andean Area held a range of beliefs and appear to have worshipped a pantheon of deities with control over different aspects of nature. Their religious beliefs developed from the earliest times, and they can be detected in the architecture and art of the earliest Andean civilizations. Many deities were universally accepted throughout the Andean Area, sometimes called by different names but having the same essential attributes, powers and roles.

A linking factor throughout Andean life was that of continuity, of how all things are connected and so part of a cycle, and this was demonstrated through the concepts of mutual exchange, duality and collectivity, which were all vital parts of spiritual and daily life for ancient Andeans. Continuity was intensely developed in Andean civilization through the pilgrimage centres, such as Chavín de Huántar and Pachacamac, that persisted over centuries and endured despite political rivalry and changing political developments.

Left: The central figure of the Gateway of the Sun, at Tiwanaku, is a ray-encircled face in the pose of the Chavín Staff Deity.

THEMES AND BELIEFS

The long sequence of development among Andean highland and lowland peoples fostered mutually beneficial relationships between cultures. Constant contact between regions brought the exchange of ideas as well as produce and commodities.

Right: An Early Intermediate Period Nazca bridge-spouted pot depicts the Oculate Being accompanied by trophy heads.

ANDEAN THEMES

Through Andean history, common themes were expressed in art and architecture. Coastal animals and motifs were copied in highland traditions and vice versa.

The early combination of temple platforms and sunken courts shows this exchange of ideas in the architectural elements of the ceremonial centre. Platforms mimic mountain peaks and plateaux, while sunken courts mimic valleys and coastal desert oases. It can be argued that ritual progression through such ceremonial complexes reflects the symbiotic relationship between highland and lowland cultures and between mountain and coastal deities.

Below: Part of the outcrop of the sacred Inca huaca *at Qenqo, north of Cuzco, was believed to be a giant seated puma turned to stone.*

This architectural combination also shows the early appearance of the Andean concept of duality. The late Preceramic Period union of platform mound and sunken court, both in highland and lowland sites, constituted the first widespread Andean 'religion'. To agricultural peoples, the sunken court was probably the focus for the worship of 'mother earth' – for the ritual re-enactment of birth or creation represented by spring crops. The ascent of the platform may have been the recognition of the upper world in which the god of creation dwelled, or from which came the waters that made agriculture possible.

The highland site of Chavín de Huántar not only combined the elements of platform and sunken court, but also introduced the idea of a sacred location widely accepted as the focus of worship for peoples throughout the central Andes and coast. The Chavín Cult developed the labyrinthine temple complex within which cult statuary was secreted, with all its obscure meaning, perhaps interpretable only by shamans.

With the development of the Chavín cult also came religious art expressing duality and a prototype supreme creator god, forerunner to representations of Viracocha in later Andean civilizations. The Staff Deity, significantly represented both as male and female, was an undisguised representation of duality. In varying forms, a deity holding staffs with outstretched arms was an artistic motif from Chavín to Inca times. In the courtyard of Chavín de Huántar's New Temple stood the 0.5m (1½ft) stone sculpture of the supreme deity. Holding a *Strombus* shell in one hand and a *Spondylus* shell in the other, the deity also manifested duality, as a metaphor for the balancing of male and female forces in the universe, and the union of opposing forces, providing completion through unity.

COMMON BELIEFS

Thus, despite variations in regional and cultural detail, the earliest ceremonial centres reflect common elements of belief.

The continuing highland–lowland interchange was cemented in the recognition of certain ceremonial centres as places of pilgrimage, Chavín de Huántar being the first. Platforms with sunken courtyards and pilgrimage centres were elements of Andean civilization for 2,500 years. Pilgrimage centres were recognized by both highland and coastal states, linking regions and persisting through political change. The cult centre of Chavín de Huántar endured for more than 500 years, while the site and oracle of coastal Pachacamac, beginning in the 1st century AD, lasted more than a millennium.

The Incas had a complex calendar of worship based on the movements of heavenly bodies, including solar solstices and equinoxes, lunar phases, the synodic cycle of Venus, the rising and setting of the Pleiades, the rotational inclinations of the Milky Way, and the presence within the Milky Way of 'dark cloud constellations' (stellar voids). Consultation of auguries concerning these movements was vital at momentous times of the year, such as planting time, harvest time and the beginning of the ocean fishing season. Inca practices represent the final stage of the development of such beliefs.

Sacrifice, both human and animal, and a variety of offerings were common. Ritual strangulation and beheading are well attested in burials and art such as ceramic painting, murals, architectural sculpture, textiles and metalwork.

As well as pilgrimage sites, tens of thousands of places – *huacas* – were held sacred. Like pilgrimage centres, their importance could endure for centuries. *Huacas* could be springs (emphasizing the importance of water), caves (prominent in human origin mythology), mountains, rocks or stones, fields or towns where important events had taken place, lakes or islands in them, or man-made objects such as stone pillars erected at specific locations. Shrines and temples were sometimes built at *huacas*, but just as often the object/place was left in its natural state.

The ritual use of hallucinogenic drugs was widespread. Coca (*Erythroxylon coca*) leaves were chewed in a complex and multi-stage ritual connected with war and sacrifice. Cactus buds and hallucinogenic mushrooms were also used.

The reverence for ancestors is evident in the special treatment of mummified burials in the Chinchorros culture of northern coastal Chile. Such practice developed into ancestor worship and became charged with special ritual, governed by the cyclical calendar by Inca times. Mummified remains of ancestors were carefully kept in special buildings, rooms or chambers, or in caves, and were themselves considered *huacas*. They were brought out on ritual occasions to participate in the festivals and to be offered delicacies of food and drink, as well as objects and prayers.

Preoccupation with death included the underworld. Skeletal figures, depictions of priests imitating the dead to visit the underworld, and skeletal figures with sexual organs or the dead embracing women were associated with fertility beliefs and the source of life in the underworld.

Above: An Early Intermediate Period Nazca sheet-gold burial mask. A burial with such a mask indicates high-status.

Below: A Late Intermediate Period Chimú mummy bundle with a copper burial mask, painted red, feather headdress and two flutes.

PACHACUTI – THE ENDLESS CYCLE

To the ancient Andeans everything around them, in all directions, was sacred. They believed themselves to be in a universe that was forever in cycle, *pachacuti*, in an endless revolution of time and history. The concept of *pachacuti* is further revealed in the Andean belief that humankind went through several phases of creation, destruction and re-creation. This progression was held to reflect the gods' desire to create an increasingly perfected form of humans. Honour and worship of the gods was so important that it took several efforts to create beings of proper humility. This veneration was essential because it was 'known' that at the slightest provocation they were capable of destroying the world.

Above: Warrior figures on this Paracas burial textile, c.500BC, are shown in the symbolic pose of the Chavín Staff Deity.

A DIVIDED UNIVERSE

The ancient Andeans' universe comprised three levels: the world of the living, which the Incas called Kai Pacha, the world below, called Uku Pacha, and the world of the heavens, called Hanan Pacha. Kai Pacha comprised the relatively flat surface of the earth and lay between the other two. As the world of humans, Kai Pacha was also called Hurin Pacha – lower world. As well as this vertical arrangement, the Inca universe was divided by two horizontal axes running through the points of the compass. The centre of both realms ran through Cuzco, where the vertical axis of the three realms and the horizontal axes intersected.

Pervading the entire universe was the creator god – the all-powerful, "formless" one – Viracocha (as the Inca and many others knew him).

AN ECOLOGICAL RELATIONSHIP

The relationship maintained between ancient Andeans and their universe can be characterized as 'ecological'. Because they perceived their environment as sacred, they believed that they were on earth not to exploit it but rather to enjoy its benefits through the grace of the gods. The relationship was one of deity power and human supplication. Humans considered themselves to be not the centre or focus of the world but only one group among all living things – including animals, plants and the stars. Thus humans appealed to the gods for their permission to make use of the various other elements of the world. Indeed, the animals, plants and stars were rather more important than humans, for it was in them that the gods were personified.

Left: Long-distance trade contacts also spread imagery. Here a rainforest monkey decorates a coastal desert Nazca ceramic vessel.

Right: An Inca textile showing a deity or a shaman, impersonating a god with sky-snake image and the stance of the Staff Deity.

AN EVOLVING RELIGION

More is known about Inca beliefs than other beliefs of the Andean Area because they were formed into an official state religion and cult of the emperor, Inti, as the earthly representative of the sun. Inca religion itself was the final stage in a long sequence of development from primitive beliefs. Inca conquest brought their people into contact with many other cultures and regions, each of which also had its own religious development.

Upon conquest, Spanish clergy and administrators recorded Inca beliefs and concepts in their attempts to understand more about the peoples of the empire. Archaeologists believed that the concepts and physical remains of Inca religion can be projected into the pre-Inca past. They also detect many common themes in ancient Andean development because the archaeological evidence indicates that pre-Inca deities, whose names are mostly unknown, nevertheless represented the same or very similar concepts to those of Inca deities.

Left: Fish, perhaps in a river channel, decorate the sculpted compound mud walls at the Chimú capital of Chan Chan.

FUNDAMENTAL DUALITY

Following the fundamental Andean belief in duality, the universe and everything in it comprised two parts in opposition, but striving for completion through unity, thus male/female, light/dark, hot/cold, good/evil, the sun/the moon.

To civilizations based primarily on agriculture for their day-to-day existence, the natural world and its physical forces represented essential elements of survival. The natural elements were considered divine and ruled human existence as evidence of the gods' powers. Ancient Andeans naturally sought to give the deities and their powers 'forms' in representational art and architecture, and common themes can be detected from at least the Initial Period in its ceremonial architecture. A pantheon of deities and beliefs is evident from at least Chavín times in the Early Horizon.

The Andean pantheon in its entirety was extremely complex and varied throughout the regions. Almost universal, however, was the belief in a creator god, known as Viracocha in the highland and inland regions and Pachacmac among Pacific coastal cultures. In addition, the sun and the moon were deities called by numerous names in different cultures and through time. Usually, but not always, the sun was regarded as male and the moon as female.

EVERYTHING IS CONNECTED

Mutual duality, or reciprocity, was a major feature of the ancient Andean world-view. It comprises the viewpoint that for every idea or object there is a reciprocal part or counterpart. Through reciprocity, therefore, all things in the world are connected.

FORMS OF RECIPROCITY

The concept of reciprocity is not unique to Andean culture, but it is heavily emphasized in the civilization and permeates every aspect of culture – from the physical exchange of goods between highlands and lowlands to its mental realization in religion, daily life and material culture. This reciprocity need not be symmetrical.

The economic face of reciprocity was demonstrated in vertically organized exchange. Traders in the products of different altitude zones such as the highlands and lowlands exchanged basic commodities including maize and potatoes, and also such exotic materials as *Spondylus* shells, available only from the far north-western coasts, or coca or hallucinogenic mushrooms from tropical regions. It occurred in political form in state organization to redistribute wealth. It was the state's recognition of its obligation to provide for all of its members.

At the same time, all members of the government recognized their duty to contribute to the continuing existence of the state and thus serve their role, whether it was rulership or the contribution of labour.

Above: *The colours of the Black and White Portal at Chavín de Huántar and the carved male hawk and female eagle symbolize duality.*

Socially, kinship divisions within the state also reflected reciprocity, with the dual social units of *hanan* and *hurin* (upper and lower) providing balance and cohesion. At the individual level, male and female represent reciprocals, and perhaps they were essential to understanding the concept in Andean culture, since they were the fundamental arrangement formed by the gods in creation.

The physical divisions of the Inca Empire and its products reflected groups of dual regions or opposed areas, such as mountain valleys and coastal valleys, dry deserts and rainy mountains, hot plains and cold sierra, lush tropics and sparse deserts.

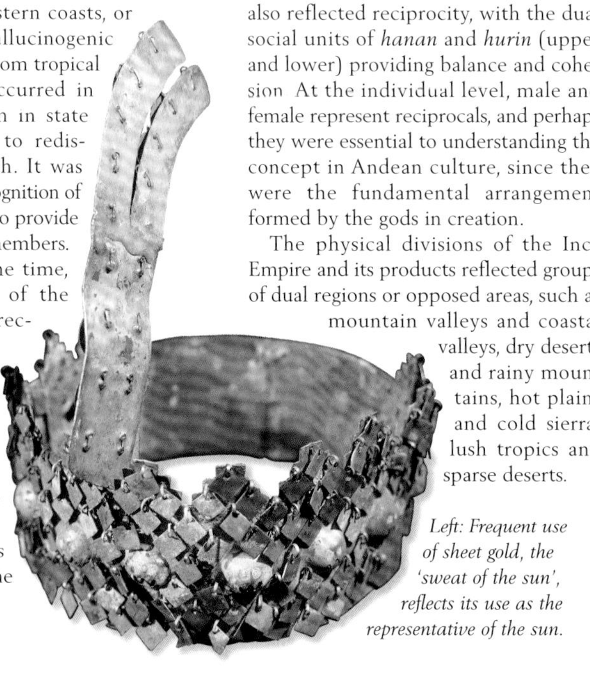

Left: *Frequent use of sheet gold, the 'sweat of the sun', reflects its use as the representative of the sun.*

DUALITY IN RELIGION

Humankind and the deities themselves were a perfect manifestation of dualism and counterpoint, both in their existence and in their hierarchical positions – the one to worship and obey, the other to be worshipped and to rule. Life and death itself were perhaps the ultimate dualism. The parts were intimately linked, as the concept demanded, through the intermediary of shamanism, keeping the dead among the living and including the dead in ritual ceremony.

Philosophically and cosmologically every idea had its opposite or counterpart: light/dark, dry/wet, high/low, happy/sad, courage/cowardice – all fundamental and observable qualities evident in everyday life. Even the divisions of the universe reflected reciprocity, with the earth and the world of the living between reciprocal worlds above and below.

Right: This jaguar, revered for its power and cunning, on a Chavín stele represents contact between mountain and rainforest cultures.

Reciprocal or dualistic thinking might have been inspired and indeed validated by the appearance of the sky in the Southern Hemisphere. The familiar individual stars and star-to-star constellations were seen as architectural structures or agricultural implements – physical things. Countering these both in type and visual appearance were the dark constellations, the spaces or dark voids between the stars, which were seen as animals – living things. Further, the animals themselves represented the conceptual counterparts of the living animals on earth because they were regarded as responsible for procreation on earth. For example, the Incas (and presumably their predecessors) saw a balance between the dark-star llama (*Yacana*) in the Milky Way, with stars for its eyes, and the living llamas in their herds. *Yacana* drank nightly from the ocean to prevent it from flooding the earth.

DUALITY IN ART

Throughout Andean art there is an emphasis on duality, on interlocking parts or pairs, and contrasts between light and dark or complementary colours. These features can be seen in ceramics and their shapes, in textiles and their colours, and in the beings shown on both. There is doubling and mirror-imaging of all kinds. Textiles and their interlocking images show dovetailed creatures, mirrored at each side, for example as two identical crabs or birds, or as double-headed creatures facing in opposite directions. The Staff Being from the Chavín Cult of the Early Horizon represents a perfect example. Holding two staffs, one on each side, and represented as either male or female, it is the ultimate example of dualism and is shown in textiles, on pottery and in architectural sculpture, persisting from the Early Horizon to Inca times.

Left: This Nazca ceramic effigy vessel depicts perhaps the most universal symbols of reciprocity – man and woman.

Architecturally, Andean structures are counterparts to natural earth shapes. In some cases, naturally shaped stones were modified by sculptors and became locations for ritual as *huacas* – linkages of the natural and man-made and of the ordinary world and religion. Structures sculpt the world in light and shadow, space and solid. The dual nature of many Andean ceremonial centres in the Initial Period and Early Horizon reflected a worldview of dualistic nature. Pyramidal platforms and sunken courts demonstrate the organization of space into solid and void, positive and negative spaces, elevated and subterranean areas, upper world and lower world, and even into concepts of descent, birth and the Earth Mother, and ascent to the Sky Father.

COLLECTIVE THINKING

Reciprocity within society was complemented by another concept, collectivity, which permeated life at all levels.

A COLLECTIVE SOCIETY

Collectivity was the overriding mode of operation in Inca (and their predecessors') society. Corporate thinking demanded that the group always took precedence over the individual, since the individual was part of the whole and could not function effectively except as part of the whole. Collectivity complements reciprocity in the idea that all things are connected and therefore part of a whole and of the cycle of the universe. As a supreme example, the Inca Inti shows reciprocity and collectivity at the same time. As the earthly representative of Inti the sun, he was an intermediary between the people and the gods – and thus part of the collectivity that was necessary for the whole to function effectively. In contradiction of this, however, he was individual and supreme above all other Incas.

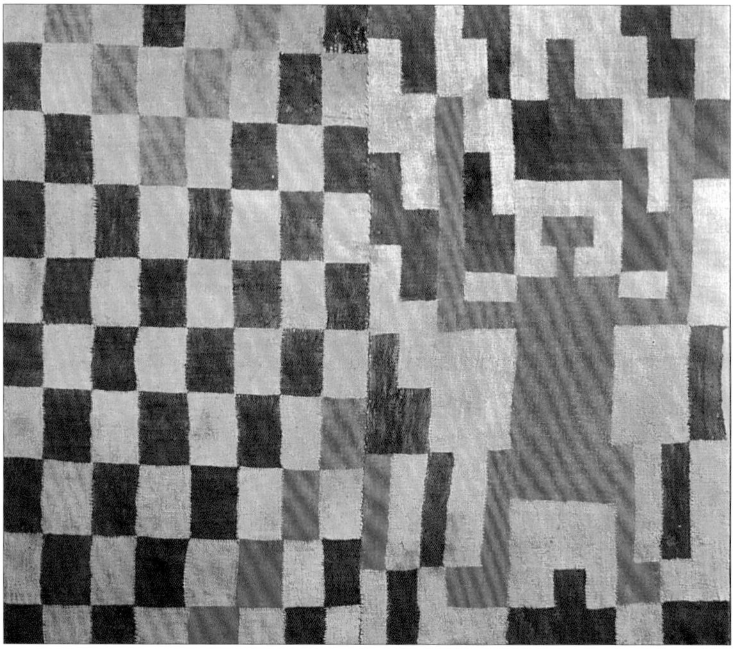

Above: A less elaborate burial textile from Nazca shows a stylized human figure within a simple, repetitive pattern.

The varied and often harsh environments of the Andean Area favour, perhaps even demand, a need to adapt in order to achieve group organization in most activities. Like reciprocity, collectivity does not necessarily render all individuals within the group as equals. Most aspects of Andean cultures are hierarchical, showing an uneven distribution of power and wealth. Most obvious are differences in burials, from royal and rich elite tombs to common graves, and from elaborate 'natural' interment to ritual sacrifice.

The concept can be traced to the earliest Andean civilizations. Architecture, from these times, demonstrates such hierarchy in quality of construction, decoration and apparent function. Common dwellings surrounded great ceremonial centres that were the hubs of the cities. Such architecture, however, represents the ultimate in corporate thinking in the marshalling and command of the labour to build ceremonial structures to serve the community. The Incas

Left: A mass-produced Inca chicha *jug and* kero *drinking cup represent state-controlled industry and the redistribution of goods.*

Above: The Incas collected agricultural produce into state-controlled warehouses for redistribution according to need and rank.

ingeniously incorporated subject peoples into the empire, embracing myriad cultures and nuances of belief and local political, social and economic arrangements. Yet, they also represent the extreme of inequality within collectivity – the few ruling the many in the pyramid of power; the Incas, who numbered about 100,000, ruled more than ten million people.

The social fission that might result from challenging environments and from such inequality was mediated by ritual, to re-emphasize social collectivity or corporateness. The Inca Quechua term for such ritual was *tinku*, referring to the joining of two to form one.

THE IMPORTANCE OF ROLE

Andean artistic collectivity is shown by a general sparsity of portraiture, historical detail and narrative. The details of special features, physical location or the actions of specific people are usually unimportant: it is the person's role that is important to show, and religious art overridingly features supernatural imagery. The deities have aspects by which they can be recognized, and it is these aspects that must be shown accurately. Artistic decoration emphasizes continuous and repetitious patterning, itself an obvious manifestation of 'corporateness'. As early as the Initial Period, the architectural monolithic mosaic at Cerro Sechín shows this concept, forming converging processions of figures and banners. Rather than representing individuals, the figures are stylized representations of warriors and captives in a procession of conquest, triumph and sacrifice – a *tinku* ritual and convergence of duality in ceremonial temple architecture.

Moche art is a notable exception to these concepts. Recent research and discoveries show portraiture and narrative, especially in Moche ceramics and in the scenes painted on them, and historical details, in which the entombed in elite burials represent the deities or priests and priestesses depicted on pots and murals.

ARTISTIC ANONYMITY

The extensive use of moulds in ceramic production and repetitious dual- and mirror-imagery also show collectivity. Although the names of individual artists are unknown, scholars recognize their particular styles. The distinctive 'makers' marks' on the millions of adobe bricks used in the construction of the pyramid platforms of the Moche capital are another demonstration of corporate thinking. The idea was not to distinguish the brick-makers but rather to account for the labour or quota required of collective work units.

Right: Llama effigy figures. Llama herding for wool and other products was also state-controlled.

The seemingly intentional anonymity of ancient Andean artists, craftsmen and labourers does not render their art generic. Individual sculptures, pots, murals and metalwork are idiosyncratic, dynamic and distinctive. They can be recognized by archaeologists today and therefore must have been identifiable when made. The specific styles of ancient Andean cultures and regions are certainly distinctive. However, within these there are styles of imagery, some of which lasted for more than 1,000 years, even though some details changed over time.

Nevertheless, it is the image and concept of a piece that are important, not its maker. The religious message was paramount, and that subsumed the whole. This combination of collectivity and stressing the abstract in art rendered ancient Andean culture highly sophisticated yet unconcerned with specific or individual conspicuousness or eminence.

TRANSFORMATION

Ancient Americans throughout the North and South American continents believed that the universe existed on multiple levels. The Inca tripartite realms of the living world, a world above and a world below were the culmination of developments from the beginning of Andean religion. The realms were not held to be exclusive, nor were they necessarily separated in time. Rather, they existed in parallel, and each was vital to the existence of the other two.

Communication between these worlds was achieved through transformation. Birth, living and death were therefore considered states of existence in an endlessly continuing cycle of time, rather than as mutually exclusive states. Each realm could influence the others, and actions in the realm of the living could influence the effects of the other realms on it. Thus, it was important to maintain communications between the realms by worshipping the gods and by honouring one's ancestors, who were believed to be 'living' in the realm of the dead. Shamanism provided the medium that enabled communication between worlds, and it was through shamans or 'priests' that instructive and corrective messages could be obtained in the world of the living.

A BALANCED ORDER

The world was ordered according to specific rules that governed how things should be and how they should work. Social and economic order had to be upheld in order to maintain the balance between the worlds.

As with reciprocity and collectivity, equal power among individuals was not required, only that all were included within the scheme and received sufficient necessities. In this way, social and economic functions can be seen as constant factors within the different political systems that evolved over time in the Andean Area. For example, the architecture of ceremonial centres, from the early U-shaped structures and sunken courts of the Initial Period, through to Chavín temples in the Early Horizon to Late Horizon Inca state religion, continued the theme of dualism, as did the practice of the collection and redistribution of goods and divisions of labour, despite the rise and fall of kingdoms and empires.

STATES OF CHANGE

The universe was considered to be in a state of flux, but its changes were cyclical and orderly. The seasons changed in regular succession, the climate altered between wet to dry seasons. Moisture was collected into and channelled by earthly rivers, taken up into the celestial river, and fell back to earth as rain and snow in a never-ending redistributive cycle. Planting, harvest, storage and redistribution formed an endless cycle. The movements of the sun, moon, planets and stars were observed to be regular, as was the progression of the Milky Way through the night sky. Thus, orderly regularity governed all realms.

Likewise, individual lives were in states of flux, from birth to youth to old age, and continued in death as the next plane of existence.

Such cyclical thinking was (and continues to be) the key to the Andean worldview. Human history progresses but is perceived to repeat itself constantly. For example, the Incas saw in the ruins of Tiwanaku a former earthly kingdom that preceded their own and thought of themselves as the inheritors of Tiwanaku power in the Altiplano.

HUMAN TO SUPERNATURAL

Andean art served to reflect these planes of existence and to unite them. It captured transformations such as the metamorphosis of shamans into supernatural beings. Artists strove to develop methods and media to depict the world as dynamic and to show two things as one, or the existence of a shaman beyond terrestrial space. Transformational examples can be seen in the statuary of Initial

Right: This Sipán sheet-gold burial mask represents various Andean themes: the sun and the shamanic transformation or human representation of a deity.

impersonating and transforming into animals – subjects of this world as representations of the superhuman world. Likewise, the importance of communication between realms is clearly shown in numerous Moche ceramics depicting shamanistc acts, and in the inclusion of Inca mummies in the annual ritual cycle.

Finally, Inca religious narrative abounds in examples of transformations: ancestors to stone, animals to stone, humans /deities to stone, humans to animals, and stones to supernatural warriors. Early Cuzco itself owes its survival to 'stones transformed into warriors'.

Above: The transfixed stare of this effigy figurine represents a shaman under the influence of hallucinogenic drugs, a frequent theme in Moche ceramic art.

Right: A deer-headed human-like ceramic figurine, representing the completed transformation of a shaman into a revered animal. His headdress bears a knife for ritual sacrifice.

Period sites such as Huaca de los Reyes, in the fibre human effigies at Mina Perdida and in the painted adobe sculptures at Moxeke. The composite features of these beings, which were represented by non-human eyes with pendent irises, feline noses, fangs, drawn-back lips and facial scarifications, and condor markings on the Mina Perdida fibre effigy, are all indicative of human transformation. Such elements heavily influenced the Chavín style of the Early Horizon in jaguar and serpentine animal–human transformers. The Staff Being him/herself carries all these elements, as do the various monumental stone sculptures of Chavín, especially the more than 40 sculptures, stone heads and relief panels on the walls of the New Temple, showing a time-lapse sequence of human to supernatural transformation from shaman to feline.

The care with which Paracas and Nazca burials were wrapped and preserved, the sumptuous burials of Moche and Sicán lords and the ritual preservation of Chimú and Inca rulers are all indicative of the importance of transformation between states of being. Many Paracas and Nazca textiles depict humans ritually

A UNITED WORLDVIEW

Essence is a fourth fundamental concept or theme in ancient Andean belief and artistic expression. Essence united the Andean peoples' worldview, incorporating reciprocity/duality, collectivity and transformation. It expressed their belief that the core element or underlying substance was more important than appearance.

REALITY AND MEANING

The symbol of an object represented its reality, even if it was hidden by its outward appearance. It was not important for an image to be visible, or for the material of an object to be pure, for its essence was still present and governed belief. Objects were created for their own sakes and in this sense de-humanized. Such lack of emphasis on the importance of the human audience underscores Andean regard for humans as only one part of the universe in their worldview. Even the depiction of humans in ancient Andean art was not necessarily the most important component. With the exception of Moche art, there was little individualism or recognition of people. Individuals normally played a part in the whole and are subservient to the theme of the work.

Symbolism was far more important. It was used to convey the idea and to represent the thought or the character of a deity or of a scene. The idea was to characterize someone or something through the use of recognizable traits commonly known and spread with the movement of religious cults.

Above: Beneath the stonework of the Machu Picchu Observatorio lies a ritual room made with minimal sculpting of the natural rock.

Below: The essence of gold is conveyed through the gilding of less precious copper and silver in this Moche Sipán funeral mask.

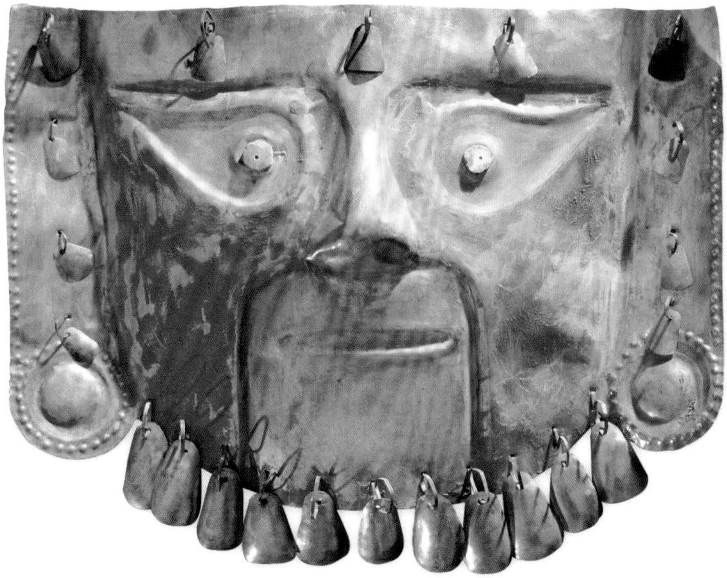

ESSENCE IN ART

A large part of artistic production was not created for daily use but was made for its own sake by craftworkers, and by artists who were subsidized by the political elite. Thus, Andean potters used moulds to make hundreds, if not thousands, of identical pieces representing aspects of Andean life and religion. Metallurgists would mask a base or less precious core with a more precious metal, or gild objects made of alloys. Architectural sculpture emphasized interior decoration and symbolic representation of deities and sacred acts. Elaborate, rich burials were filled with products made solely to be included in the burial. Textile weavers executed such elaborate patterns that the subject often became illegible but was still true to the supernatural subject.

Essence explains why it was not necessary for the Nazca geoglyphs and other ground drawings to be seen in their entirety: it was quite acceptable that the ritual pathways they prescribed could be followed and that the lines fulfilled their function in religious devotion. Thus, their essence was conveyed in the doing rather than in the seeing.

Similar reasoning may explain the use of openwork weaving in Late Intermediate Period Chancay textiles. The designs could be seen as the weaver worked them on the loom, creating interlocking animals and birds, but once removed from the loom the threads contracted and their symbolic imagery became illegible when the garment was worn. Only when spread out against a dark background could the imagery be appreciated – an example of the value of essence over appearance.

Likewise, sacred images were often placed in obscure or hidden locations within temples. The meaning and essence was conveyed to the people by shamans, sometimes personifying the deity concerned, sometimes representing the deity through transformation. Similarly, the symbolic images could be so complex, or arranged so strangely over a stone or a pot, as to render them accessible only to an elite few. For it was what the images stood for that was important rather than that all should be able to stand before them and 'read' their intimate meaning.

Most artistic production was created for its own sake, for the afterlife, for its ritual efficacy or for use within the realm of the supernatural.

Above: Traces of red paint on this sheet-gold Chimú funerary mask show that its essence (pure gold) was hidden in a reverse of the idea represented by gilding (see opposite).

Left: Moche red-on-white 'story' vessels depicted common activities as well as ritual: here a fisherman uses a pelican to fish.

RHYTHM AND ENERGY

Reciprocity, collectivity, transformation and essence facilitated the rhythms of ancient Andean life. Their interconnections guided the flow of the world and manifested the Inca concept of *ayni*, the principle that governed cyclicity. In the words of one scholar, reciprocity was 'like a pump at the heart of Andean life'. Together these concepts represent the energy that bound the cycle of the universe, the *ayni* and *mink'a* – the positive and negative, the give and take that made the Andean universe work.

MULTIPLE MEANINGS IN ART

Art often elicits dual meanings, inviting opposite or multiple interpretations. Such double readings are common in Andean art. Textiles from the earliest times right through to Chancay and Inca weaving in the Late Horizon dovetail mirror images of birds and animals. Two-headed supernatural creatures are shown in textiles, painted decoration and sculpture. Inca architecture plays with opposites, 'sculpting' natural stone to display light and shadow. Beings, real and supernatural, with double meanings, portrayed as a single motif with multiple identities abound in Early Horizon Chavín and Paracas art and continue through the ages in the art of later highland and coastal cultures.

Below: The shape of this Nazca effigy vessel makes it difficult to interpret. The mythological themes on its faces may be individual or may comprise a narrative.

EARLY SYMBOLIC ART

The idea that essential meaning could be depicted visually, and that a representation could contain multiple meanings and show a composite being was present in some of the earliest Andean art. Cotton textiles from Huaca Prieta employed a relatively simple twining technique. More than 9,000 cloth fragments were excavated. The most famous piece, only known as a photographic reproduction, shows a clearly recognizable raptor with a hooked beak and outstretched wings. Closer inspection shows a coiled snake within its stomach. The subject's basic symmetry, broken by its left-facing beak, is balanced by the right-facing slant of the snake.

The embedded serpent reveals a multi-layered meaning. Here is a raptor and its prey. The obvious victory of raptor over snake, however, may represent a religious belief or hierarchy. The zigzag contours of the piece indicate that it was held sideways as it was twined, revealing that the weaver was able to visualize the final design during execution. The use of this method may also have been so that the visual impact of the zigzag was of beating wings. Thus, complexity of meaning and mode of manufacture reveal how essence of meaning was paramount and more important than both simple imagery and method.

Another example of multiple meaning and of the early portrayal of a composite being also comes from Huaca Prieta. A twined cotton fragment shows the symmetrical figure of two crabs in a rhomboidal composition. One crab occupies the lower left and the other the upper right. Outstretched legs indicate that they are scuttling. Curiously, one has eight legs while the other has six. However, they are not just crabs. The bases of the crabs are united by one pair of their claws across the centre of the composition. Each of the other claws, however, bends in an acute angle back towards the head of the twin crab and turns into a snake's head. The angular representation hints at the nature of the animal. Not only is there double meaning in this piece in the representation of a land and a sea animal, but also the multi-layered meaning of one animal turning into the other. Perhaps the wearer was meant to become infused with the character of the animals.

Above: This vessel may depict shamanic transformation or earthly representation for a ritual involving a sky deity. Many Moche effigy vessels contain obscured meaning.

MEANING WITHIN ARCHITECTURE

At the other end of the Andean chronological scale, the Inca *huaca* of Qenqo, just north of Cuzco, shows the same concepts rendered in architecture and stone sculpture. The natural outcrop has been heavily modified, its protruding surfaces

carved extensively with steps, shelves, indentations and niches. There is also a zigzag channel that branches and rejoins, which may have been for libations. Such heavy alteration rivals the outcrops' natural irregularity. It is difficult to decide whether the modifications are meant to mimic, oppose or balance the natural irregularities. The play on light and shadow is carried to the extreme, yet some flat surfaces reflect the sun's rays so fiercely that the 'play' becomes one-sided.

Beneath the huge boulder lies hidden meaning. A large natural cleft has been carved into a small chamber. The natural 'heart' of such a stone was a quintessential Andean place of sacredness, and the modification of it recognized this and rendered it available for ritual purposes. It is the essence of the outcrop that is important; its modification by humans emphasizes and enhances its sacredness. Its use recognizes its vitality.

To ancient Andeans, Qenqo and other such sites were not inanimate objects but living beings, part of the universe. The hidden heart at Qenqo's base isolates it from the secular world; its alteration and use bring it into the spiritual world.

A separate, protruding monolith to one side of the main outcrop is naturally triangular and has been left uncarved. When viewed from a certain angle, its shape resembles that of a seated puma. It is framed by a small square wall and by an enclosing curved courtyard wall. Once again, the recognition of its shape and use as a place of ritual draws it into the Inca universe. A rainforest creature in this mountain setting unifies the realms of the world.

Above: Eagle and hawk carvings on the columns of the Black and White Portal of the New Temple at Chavín de Huántar.

Left: Rolled-out reconstruction drawings of the female eagle (left) and male hawk (right) carved on the columns at Chavín.

HIDDEN RITUAL AND MEANING

Every form of ancient Andean art contains layers of meaning. Obscuring this meaning within many possible interpretations and in a complex design became fully developed in Early Horizon times at Chavín de Huántar, like so many features of ancient Andean religion. Earlier elements of Chavín religion can be seen in the preceding Preceramic and Initial Periods.

PLATFORM MOUNDS

The architectural tradition of Preceramic platform mound sites began the practice of building small courtyards and chambers or groups of chambers on top of platforms. It is not possible to describe in detail what rituals took place in them, but they were clearly meant to hide whatever activity they enclosed. The platforms' location at the centres of ceremonial complexes and above domestic buildings isolated them, and their relatively small size made them accessible to only a chosen few. The steps leading up to such platforms presumably provided the venue for ritual display to multitudes. In this way, what different groups within society witnessed could be selected and controlled.

The deliberately broken and buried figurines at Huaca de los Idolos at Aspero represent one of the earliest examples of such hidden, selective ritual, as do the infant and adult burial at its companion mound of Huaca de los Sacrificios.

Above: The high, thick compound walls of the Huaca el Dragón, near Chan Chan, enclose the people performing the rituals within them.

Left: The Semi-subterranean Court beyond the Kalasasaya portal at Tiwanaku is an example of a sunken ritual courtyard.

The tradition was elaborated in the Initial Period at sites such as La Galgada, Kotosh, Caral and Chiripa. Twinned and multiple mounds were built at many sites, and chambers were either detached but grouped, a tradition that continued through to Inca times, or became combined in complexes divided into rooms. Larger halls were subdivided into separate chambers or divided partially to hide one part within another. Parts of complexes were made difficult to enter through long galleries leading around behind a main complex.

Kotosh, La Galgada, Aspero, Piedra Parada, El Paraíso, Sechín Alto, Cerro Sechín, Huaca de los Reyes, Garagay and numerous other sites went through such transitions. In the Titiucaca Basin, Chiripa shows the emphasis on symmetrically grouped detached chambers built on top of a platform.

HIDDEN PLAZAS

The tradition of hidden plazas (*plazas hundidas*) established an opposing organization of space by enclosing and isolating ritual within negative space. Hidden plazas may have been venues for ritual re-enactments of creation and earth veneration. The combination of the two traditions became common at sites in the late Initial Period and Early Horizon and is most elaborately represented at Chavín de Huántar. Hidden plazas were initially circular at northern Andean sites. The transition from circular to rectangular took place at Chavín de Huántar in the 1st millennium BC. Within the arms of the U-shaped platform housing the Old Temple stood the circular sunken court, while the plaza of the New Temple incorporated a square sunken court, and heralded the persistence of the rectangular form in the Altiplano until the demise of Tiwanaku at the end of the 10th century AD.

The objects of worship and the chambers that housed them also became more complicated, hidden and controlled. The labyrinthine chambers of the Old and New Temples at Chavín de Huántar are the classic example. Deep within its galleries and corridors, a dimly lit room in the Old Temple held the Lanzón Stone monolith and in the New Temple stood the Raimondi Stela. A third monolith, the Tello Obelisk, stood in the sunken court of the New Temple.

ORACLES AND IMAGES

The use of oracles at Chavín de Huántar and at Pachacamac represents another aspect of ritual obscurity. Only specialists could interpret the oracles' pronouncements. The supplicant required shamanistic intervention and interpretation. At Chavín de Huántar, the base of the Lanzón Stone stood in the lower chamber, while an upper chamber, into which its top protruded, provided a hidden chamber for the voice of the oracle. The principal idol at Pachacamac was a wooden statue kept in a windowless room at the summit of the main terraced platform.

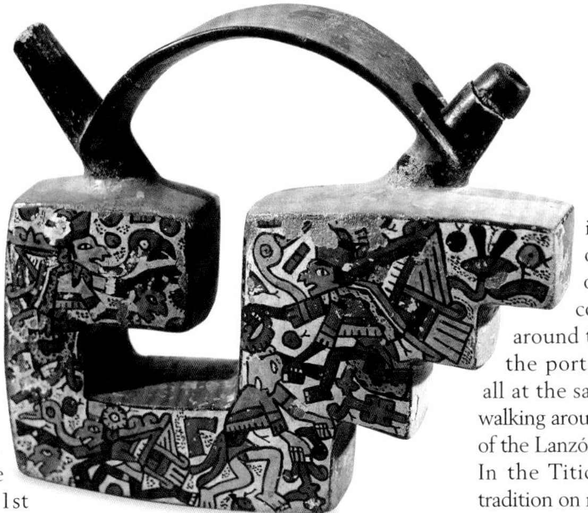

Above: Detailed scenes or mythical events painted on Nazca pottery must be read carefully to obtain their full meaning.

The symbolic images of the Chavín monoliths and of the Black and White Portal of the New Temple show multiple meaning and obscurity in several ways. All three sculptures depict supernatural beings and include snarling faces. They are three representations of the supreme being, and the features on them are repeated in modified form in Chavín portable art found throughout the central Andes and coast regions in Early Horizon settlements.

The positioning of the images enhances the obscurity of their meaning. They are not only extremely intricate and complex but are also wrapped around the monoliths or columns of the portal and thus cannot be seen all at the same time or in total without walking around the scultpure. The location of the Lanzón Stone makes this impossible. In the Titicaca Basin the Yaya-Mama tradition on monolithic slabs at Pukará and other sites, showing a male (*yaya*) and a female (*mama*) figure on opposite faces, demonstrates a similar principle.

These traditions of isolating and secluding ritual continued to the Late Horizon. The Late Intermediate Chimú capital at Chan Chan comprised a huge complex of individual rectangular complexes. The Inca Coricancha in Cuzco enclosed a group of chambers dedicated to individual deities and secluded ritual for specialized priests, who thus controlled the rare display of venerated objects.

Below: The Circular Sunken Court at Chavín de Huántar brought a coastal ritual feature to the mountain cult.

SYMBOLS OF DIVINITY

The integrated nature of the ancient Andean worldview regarded natural objects as sacred. Mountains, water and caves were universal divine symbols. Within ancient Andean belief there was an intentional melding of what modern Western cultures regard as natural and cultural; both were regarded as 'living'.

SUN AND MOON

Tracking the cycles of the sun and moon is important to agricultural peoples, and the ancient Andeans were no exception. The sun, Ai Apaec (Moche and Chimú) or Inti (Inca), and the moon, Si (Moche and Chimú) or Quilla (Inca), were universal symbols of reverence and were believed to exercise enormous influence on human life. They were associated with precious metals: gold with the sun, silver with the moon. The association became a physical metaphor to the Incas: sweat of the sun and tears of the moon. Most cultures considered the moon to be the consort of the sun. They symbolized opposing forces, and their intermingled cycles achieved the unity necessary to the world's balance. Their controlled cycles gave stability to the pre-Hispanic world.

The Incas epitomized the importance of the sun in their state cult, in which the emperor was the sun's earthly representative – son of the sun. The Incas regarded themselves as the children of the sun and moon, and in the creation myth Viracocha, the creator god, is also described as the sun.

The sun is not easily identified in pre-Hispanic art. Gold generally symbolizes it, but a specific solar deity is not obvious. Inca gold-rayed masks clearly represent the sun, and the god in the centre of the lintel of the stone portal at Tiwanaku may represent the sun, hence its name Gateway of the Sun.

The moon was intimately related to earthly matters. Images of a crescent moon feature especially in pre-Inca Moche and Chimú art.

Below: The cult of Inti, the Inca sun god, centred on Intihuatana (Hitching Post of the Sun) sites, such as this one at Machu Picchu.

JAGUARS AND OTHER CREATURES

The religious imagery of Andean and Pacific coastal cultures was influenced from the earliest times by rainforest animals – jaguars, serpents and other reptiles, monkeys and birds. Aquatic animals, both oceanic and fresh water, and birds were also widespread outside their natural habitats. Such common imagery undoubtedly reflects a basic animism and naturalism in Andean belief. It is also reasoned that the widespread occurrence and repetition of themes infers an underlying universality in the beliefs of Andean cultures.

In particular, both highland and lowland civilizations shared a fascination with the jaguar. The jaguar face inspired the imagery

Right: A sky deity is shown on this Paracas textile with the Oculate Being, complete with serpent tongue, feline whiskers, slithering snakes and streaming trophy heads.

Right: Spiders feature frequently in Andean art, from tiny golden figures on Moche jewellery to this giant Nazca desert geoglyph.

of fanged deities from the earliest times to the Inca Empire. Jaguars were depicted frequently on stationary and portable artefacts –wall paintings, stone carvings, ceramics, textiles and metalwork. Before the prominence of Chavín de Huántar, numerous U-shaped ceremonial centres in the coastal valleys of Peru show an apparently widespread religious coherence, with carvings and paintings of fanged beings at Cardál, Garagay, Sechín Alto, Cerro Sechín, Cabello Muerto, Moxeke and other sites. The plan of Cuzco itself was a feline profile (the shape of a crouching puma), and even the rock at Qenqo, a 'natural' object, was regarded as the profile of a seated puma.

COMPOSITE BEINGS

Composite creatures, combining the features and characteristics of several animals, and human-like beings were also common. Feline-human hybrids, the staff deities (with composite feline face and human body), winged beings, and falcon-headed or other bird-headed warriors all symbolized divinity and were painted and sculpted on ceremonial architecture. The variety of fanged beings implies a wealth of imagination in conjuring up fearful deities to strike awe in the intended worshippers.

In addition, creatures were often shown in cultures that were alien to them. For example, the Tello Obelisk at Chavín de Huántar shows the creation myth and features the cayman (a jungle creature) in a sierra culture. Mountain raptors appear frequently on coastal textiles. Pacific shells, especially *Strombus* and *Spondylus*, are found as grave goods and are depicted on pottery and architecture throughout the Andean Area. Finally, the ritual pathways of the Nazca trace the outlines of creatures that were alien to the desert, for example a monkey and a whale. Their sacredness was incorporated in the act of following the ritual route. Such representations of 'misplaced' creatures show links between highland and lowland cultures and demonstrate universal reverence.

The Staff Deity of Chavín became a persistent symbol for 1,500 years, with full-frontal beings in various forms featuring widely in Andean art. Its portrayal on the Raimondi Stela epitomizes the Chavín Cult. The full-frontal, standing figure is a composite of animal and human characteristics. Symbols of the Staff Deity, ubiquitous in Chavín imagery, were spread throughout the central and northern Andes and coast on portable art.

Serpents, like felines, were also pan-Andean and were used often in all media: wall paintings, stone carvings, ceramic decoration, textiles and metalwork.

Right: On this Nazca effigy vessel a bird shape is combined with a human face, feline masks and an Oculate Being-like face on the breast.

CHAPTER EIGHT

HONOURING THE GODS

In his *Historia del Nuevo Mundo*, the 17th-century Spanish chronicler and historian Father Bernabe Cobo names 317 different shrines in Inca Cuzco alone. From this, there is no doubt that religion permeated Inca society.

From the earliest times, it is evident that ancient Andean cultures honoured their gods. The treatment shown in special burials and in the construction of special architecture in the midst of domestic dwellings in towns and cities reveals a deep reverence for things beyond day-to-day survival. Whatever their nature, religious considerations were intermixed.

Political arrangements came and went. Rulers were seen to participate in religious ritual, and to be representatives of the gods on Earth. Yet when kingdoms fell and regions were broken up into smaller political entities, the gods remained. In this sense, religion was both integral to and independent of politics in ancient Andean civilization.

The gods and goddesses were depicted on all media: ceramics, textiles and metalwork, and on small and monumental stone, clay and wooden sculpture. They were both portrayed directly, as men and women dressed to represent them, and symbolized in architectural complexes. Features of the landscape were held to be imbued with their presence and therefore representative of them.

Left: Supernatural beings, including a figure reminiscent of the Staff Deity, on a Moche dyed and finely woven cotton textile.

RELIGIOUS CONQUEST

It is not certain, especially in the earliest Andean civilizations, if religion was spread through military conquest. The evidence of the distribution of the art styles and supernatural imagery of different cultures might be interpreted as having been spread through conquest, and the Moche, Wari, Tiwanaku, Chimú and Inca were certainly warlike states engaged in the acquisition of territory through military conquest. The image of the severed head or trophy head was common from the Initial Period onward in virtually every culture. The close association of rule, Inca conquest and the spread of the state cult in the Late Horizon might have been the culmination of a widespread practice.

RELIGION AND ADMINISTRATION

Archaeologists argue that sunken courts and raised platforms, found in both lowland and highland cultures, represent earthly and heavenly deities and themes as well as reflecting the landscapes of the two regions. The central locations of ceremonial complexes among domestic sprawl, or in other cases the isolation of them among surrounding domestic settlements, shows that architectural ceremonial complexes were places for the gathering of people for special rituals. The increasing complexity of elements of ceremonial complexes – divisions into rooms, labyrinthine temples, multiple groupings of platforms, and intricate images of supernatural beings – demonstrates the development of a specialized priesthood to hold the truths of belief and to perform the rituals associated with them.

These centres must also have been places for carrying out civil duties. The sacredness of vital elements – sunshine, water, the well-being of the crops and herds – may have been under the control of the gods, and soliciting the gods' favour may have been the responsibility of the shamans on the peoples' behalf. However, once the crops had been gathered it was the responsibility of a civil structure that had had no direct physical input into their production to administer their distribution. Thus, the distinction between religion and politics can never have been very clear-cut in ancient Andean cultures.

THE ROLE OF CERRO SECHÍN

The ceremonial complex at Cerro Sechín was built, used and modified over a period of several hundred years. It eventually covered 5ha (12 acres) and must have served as a political and religious centre for a considerable region. Its principal pyramidal structure formed a quadrangle with rounded corners, 53m (174ft) on a side, and its outer wall was adorned with some 400 stone sculptures. The sculptures of the late platform portray humans marching towards a central entrance. They are clearly warriors, and among them are dismembered bodies, severed heads and naked captives. One warrior has severed heads hanging from his waist as trophies.

Below: The cult of Inti was spread throughout the empire through the establishment of Inti-huatana (Hitching Post of the Sun) temples.

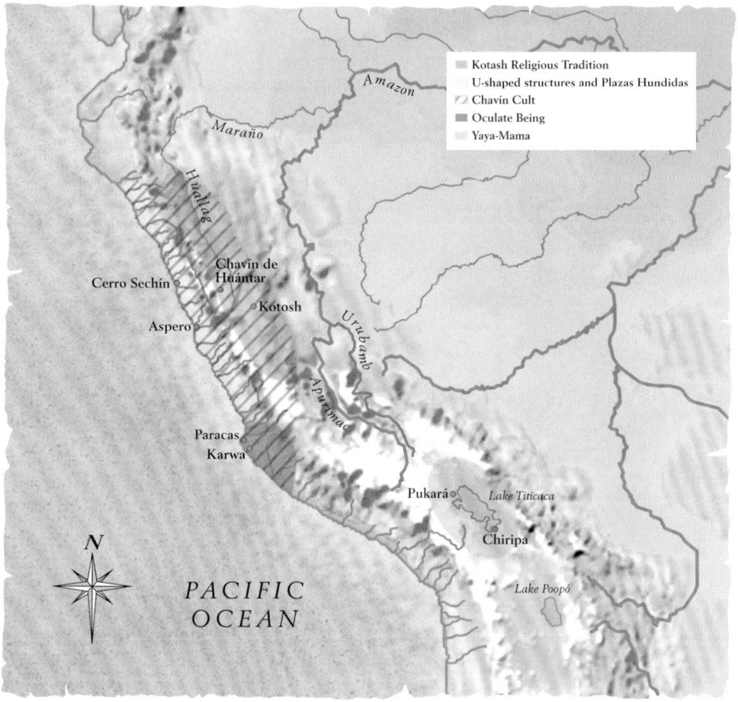

Left: Map showing early religious cults and traditions, including the Kotosh Religious Tradition, the Chavín Cult and Yaya-Mama.

A CONQUERING CULT?

Legends recorded by Spanish chroniclers describe how northern coastal dynasties had been established through invasions from the south. They may be the hazy records of the establishment of the dynasty of Moche lords. Among the Moche, narrative scene painting on pottery and textiles depicts ritual combat and ceremony, including ritual sacrifice. Blood offerings are made to deities impersonated by men and women, presumably priests and priestesses. Burials have been found with elite corpses wearing the costumes depicted in the scenes. This sequence and the scenes might represent the spread of religious ideas with territorial conquest.

The scene seems to show the successful return of an army and can be interpreted as endemic of regional warfare. Yet, this scene is of a late renovation of the Cerro Sechín complex. Was it a war memorial? A stone pilaster of much earlier date depicts essentially the same scene. Or does such repetition over time represent a mythical or legendary battle and victory rather than a specific event? Is it, rather, symbolic of religious conversion combined with territorial claims?

A PEACEFUL CULT?

Archaeologically, the distribution of the symbolic imagery of the Chavín Cult demonstrates it was spread across a large region and that the gods of Chavín were revered among both highland and coastal peoples. Architecturally, Chavín de Huántar was both the inheritor of and participating member in the elements of the ceremonial complex that had developed through the Initial Period and Early Horizon. Yet much of the spread of Chavín religious imagery, especially through portable art, appears to have been achieved alongside the spread of technological innovation.

Like all religious missionaries, those spreading the Chavín Cult would have been faced with explaining complex concepts and evoking other-worldly experiences through objects and representations of them based ultimately on analogy and metaphor.

Chavín artists, either instructed by or acting as shamans, made these themes central to their art. The complexity of Chavín imagery conveys 'otherness'. New techniques in textiles and metallurgy seem to appear suddenly and spread rapidly, conveying the Chavín Cult. This appears to be not military conquest, but rather the perpetuation of regional links already established for economic reasons.

Right: An elaborately decorated Inca wooden kero *or drinking vessel in the shape of a head, decorated with figures carrying* keros.

ANIMAL AND SUPERNATURAL SYMBOLISM

Above: Detail on an early Nazca burial shroud of the sun god, symbolically shown in human form with main and fine rays.

The fantastic imagery on ancient Andean pottery, textiles, metalwork and stone sculpture is clearly highly symbolic, and it conveyed important meaning to those who knew how to interpret it. Its complexity increased with time to the point where specialized individuals were needed to act as intermediaries between the deities and powers the symbolism represented on the one hand and the general populace on the other.

SHAMANS AND NARRATIVES

The feline and serpentine features that adorned the faces of supernatural beings and humans representing, or being transformed into, them constitute perhaps the most notable imagery used through time and throughout the civilizations of the Andean Area. Close seconds are the uses of birds of all kinds, and of spiders and crabs, particularly in coastal cultures, and the use of double-headed imagery. The general image of the Chavín Staff Deity, by repetition over a widespread area and through time, is a familiar symbol of sacredness and representative of a god and goddess.

More generally, there are several themes that can be identified. Shamanic expression is one that seems easy to recognize. The staring eyes, deep incisions and transfixed expressions on many painted, woven and sculptured faces depict shamans in the state of trance experiencing visions under the influence of hallucinogenic drugs. The contexts of their portrayal, for example a shamman administering to a 'patient' or in a state of transformation into an animal or into a supernatural being, makes this clear.

Another theme is the narrative. Many scenes show a ritual in the process of being performed. This is the case on much Nazca and Moche pottery, on which sacrifices and ritual combat are depicted. Series of images, such as those of shamans and jaguars on the walls at Chavín de Huántar, give a still-photo-like sequence of transformation. Other scenes imply movement and a 'story', as they depict a hunting or a fishing scene. A sense of perspective is given by overlapping limbs and other elements. Some other scenes show what appear to be obvious themes, such as hunting or fishing, or the harvest on Nazca pots, or battle scenes on Moche and Wari pottery, but these pictures can also carry more complex, extended or additional meanings.

ADDITIONAL MEANINGS

The Nazca 'harvest festival' textile, at face value, shows the produce of the harvest. In detail, however, the Staff Deity-like stance of the figures, their masked or supernatural faces, their complex interlocking pattern and the fact that some are upright and others upside down all contribute to an appearance of hidden or

Right: Regional deities incorporated symbolic themes, as in this Paracas embroidered burial mantle depicting a feline with eyes reminiscent of the staring Oculate Being.

less obvious meanings connected with the ritual significance of the harvest in Nazca religious belief.

Similarly, in the Moche mural (now destroyed) called *The Revolt of the Objects*, everyday objects employ weapons to attack humans. For every human depiction, there is a reciprocal object, such as a warrior with a fox head or a boat with legs, representing duality.

MYSTERIOUS SYMBOLISM

The Moche culture had waned by about the end of the 8th century AD, yet in the 16th century a story about the revolt of 'inanimate' things was told to the Spaniards, seemingly as a general folk story or myth. The survival of the legend for nearly a millennium reveals its apparent common acceptance.

Knowledge that the Inca (and presumably pre-Inca cultures) viewed their world differently from Europeans by regarding virtually everything, including the actual landscape, as living parts in the universe gives a symbolic meaning to a story that Westerners find difficult to interpret. Other themes are equally complex and difficult to interpret, if they can be interpreted now at all. The symbolism of the Lanzón monolith at Chavín is easier to identify than to interpret. There are two caymans. But why is a river creature featured as the primary deity in a sierra culture? And why, in a culture that existed more than a millennium and a half before the Incas, with their belief in the upper and lower world spheres, are the caymans pointing in celestial and earthly directions?

Left: Detail of three supernatural beings on a Moche cotton textile, one with a staff and, perhaps, a representation of the cratered moon, Si, the northern coastal moon goddess.

SYMBOLIC MEANING

The complexity of Andean Area religion and its different worldview have led scholars to conclude that ancient Andeans infused all their art with potential double meaning. There are images that are real, others that are unreal, and yet others that are purely symbolic. Even real images may operate on a higher symbolic level as well as simply depicting, for example, a man leading a llama or a woman weaving. Does a Moche scene of a man hunting simply portray the act of hunting, or are we meant to be reminded of male characteristics, man's role in society or, perhaps, of a symbolic hunt? Does a female figurine represent a woman, or should it indicate fertility, or, higher still, the mother of humans?

The frequent repetition of such 'scenes' indicates that they are not to be taken at face value. It seems that on one level the essence of appearance is operative and on another level that a hidden, double or reciprocal meaning is operating.

Below: Agricultural abundance is symbolized in this Nazca bridge-spouted vessel, showing a man grasping a maize plant with bulbous roots and laden with ripening cobs.

Many Moche faces painted on pottery, as ceramic effigies or in precious metal, show what appear to be laughing faces but could be snarling or shamanic hysteria.

Some ritual practices are plainly depicted on pots, especially on Moche fine-line red-on-white narrative scenes. Some show blood sacrifices and offerings to deities, or to humans representing deities. Others show individuals engaged in combat. However a closer examination is necessary to see that the combat scenes, for example, show Moche fighting Moche, not a war against Moche enemies. A Nazca stepped-bridged double-spouted vessel painted with a battle scene of interlocking warriors in brilliantly coloured regalia appears equally straightforward. But is this a war of conquest or a depiction of a mythical battle, a symbolic representation of some universal religious 'event' to remind viewers of how the world began and how it operates?

COMPOSITE IMAGERY

Humans with animal heads and other features, a conflated man and peanut or an owl with a trumpet are clearly unreal but may be deeply symbolic of something that we cannot now fully understand. Male and female effigies are clearly shamans by their contexts and visages, but we are unable to understand the full symbolism of the imagery within its own cultural context. The conclusion that the scenes on Moche pots were mythologically symbolic of general religious belief, however, is strengthened by the elite burials of individuals dressed in the identical regalia shown in the narrative scenes.

SYMBOLIC ORGANIZATION

The manner of the organized production of ceramics is itself symbolic. In the Moche and later states, if not earlier, specialists were employed to make thousands of highly crafted pieces as a state-supported enterprise. Many are from burials and seem to have been produced specifically for the burial rite. Such a set-up was representative of the power of the state – to command and control ceramic manufacture – and of social organization – part of the populace producing essentials and sharing them with another part through state redistribution of wealth. They are symbolic of the ancient Andean belief that such an arrangement was necessary because not having it would neglect religious belief. Similar arrangements prevailed for the manufacture of precious metal objects, textiles, featherwork and other materials.

Above: The meaning of this Moche prisoner effigy vessel is unmistakable: bound wrists and a rope around his head and penis show capitulation, defeat and domination.

For example, there were ceramic workshops at the Moche towns of Galindo and Cerro Mayal. The Cerro Mayal workshop occupied 29,000 sq ft (9,000 sq m). These towns were the western equivalent, perhaps, of a town with a car factory, wherein much of the local economy was focused on the factory employment.

LOCAL HEROES

The sacrificial scenes on Moche red-on-white painted narratives show not just ordinary citizens, but also combatants who were elites. If not actually of the ruling class, they were at least specialists in their role in ritual combat. Just as potters were state specialists, they also were chosen and trained into the role that they are shown performing. Recent research on Moche effigy pots by Christopher Donnan has produced convincing arguments that the Moche, seemingly unique among pre-Hispanic Andean cultures, actually produced portraiture. More than 900 examples are known to show individuals with such distinctive facial features that they cannot be anything other than true likenesses. If they had other meaning as well, this may have been in combination with the use to which they were put, rather than what they depicted.

Their symbolism is revealed by the fact that they were not just one-off portraits, but that groups of them were portraits of the same individual as he grew up. One group, for example, portrays just such an individual who was chosen, trained for ritual combat, was successful in his youth, but was eventually defeated and submitted to sacrifice. His body was dismembered and his blood offered to the gods. The entire sequence of his life, including the manufacture of the effigy vessels to record it, represents a sort of legend and symbolic example. This is symbolism on the order of commemorative event ceramics, coronation crockery, and modern celebrity memorabilia.

Above: Drawings of the Revolt of the Objects, *an Andean mythological theme that survived to Inca times. The original was at the Moche Huaca de la Luna.*

Below: Detail of a Nazca embroidered textile showing a priest in a tunic displaying the ray headed Staff Deity, and himself in a similar pose, holding a staff and a trophy head.

REPETITIVE ADDITIONS

Such symbolism and theme-related 'decoration' continued to be the practice in later periods, with certain modifications. Much Wari decoration is geometric and reflects systematic divisions of space similar to their architecture. Late Intermediate Period art shows a tendency to be additive and non-individualistic, to represent an assembly of elements in repetitive patterns. Yet, among the repetition there is often an anomaly – a singular shape and/or colour that contrasts with the rest of the pattern. Does this represent individual expression in an otherwise rigid society? Or perhaps some understood, and necessary, break in perfection?

Royal and elite cult practice became even stronger, particularly in the Chimú state, in which a huge area of the capital was devoted to enclosed compounds as the palaces of deceased royals, their relations, and their living entourages and dedicated caretaker priests. The entire arrangement was state supported, like the manufacture of pottery and other artefacts, as part of the cult. Once again, the organization symbolized and reinforced the rigid social framework, state power and territorialism.

RITUAL SYMBOLISM IN ARCHITECTURE

Ancient Andean architecture, like portable artefacts, incorporated multiple meanings. From the earliest ceremonial complexes of the Initial Period, once special architecture became the focus of settlement ritual, the architecture and its decoration symbolized religious belief.

Above: The double-headed rainbow deity in sculpted mud plaster decorates the platform walls at Huaca el Dragón, near Chan Chan.

Below: Stone heads at Tiwanaku perpetuated a long tradition of decapitation and trophy-head cults, also prominent in the Chavín Cult.

CLASSIFICATIONS OF SPACES

Ritual space comprised positive volume, negative volume and neutral areas. Platforms and stepped pyramids were positive structures that mimicked the surrounding landscape of hills and mountains. Negative spaces – sunken courtyards, temple interiors and walled compounds – mimicked natural voids such as caves, valleys and gullies. Walled compounds divided space into territories to confine people, things and activities within the compound, and to restrict some people from the space. Neutral space can be conceived in the more open areas of ceremonial complexes, such as larger courts at ground level, or particularly large walled areas, in which the general public could be accommodated to witness and participate in part in ritual ceremonies. Within neutral space the public could be included as far as they were allowed by the specialists. Their activities could thus be controlled by the ruling elite and specialist religious leaders.

Architectural spaces thus represented specialized areas where ritual enactment could proceed in a controlled manner. The spaces themselves symbolized part of the ritual.

COLOURS AND SOUNDS

Decoration on architecture also symbolized religious concepts. The bright colours painted on sculptural adornment were signals, although their meanings are only generally understood by reference to Inca records from the Spanish chroniclers. The effort to produce the pigments and the use of such bright and numerous shades indicates an early significance, even if their exact meanings are unknown. Apart from anything else, the colours drew attention to the sculpture and architecture, enforcing the presence of the deities portrayed and invoking awe within the beholder. For example, the gaze of the fearsome-looking supernatural face

Above: Even minor detail was symbolic. Here two shaped white stones represent the sacred condor's bill at a fountain at Machu Picchu.

of the Decapitator God on the platform walls and Great Plaza of the Huaca de la Luna at Moche cannot be escaped.

Similarly, there is some evidence for the use of sound. Various shell and pottery trumpets, and drums, must have been used in ritual, and their full effect would have been best appreciated from the heights of platforms by a congregation below. The ritual use of water, channelled through temples and compounds, is notable at Chavín de Huánta (where it is linked to sound), at Tiwanaku and in Cuzco, showing that the practice was a long tradition from the Early to the Late Horizon. It can only reflect the importance of water in ancient Andean survival and agriculture, as benign and life-giving rains filled the lakes and rivers, but also as the power of the weather gods and the forces of storms and thunder. It has been argued that the intricate channelling of water within the temple interiors at Chavín de Huántar was deliberately used to replicate the roar of the elements, from the temple to a presumably awestruck congregation in the courtyard outside.

PATHWAYS AND PROCESSIONS

The ritual pathways of the Nazca lines and of the Inca *ceque* lines represent architectural extensions. 'Owned' by selective groups, they represented symbolic procedures and procession routes. As well as geometric designs similar to those used on pottery and textiles, the Nazca lines and other geoglyphs form the shapes of animals and plants that were held sacred. Such animals were recognized as representative of religious concepts and powers. Large cleared rectangular areas among the Nazca geoglyphs presumably also served as arenas for group ceremonies.

The *ceque* routes of the Incas were both physical and theoretical. They were actual roads followed by intended victims, leading up to their ritual sacrifice, and also lines of sight for astronomical observation and priestly divination. *Ceque* lines divided up the space between them into sacred parcels. Along them, architectural elements were encountered (natural rock outcrops, sometimes modified, caves and springs) and man-made temples.

Moche murals display ritual processions, again in bright colours. They hark back to the single-colour procession of warriors around the platform at Cerro Sechín, one of Moche's predecessors in the north coast valleys. These murals, along with similar scenes on ceramics and elite burials with the costumes of the scenes' participants, are known to depict ritual combat, sacrifices and blood-offerings dedicated to powerful and demanding gods and goddesses.

PAN-ANDEAN SYMBOLISM

Such careful organization of space and the use of prescribed ritual routes were incorporated into Andean religious thought from the first ceremonial complexes. They are recognizable in the U-shaped complexes of the northern coastal valleys and sierra; in the Nazca platforms and plazas of Cahuachi; in the carefully laid-out courts and temples of Chavín de Huántar; in the great mound complexes of 'mountains' on the coast built by the Moche; in the temple-topped pyramid and open plazas of Pachacamac; in the multiple platforms and walled courts of Tiwanaku; in the rigidly organized architecture of Wari central sierra cities; in the sacred royal compounds of Chan Chan of the Chimú; and in the ritual layout of puma-shaped Cuzco and the Sacsahuaman angular-walled Temple to the Sun. The repeated use of the same fundamental forms reveals the underlying essence of the most ancient Andean creation beliefs.

Below: A procession of naked slaves or war captives decorates the Moche pyramid-platform of El Brujo.

COLOURS AS SYMBOLS

The use of bright colours to decorate ceramics, textiles, and adobe and stone sculpture in ancient Andean cultures was universal. From the earliest times, ceramics were painted, textiles featured a variety of dyed colours and were painted on, and murals and sculptures were painted. Stone and metal were often chosen for their colours to create contrast and symbolic statements.

Black, white, green, blue, yellow and shades of red were the primary colours used. Although such deliberate use of colour must reflect metaphorical meaning, its specifics cannot be known with certainty.

Above: Black llamas, much rarer than white and grey ones, were especially sacred and valuable for sacrifices as well as their wool.

EARLY COLOURING

The Initial Period adobe sculptures at Moxeke and Huaca de los Reyes/Caballo Muerto, and the Cerro Sechín sculptured stone slabs were all originally painted in reds, blue and white. The use of black limestone and white granite on the Black and White Portal of the New Temple at Chavín de Huántar was a deliberate choice, and must have been meant to convey a statement: juxtaposing two opposites, and reflecting duality and the opposing forces of nature. As well as the choice of stone colours, the two columns were carved with a male hawk and a female eagle, reinforcing the message.

Below: Vivid use of red on an Inca wooden kero *drinking cup symbolizes domination and perhaps blood in a llama-herding scene.*

On Chavín textiles, the background colour was laid out first, then design lines filled in with blue, gold and green threads. Nazca potters perfected no fewer than 13 ceramic slip colours, and such deliberate craftsmanship and choice reflects the importance that colours had in the culture.

The juxtaposition of contrasting colours was a universal practice, presumably a visual symbol of duality and opposition. In Wari art the use of one contrasting colour within a general scheme of harmonious colours must have conveyed some meaning to those who knew how to interpret it. Metallurgists' choice of metals frequently contrasted gold and silver, presumably for the same purpose.

BLUE

Spanish chroniclers recorded some colour meanings among the Inca. How far this can be projected into pre-Inca times is unknown.

The *Huarochirí Manuscript* describes Huatya Curi, son of the sky god Paria Caca. In one of his many contests with his hostile brother-in-law, he danced in a blue feather tunic and white cotton breechcloths, the colours of the sky and clouds, worn, presumably, to honour his father. The Inca rarely used blue, but this colour became more common in clothing in colonial times.

RED

This colour was favoured in Moche ceramics and textiles. Red-on-white fine-line narrative drawings were a Moche speciality. Many narrative scenes show ritual sacrifice, and it is assumed that red is therefore symbolic of blood. It might also be representative of the dawn and dusk skies, when sacrifices might have been performed, also of mud-laden rivers during the rainy season in north coast valleys.

The Incas associated red with conquest and rulership, as blood and perhaps symbolizing conspicuousness. The Inca state insignia, Mascaypacha, comprised a crimson tassel hung from a braid tied around the head. The chronicler Murúa

Above: An Inca noble painted on a wooden kero *drinking cup is dressed in symbolic red, representing conquest and rulership.*

says that each woollen red thread represented a conquered people and the blood of an enemy's severed head. Red seems to have become symbolic of the long tradition of severed heads that began as early as the stone panels at Initial Period Cerro Sechín.

The Inca founder Manco Capac wore a bright red tunic when he stood on the hill of Huanacauri to impress the populace. His 15th-century successor Pachacuti wore a long red robe when he confronted the giant storm god who came down the River Urubamba wreaking destruction.

Inca ritual face-painting featured a red stripe from ear to ear across the bridge of the nose. Sometimes pigment was used, but at other times the blood of a sacrificed llama or the blood of a child *capacocha* sacrifice was used. The blood was smeared across the face of the deceased Inca's mummy to emphasize and enforce the bond of conquered peoples to the living emperor.

Below: This Moche scene shows a sacred sky serpent across the stirrup spout and a fishing boat representing the abundance of the sea.

Coloured threads and combinations of threads in *quipu* recording devices were also used to represent commodities and perhaps directions, places and numbers.

GREEN

In contrast to red, the Incas associated green with tropical peoples and lands. When Inca Roca, sixth emperor, marched against the rainforest Chunchos of Antisuyu, he went in the guise of a jaguar, donned a green mantle and adopted tropical habits such as chewing coca and tobacco, both green.

The significance of the green stone idol, Yampallec, brought by the legendary conqueror and dynasty founder Naymlap to the north coast, is unknown. The dynasty must have associated green stone with ritual and rule.

Green was also associated with the rainy season, a somewhat obvious link with plant growth and, by extension, with sorcery, drugs and love. Finally, the chronicler Betanzos describes the association of green with ancestors: Pachacuti Inca's kin group washed and dyed themselves with a green herbal plant.

BLACK

Black was fundamentally a metaphor for creation and origins. The Incas, and presumably pre-Inca cultures, associated black with death. In the Camay Quilla ceremony (January/ February) to officially end the rainy season, celebrants dressed in black clothing and blackened their faces with soot. They held a long rope wrapped around the emperor, and newly initiated teenage boys held a mock battle in black tunics. A year after the death of an emperor, his kin group painted their faces black and held a ceremony with his mummified body. Four men with blackened faces concluded the ceremony at the time that it was believed the spirit of the dead Inca arrived at its destination.

Black llamas were sacrificed in the same month, to signify reciprocal ties between the Inca ruler and his subjects. Men dressed in black performed the Mayucati ritual – throwing the ashes of the year's sacrifices into the River Ollantaytambo and following it out of Cuzco by night. The ashes were carried though conquered lands and ultimately to sea as offerings to Viracocha, the supreme deity.

The black-cloud constellations of Inca cosmology, comprising the spaces between stars, were believed to be sources of life and fecundity. They were linked to the colours of the rainbow by association with the deep purple stripe, which the Incas considered the first colour, representing Mama. The remaining colours, called 'lower thing' and 'next thing' descending in colour intensity, were held to descend from Mama.

PILGRIMAGE AND ORACLE SITES

The difficulties inherent in explaining supernatural concepts through images difficult to produce with the existing technology may have fostered the growth of pilgrimage centres. Their symbolic art, meant to show the complexities of supernatural belief, could be combined with complex architecture and mystery in a central place. The spread of religious ideas could be accomplished by bringing converts to a place held most sacred and then dispersing them again, convinced of or reinforced in their belief in the cult. Portable art decorated with the symbolic images of the religious concepts would help remind those living at distance from the cult centre of the tenets of the cult.

Similarly, the sacredness of a cult centre, where the truth was held and expounded by its priests, would become a focus for other-worldly experience. The architecture of the centre could provoke and enhance such an experience.

Above: The city of Pachacamac endured as a powerful centre of religious devotion to the supreme being for more than a millennium.

A WESTERN VIEW?

These general concepts seem self-evident, yet they are overlain with concepts of conversion and missionary work as documented in Western European and North American historical experience. This experience may be different from, and so not directly applicable to, ancient Andean religious experience, for which there is essentially no archaeological evidence.

The growth in the importance of special sites as religious cult centres is not unique to Andean civilization. It is, however, a centrally important part of ancient Andean belief from at least the Early Horizon. The central location of ceremonial complexes either within a domestic settlement or among surrounding domestic settlements began in the preceding Initial Period. Many sites are identified by scholars as pilgrimage sites: Chavín de Huántar, Cahuachi, Pukará, Tiwanaku, Pachacamac and Inca Cuzco itself.

Below: The Semi-subterranean Court enclosed formal ritual space at Tiwanaku, capital city of the Titicaca Basin.

THE PACHACAMAC MODEL

It is the Spanish colonial records describing the cult and oracle at Pachacamac that provide the basis for the model of ancient Andean pilgrimage and oracle sites. Essential elements of the Pachacamac model were a special chamber housing a cult idol, access to which was restricted to specialist priests; oracular predictions; public plazas for general ritual; and the establishment of a network of affiliated shrines in other communities.

CHAVÍN DE HUÁNTAR

The earliest widely recognized cult centre in ancient Andean civilization was Chavín de Huántar, for it appears to fulfil at least some of these criteria. Its complex architecture deliberately instilled a sense of mystery, supernatural presence and exclusiveness. First the Old Temple, then

the much larger New Temple, comprised numerous interconnected chambers holding a cult monolith carved with the symbolic image of a supernatural being. Its isolation within the temple clearly restricted access to it and made it more awesome and powerful. Its complex symbolic imagery made it necessary for specialists to interpret it.

The Old Temple contained the Lanzón, or Great Image, monolith and the New Temple held the Raimondi Stela. The curious position of the former, piercing through the roof of one chamber to a hidden upper chamber, implies an oracular room. The acoustics of the water channels of the temples also implies the mysterious use of echoing and mimicry of the elements.

Both the Old Temple and the New Temple were accompanied by open plazas. These were wide, flat spaces between the arms of the U-shaped platform mounds, and within each was a sunken ceremonial courtyard: round in the Old Temple, square in the New Temple.

The imagery of several Chavín deities became widespread: the Staff Deity and feline and serpent imagery in particular. Yet, felines and serpents were common elements in earlier cultures throughout an even wider area. Several sites, however, show imagery, though locally produced, that is identical to that from Chavín.

Above: The Inca trail has become a modern 'pilgrimage' route. This is the sentry post of Runkuaqay on the way to Machu Picchu.

At Huaricoto, north-west of Chavín, the Early Horizon ritual precinct contained a carved stone 'spatula' depicting the deity of the Lanzón. There is also decorated pottery of Chavín design. Other sites in adjacent highlands also have portable artefacts of Chavín style. It may be, however, that the Chavín Cult was adopted in addition to established local patron deities.

More revealing is Karwa on the southern coast, near the Paracas necropolis site. Textiles from the Karwa tomb are decorated not in the local Paracas style but in the bright colours and images of the Chavín Cult, including their composition, bilateral symmetry and double profiling. The Chavín Staff Deity, here in female form and sometimes called the Karwa Goddess, is unmistakable. Such faithful adherence to the Chavín orthodoxy seems to betray Chavín presence or a shrine in a network of Chavín shrines.

In the northern highlands, Chavín stone sculpture from Kuntur Wasi and Pacopampa clearly displays Chavín imagery. In the upper Lambayeque river drainage, two matching carved stone columns were found, reminiscent of the Black and White Portal columns at Chavín de Huántar. Further, in the Chicama Valley there were painted adobe columns (now destroyed), one of which was painted with a winged creature like those on the Black and White Portal.

The distribution of these sites across cultural spheres and production zones indicates the establishment of Chavín shrines and may imply the integration of the cult into local community structures.

Left: Chavín de Huántar became the earliest widely recognized pilgrimage and oracular site in the Early Horizon.

TEMPLES AND SUNKEN COURTS

The earliest ceremonial complexes in the northern coastal valleys and adjacent northern Peruvian sierra organized both positive and negative space in the forms of platforms and sunken courts. The forming of a U-shape, comprising a tiered platform at the base and two elongated platform wings enclosing a sunken court and a level, open plaza around it, was clearly symbolic. The form was repeated at numerous coastal valley and northern and central Peruvian highland sites. Its mere repetition underlies a core of common religious belief.

Above: The great temple pyramid platform of Huaca Larga incorporated La Ray Mountain in the centre of the Moche city Tucume Viejo.

U-SHAPE ORIGINS

The U-shaped ceremonial structure was the culmination of the development of two elements: platforms and subterranean courts. The U-shaped temple established at Chavín de Huántar as the centre of a religious cult had representations as far afield as the southern coastal valleys. But the form began much earlier, in the Initial Period.

The building of platform mounds began at least as early as 3000BC. The earliest were those at Aspero in the Supe Valley: the Huaca de los Idolos and the Huaca de los Sacrificios, among a ceremonial complex of as many as 17 platforms. Within the next few centuries smaller complexes of mounds had been built at Piedra Parada, also in the Supe Valley, El Paraíso in the Chillón Valley, Río Seco in the Chancay Valley, Bandurria in the Huaura Valley, Salinas de Chao and Los Morteros in the Chao Valley, and at Kotosh, a highland site in the Río Huallaga-Higueras Valley.

Below: The mud-plaster walls of the Middle Temple at Garagay feature a fanged being with spider attributes and water symbolism.

Ancient Andeans were thus building ceremonial architecture as early as the first royal pyramids in Egypt and temple platforms, called ziggurats, in ancient Mesopotamia; and Andean ceremonial platforms are the earliest in the New World, predating the first Olmec earthen pyramids in Mesoamerica by at least 1,000 years.

Two 'traditions' of raised platforms developed, both based on ritual on top of the platform and open ceremonial space at the base for an attendant congregation: the Supe-Aspero Tradition and the El Paraíso Tradition. Chambers and niches to house ritual objects were built on top as the traditions evolved.

The practice of building circular sunken courts (*plazas hundidas*) also began in northern Peru during the 2nd millennium BC. Most often they were built in association with a platform at its base and aligned with the platform's staircase. Early examples include Salinas de Chao, Piedra Parada and highland La Galgada. Only occasionally was a sunken court built as the sole ceremonial element, for example at Alto Salavery.

By about 2000BC the stone-built civic-ceremonial centre at El Paraíso was the largest Preceramic Period civic-ceremonial centre on the coast. With a group of small temples forming a base and two elongated parallel platforms, it was a configuration transitional to the classic U-shaped structures of the Initial Period.

Below: Huaca de la Luna, mimicking the hill behind it, another Moche mud-brick temple of the Early Intermediate Period.

Above: The high stone walls of the rectangular Semi-subterranean court at Tiwanaku were decorated with stone trophy heads.

SECHÍN ALTO

By 1200BC the U-shaped ceremonial complex at Sechín Alto was the largest civic-ceremonial complex in the New World. At its fullest development it included all the elements of the classic U-shaped ritual centre. Construction began in about 1400BC (although one radiocarbon date from the site is as early as 1721BC). Its principal platform ruin still stands some 44m (144ft) above the plain and covers an area 300 x 250m (985 x 820ft). The huge U-shape is formed by sets of parallel platform mounds extending from the base corners of the pyramid, and forming part of a ritual area 400 x 1,400m (1,310 x 4,600ft). Running north-east from the principal pyramid is a succession of plazas and sunken courts.

The principal wings enclose a plaza with an early, small sunken court. Beyond the ends of these mounds there is a larger circular sunken court, then another open area formed by two long, thin parallel platforms flanking a plaza approximately 375m (1,230ft) square. Forming the end of the complex, 1km (½ mile) north-east of the principal platform, an H-shaped platform faces the main pyramid and flanks the largest circular sunken court, 80m (262ft) in diameter. The principal pyramidal platform is faced with enormous granite blocks set in clay mortar. Some of the blocks are up to 1.4m (4.5ft) on each side and weigh up to 2 tonnes (tons).

Surrounding the Sechín Alto complex there was 10.5 sq km (2,560 acres) of buildings and smaller platforms. Like other U-shaped complexes, the site must have been a religious centre that served its surrounding area. Judging by its size, it may have served a considerable region as well.

RITUAL MEANINGS

The practical aspects of the arrangements of the U-shaped complex seem obvious: a raised platform from which to address a crowd, an open area for the crowd to stand in and a sunken court for exclusive ritual. There is an element of implied control in the arrangement: the congregation was partly confined between the arms of the U-shape, and their attention could be monitored from the height of the platform or focused on the sunken court.

Perhaps the two elements symbolize the concepts of a sky deity and an earth deity. Ritual may have involved procession from one to the other. Assuming strong naturalism in early Andean religious thought, the gods were believed to inhabit or infuse the natural landscape. Thus platforms were representative mountains and sunken courtyards representative valleys or caves. Further, their shapes might have represented the sky father and the earth mother, the womb and the symbolic shapes of man and woman. In seeming recognition of the source of life-giving water as the mountain thunder and rainstorms, the open ends of U-shaped complexes were oriented towards the mountains, their U-shapes imitating the collecting valleys.

Below: The ultimate sacred circular court of the great Sacsahuaman Temple of Cuzco formed the puma's head of the Inca capital.

SACRED CEMETERIES

Honouring the gods in the southern coastal desert cultures was focused on cemetery rites and ancestor worship. The dry climate has been instrumental in preserving the buried bodies and artefacts in the tombs.

SHARED TRADITIONS

The Paracas and Nazca cultures developed in continuous succession through the Early Horizon and Early Intermediate Period in the southern valleys and deserts of Peru, focusing their settlement and economy around sea fishing and shellfish collecting, and later on maize and cotton agriculture. Early Paracas ceramics and textile decoration shows much influence from Chavín de Huántar. At Karwa, near the early Paracas necropolis, textiles from an elite tomb are decorated with one of the best representations of the Staff Deity. Here she is the Staff Goddess, thought to honour a local goddess while at the same time acting as a 'wife' or 'sister' shrine to the Chavín Cult in the north.

Below: Stone slab circles at the Sillustani necropolis of the Colla people possibly served as the sites of burial ceremonies before bodies were taken to their kinship chullpa *tower.*

The Paracas and Nazca developed their own distinct style and deities. Quintessential was the Oculate Being, a wide-eyed distinctively local deity depicted in brightly painted ceramic masks and portrayed, flying, on pottery and textiles.

THE CAVERNAS CEMETERY

Paracas settlements covered an area of some 54ha (133 acres) around a core area of about 4ha (10 acres) on the low slopes of the Cerro Colorado on the Paracas Peninsula. Among the sprawling habitation remains, special areas were used as cemeteries for hundreds of burials, possibly the foci of family cults for nearby and more distant settlements.

Great care was taken in the burial of the dead in the Cavernas cemetery area. The naked corpse was tied with a cord into a flexed seated position. The body was wrapped in several layers of richly coloured textiles, both cotton and wool, revealing trade contact with highland cultures for llama wool. Placed in a basket and accompanied by plain and richly decorated ceramics, and sheet-metal jewellery, the whole was finally wrapped in plain cotton cloth. Such 'bundles' were then enshrined in large subterranean crypts, which were reopened and used repeatedly over generations, presumably by kin groups as family mausoleums.

Above: Cahuachi, a sacred 'city' of about 40 temple mounds, served as a funerary and pilgrimage centre for Nazca religion.

PARACAS INFLUENCE

A prominent element in Paracas and Nazca religious ritual was decapitation. Trophy heads adorn pottery and stream from the waists of Oculate Beings on textiles. In addition, the skulls of many Paracas burials show evidence of ritual surgery, with small sections of the cranium being removed by incision and drilling. The exact purpose of this operation is unknown – it may have been ritual or medical. The Nazca inherited veneration of the Oculate Being from the Paracas culture.

Highland drought had caused increasing aridity in the coastal plains. It seems likely, therefore, that the Oculate Being was

associated with water and precipitation. Flying Oculate Beings perhaps betray a fixation with the sky. As a practical measure, the Nazca developed an elaborate system of underground aqueducts to collect and channel the maximum amount of water around Cahuachi. Great stepped spiral galleries, cobbled with smooth river stones, gave access to the wells.

Two of the most important Nazca settlements were Cahuachi and Ventilla, the first a ritual 'city', the second an urban 'capital'. Ventilla covered an area of at least 200ha (495 acres) with terraced housing, walled courts and small mounds. It was linked to Cahuachi by a Nazca line across the intervening desert.

Revealing their wide Andean contacts, Nazca ceramics and textiles are also decorated with a multitude of supernatural, clearly symbolic images. As well as sea creatures, crabs, insects and serpents that would have been familiar local sights, images of monkeys, felines and tropical birds from the rainforests were also used.

Below: In the Nazca cemetery (and Paracas, shown above) of the southern desert coast cultures, the desiccated conditions preserved the hair, fibres and textiles of the deceased.

The trophy-head cult extended to caches of trepanned, severed skulls of sacrificial victims being found among the remains in Nazca cemeteries.

Above: The Paracas cemetery (and Nazca, shown below left) of the Early Horizon and Early Intermediate Period served numerous cities as kinship burial mausoleums.

LINES AND CEREMONIAL MOUNDS

Nazca religion is defined by two elements. Cahuachi was a ritual complex concerned with spiritual matters rather than daily life. Covering an area of 150ha (370 acres), it comprised a complex of 40 ceremonial mounds made by shaping natural hillocks into terracing and associated plazas. It was used from about AD100 to 550, and thereafter continued in use as a mortuary ground and place of votive offering. The entire site appears to have been devoted to mortuary practices, probably as family vaults following the Paracas tradition.

The largest mound was 30m (98ft) high, modified into six or seven terraces with adobe-brick retaining walls. Most of the tombs have been looted, but the few unlooted tombs excavated yielded mummified burials accompanied by exquisitely decorated, multicoloured woven burial coats and ceramics. Some contained animal sacrifices and ritual human sacrifices of Nazca men, women and children. Some skulls had excrement inserted into the mouths; some had been perforated and a carrying cord inserted; some had blocked eyes, cactus spines pinning the mouth shut, and tongues removed and put in pouches.

The second element was the Nazca lines, the geoglyphs forming geometric patterns, clusters of straight lines and recognizable animal and plant figures. There are some 1,300km (808 miles) of such lines, including 300 figures. A huge 490m-long (1,600ft) arrow, pointing towards the Pacific Ocean, is thought to be a symbol to invoke rains. The lines were undoubtedly associated with the Nazca preoccupation with water and crop fertility, together with worship of mountain deities – the ultimate source of water.

Cahuachi was abandoned as the coastal valleys became more arid. Simultaneously, there was an increase in the number and elaboration of Nazca lines. Regarded as ritual pathways, perhaps like the family vaults dedicated to kin groups, the increase in their use represents desperate efforts to placate the gods who had forsaken them. As Cahuachi was abandoned, people covered the mounds with layers of sand.

CEREMONIAL COMPOUNDS

Platforms and U-shaped complexes continued to form the core elements of ceremonial centres in the northern coastal valleys and highlands through the Early Horizon. In time, Moche platforms of the Early Intermediate Period achieved both the shape and proportions of hills, as if the people were building their own mountains on the coast. The Huaca del Sol and Huaca de la Luna at Moche are the largest adobe-built pyramidal platforms ever constructed in the Americas.

ALTIPLANO TRADITIONS

In the southern highlands of the Titicaca Basin architectural symbolism also mirrored the landscape. Here there developed a tradition comprising a central platform mound with a central, square sunken court at the top surrounded by rectangular temples arranged symmetrically around the court. This 'tradition' of a sacred compound flourished in the late 2nd and 1st millennia BC and is named after its principal example, Chiripa, near the southern end of Lake Titicaca. Compared to the huge mounds built at U-shaped complexes, Altiplano mounds were relatively modest in scale. The final height of the Chiripa mound, reached late in the 1st millennium BC when the site was used by people from Tiwanaku, was a mere 6m (19½ft).

Below: The ciudadelas *of Chimú and Chan Chan comprised courtyards and chambers for ritual and ceremony as 'cities' of the dead.*

Above: The mud walls and rooms at the Tchudi ciudadela *at Chan Chan were sculpted with attention to detail throughout.*

THE PUKARÁ TRADITION

In the Early Horizon, religious and political focus shifted north of the lake during the latter half of the 1st millennium BC and became centred at the site of Pukará, northwest of Lake Titicaca. Unlike U-shaped complexes, the Pukará Tradition comprised monumental masonry-clad structures terraced against hillsides. The principal terrace had a monumental staircase and was topped by a rectangular sunken court with one-room buildings around three sides – a style that was reminiscent of Chiripa.

The Pukará Tradition's religious focus was on the Yaya-Mama cult of male and female symbolism, although it also shared the feline and serpentine imagery prevalent throughout contemporary Andean civilization. This emphasis on father sky and mother earth is reflected not only in the carved images of Yaya and Mama monoliths, but also in the combination of platforms and sunken courts in association with ritual architecture.

These developments were not isolated, however. The economy of the Altiplano was largely based on llama pastoralism and the wool was traded with the southern coastal cultures of Paracas and Nazca and farther afield. Thus, religious ideas must have been encountered from northern regions through the Chavín Cult and its aftermath.

THE TIWANAKU COMPOUND

Pukará dominated the Titicaca Basin Altiplano for about four centuries. Its inheritor in the later Early Intermediate Period and the Middle Horizon was Tiwanaku, a ceremonial city of proportions and complexity to rival the waning Chavín de Huántar and any northern and southern coastal valley contemporaries of the Moche and Nazca.

Two rival empires eventually dominated the Middle Horizon: the highland peoples of Tiwanaku and Wari. Although they shared religious concepts, they conquered respective areas and reached an uneasy settlement with each other at a highland boundary in the La Raya Pass south of Cuzco.

Ceremonial buildings at Chiripa and Pukará herald those at Tiwanaku. The tradition of the enclosed courtyard was continued and expanded into large public, walled ceremonial areas and semi-subterranean courts. Platforms remained relatively low and sunken courts stayed rectangular in shape.

From Tiwanaku, Mt Illimani dominates the view and is perhaps replicated in the platform mound of the Akapana pyramid. In nearby Lake Titicaca sit the Island of the Sun and the Island of the Moon, believed to be the birthplaces of the sun and moon. The moat around the Akapana and Kalasasaya structures renders the complex a symbolic island, although it can be argued that in the flat compound the water in a moat would flood the structural footings and drains. Nevertheless, the essence of the symbolic island is there.

Above: Wari's southernmost provincial centre, Pikilacta, was laid out as repetitive, adjoining, symmetrical stone-walled compounds.

AKAPANA AND THE PUMA PRIEST

The Akapana temple comprised a six-stepped mound in the shape of half a stepped diamond, known as the Andean Cross. The top was occupied by either a palace/temple or by a sunken court in the shape of a full-stepped diamond cross. Excavations revealed that ritual eating and burials took place there, including the primary burial of a man seated and holding a puma effigy incense burner. There was also a cache of sacrificed llama bones, and most of the skeletons found buried on the first terrace and under its foundations were headless. The upper terraced walls of the platform were decorated with tenoned stone puma heads, and at the base of the western staircase a black basalt image of a seated, puma-headed person (*chachapuma*) holding a severed head in his lap was found. Another *chachapuma* sculpture is a standing figure holding dangling severed heads.

Such symbolism – severed heads, pumas, the western location indicative of the setting sun and night – implies shamanic ritual, puma transformation and death.

On the huge Sun Gate at Tiwanaku, the central figure has often been associated with the sun, owing to his rayed head. The frontal stance and arms holding staffs equally associate the figure with the Staff Deity of Chavín. Another interpretation, however, can be based on the stepped dais on which the figure stands. It is identical to the half-stepped diamond court of the Akapana and could imply association with the *chachapuma*.

Such complex, composite, enigmatic imagery is typical of the tradition of multiple meanings and hidden or obscure meaning in Andean religious symbolism. Specialists are needed to interpret the imagery, perhaps according to the ceremony and occasion.

Left: In its remote mountain location, Machu Picchu was a sacred Inca city and religious retreat at the heart of the empire.

THE PACHACAMAC NETWORK

The religious network of Pachacamac was organized in sympathy with Andean concepts of community, mutual exchange, taxation and kinship.

THE ORACLE SITE

The cult centre was the city of Pachacamac at the mouth of the River Lurín, south of modern Lima. It comprised a complex of adobe platforms and plazas. An isolated chamber at the summit of the principal platform housed an oracle. There were open plazas in which pilgrims could fast and participate in public ceremony. Access to the oracle chamber was strictly limited to cult specialists. Oracular messages were given by these specialists concerning life and the future: predictions about the weather, favourable interventions of the gods with the elements, protection against diseases, specialized knowledge about the best times for planting and the harvest. Earthquakes, crop failure and other disasters were believed to be the result of antagonizing the god Pachacamac.

Much of what is known of the Pachacamac oracle site is from descriptions from Inca and early Spanish colonial sources. The elements of the central coastal ceremonial city incorporated the full range of Andean religious architecture: platform mounds, sacred compounds and plazas for congregational worship, and exclusive chambers for restrictive ritual performed by specialists.

Distant communities solicited the priests for permission to establish branch shrines to Pachacamac. If deemed to have the ability to support cult activities, a priest from Pachacamac was assigned to the new shrine and the community supplied labour on and produce from assigned lands to support him and the shrine. Part was kept for the shrine and the rest sent to the Pachacamac oracle site. Such branches were thought of as the wives, children or brothers and sisters of the main cult complex.

Below: Pachacamac, established in the 3rd century AD, soon became a cult centre for the supreme deity, Pachacamac.

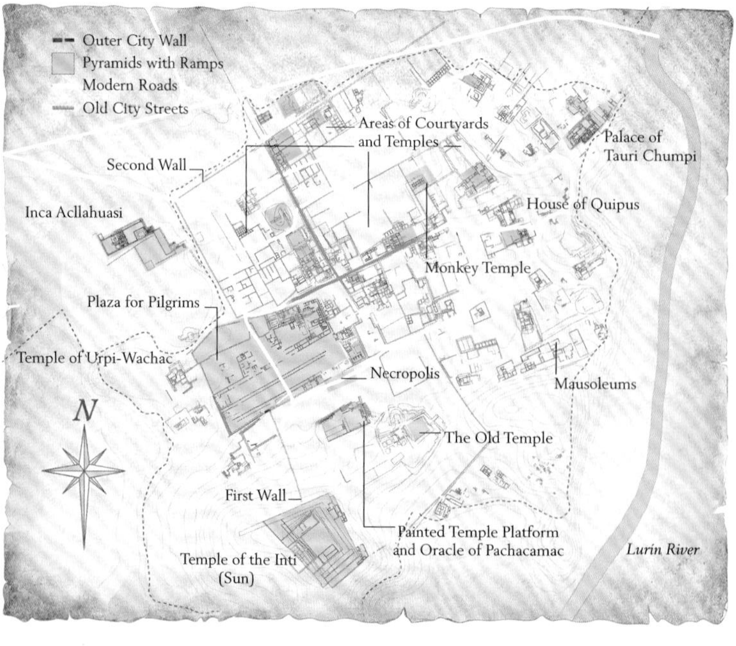

THE CULT

Pachacamac – 'earth/time maker' – was the creator deity of the peoples of central coastal Peru and the adjacent Andes. The Pachacamac cult and shrine began to become important in the latter half of the Early Intermediate Period. By the 16th century a network of shrines spanned the range of Andean Area production zones from the coast into the highlands, as well as north and south along the coast.

The cult itself spread from the coast, first north and south, then inland into the highlands, where worship of Pachacamac rivalled the highland creator deity Viracocha. Its spread inland is associated with the inland spread of the Andean Area Quechua language.

In the Middle Horizon and Late Intermediate Period the cult and oracle site overtook the importance of local deities to the north and south coasts – those of the Nazca and Moche. Even when the mountain empire of Wari rose and its armies threatened the coast, ultimately to conquer Pachacamac and incorporate the city into its empire, Pachacamac remained independently important as an oracle site. In fact, despite being politically demoted to an outpost of Wari power, Pachacamac remained religiously important throughout the Late Intermediate Period.

When the Incas arrived in the Late Horizon they immediately recognized the importance of the oracle, not only locally but also throughout the region and beyond. They recognized Pachacamac's importance in relation to Viracocha and sought to accommodate the religious concepts that both gods embodied.

The cult thus endured for more than a millennium. In addition to its primary religious purpose, it became entrenched in

the community and its social structure, in its agricultural production and in the redistribution of wealth. There is, however, no recorded evidence of the use of missionaries to spread the cult's ideology.

EARLY ORIGINS

The site of Pachacamac became important locally from the latter half of the Early Intermediate Period, when the first phases of the pyramid platform to the sun and adjoining Temple to Pachacamac were built. It became an important political power during the Middle Horizon, and may have been partly responsible for the northern shift of Moche power in the late Early Intermediate Period/Middle Horizon.

Wari presence is attested by the architecture and a Wari cemetery, and the continuance of the site's religious importance is implied by a wooden post carved with figures of Wari-like divinities, as well as stone figurines. The upper part of the post depicts a man holding a bola and wearing a chest ornament; the lower part is carved with double-headed serpents, jaguars and a figure with attributes like those of the 'angels' on the Gateway to the Sun at Tiwanaku.

LATE HORIZON PACHACAMAC

The 16th-century chronicler Cieza de León noted the importance of the shrine and Inca reverence for it, while the 17th-century writer Father Bernabe Cobo devoted an entire chapter to a detailed description of the ancient site.

Cobo describes how devotees of the Pachacamac Cult visited the centre specifically to petition the priests there to establish satellite shrines in the cities of their homelands, and to permit them to erect 'wife', 'son' or 'daughter' shrines of their local deities, to Pachacamac. Prophecy from the oracle was sought for everything from health, fortune, the well-being of crops and flocks, the weather and even the prognosis of Inca battle plans. Defying or neglecting Pachacamac was believed to provoke earthquakes. Offerings in solicitation of oracles included cotton, maize, coca leaves, dried fish, llamas, guinea pigs, fine textiles, ceramic drinking vessels and gold and silver – no doubt useful to the priests.

The arrival of aliens – the Spaniards – caused the oracle to fall silent, although worshippers still visit Pachacamac today to make offerings.

Above: The main pyramid platform at Pachacamac was surrounded by a vast complex of courtyards and platforms.

Below: The Incas recognized Pachacamac's importance, but also built a temple to Inti, the sun god, here.

STATE RELIGION

Although the Incas embraced the cults of all those they conquered, and worshipped a pantheon of deities, they insisted on the supremacy of a state religion or cult centred on their own two principal deities: Viracocha and Inti.

Viracocha was more of an all-embracing entity than a specific god or idol. He was not exclusively Inca, rather a long-standing highland creator god. The Inca traced the origin of their right to rule the Andean Area to Viracocha.

Inti, the sun god, was increasingly favoured in day-to-day worship in the late 15th and early 16th centuries, as the empire grew. The importance of the person of the emperor himself was emphasized more, in an attempt to focus the various peoples of the empire on a state cult, not in replacement of long-held beliefs, but to empower the state and enhance the importance of the new regime the Incas brought.

In keeping with Andean pantheism, other major Inca deities were Quilla (moon goddess), Chaska-Qoylor (goddess of Venus), Illapa (weather god: thunder, lightning, rain) and Cuichu (god of the rainbow). The two principal temple complexes in Cuzco were the sacred Coricancha precinct and the imposing Sacsahuaman edifices.

Below: The carved stone walls of the Temple to Inti at the fortress of Ollantatambo – one of many temples spreading the state cult.

Above: This La Tolita (Ecuador) sheet-gold mask of the sun god is similar to the golden image of Inti in the Coricancha Temple.

THE CULT OF INTI

The universality of the sun notwithstanding, the Inca cult of Inti was in many respects unique. The emperor's person became regarded as the earthly embodiment of the sun. His presence and well-being were vital to the life of every subject, and to the prosperity of the land in general. Although the emperor's power was absolute, Inti was believed to be benevolent and generous. Solar eclipses were regarded as signs of his anger and required sacrifice and the solicitation of the return of his favour. As the power of the state cult grew, Inti came to be regarded as Viracocha's intermediary.

By the 16th century Inti/the emperor was so central to the state's well-being that an incident witnessed by priests during ceremonies in his honour appeared to foretell the empire's end. In the reign of Huayna Capac, priests witnessed the fall of an eagle from the sky mobbed by buzzards. The event coincided with reports of the spread of an unknown deadly disease – now known to have been smallpox brought by the Spaniards and spreading from Mesoamerica.

The Coricancha was the centre of the state cult dedicated to Inti's worship. A great mask of sheet gold, moulded into a human face, wide-eyed and grinning, and with rays of zigzag sheet gold ending in miniature masks was housed in its own chamber within the temple.

Rituals and offerings to Inti served constantly to reinforce his power and to confirm the acceptance among the people of the emperor as representing Inti himself. The dead emperor's mummified remains were brought out on ritual occasions, and offered food and drink, and sacrifices, in the belief in the ultimate immortality of Inti.

Above: The Observatorio at Machu Picchu was the focus of the cult of Inti. Its central window is placed to align with the rising of the sun on the winter solstice (21 June).

THE RIGHT TO RULE

Inca right to rule was integral in the state cult. The Incas were painstaking in their efforts to establish, and to alter as necessary, an elaborate mythology to support this close association of Inti, the emperor and power. The Incas demonstrated their right to rule, and unified the empire, by proving that all peoples were descended from the same ancestors, namely the Inca ancestors. The beliefs and cosmologies of those they conquered had to be incorporated into the state religion. To do this alongside continuous acquisition of territories and peoples required an unremitting effort to add to and alter the state mythology. It was important to extend this continuity right back to the first ruler of Cuzco, Manco Capac, and to link the state foundation myth with creation mythology itself.

Official mythology describing the wanderings of the ancestors after their emergence from Tambo Toco cave included the sun's sanction of the founder Manco Capac to rule in his name. In another version Manco Capac is said to have bedecked himself in gold plates to give credulity to his divine appearance when he presented himself at dawn to the people of Cuzco. As the myth was developed, Pachacuti Inca Yupanqui (AD 1438–71) added his dream visit and discovery at the spring of Susurpuquio of a crystal tablet bearing the image of Viracocha, who sanctioned his right to rule.

Below: Machu Picchu was an imperial retreat and sacred city devoted to Inti. This stone-walled chamber was possibly a royal tomb.

Pachacuti and his son Tupac Inca Yupanqui (1471–93) rebuilt much of Cuzco to accommodate the state cult, including the rebuilding of the Coricancha to enhance the importance of Inti. Thus, the creator, the sun and the emperor were united in one stroke.

ONLY ONE RIVAL

Viracocha's, and therefore Inti's, only serious rival was the cult and oracle of Pachacamac. The site was duly included in the wanderings of Viracocha. The Incas recognized Pachacamac's ancient importance, but to establish the state's supremacy they built a temple to Inti alongside that of the Pachacamac oracle. Pachacamac's importance was noted, but the temple to Inti in the city was more than a reciprocal shrine dedicated to a regional deity.

The peoples of the empire were also continually reminded of their bond with Inti by *capacocha* sacrifices. Annually, chosen victims were brought from the provinces to Cuzco, then marched back out to their respective provinces again for ritual sacrifice in the name of both Inti and the emperor.

THE SACRED CORICANCHA

The Coricancha or Golden Enclosure of imperial Cuzco, was the centre of the Inca cosmos. It was the supreme ceremonial precinct of the capital, the most sacred *huaca*. It housed the images of Viracocha, the creator, and Inti, god of the sun, and other principal Inca deities. From it emanated the sacred *ceque* lines, both physical roads and cosmic routes of sacred meaning. Forty-one *ceques* led to 328 sacred locations: *huacas* such as caves, springs, stone pillars and points on the surrounding horizon, and important locations such as critical junctions of the city's irrigation canals. One Spanish chronicler, Bernabe Cobo, listed 317 shrines.

These lines bound the Inca world, physical and religious, to the Coricancha 'navel' of the world. From points within the precinct, priests plotted the movements of Mayu (the Milky Way) across the night sky – for example from the Ushnua Pillar, from which sightings of Mayu were taken between two pillars on the distant horizon.

The complex was in the tail of the puma image profile that formed the plan of Cuzco, at the confluence of the rivers Huantanay and Tullamayo, emphasizing the importance of water in the Andean psyche. The second most sacred shrine of the city, Sacsahuaman, formed the puma's head at the prominence above the rivers.

THE SACRED WASI

The complex is sometimes referred to as the Temple of the Sun (Inti), but in fact, the temple to Inti was one of several temples forming the precinct. It was built of stone blocks so carefully fitted together that there was no need for mortar. Its walls were covered with sheet gold – referred to as 'the sweat of the sun' – while another of the temples, to Quilla, was covered in silver ('tears of the moon').

Above: The entrance to the Golden Enclosure of the Coricancha in Cuzco, centre of the state cult of Inti (the sun god).

The precinct comprised six *wasi*, or covered chambers, arranged around a square courtyard. Each *wasi* was dedicated to one of the six principal Inca state deities: Viracocha, Inti, Quilla, Chaska-Qoylor (Venus as morning and evening star), Illapa (weather, thunder, lightning) and Cuichu (rainbow), ranged hierarchically in that order, although Viracocha and Inti were near equivalents.

Each temple housed an image of the deity and the paraphernalia of ritual and worship. A special room was reserved for the storage and care of the mummies of deceased emperors (*mallquis*). On ritual days – for example the winter and summer solstices of Inti Raymi and Capac Raymi – the *mallquis* were brought out in their rich vestments, carried on royal litters in procession around the capital and offered food and drink while court historians recited their deeds. The temple courtyard was also the venue for incantations to and the sanctification of *capacochas* – specially selected sacrificial victims. From the Coricancha they set out

Below: The sacred Coricancha included separate chambers dedicated to and housing the idols of the principal Inca deities.

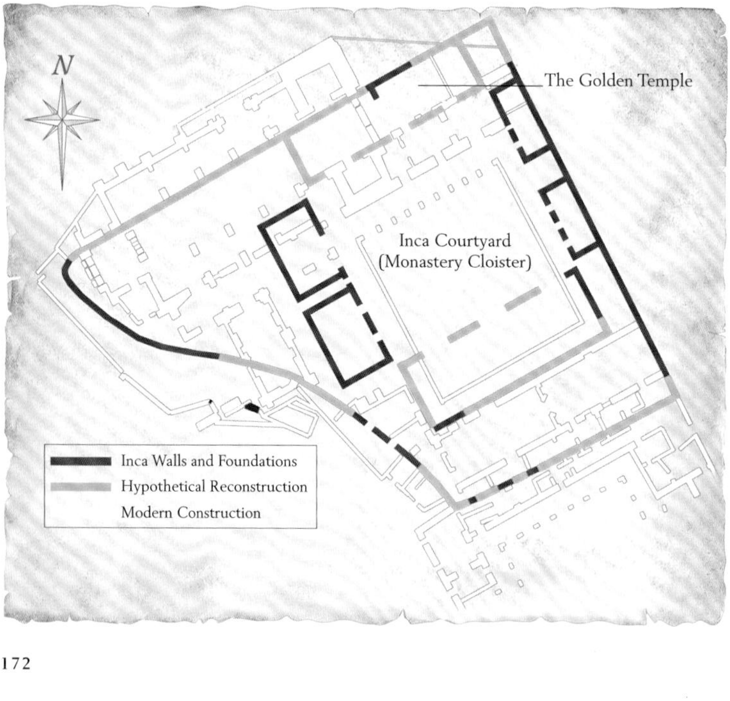

Above: Exterior of the Temple of the Moon in the Coricancha, Cuzco, showing the closely fitted blocks without mortar.

on their ritual journey following *ceque* lines back to their provinces, where they were sacrificed.

Other rooms were used to store the sacred objects taken from conquered provinces, including a *huaca* from each subjugated population. These *huacas* were kept in perpetual residence as hostages, and nobles from each subject population were forced to live in the capital for several months each year.

A GOLDEN GARDEN

The intimate mythological connection between Inti and gold was manifested in the temple garden. Here were gold and silver sculptures of a man, a woman, animals and plants representing creation. There were not only jaguars, llamas, guinea pigs and monkeys, but also birds, butterflies and other insects.

The arrangement of the Coricancha was established by the tenth emperor, Pachacuti Inca Yupanqui, in the 15th century, along with his rebuilding of much of the capital.

Something of its splendour was captured in the words of the conquistador Pedro de Cieza de León, as recorded in his *Crónica del Peru*, published in Seville between 1550 and 1553:

'[The temple was] more than 400 paces in circuit...[and the finely hewn masonry was] a dusky or black colour... [with] many openings and doorways... very well carved. Around the wall, half way up, there was a band of gold, two *palmos* wide and four *dedos* in thickness. The doorways and doors were covered with plates of the same metal. Within [there] were four houses, not very large, but with walls of the same kind and covered with plates of gold within and without.... In one of these houses...there was the figure of the Sun, very large and made of gold...enriched with many precious stones.

They also had a garden, the clods of which were made of pieces of gold; and it was artificially sown with golden maize, the stalks, as well as the leaves and cobs, being of that metal .... Besides all this, they had more than 20 golden sheep [llamas] with their lambs, and the shepherds with their slings and crooks to watch them, all made of the same metal. There was [also] a great quantity of jars of gold and silver, set with emeralds; vases, pots, and all sorts of utensils, all of fine gold.'

It was with this golden wealth of the Coricancha that Atahualpa attempted to secure his freedom when he was captured and imprisoned by Francisco Pizarro at Cajamarca in 1532.

Below: Each of the six deity chambers of the Coricancha temples was made with finely dressed stone masonry.

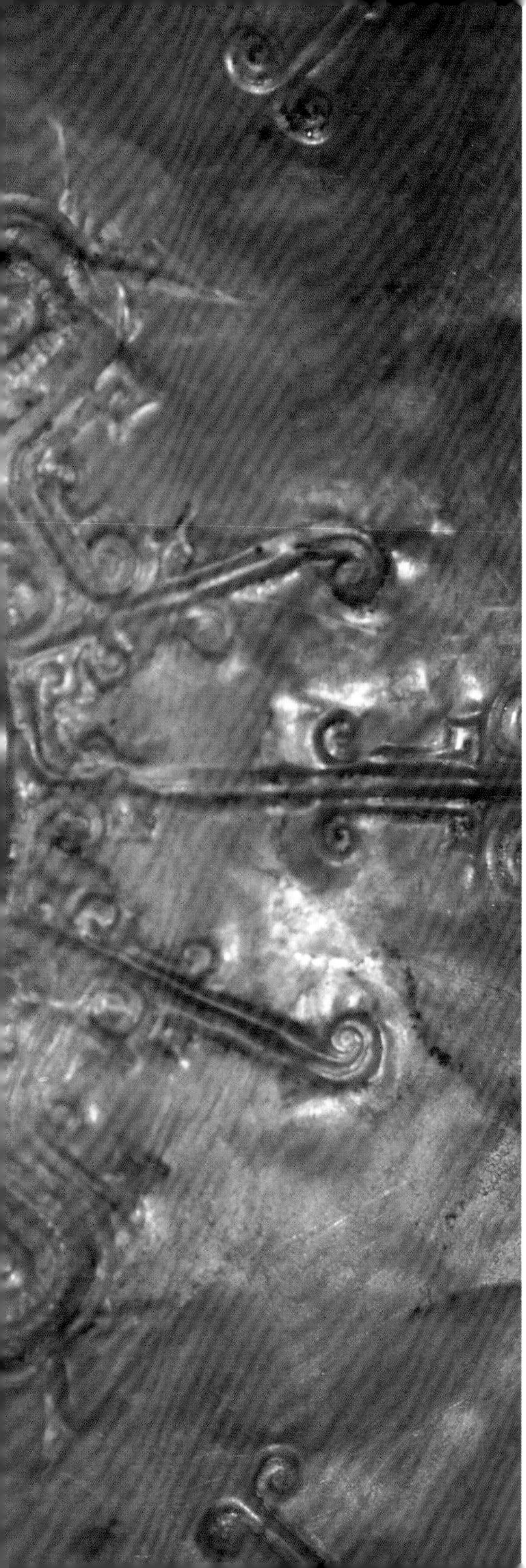

CHAPTER NINE

TALES OF THE GODS

Andean religious beliefs are replete with tales and stories of the deities and their representatives on Earth. However, it is not until the final stages of Andean history that we have this literature, and it is only because the stories were recorded by Spanish chroniclers, priests and administrators from their Inca informants.

These stories concentrate on Inca belief, creation and the rise of the Inca state. Some of the tales hark back to earlier cultures – those collected by the Inca in their conquests. For most of the pre-Inca cultures, however, we have only the archaeological evidence. For the Moche culture in particular, there is a rich 'narrative' of painted scenes on pottery, but most other imagery is of a more static than narrative nature. Nevertheless, an event in progress can be detected in the series of marching figures at Initial Period Cerro Sechín and in the tenoned stone heads on the walls of the temple court at Chavín de Huántar, showing the transformation of a shaman into a jaguar.

The use of creatures from distant, alien environments in the art reveals the contact of cultures across widely dispersed regions. By comparing the images with Inca history and mythological tales, it may be possible to find the origins of belief in pre-Inca cultures. Common imagery, modified through time, inevitably reflects continuity in belief.

Left: The face of the sun god on a gold dish made by a Manteño craftsman (Ecuador) at the far north of the Inca Empire.

SUN GOD AND MOON GODDESS

Ancient Andean traditions link the sun and moon as consorts, the sun being male and the moon female. Both were created and set into motion in the sky by Viracocha, the creator. His association with the sun in particular is made in the east–west orientation of his wanderings. The Islands of the Sun and of the Moon in Lake Titicaca were believed to be their birth places.

There is no doubt that the regular cycles of the sun and moon established recurrent, cyclical ritual calendars in ancient Andean cultures. The association of the sun with celestial matters and the moon with earthly cycles was probably reflected in the first ceremonial architecture – raised platforms symbolizing proximity to the sun and sunken courts providing links to the Earth.

Below: Silver and gold, 'tears of the moon' and 'sweat of the sun', represented an essential Andean duality.

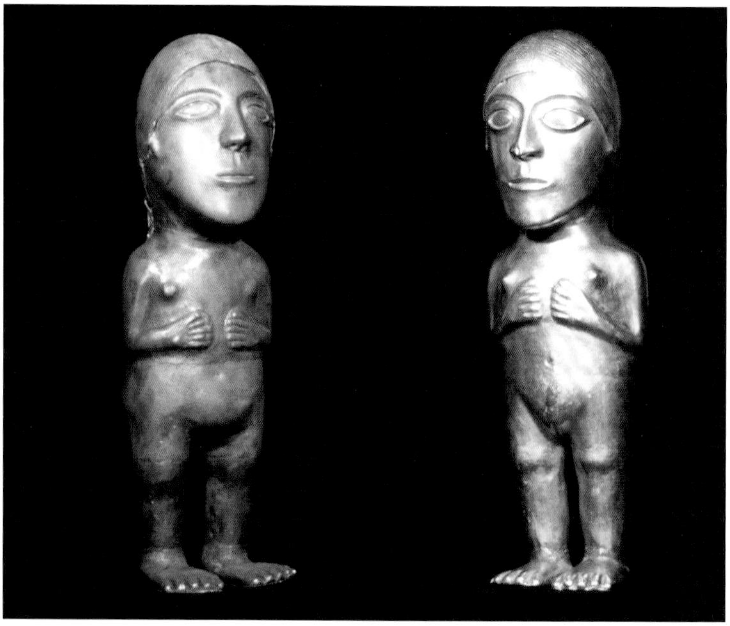

The sun and moon were the epitomy of the Andean concept of duality. As opposites they represented light and dark, warmth and cold. However their importance to life and its everyday cycle was balanced, and thus they achieved oneness through the unity of their cycles.

Neither the Incas nor more ancient Andeans made obvious images of the sun or moon. Faces with radiating appendages are common but cannot be categorically identified as the sun. Images of a crescent moon, however, are found among the pre-Inca northern coastal Moche and Chimú cultures, hinting at a complex mythological tradition now obscure. It may be that the Inca suppressed the Chimú's closer association with the moon by their advocacy of the state cult of Inti, the sun.

AI APAEC AND SI

Among the Moche and Chimú the sky god Ai Apaec was perhaps combined with the sun. He was a somewhat remote and

Above: Niches in the interior of the walls of the Temple of the Moon at Pisac resemble those in the Coricancha in Cuzco.

mysterious creator god who, like Viracocha, paid little attention to the daily affairs of humans. Pictured in art as a fanged deity, his throne was regarded as being the mountaintops. His perception as a sky god appears to be implied by his association with a tableau of two scenes separated by a two-headed serpent. In the upper part appear gods, demonic beings and stars; in the lower part are musicians, lords, or slaves, and rain falling from the serpent's body, implying a celestial and terrestrial division.

Si was the Moche and Chimú moon goddess or god, sometimes regarded as the head of the Moche and Chimú pantheon. He/she was a supreme deity, omnipresent, who held sway over the gods and humankind, and controlled the seasons, natural elements, storms and therefore agricultural fertility. His/her origins can be traced to an un-named radiant and armoured war deity who rivalled or even replaced Ai Apaec in importance among the Chimú. One source refers to a Temple of Si-an dedicated to Si, interpreted as the Huaca Singan in the Jequetepeque Valley, possibly the structure known today as the Huaca del Dragón.

The Moche and Chimú realized that the tides and other motions of the sea, and the arrival of the annual rains, were

Above: The sacred Intihuatana Temple to Inti the sun god at Pisac, a palace city of Pachacuti Inca Yupanqui, north-east of Cuzco.

linked to the phases of the moon, and thus allocated great power to Si because the food supply and well-being of flocks depended upon his/her beneficence. In contrast, the sun was considered to be a relatively minor deity. Si was regarded as more powerful than the sun because he/she could be seen by both night and day, and eclipses were believed to be battles between the moon and sun. An eclipse of the moon was considered a disastrous augury and regarded with fear; an eclipse of the sun, however, was treated as a joyful occasion.

INTI AND QUILLA

The Incas specifically claimed descent from the sun, but refer less frequently to the moon as their mother, and her role in Inca creation myth is less obvious. Nevertheless, the chronicler Garcilaso de la Vega describes the moon as sister and wife of the sun, and thus mother of the ancestral Incas.

The Incas worshipped Inti, the sun, but did not frequently portray him. The emperor was regarded as the 'son of the sun' and therefore Inti's embodiment on Earth. They associated the sun with gold, calling it the 'sweat of the sun', and the moon with silver, calling it the 'tears of the moon'. The sun and moon had separate chambers in the Coricancha Temple. The sun was represented by a sheet-gold mask with radiating gold appendages; the moon by a silver image in the shape of a woman.

The solstice days of Capac Raymi (summer/ December) and Inti Raymi (winter/ June) were auspicious days in the Inca ritual calendar.

The Inca empress was regarded as the earthly embodiment of the moon, Quilla, and in her role regulated lunar worship in the capital at Cuzco. A spring moon festival was held in October. An eclipse of the moon was believed by the Incas to be an attempt by a huge celestial serpent or mountain lion to eat Quilla. During such events they would gather in force in their sacred precincts and make as much noise as possible to scare off the creature.

Below: The Temple of the Moon at Machu Picchu was formed from fine masonry and built within a natural rock overhang.

FELINES AND SERPENTS

Feline, serpentine and reptilian imagery pervades Andean religion. Religious animism took the characteristics of such creatures and revered their power, guile and cunning. This was indicative of underlying religious ceremony. Shamans were frequently shown transformed, or transforming, into jaguars or snakes. The cayman was also prominent from early times. The use of feline and reptile imagery also reveals the widespread contacts between cultures that characterized Andean civilization.

Fangs are the most common feature, and they are sometimes indistinct; with claws and a cat-like face, or with a writhing body, the meaning becomes clear. Both images are frequently used in the same compositions.

JAGUARS AND OTHER FELINES

Jaguars and jaguar-humans are universal in the mythology of peoples throughout South America. Among Andean and Pacific coastal cultures the jaguar's face clearly inspired much of the 'fanged god' imagery from the earliest times to the Inca Empire. Its presence confirms the importance of the jungle and of jungle products from the earliest times. Feline creatures were frequently depicted in wall paintings and stone sculpture, and on ceramics, textiles and metalwork. Feline features, especially prominent curved canines, were used on humanoid beings representing shamans and inspired the monster gods of pre-Chavín, Chavín, Moche and Chimú art.

Left: A Late Intermediate Period Chimú wooden jaguar figure, inlaid with bone and mother of pearl, supporting a decorated gourd container.

Below: A complex row of cayman-like teeth on the cornice at the entrance to the sunken court of the New Temple at Chavín de Huántar.

An early example comes from the Initial Period Caballo Muerto Complex in the Moche Valley. The façade of the Huaca de los Reyes two-tiered platform is adorned with six huge, high-relief feline heads, each 2m (6½ft) high, framed within niches. Sculpted in adobe, they have wide feline noses, fangs protruding from drawn-back lips, pendant irises and deep facial scarifications – features that influenced later Chavín imagery. They were probably painted.

Jaguar imagery at Chavín de Huántar shows classic shamanic transformation. The Circular Sunken Courtyard within the wings of the U-shaped complex of the Old Temple had two sets of steps descending into it, aligned with the entrance to the central passageway of the temple. The stone-lined walls are made with two strata of large, flat rectangular (lower) and square (upper) slabs, separated by smaller rectangular blocks.

SHAMANIC TRANSFORMATION

The panels are carved in low relief. The upper panels show a parade of composite beings, depicted in profile and many carrying San Pedro hallucinogenic cactus stems. Their stance is human-like but their feet and hands have claws and their grimacing mouths with interlocking fangs show them to be transforming into jaguars. From their headdresses and waists hang snakes, the symbol of spiritual vision. The lower panels form a line of prowling jaguars. Upper and lower panels form

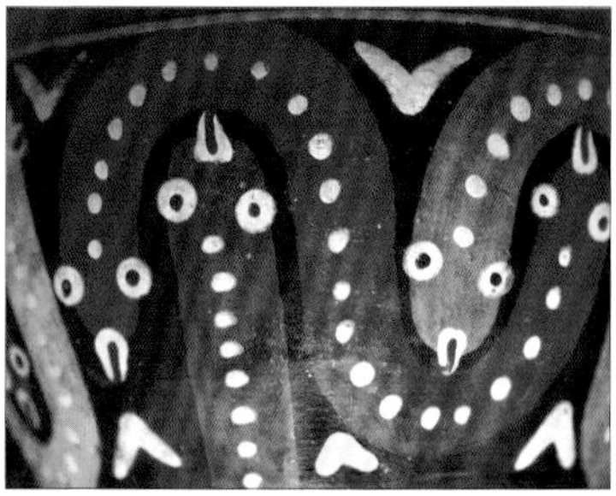

Below: Intertwined desert serpents decorating an Early Intermediate Period Nazca painted bowl.

Above: A feline head tops the sinuous serpentine body of an Early Intermediate Period Recuay effigy vessel.

human-like and animal pairs around the walls. Revealingly, the felines have coat markings that distinguish them as jaguars rather than as highland pumas, with their monochrome coats, and so confirms the mountain–jungle liaison.

The more than 40 tenoned stone heads adorning the New Temple walls of Chavín de Huántar give an equally graphic display of shamanic transformation. They were placed high up, spaced every few metres (yards). Although only one remains *in situ*, reconstruction based on the logic of changes in their features shows them to be a sequence of human to supernatural transformation, from shaman to feline.

Fanged beings remained prominent in the art of later cultures. The Moche Decapitator God has distinctive protruding fangs and double ear-ornaments and the Moche-Chimú sky or creator god Ai Apaec also has a distinctive feline mouth.

SNAKES

Serpentine imagery was as early as feline and, like fanged beasts, was pan-Andean and used in all media: wall paintings, stone carving, ceramic decoration, textiles and metalwork. Snakes feature on the earliest textiles from coastal Preceramic Huaca Prieta, shown in a typical double-meaning composition of snakes and crabs. The combination of a feline head with a serpentine body is also not infrequent.

Initial Period Moxeke has three high-relief, painted adobe sculptures on a 4m (13ft) wide panel on its principal platform. The left and central figures are headless torsos, probably deliberately decapitated; the right-hand sculpture is a colossal head, also probably a decapitation. The two torsos are caped figures, and the central figure has four snakes writhing down its front. The identities are uncertain, but the snakes on the central figure highlight its spiritual role, probably that of a shaman. The composite imagery and presence of snakes are indicative of transformation and spiritual vision. Similar adobe sculptures at Huaca de los Reyes show human-like figures with snakes hanging from their waists, as do figures in the circular sunken courtyard at Chavín de Huántar described above.

LANZÓN CAYMANS

The Lanzón monolith in the Old Temple at Chavín de Huántar displays many of the features described for later Chavín imagery, but is less specific. It portrays a fantastic beast with a tusked mouth and thick, up-turned lips and clawed hands and feet, but is not distinctively feline or reptilian. With only upper fangs, rather than the crossed canines of the jaguars of the circular sunken courtyard, its fanged mouth could have been inspired by several animals. More important is its association with snakes: they adorn its eyebrows, form its hair and dangle from its waistband. Its headdress comprises stacked feline heads, and its waistband is a row of similar feline faces. Significantly, one hand gestures up, the other down, indicating a supreme being whose rulership embraces the universe.

Below: A snarling jaguar-faced, bridge-spouted effigy vessel from the Early Intermediate Period Lima culture.

The New Temple Tello Obelisk depicts the creation myth and features two almost identical caymans, identifiable because a cayman's upper row of teeth shows even when its mouth is closed. Additionally, 'flame eyebrows' resemble the heavy brow-ridges, and the form of the legs and feet resemble those of crocodilians. Snakes' heads and other fanged faces also adorn the stone. The dual cayman image represents an early manifestation of duality. The arching figures of 'dragons' at Chimú Huaca del Dragón appear to combine feline, serpentine and celestial elements in a single rainbow-like image.

THE STAFF DEITY

The Staff Deity was the earliest widespread pan-Andean deity. The image originated in the Early Horizon with the Chavín Cult and endured to the Late Intermediate Period. The Staff Deity was portrayed frontally with outstretched arms holding staffs, and could be either male or female. He/she epitomizes the Chavín Cult and the early development of pan-Andean religious belief.

COMPOSITE BEING

Much Chavín imagery was inspired by the natural world. The Staff Deity was a composite human-like being, with male, female or non-distinct genitals. Like other Chavín imagery, the hands and feet end in claws, the mouth displays curved feline fangs, pendant irises hang from the curve of the eyes and the ears are bedecked with all kinds of ornaments. Outstretched arms clutch staffs in one form or another, and they are themselves often festooned with spikes and plume-like decorations. In many cases the staffs held by the Staff Deity are writhing snakes.

THE RAIMONDI STELA

At Chavín de Huántar, the pilgrimage centre of the cult, the most distinctive portrayal of the Staff Deity is undoubtedly the Raimondi Stela (1.98m/6½ft h). Its stylistic similarity to the human-like creatures on the columns of the Black and White Portal of the New Temple suggest that it once stood within one of the New Temple's chambers.

The image on the Raimondi Stela is an incised composition on a highly polished granite-ashlar slab. It has all the hallmarks of the Staff Deity: clawed feet, taloned hands, down-turned, snarling, fanged mouth and pendant irises. Curiously, its genitalia are non-specific. Perhaps, as the most important cult deity at the central cult city, it was meant to represent the unity of opposites (male and female) in order to achieve balance in the Andean worldview.

DUAL MEANING

The Raimondi Stela is not simply a portrait of the Staff Deity. It is an early example of complex, multiple meanings within one image. When viewed as a standing figure, the stela is clearly a Staff Deity wearing an elaborate headdress. The staffs are made up of faces, snakes, vegetation and curved embellishments. Viewed more closely, the headdress comprises similar vegetation, feather-like projections and what appear to be two stacked faces or miniature-bodied standing figures.

This is not all: if the entire image is inverted it shows a different figure. The same principal incised lines of the

Left: A bizarre Staff Deity-like warrior figure on a shallow dish of the Middle Horizon Cajamarca culture of northern Peru.

Above: Andean representations of the Staff Deity in art would be either male or female. This version is male.

Staff Deity face form a new face. What were the irises become nostrils above an upturned, toothy and be-tusked mouth; what were the nostrils of a pug nose become upraised irises; and what were apparent chin dimples beneath the down-turned mouth become the eyes of a grinning face on the forehead of the new face. Finally, the elements that made up the headdress of the Staff Deity image become three sinister-looking faces in which the pendant irises of the headdress faces become nostrils and the new dark areas become widely spaced squinting sets of eyes.

The Staff Deity image appears to be rising, and its various sets of eyes appear to gaze skyward. The inverted features, however, appear to plunge from the sky.

WHO WAS THE STAFF DEITY?

The exact significance and meaning of the Staff Deity is uncertain. His/her power is attested by the number images at Chavín de Huántar on stones and walls, and throughout the central Andes and coast on portable objects. He/she appears to be predominantly associated with agricultural fertility, which is incorporated in the composite features.

The Raimondi Stela image, however, clearly demonstrates aspects of the earliest universals in Andean religion. The profound complexity of the image gives an equally profound religious message of duality within unity. The celestial orientation of one image and the earthly orientation of the other reveal two deities within one composition. The very viewing point for each of the images points to its respective realm. In context with a platform mound and sunken court at Chavín de Huántar, the theme of dual divinity – sky god and earth goddess – was disclosed. Further, the deep recesses of the New Temple secreted meaning and divided worshippers into inclusive and exclusive groups.

Above: The Raimondi Stela, depicting the supreme deity of the Chavín Cult, can be viewed with meaning either way up.

Above: A female representation of the Staff Deity, showing outstretched arms clasping staffs festooned with decorations.

AN ENDURING DEITY

The Staff Deity's potency is likewise demonstrated by endurance. The imagery is interrupted in the Late Intermediate Period, but early colonial depictions of the Inca kings show them holding a staff in each hand. Such exceptional importance through longevity imbues the Staff Deity with a distinct 'personality' and the supernatural power of an early creator god.

Chavín Staff Deity images were found everywhere throughout central Andean and Pacific coastal sites in the Early Horizon, on stone sculptures, ceramics and textiles. Of particular note are the Staff Deity images painted on cotton textiles from the Karwa culture of the Paracas Peninsula. There are more than 25 of them, all clearly female. Appendages of cotton growing from the staffs and headdress symbolize the principal agriculture of the coast, and perhaps reveal her to be wife or consort of the Chavín deity, in a locally focused cult.

The most prominent Middle Horizon representation of the Staff Deity is the central figure on the monumental portal at Tiwanaku. Staff Deity images are frequent in both Tiwankau and Wari art.

MUMMIFICATION AND THE OCULATE BEING

The Paracas culture of southern coastal Peru was one of the first Andean cultures to practise mummification. Great reverence is shown by the elaborate preparation of the bodies. The mummies were 'bundled' in tight, foetal positions, placed in baskets and wrapped in layers of high-quality cotton and llama-wool textiles displaying a wealth of natural imagery and supernatural iconography – a rich mythology associated with ritual practices. The burials were accompanied by decorated and plain pottery, many in the shapes of animal effigies, and by sheet-gold ornaments. The freshness of the textiles indicates they were made specifically for burial. Some pieces were even unfinished before needed!

Above: In this woven example, a human-like Oculate Being has whiskers, eyes with pupils, a golden diadem headpiece, and trophy heads.

Among and between sprawling areas of habitation, special necropolis sites had been chosen for hundreds of burials. These might have been the foci of family cults. As the numbers of burials appear to exceed the needs of the immediately adjacent settlements, it is thought that the Paracas necropolises might also have been pilgrimage centres for a regional cult, with honoured individuals being brought from more distant settlements for burial.

A LOCAL DEITY

The Paracas style was heavily influenced by the Chavín style of the north-central Andes, but had soon developed its own regional flavour. Without written records we can only surmise the names and details of Paracas deities and ceremonial practices. Fanged creatures – highly stylized feline faces – feature frequently on textiles and ceramics, but among them one is especially prominent: the Oculate Being.

Left: The Nazca inherited the Paracas Oculate Being. In this rather stylized version, the Oculate Being is shown with his essential feature: blank, staring eyes.

The Oculate Being was most often portrayed horizontally on textiles and ceramics, as if flying, often upside-down (perhaps looking down on humankind), and crouching. With no distinctively female attributes, 'he' is assumed to be male. He has a characteristic, frontal face with large, circular, staring eyes – hence the name. Long, streaming appendages originate from various parts of his body and end in trophy heads or small figures.

He is depicted on textiles and pots, and in the form of distinctive ceramic masks brightly painted with his countenance. Significantly, the Oculate Being is the only image shown on these masks, a fact, it is argued, that emphasizes his importance as a regional deity. His face is often heart-shaped on pottery and in textiles, and sometimes sprouts a smaller head from its top. On other figures, he wears a headband identical to sheet-gold headbands found in some Paracas burials.

SHAMANS AND SERPENTS

Dilated eyes are characteristic of shamanic vision, perhaps inspired by the perceived powers of the round, reflective eyes of nocturnal animals. Numerous birds are depicted in Paracas and Nazca art, in all media, and it is not surprising that the owl was known in later Andean religion as an alter-ego of the shaman.

Despite his regional ownership, the Oculate Being employs the universal Andean iconography of the serpent. Flying Oculate Beings often have long, trailing serpentine tongues; on one textile, two images share a tongue, forming a duality. They often wear writhing belts of snakes trailing behind their legs, demonstrating a sense of artistic perspective. Oculate Being masks have undulating double-headed snakes across the face; on some such masks the forehead snake forms the arms of the miniature figure on the brow, and the figure itself also has a serpent across its forehead.

Above: Here the Oculate Being is shown several times inside a ceramic bowl with typical feline attributes, serpentine tongue, snakes and sky symbols.

DECAPITATION

There are also indications of ritual decapitation. One textile shows a group of flying Oculate Beings each carrying a crescent-shaped knife typical of the *tumi* shape known to be used for decapitation, especially among the Moche, Lambayeque (Sicán) and Chimú cultures of the Early Intermediate to Late Intermediate Periods. Other images of the Oculate Being show him holding a staff, not in a frontal stance with two staffs, like the Staff Deity of the Chavín Cult, but still possibly inspired by Chavín iconography. Later Paracas textiles show the Oculate Being more stylistically, owing partly to the use of a new weaving technique known as discontinuous warp and weft.

In the Early Intermediate Period, the Oculate Being cult continued to form an important part of the art images of the succeeding Nazca culture in the same region. One Nazca painted textile shows figures facing forwards and holding agricultural products. Their visages appear bespectacled and they have strange flaring moustaches and beards. One holds a mask. Another painted textile, known as the 'Harvest Festival', shows a crowded scene of little figures, facing front, with outstretched arms holding agricultural produce. Their stances resemble the Staff Deity, while their faces have the wide-eyed stare characteristic of the Oculate Being or of shamanic trance.

THE MEANING OF THE BEING

The role of the Oculate Being is difficult to determine. His round visage, association with flying and burial, and depiction with decapitation knives all indicate attributes of a god of the sun, sky, death or sacrifice. With such combined characteristics, perhaps he was an early manifestation of the supreme deity. The relationship between the Oculate Being and the Chavín Staff Deity is equally unknown, despite the appearance of unmistakeable Chavín influence at Karwa, just south of the Paracas cemeteries.

THE DECAPITATOR GOD

In a diamond frame, the grimacing face of a fearsome-looking half-human, half-jaguar peers from the walls of Platform I and the Great Plaza of the Huaca de la Luna at Moche. Stylized, stepped supernatural faces surround it, linked by a common 'thread' as if woven in textile. The face is outlined in red. Black hair and a beard curl from the head and chin. A sausage-shaped, down-turned mouth snarls, displaying human-like rows of white teeth and interlocked feline canines. His ears appear to be pierced and decorated with double ear-ornaments. Huge white eyes underlined in black and with heavy red brows stare menacingly with large black pupils. Curious, alien-looking miniature faces surround the head. This mural depicts the Decapitator God. What fear and reverence might he have struck in citizens as they stood beneath his gaze watching priests perform ritual sacrifice?

Above: There is no mistaking this sheet-metal and shell inlay depiction of the Decapitator God, with his grinning sinister expression, tumi *sacrificial knife and his latest victim's head.*

Below: Murals at the Huaca de la Luna depict a wide-eyed shamanic face with pierced ears, human teeth and feline canines.

RITUAL BLOOD-LETTING

The Decapitator God so graphically dominating the Moche capital was depicted in friezes and murals in temples and tombs, and on ceramics and metalwork at Moche and other north coastal valley sites, including Sipán in the Lambayeque Valley. He has several guises: as an overpowering face that grips one's attention, or full-figured, holding a crescent-shaped *tumi* ceremonial knife in one hand and a severed human head in the other. The elaborate plaster friezes at the Huaca de la Luna of Early Intermediate Period Moche are the most renowned, but the development of his imagery can be traced back to the Early Horizon in the preceding Cupisnique culture of the same region.

The Decapitator God is portrayed in an elaborate blood-letting rite painted on pottery and on temple and tomb walls. His role, acted out by priests, embodied a gruesome sacrificial ritual. Although once thought to be merely representational of a mythical event, archaeological evidence discovered in the 1980s attests to its reality. An enclosure behind the Huaca de la Luna platform contained the buried remains of 40 men, aged 15 to 30. They appear to have been pushed off a stone outcrop after having been mutilated and killed. The structure, outcrop and enclosure seem to mirror the nearby Cerro Blanco and valley. Some skeletons were splayed out as if tied to stakes; some had their femurs torn from the pelvis joints; skulls, ribs, fingerbones, armbones and legbones have cut marks. Several severed heads had their jaws torn away.

A thick layer of sediment, deposited during heavy rains, covered the gruesome scene, and it is suggested that the sacrifice was performed in response to an El Niño event that might have disrupted the economic stability of the realm.

RITUAL COMBAT

The Decapitator God and sacrificial ritual are put into context by scenes painted on Moche ceramics and walls. Friezes show warriors in paired combat, almost always both wearing Moche armour and bearing Moche arms. The combatants are shown in narrative sequences: instead of killing a vanquished foe, the loser is next shown stripped and tied by the neck with a rope, being marched off for their arraignment. The final scenes show the captives naked, having their throats slit. Their blood is given in goblets to four presiding figures.

The most elaborate of these is the Warrior Priest. He wears a crescent-shaped metal plate to protect his back, and rattles hang from his belt. To his right sits the Bird Priest, wearing a conical helmet bearing the image of an owl and a long beak-like nose-ornament. Next to him is a priestess, identified by her long, plaited tresses, dress-like costume and plumed and tasselled headdress. The final figure, with a feline face, wears a headdress with serrated border and long streamers.

THE REAL THING

These scenes show ritual warfare in fields near Moche cities for the purpose of 'capturing' victims for sacrifices to the gods. Excavations in the 1980s of unlooted Sipán tombs in the Lambayeque Valley dated *c.*AD300 corroborate their actual occurrence. The elite citizens buried in the tombs, accompanied by sacrificial victims, were richly adorned and surrounded by the artefacts of sacrifice and ritual; the bodies were decorated with gold, silver, turquoise and other jewellery, and textiles. They wore costumes identical to those of the four figures in the sacrificial ceremonies.

Right: A Chimú gold sacrificial knife handle, representing the legendary leader and conqueror Naymlap.

The principal body personifies the Warrior Priest. He wore a crescent-shaped back-flap and belt rattles, just as in the scene. The Decapitator God image decorates both back-flap and rattles – in this case the face is symbolized by a spider with a human face, perched on a golden web. The spider imagery is thought to reflect the parallel of the blood-letting and sucking the life juices of its prey. Offerings included three pairs of gold and turquoise ear-spools – one of which shows a Moche warrior in full armour – a gold, crescent-shaped headdress, a crescent-shaped nose-ornament, and one gold and one silver *tumi* knife. At the Warrior Priest's side lay a box-like gold sceptre, embossed with combat scenes, and a spatula-like handle of silver studded with military trappings.

Near by, another tomb, less rich, contained the body of a noble with a gilded copper headdress decorated with an owl with outspread wings – clearly the Bird Priest. Sealed rectangular rooms near the tombs contained more offerings, including the bones of severed human hands and feet.

Two tombs dated *c.*AD 500–600 at San José de Moro in the Jequetepeque Valley contained the skeletons of women. Their silver-alloyed copper headdresses had tassels and other accoutrements of the priestess figure. Finally, at El Brujo in the Chicama Valley, a terrace frieze shows a life-size warrior leading a procession of ten nude prisoners by a rope placed around their necks. On a terrace above (later destroyed by looters) was a huge spider or crab with a fanged mouth and double ear-ornaments, one leg brandishing a *tumi* knife – the 'arachnoid decapitator'.

CON THE CREATOR

Con created and shaped the natural world, made the first generation of humans and gave life to the animals and plants. He is central in a generic creation myth, but is not always benevolent. His name forms part of other Andean creator deities such as Con Tici (or Titi) Viracocha Pachayachachic, Coniraya Viracocha of the early 17th-century *Huarochirí Manuscript*, and Wakon. The word 'con' is indicative of heat, energy and creation.

CON VERSUS PACHACAMAC

Con was a formless figure, without bones or joints, who came from the north and was a child of the sun and the moon. After walking up and down the coast, shaping the land and creating all things in it, he disappeared into the sea and ascended into the sky.

The central Andean Colloas believed that Con created the sun, then made stone figures of the various Andean peoples, whom he placed throughout the valleys before bringing them to life and instructing them in his worship.

Con's rival or opposite was Pachacamac. Because he had left the world's inhabitants without a leader or protector, Pachacamac, who came from the south, transformed these first humans into pumas/jaguars, foxes, monkeys and parrots.

WAKON AND THE SPIDER

In a later tradition, Wakon was a malevolent being opposed to Pachacamac, who, with his consort Pacha Mama, were sky and earth deities respectively. Their union produced twins, a boy and a girl, after which Pachacamac died and disappeared into the sea, leaving Pacha Mama and the twins alone.

Wakon, who lived in a cave, appeared semi-naked to the twins. He asked them to fetch some water and while they were away seduced Pacha Mama. He ate part of her and threw the rest of her body into a cooking pot. When the twins returned and learned of her fate, they fled. Wakon asked

Above: A puma-headed reed boat on Lake Titicaca on whose shore the survivors from the flood landed.

the animals and birds where the twins were hiding. Spider suggested that he go to a mountaintop and call to the twins, imitating Pacha Mama's voice. Spider, however, had prepared a trap, a chasm on the mountain, into which Wakon fell and was destroyed, causing a violent earthquake. Pachacamac then returned, apologized to the twins and transformed his son into the sun and his daughter into the moon. Pacha Mama 'survived' as the snow-capped mountain La Viuda (the widow).

In later myths, Con became blended with Viracocha. The central Andean Cachas, for example, called him Con Tici Viracocha Pachayachachic, literally 'god, creator of the world'.

CON TICI OF THE TIWANAKU

In one version of the Inca creation myth, related by the 16th-century chronicler Cristobal de Molina, the world was already peopled when a great flood destroyed all except one man and one woman. They were cast up on land at Tiwanaku, where Con Tici Viracocha appeared to them and created a second race of humans of clay and stone in the Titicaca Basin, including the Inca ancestors. He also made birds and animals, two of each, and spread them among their habitats, designated their foods, and gave each bird its song.

He named two of his creations (sometimes said to be his sons) Imaymana Viracocha and Tocapo Viracocha, the inclusion of 'Viracocha' imbuing them with divinity and supernatural power. With them he travelled throughout the land giving life to the peoples, animals and plants that he had created. Imaymana Viracocha went north-westwards along the forest and mountain borders, Tocapo Viracocha went northwards along the coasts, and Con Tici Viracocha went along a route between them,

Below: Con/Viracocha, the bodiless or formless deity, is appropriately represented in this blocky, rather abstract form.

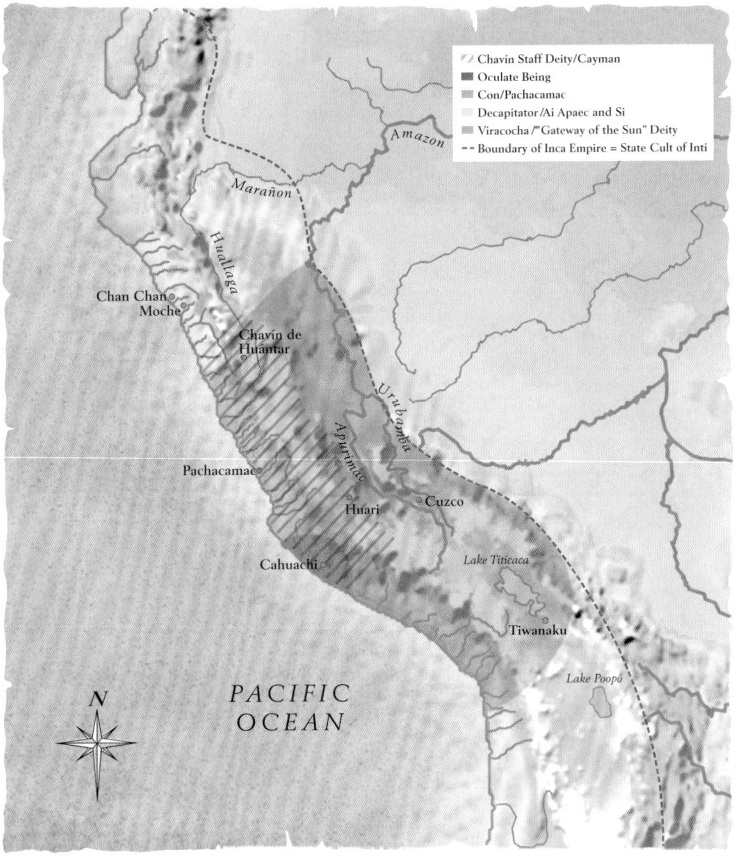

Above: Map showing the distribution of the major creator deities, from the Decapitator in the north to the Oculate Being in the south.

through the mountains. They continued to what became the north-westernmost edge of the Inca Empire, to the coastal site of Manta, where they walked out across the sea until they disappeared.

Coniraya Viracocha of central Andean Huarochirí mythology, like Con, was a coastal creator deity who wandered throughout the world, reshaping the landscape before disappearing across the western sea. Like Wakon, Coniraya sought Pachacamac's children by asking the animals and birds about them.

HISTORY BEHIND A MYTH?

The conflict between Con and Pachacamac might represent the later mythologizing of historical consciousness, a shared general memory of past events in a culture without written records. In the versions related above, Con comes from either north or south, and travels up and down the coasts, mountains and forests. From the north, he would have represented a Moche or earlier deity of the northern coastal valleys. It has also been suggested that the shapeless Con is represented by the flying human-like sky deities on the textiles and pottery of the Paracas and Nazca peoples of the southern coasts, and continued as the winged attendants associated with the Staff Deity at Tiwanaku. Together, these cultures span the Early Horizon, Early Intermediate Period and Middle Horizon.

The conflict between them and the replacement of Con by Pachacamac would thus reflect the decline of southern cults and the rise of the importance of middle coastal Pachacamc as a deity, and of his associated temple and pilgrimage cult.

THE YAYA-MAMA RELIGIOUS TRADITION

A tall stone post from Taraco on the northern shore of Lake Titicaca is carved on all four faces. Two opposite faces have a male and a female figure, giving the name Yaya-Mama – father and mother – to a regional cult. Below each figure, and on the other two faces, there are writhing serpents. Three of the four serpents on the faces adjacent to the figured faces are double-headed.

Above: At Lake Titicaca the cult of Yaya-Mama/Pukará was established at ceremonial centres around the lake.

A REGIONAL CULT

Pukará, another Yaya-Mama site north of the lake, flourished as a regional cult centre in the late Early Horizon and Early Intermediate Period, before the rise of the Wari and Tiwanaku states to the north and south. Yaya-Mama developed independently of the Chavín Cult to the north, and provided the template for later south-central Andean civilization. Tiwanaku people revered the Yaya-Mama tradition, as evidenced by their incorporation of Yaya-Mama sculptures in their own ceremonial complexes. For example, Yaya-Mama Stela 15 (2m/6½ft high) was erected beside the much taller Bennett Monolith (7.4m/24ft high) in the Semi-subterranean Temple at Tiwanaku; and the lower part of the Arapa-Thunderbolt Stela was taken from Arapa, at the north end of the lake, and placed in the Putuni Palace at Tiwanku. Altogether there are a total of seven Pukará sculptures at the city of Tiwanaku.

Pukará stone sculpture is blocky and columnar. Its imagery features flat, squared-oval eyes. Movement is indicated in the poses and limbs of figures, and ribs show prominently. Hands sometimes hold objects. Heads are frequently rayed with feathers and animal images emanating from the main heads. As well as monumental stone sculpture, there were roofless temples and sunken courts, complex supernatural artistic symbols and ritual paraphernalia.

Dozens of Pukará temple sites are distributed more or less equidistantly around Lake Titicaca, located on hill summits, on artificial platforms and at the bases of cliffs. Yaya-Mama temples typically comprise a rectangular sunken court, which is surrounded by individual, multi-chambered structures arranged symmetrically around the court. The courts are stone lined, either plain or carved with heads that have appendages radiating from them. Sometimes there are burials around the court.

Left: Pukará ceramics shared features that resemble later Tiwanaku styles in the use of incised decoration and colours.

A TWO-PHASED TRADITION

Most Yaya-Mama stone sculptures have not been found *in situ*. Some are still objects of local veneration. Lasting about a millennium, the style comprises two phases, characterized by examples from Chiripa (earlier) and Pukará (later). Earlier pieces are mostly pecked designs of geometric symbols, animals and humans on stone slabs or four-sided posts. Later examples are incised and carved in the round, showing greater finishing. Generally, human figures are carved in the round while animals and geometric motifs are in low relief.

Early Yaya-Mama stone imagery shows pairs of figures, male and female, with arms raised to their chests. Human heads have appendages radiating from them that often end in triangular serpent heads. There are also severed human heads.

Above: The characteristic Pukará-style Yaya-Mama features a life-size or larger stone head with a turban-like headdress.

Animals include felines, birds with outstretched wings, frogs and/or toads, snakes, or supernatural serpentine creatures with flared ears and zigzag bodies. Geometric designs include checkered and Maltese-like crosses, chevrons and rings.

The most common animal on pottery is the spotted feline – the spotted coat indicating the jaguar rather than the monochrome mountain lion. There are also trophy heads and dismembered sacrificial victims, birds, coiled snakes and camalids. The characteristic vertical division of eyes into black and white halves of Tiwanaku and Wari imagery is first seen in Pukará art, as are tears below the eyes.

Later Pukará stone sculptures feature large slabs carved with felines, coiled snakes, frogs and/or toads, steps, volutes and zigzags. Humans are carved in the round. There are seated and standing males figures, one wearing a serpent-head decorated hat. The Pukará Decapitator depicts a seated male figure, holding an axe in his right hand and a severed head in his left. His cap is decorated with supernatural faces. He is either a supernatural composite being, or a man wearing a representative mask with a fanged mouth. The round, staring eyes are indicative of shamanic trance or transformation.

RITUAL PARAPHERNALIA

Yaya-Mama ritual paraphernalia includes ceremonial burners, ceramic and *Strombus* shell trumpets, miniature pottery vessels, including painted and effigy-shaped pieces, and architectural models. Pottery vessels are invariably found in pieces and contexts that indicate deliberate breakage.

Two prominent ceramic themes are the 'feline man' and the 'woman with alpaca'. The first depicts pairs of fanged men lunging forward or running, facing each other or one chasing the other. Each figure carries a severed head and a staff. Some figures wear feline pelts. The 'woman with alpaca' shows a single, skirted, frontal-standing figure leading an alpaca by a rope. She carries a bag and holds a distinctive staff with an I-shaped head, and she wears a plumed cap. She is associated with plants and sometimes a rayed-head motif.

From the Pukará temple come rectangular stone boxes, subdivided and externally decorated on six equal panels with stylized faces, each with 16 appendages ending in a variety of serpent or circular heads. Ceramic models are of miniature temples, complete with the details of their windows and doors.

These objects and images imply ritual combat, agricultural and pastoral themes, and fertility. Ritual clearly included incense burning, feasting and music-making. Images of severed heads – a feature of religious symbolism throughout the Andean Area – and dismembered bodies, and a cache of human mandibles found at Pukará, indicate ritual sacrifice and/or warfare, either in the real world or in the world of mythological concept.

Below: Accurate, individual and natural features are complemented by ringed/lidded eyes, but without pupils.

VIRACOCHA: THE SUPREME ANDEAN DEITY

Viracocha was the supreme deity, almost universally regarded throughout the Andean Area as the creator of the universe, the human race and all living things. He became a rather remote and inaccessible deity, although regarded as omnipresent and inescapable.

In Cuzco he was represented in his own shrine by a golden statue slightly smaller than life. He was white, bearded and wore a long tunic, as described by the Spaniards who first saw him there. In Inca legend, he travelled south to Cacha, *c.*100km (60 miles) south of Cuzco, where another temple and statue were dedicated to his worship. Another shrine and statue were at Urcos.

THE PRIMORDIAL CREATOR

To the Incas, Viracocha was primordial. He remained nameless, and instead was referred to by descriptive terms befitting his role in the various permutations of the creation myth. He was Illya ('light'), Tici ('the beginning of things'), Atun Viracocha ('great creator), or Viracocha Pachayachachic ('lord, instructor of the world'). The earliest Spanish chroniclers to describe him, Cieza de León and Juan de Betanzos around 1550, personify him, but to ancient Andeans 'he' represented a concept – the force of creative energy. The Quechua elements of his name, *vira* ('fat, grease, foam') and *cocha* ('lake, sea, reservoir'), can be rendered as 'sea fat', 'sea foam', or 'the lake of creation'.

As supreme deity, Viracocha's name has been used for the creator god in the pantheons of many pre-Inca cultures. Much of his history and legend therefore owes to the Inca's adoption of him from their conquered subjects. For example, his portrayal with weeping eyes was a characteristic almost certainly adopted from the weeping god imagery of Tiwanaku. In Inca legend he bestowed a special headdress and stone battle-axe on Manco Capac, the first Inca ruler, and prophesied that the Incas would become great lords and would conquer many other nations. Viracocha Inca, the 15th-century eighth Inca ruler, took his name, presumably as representing strength and creative energy. As a concept, he could also be regarded as "shapeless" or "boneless".

Above: Viracocha came to be associated with other sky symbols such as the double-headed rainbow serpent found in Chimú art.

CREATION AND LAKE TITICACA

Many Andean cultures believed that Lake Titicaca was where the sun, moon and stars were created, and that the lake waters were the tears of Viracocha acknowledging the sufferings of his creations.

Viracocha first created a world of darkness, then populated it with humans fashioned from stone. But he was disobeyed, so he destroyed them with a flood or by transforming them back into stones. These beings could be seen, it was thought, at ruined cities such as Tiwanaku and Pukará. Only one man and one woman survived, and were magically transported to Tiwanaku, where the gods dwelled.

Viracocha next created a new race of humans, and animals, of clay. He painted distinctive clothes on the humans and gave them customs, languages, songs, arts and crafts, and the gift of agriculture to distinguish the different peoples and nations. Breathing life into them, he instructed them to descend into the earth and disperse, then to re-emerge through caves, and from lakes and hills. These places became sacred, and shrines were established at them in honour of the gods.

Above: *A portrayal of Viracocha's face in sheet gold features typical Tiwanaku sun rays around the head, and weeping eyes.*

The world was still dark, so Viracocha ordered the sun, moon and stars to rise into the sky from the islands in Lake Titicaca.

SPREADING CIVILIZATION

After his creations, Viracocha set out from the Titicaca Basin to spread civilization, but he did so as a beggar, bearded, dressed in rags, and under many names, and dependant on others for his sustenance. In other accounts he was described as a tall white man wearing a sun crown. Many of those he encountered reviled him. He was assisted by two of his creations, variously called his sons or brothers: Imaymana Viracocha and Tocapo Viracocha. The inclusion of the name 'Viracocha' imbued them with divinity and supernatural power.

He commanded Imaymana Viracocha to travel north-westward along a route bordering the forests and mountains and Tocapo Viracocha to journey northward along a coastal route. He himself followed a route between them, north-westward through the mountains. As they passed through the land, they called out the people, named the trees and plants, established the times when each would flower and bear fruit, and instructed the people about which were edible and which medicinal. They taught humankind the arts and crafts, agriculture and the ways of civilization, and worked miracles among them, until they reached Manta on the Ecuadorian coast (the most north-western edge of the Inca Empire), where they continued across the sea, walking on the water until they disappeared.

Below: Temples were dedicated to Viracocha throughout the Inca Empire, as here at Rachi in the Vilcanota Valley.

Another version, recorded by Cristobal de Molina, begins with the world already peopled. A great flood destroyed all except one man and one woman, who were cast up on land at Tiwanaku. Con Tici Viracocha appeared to them and ordered them to remain there as *mitimaes* (people resettled by the Incas), then repopulated the land by making the Inca ancestors out of clay, and as before, giving them customs, languages and clothing.

This active role on Earth likens Viracocha to the preacher heroes in much pre-Inca legend. To the Incas, Viracocha remained remote, interacting with humans through other gods, particularly Inti, the sun god, and Illapa, god of weather. His purposeful travels relate to ancient Andean pilgrimage traditions. The trinity implied by the three Viracochas suggests a strong element of Christian interpretation in the descriptions of the Spanish chroniclers.

PACHACAMAC THE CREATOR

Pachacamac, 'earth/time maker', was the creator deity of the peoples of the central Peruvian coast. His Quechua root words, *pacha* ('time/space', 'universe/earth', 'state of being') and *camac* ('creator', 'animator') render him as potent as Viracocha and reveal lowland–highland association through the spread of Quechua from coastal regions to the Andes.

AN ANCIENT ORACLE

The centre of Pachacamac's worship was the pilgrimage city and oracle of the same name near modern Lima. The 16th-century chronicler Cieza de León noted Inca reverence for the shrine, and the 17th-century writer Father Bernabe Cobo describes it in detail. The Earth Maker was represented by a wooden staff (destroyed by Hernando Pizarro, brother of the conquistador) carved with a human face on both sides and housed in an oracular chamber, epitomizing the Andean concept of duality. Other carved wooden idols, which were scattered about the city, survive from other parts of the site.

Below: For more than a millennium, complexes of courtyards at Pachacamac accommodated pilgrims.

Pachacamac's following was ancient and widespread among central coastal civilizations, enduring from the Early Intermediate Period for more than a millennium. The oracle, like Early Horizon Chavín de Huántar, drew visitors from throughout the lowland plains and valleys, and the adjacent Andes. The principal temple platform was surrounded by a vast complex of courtyards and subsidiary platforms for the accommodation of pilgrims. Like Lake Titicaca and the Coricancha in Cuzco, it was one of the most sacred sites in the Inca Empire.

THE CREATION MYTH

There are many threads to Pachacamac's mythology. He was a serious rival to Viracocha. His cult developed independently and much earlier than that of Inca Inti, but the predominance of ancient contact between the coastal lowlands and the Andean highlands inevitably brought the two creator gods into 'contact' at an early date, long before the Inca compulsion to incorporate all their subjects' myths and pantheons of gods.

Mythology shows the two deities to have distinct identities, yet many similar traits: they created the world; they held control over the creation and destruction of the first people; they travelled throughout the lands and taught, often in the guise of a beggar, and punished those who mocked them for this; they met, named, and gave their characters to the animals and plants.

Above: Guaman Poma de Ayala's depiction of a child sacrifice to Pachacamac in his Nueva Crónica y Buen Gobierno, *c.1613.*

In the principal myth, Pachacamac was the son of the sun and moon. An earlier deity, Con, had created the first people, but Pachacamac overcame him, and transformed the first people into monkeys and other animals.

Pachacamac then created man and woman, but, because he did not provide them with food, the man died. The woman solicited the sun's help, or in another version accused the sun of neglecting his duty, and in return was impregnated by the sun's rays. When she bore a son, she taught him to survive by eating wild plants. Pachacamac, jealous of his father (the sun) and angered by this independence and apparent defiance, killed the boy and cut him into pieces. He sowed the boy's teeth, which grew into maize; planted the ribs and bones, which became yucca, or manioc, tubers; and planted the flesh, which grew into vegetables and fruits. The story appears to be a mythical précis of the discovery of cultivation among coastal peoples.

Not to be outdone, the sun took the boy's penis (or umbilical cord) and navel and created another son, whom he named Vichama or Villama. Pachacamac wanted to kill this child too, but could not catch him, for Vichama had set off on his travels. Pachacamac slew the woman instead and fed her body to the vultures and condors.

Next, Pachacamac created another man and woman, who began to repopulate the world. Pachacamac appointed some of these people *curacas* (leaders) to rule.

In the mean time, Vichama returned, found his mother's remains and reassembled her. Pachacamac feared Vichama's reprisal as the pursued became the pursuer, and he was driven, or fled, into the sea, where he sank in front of the temple of Pachacamac/Vichama. Wreaking further revenge, Vichama transformed Pachacamac's second people into stone, but later repented and changed the ordinary stone of the *curacas* into sacred *huacas*.

Below: The Incas established a temple to Inti (the sun god) alongside the ancient platform at Pachacamac.

SOCIAL ARRANGEMENTS

The second part of the tale explains the creation of social order among humans. Vichama asked his father, the sun, to create another race of people. The sun sent three eggs, one gold, one silver and one copper. The gold egg became *curacas* and nobles, the silver became women, and the copper egg became commoners. Thus, the world was populated. A variation describes how Pachacamac did the final deed by sending four stars to earth. Two of these were male, and generated kings and nobles; the other two were female, and generated commoners.

Other variations combine Con and Viracocha, emphasizing the latter's opposition to Pachacamac. The Huarochirí, between coast and sierra, incorporate Pachacamac's shrine, wife and daughters (including the seduction and attempted seduction of Pachacamac's daughters) into the itinerary of Coniriya Viracocha.

Such variations reflect lowland–highland and inter-coastal exchange and political tension. In the interests of empire, the Incas sought to alleviate any potential conflict by amalgamating the deities and by presenting variations as different names for the same events, as if it had always been so.

Above: Pachacamac was principally a coastal creator god who was ultimately combined with Viracocha, the highland creator deity.

INTI THE SUN GOD

The solstices were crucial days in the Inca ritual calendar. At Capac Raymi (summer/December), there was an imperial feast and initiation rites for noble boys; Inti Raymi (winter/June) honoured Inti, the sun, with feasting and the taking of important auguries. Plotting and confirming their dates was based on observations from the sacred Coricancha Temple in Cuzco.

THE CULT OF INTI

In Inca belief the sun was set in the sky by Viracocha, creator being of indistinct substance. The founding Inca ancestor, Manoc Capac, was believed to have been descended from the sun – the son of the sun – and this belief began the special relationship between the Incas and Inti. The adoption of the cult of Inti was associated especially with the ninth ruler, Pachacuti. Inca imperial expansion probably introduced a solar element into the mythologies of coastal peoples, as the father of Con and Pachacuti. Thus began the combining of creation myths with Inti, the sun.

Inti's image was most frequently a great sheet-gold mask, moulded as a human-like face, wide-eyed and showing a toothy grin. Sheet-gold rays, cut in zig-zags and ending in miniature human-like masks or figures, surrounded the face. Rayed faces were a common feature of pre-Inca imagery, but their identification as the sun is not always tenable.

Below: The Christian Church of Santo Domingo, superimposed on the Coricancha Temple, dedicated in part to Inti.

The sacred Coricancha precinct in Cuzco was the centre of the official state cult dedicated to Inti's worship. By the 16th century, the cult of Inti was so important that an incident witnessed by the priests during ceremonies in his honour appeared to foretell the fall of the empire. An eagle, mobbed by buzzards, was seen falling from the sky in the reign of Huayna Capac about 1526, coinciding with reports of the spread of an unknown, deadly disease from the north, now known to have been smallpox.

CAPTURING THE SUN

The emperor was seen as Inti's embodiment on Earth. Although regarded with awe because of his power, Inti was believed to be benevolent and generous. The sun was symbolically captured at special locations called *intihuatanas* ('hitching posts of the sun'), for example at Machu Picchu – carved stone outcrops probably used for astronomical observations. Together with set stone pillars, priests used the shadows cast by them to observe and record regular movements of the sun in order to understand it and to predict the future. Solar eclipses were regarded as signs of Inti's anger.

Above: Llamas were frequently sacrificed to honour Inti, as depicted in this colonial painting of a sacrificial ceremony.

INTERMEDIARIES

By the second half of the 15th century, as the empire reached the limits of expansion, Viracocha had become a remote deity, and Inti came to be regarded as his intermediary. Inca rulers emphasized this relationship carefully, and it became the basis for cultivating their intimate association with Inti. They became intermediaries between the sun and the people, and their presence was regarded as essential to assure light and warmth to make the world habitable. Elaboration and adoption of regional mythologies and combining them with Inca myth created an association between Inti, the emperor and power. Ceremonies and ritual offerings to Inti served constantly to reinforce this link.

Above: Perhaps the most celebrated intihuatana *is the one located at the highest point of the sacred city of Machu Picchu.*

THE RIGHT TO RULE

Historical and archaeological evidence shows that the expansion of the Inca empire beyond the Cuzco Valley began in earnest with Pachacuti Inca Yupanqui (1438–71) and with his son Tupac Yupanqui (1471–93). To unify the empire and convince their subjects of the Inca right to rule it became necessary to demonstrate a mythical common ancestry – namely the Inca ancestors. Thus, the first ruler, Manco Capac (at first called Ayar Manco), after emerging from the cave of Tambo Toco, acquired divine sanction when his brother Ayar Uchu flew up and spoke to the sun. Ayar Uchu returned with the message that Manco should thenceforth rule Cuzco as Manco Capac in the name of the sun.

Other versions of the creation myth name Inti as the father of Ayar Manco Capac and Mama Coya (also Mama Ocllo), and the other brother/sister/partners collectively known as the ancestors. Manco Capac and Mama Ocllo were sent to Earth to bring the gifts of maize and potato cultivation, establishing the Inca right to rule on the basis of their benevolence.

Below: The Intihuatana *or Hitching Post of the Sun at Machu Picchu was probably used for astronomical observations.*

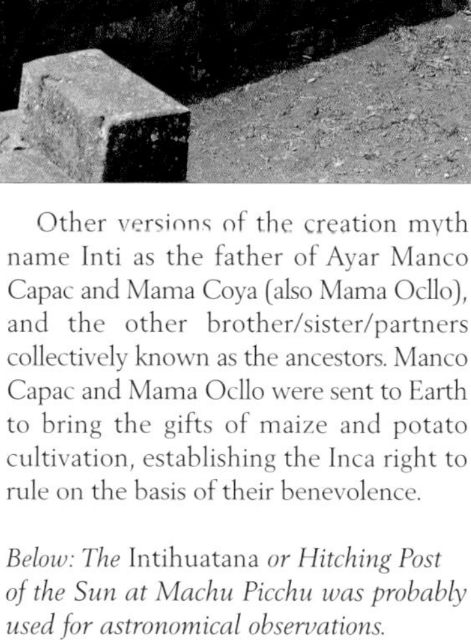

A somewhat more sinister variation says that 'son of the sun' (Inti) was the nickname given to Manco Capac by his father to trick the populace of Cuzco into handing over power. Manco Capac wore gold plates to lend credulity to his divine dawn appearance to the people of Cuzco.

The emperor Pachacuti Inca Yupanqui's discovery of the crystal tablet in the spring of Susurpuquio, with its image of Viracocha, was followed by renewed construction and rearrangement of the sacred Coricancha, giving greater prominence to Inti. It was Pachacuti, too, who visited the Island of the Sun in Lake Titicaca, where ancient Andeans believed the sun to have been born. The construction of Sacsahuaman, at the north-west end of the capital, was probably also begun by Pachacuti. It became a sacred precinct and place of sacrifice to Inti, and probably also a site for cosmological observations. All these legendary events enhanced the importance of Inti and therefore the Incas.

CHAPTER TEN

CREATION AND THE FIRST PEOPLES

The creation story of the Ancient Andean peoples involved a layered world that revolved in endless cycles of creation and rebirth. They linked these concepts to their intimate association with their landscape to explain both its bounty and the difficulties and trials it sometimes presented.

The Spaniards recorded a wealth of rival, even seemingly contradictory, tales of creation among the peoples of the Inca Empire – and indeed throughout their New World colonies. However, as among the cultures of Mesoamerica, Andean cultural accounts of cosmic origin and the creation of humankind had common elements that arose from a long and common inheritance, strengthened by millennia of trading and social contact between highland and lowland peoples.

First was the belief that humanity originated at Lake Titicaca, and that Viracocha was the creator god. Second was the concept that, wherever they lived, a tribal group identified a particular place or feature in their landscape as the place from which they emerged. Third was a dual relationship between local people and a group of outsiders, which, whether it was portrayed as one of co-operation or conflict, defined the nature of how the groups interrelated. Finally, there was the conviction that there was a correct ordering of society and place in terms of rank and hierarchy.

Left: Lake Titicaca, with its sacred waters, came to be regarded by Andean peoples as the birthplace of the world.

CAVES, TUNNELS AND ISLANDS

The Earth, the Lower World of Hurin Pacha, lay between the worlds of Hanan Pacha (the World Above) and Uku Pacha (the World Below). Also known as Kai Pacha, it was the physical world in which humans lived, and was, theoretically speaking, flat. Completing the cycle of the universe, it was connected to the worlds above and below.

The celestial river of Mayu, the Milky Way, channelled water across the heavens, having collected it from earthly sources – a perfect representation of the endless cycle, *pachacuti*. In theory, all living things on Earth had celestial counterparts in stellar and dark cloud constellations (the spaces between the stars). Connection to the underworld was through caves, underground tunnels and springs.

MOTHER EARTH

Crucial in Andean and coastal peoples' belief was worship of mother earth, or Pacha Mama, as she was known to the Incas. To peoples so closely involved with agriculture and the harvesting of the sea for their living, and thus exposed to the periodic extremes of nature, it was natural to develop belief in an all-embracing mother goddess whose whim reflected and was responsible for their environment.

The earth goddess was a primeval deity responsible for the well-being of plants and animals. Worship of her was at least as early as the first U-shaped platform groups and sunken courts, and continues to the present day in the form of offerings of coca (*Erythroxylon coca*) leaves, *chicha* maize beer, and prayers on all major agricultural occasions. She is sometimes identified with the Virgin Mary of Christianity. In one myth, the Inca founders sacrificed and offered a llama to Pacha Mama before they entered Cuzco to take it over. One of the sister/wives, Mama Huaco, sliced open the animal's chest, extracted the lungs and inflated them with her own breath, then carried them into the city alongside Manco Capac, who carried the gold emblem of the sun god Inti.

Above: The first age in Inca creation was inevitably interpreted by author Guaman Poma de Ayala as Adam and Eve.

CAVES

These were believed to be the openings from which people emerged to inhabit the Earth. In the story of the creator god Viracocha, he created the second race of human beings from clay – the Earth. Having painted his creations with distinctive clothes and given them the different languages and customs that would distinguish them, he breathed life into them and caused them to descend into the earth and disperse. In his wandering he called them forth, to re-emerge through caves, and from lakes and hills.

The cave also features in the battle between the coastal creator god, Pachacamac, and the malevolent deity, Wakon, a classic duel between good and evil. Wakon lurked in a cave, enticed the twin son and daughter of Pachacamac and Pacha Mama and sent them to fetch water so he could seduce their mother.

Left: The massive gateway entrance to the Kalasasaya compound at Tiwanaku, which was surrounded by a moat.

Having done so and then destroyed her, it was the humble spider, servant of the Earth, who tricked Wakon in his search for the twins by laying a mountain chasm trap, into which Wakon fell and was destroyed.

SACRED LINKS

Caves were linked by tunnels running beneath the earth. Using these tunnels, the peoples created by Viracocha were thus redistributed throughout the known world. In one of the many versions of the Inca creation myth, it was held that the ancestors were born on the Island of the Sun, in Lake Titicaca. The senior ancestor, Manco Capac, led them from there, underground, to Capac Toco cave at Pacaritambo, south-west of Cuzco, from which they emerged to take over the valley.

The original inhabitants of the Cajatambo region, in highland central Peru, were the Guaris. Their patron god was a giant called Huari, who lived among the caves. Another important Guari deity was the 'night-time sun' – the sun after sunset, which it was believed passed through a hidden, underground watery passage until the next day's sunrise.

Left: The first Inca 'coat of arms' showed elements of their origin: Inti, Quilla and the cave from which the Inca ancestors emerged.

Above: Inca ancestors would have approached Cuzco across the southern mountains, including sacred Mt Ausangate (centre left).

These sacred links between Mother Earth, the sky deities and the underworld were symbolized in ceremonial architecture from earliest times. U-shaped structures and sunken courts feature from the Initial Period to the Late Horizon. The inner labyrinths of temples, particularly at Chavín de Huántar, mimic cave-like mystery. Paracas and Nazca tombs were cave-like structures in which descendants could inter ancestors and re-enter to place more burials within them. They were places of symbolic rebirth through mummification, as well as of burial. The underground water channels of Cahuachi can also be regarded as links. Life-giving waters that had disappeared into the earth on their course from the mountains was tapped underground and brought to the surface for the rebirth of the crops in an endless cycle. Ritual processions through ceremonial complexes descended into the sunken court – a symbolic cave of creation – before being reborn to ascend the celestial heights of the platform to complete the link with the upper world.

ISLANDS

These were also significant in the mythology of creation. The Island of the Sun and the Island of the Moon in Lake Titicaca were believed to be the birthplaces of the celestial bodies, created by Viracocha, and from which they were caused to rise into the heavens. The sacred Akapana and Kalasasaya compound at Tiwanaku were surrounded by a moat, effectively making it an island, whether or not the moat was actually filled with water.

The Incas recognized the ancient sacredness of Tiwanaku not only because of the significance of the Islands of the Sun and the Moon, but also as the birthplace of an earlier race of beings – giants who preceded the Incas and were represented by the great stone statues at the site.

AGES OF MAN

The most important ancient Andean religious theme is continuity, progressing in cycles of events through time. Despite changes to the landscape, climatic change and the ebb and flow of political change, generations of Andean peoples developed beliefs in a sequence of ages that led through a series of creation efforts to their own times. The final expression of this theme was recorded as the Incas told it to Spanish chroniclers.

THE AGE OF GIANTS

The creator god was, to name him fully, Con Tici Viracocha Pachayachachic – 'creator of all things'. He rose from the deep waters of Lake Titicaca and created the first world, a world without light. There was no sun, moon or stars. Viracocha made giant models of beings in his own likeness, which he painted. He wanted to see if it would be a good thing to have a race of people who were that large. They lived in darkness and were unable to worship him.

Below: Lake Titicaca, the most sacred place in the Andean world, where Viracocha made the world and all its forms and living beings.

Viracocha ordered these giants to live without conflict and to obey and worship him. But they did not obey him, and in retribution he turned them into stone and other features of the landscape. The Incas regarded the great stone statues among the ruins of Tiwanaku as a record of this first age.

It began to rain and continued to do so for 60 days and 60 nights. A great flood known as *unu pachacuti* – 'water that overturns the land' – engulfed the land. Some giants, who had not been turned into stone, were destroyed by the waters and swallowed into the earth. Some people believed that all living things were drowned in the flood, but it seems that one man and one woman of normal size survived by hiding in a box or drum, which floated on the flood waters and came to land at Tiwanaku.

THE SUN, MOON AND STARS

Con Tici Viracocha next went to the Island of the Sun, in Lake Titicaca, near Tiwanaku. There he made the sun, moon and stars and ordered them to ascend into the heavens to give light to the world. He set them in motion to create the cycle of day and night, the waxing and waning of the moon and the progression of the seasons. The moon shone more brightly than the sun, and the sun became jealous. In rage, he threw ashes into the moon's face, diminishing its glow and causing the shades of grey on its surface.

Above: The Incas regarded such great stone statues as the Ponce Stela at Tiwanaku to be a record of the first age of giants.

A SECOND AGE OF HUMANS

Viracocha then returned to Tiwanaku and created a second race of humans. This time he wanted his creation to be more perfect, so he created men and women of a stature similar to his own. He sculpted these beings from 'the pliable stones' of the lakeshore – meaning clay. He painted the men and women of different nations and tribes with their characteristic costumes, hairstyles and jewellery. He gave each

designated group its own language, special songs and the precious gift of agriculture in the form of seeds to sow.

Viracocha then dispersed these peoples throughout the land by causing them to descend into Mother Earth and to migrate to their 'places of origin' (*pacarinas*). They were instructed to wait there as *mitimaes* (the name given to communities forcibly resettled by the Incas) until called forth to inhabit the land. (This arrangement clearly fitted Inca notions that they were the chosen people with a right to rule others, for Viracocha seems to anticipate what would happen when the Incas began to create their empire.)

Below: Viracocha was represented in many stone images at Tiwanaku, usually in Staff Deity pose, recalling the ancient Chavín god.

Two men, called his sons or brothers, were kept aside as his helpers. Viracocha taught them the names of the various peoples and told them to memorize their designated valleys and provinces of origin. He said, 'just as I have made them they must come out of the springs and rivers and caves and mountains'. He instructed each helper on his route, directing each to start by heading towards the sunset. Lastly, Viracocha made a sacred idol on the Island of the Sun to commemorate what had been accomplished.

CALLING FORTH THE NATIONS

The brother-son Imaymana Viracocha travelled north-west along the border of the mountains and jungles. Tocapu Viracocha went to the coast and travelled north along the ocean provinces. Con Tici himself went between them, following the highlands, towards Cuzco along the River Vilcanota. As they passed through the land, they called forth the nations, telling the people to obey the orders of Con Tici – to spread across the valleys, settle the land and multiply.

Above: The Incas recognized the Island of the Sun, in Lake Titicaca, as the birth place of the sun and moon, and built a temple there.

A third helper (in one variation), Taguapaca, refused to follow Viracocha's commands. Viracocha ordered Imaymana and Tocapu to seize Taguapaca, bind his hands and feet and throw him into the river. Cursing and vowing to return to take vengeance, Taguapaca was carried by the river into Lake Titicaca and disappeared. Much later he reappeared and travelled to preach, saying that he was Viracocha, but people were suspicious and most ridiculed him.

The three Viracochas taught the people and performed many miracles in their travels, finally reaching the end of their journey on the north-west coast. Viracocha (or, in one version, all three) continued out to sea, walking on the water (or in a boat made from his cloak).

TALES OF HEROES

Heroes and rulers of the most ancient times are unknown because there are no written sources to name them. It is not until the Later Intermediate Period and the Late Horizon that there are accounts of legendary kings and their dynasties, and several legendary heroes who stand out among the ancient Andean cultures. Apart from obvious figures in the Inca state creation myth – Manco Capac and his brothers and sisters – there are a few founders of dynasties in pre-Inca cultures whose legends have survived because they were important in some way to Inca imperial claims to rulership and territory. They have survived in turn through the Spanish chroniclers.

The ancient Moche deities are, for the most part, unnamed except by epithets created by archaeologists – for example the Decapitator God and the bird deities depicted in painted ritual scenes. If the priests impersonating these deities were also rulers, their names are likewise unknown, even though their reality is confirmed in the rich burials of the Moche Lords of Sipán, burials with all the rich trappings of rulership and a style of dress identical to the figures in the painted scenes. Royal dynasties are again attested by the rich burials of the later Sicán Lords of the Lambayeque Valley farther north.

The story of the founding of a dynasty of kings, so clearly attested by these archaeological discoveries in the northern coastal valleys, however, emerges in the legend of Naymlap, a founder hero.

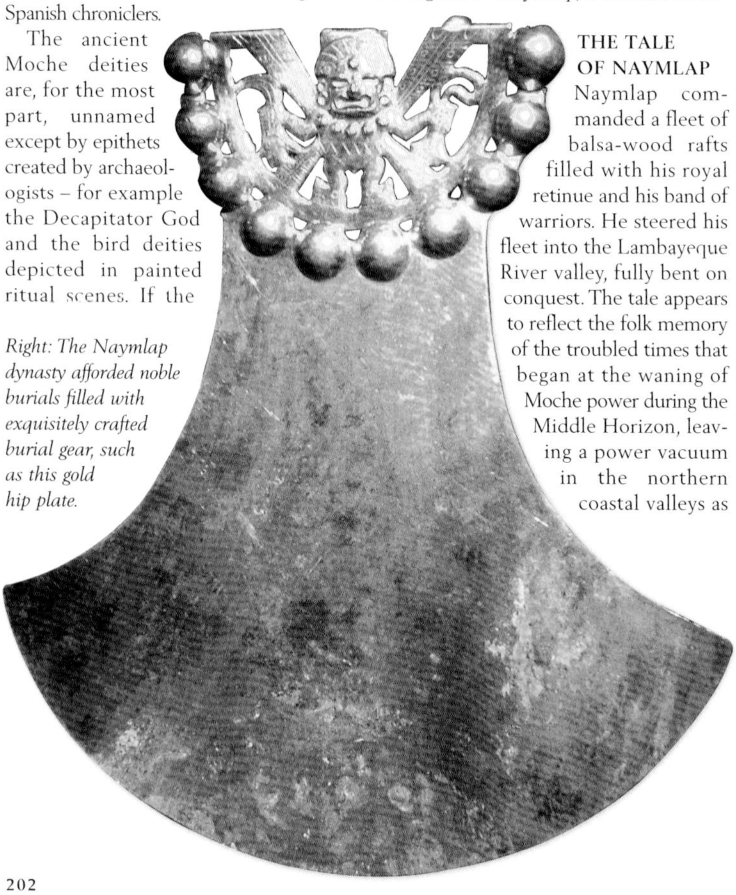

Right: The Naymlap dynasty afforded noble burials filled with exquisitely crafted burial gear, such as this gold hip plate.

THE TALE OF NAYMLAP

Naymlap commanded a fleet of balsa-wood rafts filled with his royal retinue and his band of warriors. He steered his fleet into the Lambayeque River valley, fully bent on conquest. The tale appears to reflect the folk memory of the troubled times that began at the waning of Moche power during the Middle Horizon, leaving a power vacuum in the northern coastal valleys as

Above: This pair of Moche turquoise and gold earrings from Sipán, c.AD 400, shows warriors carrying spears and ropes and reflects the richness of Naymlap's 'noble company'.

Wari and Tiwanaku rulers built powerful sierra empires farther south. It seems that Naymlap, even if only one among several powerful war leaders, stepped into the breach and may be one of the first real people of ancient Andean civilization known today. The Lambayeque (or Sicán) culture that succeeded the Moche appears to have been a loose confederation of petty states in these northern coastal valleys, possibly linked through dynastic inheritance and royal descent as the sons of kings founded sister cities in the adjacent valleys.

A BRAVE AND NOBLE COMPANY

Naymlap led a 'brave and noble company' of men and women. Accompanying him were his wife, Ceterni, his harem and 40 followers. There were Pitz Zofi, Preparer of the Way; Fonga Sigde, Blower of the Conch Trumpet; Ninacola, Master of the Royal Litter and Throne; Ninagintue, the Royal Cellerer (presumably for *chicha* beer); Llapchillulli, Provider of Feather Garments; Xam Muchec, Steward of the Face-paint; Occhocalo, the Royal Cook; and Ollopcopoc, Master of the Bath.

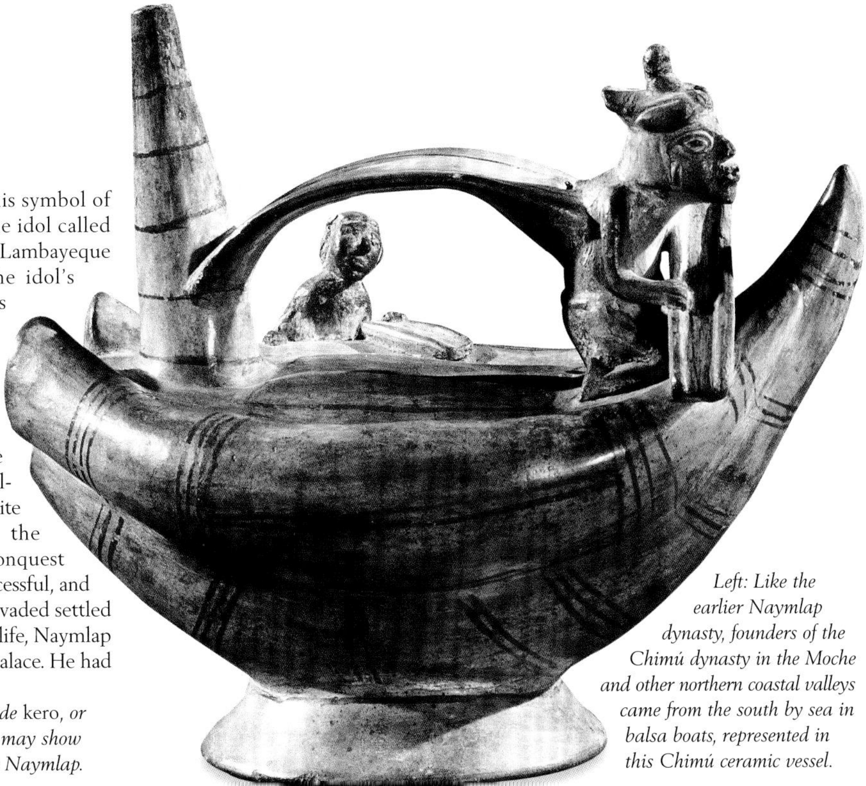

Naymlap also brought his symbol of royal power, the greenstone idol called Yampallec, from which the Lambayeque Valley takes its name. The idol's visage, stature and figure was a double of the king himself.

NAYMLAP'S DYNASTY

With his men, Naymlap invaded the valley and built a palace at the place called Chot, which archaeologists have identified as the site of Huaca Chotuna in the Lambayeque Valley. The conquest of the local peoples was successful, and together the invaders and invaded settled down in peace. After a long life, Naymlap died and was buried in the palace. He had arranged in secret with his priests, however, that they should tell his people that upon his death he had sprouted wings and flown away into the sky.

Left: Like the earlier Naymlap dynasty, founders of the Chimú dynasty in the Moche and other northern coastal valleys came from the south by sea in balsa boats, represented in this Chimú ceramic vessel.

Below: Detail of a gold and jade kero, *or cup, from Lambeyeque, which may show the legendary dynasty founder Naymlap.*

Naymlap was succeeded by his eldest son, Cium, and thereafter by ten other kings in his dynasty, until the last ruler, Fempellec. Cium married a local woman named Zolzoloñi. The Spanish text refers to Zolzoloñi by the word *moza*, 'commoner' or 'outsider', making it clear that she was not one of Naymlap's people or descendants. Cium and Zolzoloñi had 12 sons, each of whom married and also produced large families. As the population of the valley grew, each son left the capital and founded a new city within the valley.

A DYNASTY BETRAYED

Fempellec was the 12th ruler of the dynasty. Unlike its founder, however, he is noteworthy for having brought dishonour and disaster to the kingdom. He was insistent upon a plan to remove the stone idol of Yampallec from Chot to another city, an act of which his priests heartily disapproved. Before he could accomplish this sacrilege, however, a demon appeared to him in the form of a beautiful woman. She seduced him, and after his betrayal it began to rain heavily, an event all too rare in the region. It rained for 30 days, and then was followed by a year of drought and, inevitably, hunger, as the crops failed.

By this time the priests had tired of their scheming ruler. They seized Fempellec and tied his hands and feet; carried him to the sea, threw him in, and left him to his fate, thus ending the dynasty of Naymlap and his successors.

The legend of Naymlap is so lost in time that it is impossible to be certain whether his tale is to be associated with the founding of the Early Intermediate Period Moche, or one of its dynasties, or with the Late Intermediate Period Kingdom of Chimú, or indeed with the intervening Lambayeque (Sicán) civilization.

Above: The administrative sector of Chan Chan, capital of Chimú and South America's largest pre-Hispanic mud-brick settlement.

THE KINGDOM OF THE CHIMÚ

The Late Intermediate Period kingdom of Chimú (or Chimor) occupied the northern coastal valleys the Moche had previously occupied, filling the power vacuum apparently left by the collapse of the Moche and Lambayeque-Sicán dynasties. Chimú was centred in the Moche Valley, south of Lambayeque. Again there are stories of legendary rulers; early accounts were handed down through the generations before being recorded by the later kings of Chimú and the Incas, then passed on through Spanish chroniclers.

A NEW DYNASTY

Taycanamu was the first of a new Chimú dynasty established in the 14th century. Like so many pre-Inca rulers in the kingdoms subjugated by them, knowledge of the dynasty is obscured in legend. Taycanamu was said to have arrived at Moche on a balsa-wood raft, 'sent' from afar with the express mission of governing the peoples of the valley. Was he a late descendant of the northern dynasties? Several unnamed and little-known kings succeeded him until the conquest of the valley by the Inca prince Tupac Yupanqui in the mid-15th century. The *ciudadella* compounds at the capital, Chan Chan, appear to be the dedicated sacred compounds of the succeeding kings of Chimú.

Chimo Capac, literally 'Lord Chimú', was undoubtedly one of these kings. In the late 14th or early 15th century he invaded the Lambayeque Valley from Moche, possibly after the death of Fempellec and his contemporaries. Like Naymlap, he came by sea. He appointed a man named Pongmassa to rule the valley as the local *curaca* (official), then returned to Chan Chan. Pongmassa was succeeded by his son and grandson. During the grandson's time, the Incas invaded and subjugated Chimú. As was characteristic Inca policy, they continued to rule the valley through its local *curaca*, five more of whom succeeded before the Spanish Conquest.

THE SUBJUGATION OF CHIMÚ

Minchançaman (or Minchancamon) was the last of the independent rulers of the Taycanamu dynasty, the sixth or seventh ruler in that line. The account of Tupac Yupanqui's invasion demonstrates the Incas' method of incorporating new kingdoms into the fabric of the empire, firmly establishing their overlordship while at the same time recognizing the integrity and power of the ruling dynasty:

'The brave Chimú [Minchançaman], his arrogance and pride now tamed, appeared before the prince [Tupac Yupanqui] with as much submission and humility, and grovelled on the ground before him, worshipping him and repeating the same request [for pardon] as he had made through his ambassadors. The prince received him affectionately in order to relieve [his] grief ... [and] bade two of the captains raise him from the ground. After hearing him [Tupac Yupanqui] told him that all that was past was forgiven.... The Inca had not come to deprive him of his estates and authority, but to improve his idolatrous religion, his laws, and his customs.'

Above: From the Titicaca Basin, backdrop to the ancient city of Tiwanaku, the Unnamed Man appeared after the great flood.

TALES FROM THE SOUTH

The abandonment of the ceremonial city of Tiwanaku on the southern shores of Lake Titicaca occurred at the end of the Middle Horizon. Archaeological evidence indicates that the withdrawal from use of the various monumental structures and ceremonial courts was quite abrupt, even violent. We can only speculate as to why the rulers of the city abandoned it or were overthrown. However, one tale from Inca records that may be relevant tells of the legendary rulers of two city-states in the Titicaca Basin, Cari and Zapana.

Cari sought the help of the Incas of Cuzco against his rival Zapana. The Incas, however, saw this as an opportunity (or an invitation) to invade the region and to subjugate both cities. Although the story dates from long after the civilization of Tiwanaku had collapsed, the still visible ruins were revered by the Incas. They recognized that the city was ancient and had been powerful. The ruins inspired them to use these invasions to claim descent from the ancient rulers or deities of the region. Perhaps the story is a long folk memory of the break-up of Tiwanaku, recording how rival factions within the Titicaca Basin sought the help of the Incas as the rising power in the Cuzco Valley to the north-west.

Below: A drawing by Guaman Poma de Ayala showing humans from the first age cultivating the crops and tilling the land.

THE UNNAMED MAN

A mysterious figure features in the story of Inca beginnings – the Unnamed Man. The Incas divided their empire into four parts and referred to it as Tahuantinsuyu – land of the four quarters – which were named Chinchaysuyu, Antisuyu, Cuntisuyu and Collasuyu. The story of the Unnamed Man is the only substantial account of this division and of the appointment and naming of the *suyu* (quarter) rulers.

After the waters of the great world flood receded, a powerful, but unnamed, man appeared at the ancient city of Tiwanaku in the Titicaca Basin. The Unnamed Man used his powers to designate the four quarters and to appoint rulers for each of them. To Chinchaysuyu (the north) he named Manco Capac; to Collasuyu (the south) he named Colla; to Antisuyu (the east) he named Tocay; to Cuntisuyu (the west) he named Pinahua. He commanded each king to conquer his allotted quarter and to govern his people.

The brief story is recounted in Garcilaso de la Vega's *Commentarios Reales de los Incas*. The dearth of further explanation is curious, given Inca emphasis on their origins at Lake Titicaca in one version of the official state creation myth. Recognizing Tiwanaku as an ancient seat of power, they wished to bolster their claimed right to rule. Tiwanaku was, in fact, much closer to the actual centre of the empire than was Cuzco.

The rich lands of the Lupaqa Kingdoms – the late inheritors of Tiwanaku power – were important acquisitions to the Inca, as were the vast llama lands of the Altiplano.

EL DORADO AND CHIBCHA HEROES

Although the Chibcha area of present-day Colombia is not technically in the Andean Area as defined here, no book on ancient Andean mythology would seem complete without a description of the legend of El Dorado.

THE GILDED MAN

El Dorado, literally the 'Gilded Man' in Spanish, was the legendary king of the chiefdom of the Chibcha, or Muisca, of the far northern Andes in Colombia. El Dorado was a person, a city, an entire kingdom and, in time, a myth. In their lust for gold, once tales of untold wealth from that quarter had reached their ears, the Spaniards generally associated the legend with the entire region of central Colombia. In reality, the quest for gold and riches beyond belief turned out to be a chimera: El Dorado was always just one more range of mountains away, but was never found.

Below: The myth of El Dorado was represented in a multi-necklace- and earring-wearing man from the Calima culture.

The most reliable sources of the legend focus on the Chibcha/Muisca and their chiefdom around Lake Guatavita in central Colombia, north of Bogotá. Gold was extremely important to all the chiefdoms of the far northern Andes, and several distinctive gold-working styles developed throughout the region from the first century BC/AD; the Muisca style itself dates from the 8th century AD. The Spaniards learned the story of the Gilded Man from many sources, including the Chibcha, who had actually witnessed the ceremony before the Spaniards arrived. Every conquistador and chronicler of this northern area makes mention of the Gilded Man, but the most complete account is that of the mid-17th-century chronicler Rodríguez Freyle, who was told the legend by his friend Don Juan, the nephew of the last independent lord of Guatavita.

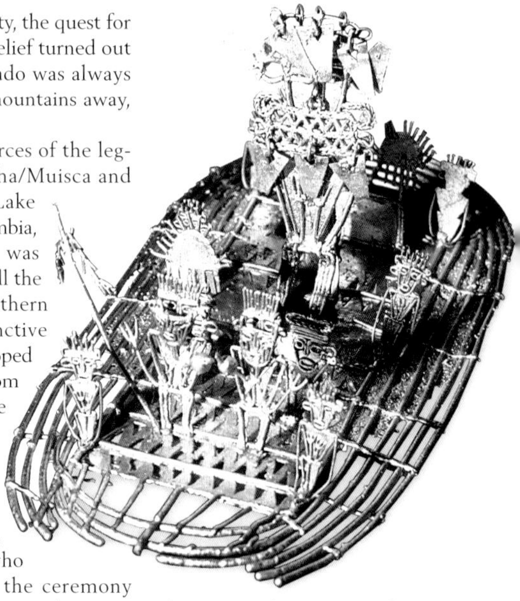

Above: On Lake Guatavita, the anointing of the Gilded Man involved a journey on to the lake and the deposition of golden gifts.

THE ANOINTING OF A KING

The ritual that gave rise to the legend was performed at the inauguration of a new king. The heir to the throne spent the days before the ceremony secluded in a cave. During this time, he was required to abstain from sexual relations with women and was forbidden to eat chilli peppers or salt. On the appointed day, he made his first official journey to Lake Guatavita, there to make offerings to the gods. At the lakeside, a raft of rushes was made and bedecked with precious decorations and treasures. Four lighted braziers were placed on the raft, in which *moque* incense and other resins were burned. Braziers of incense were also lit along the shoreline, and such a quantity of smoke was produced by them that the light of the sun was said to be obscured.

The king-to-be was stripped naked and his body smeared with a sticky clay or resin. Over this he was covered with glittering gold dust, shown being blown from a tube in an engraving of 1599. He then boarded the raft, accompanied by four principal subject chiefs, all of whom were richly attired in 'plumes, crowns, bracelets, pendants, and ear rings all of gold', but also otherwise naked. The king remained motionless on the raft and at his feet was placed a great heap of gold and precious stones (called 'emeralds' by Freyle).

The raft was pushed off across the lake, whereupon musicians on shore struck up a fanfare of trumpets, flutes and other instruments, and the assembled crowd began to sing loudly. When the raft reached the centre of the lake, a banner

was raised as a signal for silence. The gilded king then made his offering to the gods: all of the treasures on the raft were thrown into the lake, one by one, by the king and his attendants. Then the flag was lowered again, and the raft paddled towards shore to the accompaniment of loud music and singing, and wild dancing.

Upon reaching the shore, the new king was accepted as the lord and master of the realm.

CHIBCHA LEGENDS

A few Chibcha heroes are known. Bochica was their legendary founder hero. He arrived among them from the east, travelling as a bearded sage, and taught them civilization, moral laws and the craft of metalworking. Not all accepted his teaching, however. A woman named Chie challenged him by urging the Chibcha to ignore him and make merry, whereupon Bochica transformed her into an owl. Even so, she helped the god Chibchacum (patron of metalworkers and merchants) to flood the Earth. Bochica appeared as a rainbow, then as the sun. He sent his rays to evaporate the waters, and created a channel by striking the rocks with his golden staff for the water to drain into the sea. He was worshipped as the sun god Zue, and Chie became the moon goddess.

Above: Skilled gold-workers from northern cultures in Colombia produced items such as this embossed breastplate with ear disks.

Below: Guatavita, the 'El Dorado' lake in Colombia where Chibcha chiefs dived covered in clay and powdered gold.

A parallel tale concerns an old bearded man called Nemterequeteba, who came to the Muisca from a distant land. He, too, taught the Chibcha the art of weaving and civilized behaviour. His rival was Huitaca, goddess of evil and patroness of misbehaviour and drunkenness. She challenged Nemterequeteba and in one version of the legend she was transformed into the moon by him. She is therefore sometimes confused with the Muisca moon goddess Chie.

The obscurity of these tales might reflect troubles on the distant northern borders of the Inca or earlier kingdoms. Chie/Huitaca, clearly a local deity, resented the appearance of an outsider from afar, who came essentially in a guise similar to the wandering creator god Viracocha.

EMPIRE OF THE SUN

Manco Capac was the legendary first Inca ruler and founder of the Inca dynasty Hurin Cuzco. He was the principal character in Inca mythology surrounding the origins of the state and Inca power.

THE STATE CREATION MYTH

Various permutations of the Inca state creation myth prevailed simultaneously, a fact that caused the Spanish chroniclers considerable consternation. The most prominent version described how four brothers and four sisters came forth from the central one of three 'windows', or caves, in the mountain called Tambo Toco ('window mountain'). These were 'the ancestors', led by the eldest brother, Manco Capac (originally Ayar Manco), who, with his brothers (Ayar Auca, Ayar Cachi and Ayar Uchu) and sisters (Mama Ocllo, Mama Huaco, Mama Ipacura/Cura and Mama Raua), led the people of Tambo Toco in search of a new land to settle, where a capital city could be built.

Below: The endurance of Inca culture is exemplified by this characteristic Inca trapezoidal doorway in Cuzco, still in use.

Above: Manco Capac, legendary founder of the Inca dynasty and 'son of the sun'.

After much wandering they came to a hill overlooking the Cuzco Valley. Miraculous signs informed them that they should settle there, so they came down from the mountain, overcame local resistance and took possession of the land.

EMERGENCE FROM CAPAC TOCO

The standard version comes from Sarmiento de Gamboa, in his *Historia de los Incas* (1572), an early source that relied heavily on interviews with keepers of the Inca state records, the *quipucamayoqs*.

Pacaritambo, overlooking which was Tambo Toco, was the 'house of dawn', the 'place of origin'. According to the chroniclers it was six leagues (about 33km/20 miles) south of Cuzco; in fact, it is closer to 26km (16 miles). In the beginning, the mountain there, Tambo Toco, had three windows, the central one of which was called Capac Toco – 'rich window'. From this window emerged the four ancestral couples, the brother/sister–husband/wife pairs: Capac with Ocllo, Auca with Huaco, Cachi with Ipacura/ Cura, and Uchu with Raua. From the flanking windows, Maras Toco and Sutic Toco, came the peoples called the Maras and the Tambos, both Inca allies. A divine link was immediately established in the promotion of the myth when it was claimed that the ancestors and allies were called out of the caves by Con Tici Viracocha.

Ayar Manco declared that he would lead his brothers and sisters, and the allies, in search of a fertile land, where the local inhabitants would be conquered. He promised to make the allies rich. Before setting out, the allies were formed into ten *ayllus* (lineage groups) – the origin of the ten *ayllus* of Cuzco commoners. The ten royal *ayllus* (called *panacas*) were the descendants of the first ten Inca emperors.

THE JOURNEY BEGINS

Ayar Manco led his followers north, towards the Cuzco Valley. He carried a golden bar, brought from Tambo Toco. With this he tested the ground for fertility by thrusting it periodically into the soil.

Progress was slow and there were several stops. At the first stop Ayar Manco and Mama Ocllo conceived a child. At the second stop a boy was born, whom they named Sinchi Roca. They stopped a third time at a place called Palluta, where they lived for several years; but eventually the

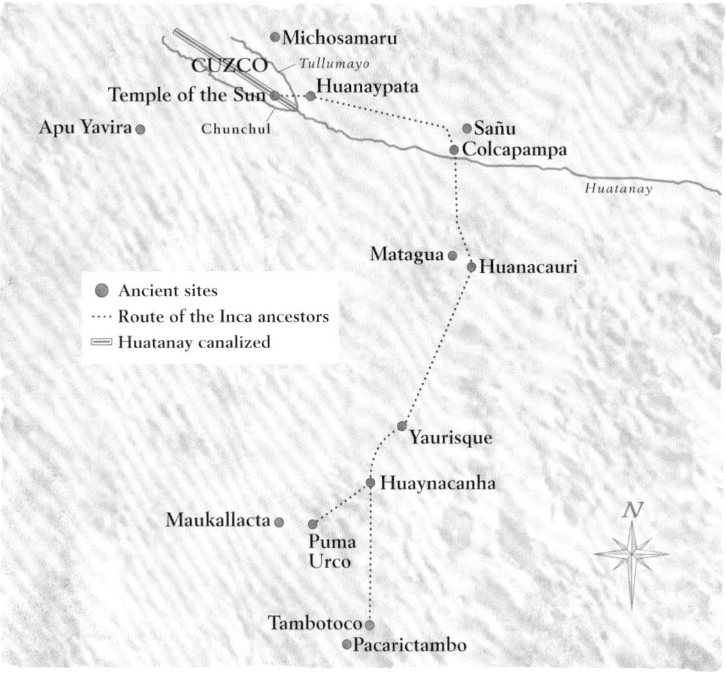

Above: After their underground migration from Lake Titicaca and emergence from a cave, the Inca ancestor pairs went to Cuzco.

land proved unfertile, so they moved on to a place called Haysquisrro. Here the company began to break up.

BREAKING UP OF THE COMPANY

Ayar Cachi was unruly and sometimes cruel. He always caused trouble with the local inhabitants through his tricks and rowdiness wherever the ancestors passed through or stopped. He was a powerful slinger, and could hurl stones so hard that he could split open mountains, causing dust and rocks to fly up and obscure the sun. The other ancestors began to consider him a liability, so they formed a plan to dispense with him. Manco told Cachi that several important objects that should have accompanied the golden rod had been left in Pacaritambo: a golden cup (*topacusi*), a miniature llama figurine (*napa*) and some seeds. Ayar Cachi at first refused to return to Capac Toco, but agreed to do so when his elder sister, Mama Huaco, herself forceful in character, chided him and accused him of laziness and cowardice.

Cachi journeyed back to Capac Toco with a Tambo companion called Tambochacay ('the Tambo entrance-bearer'). He was unaware, however, that Manco and the others had convinced Tambochacay to get rid of him. When Ayar Cachi entered the cave to retrieve the forgotten items, Tambochacay quickly sealed off the entrance, trapping Cachi inside forever. The site, later known as Mauqallaqta ('ancient town'), became an important Inca sacred *huaca*.

The ancestors' next stop was Quirirmanta, at the foot of a mountain called Huanacauri. They climbed the mountain, and from the top saw the Cuzco Valley for the first time. From the summit, Manco threw the golden rod into the valley to test the soil. To the ancestors' amazement the rod disappeared into the Earth and a rainbow appeared over the valley. They took these signs to mean that this should be their homeland.

Before they could descend the mountain, Ayar Uchu sprouted wings and flew up to the sun. The sun told him that, thenceforth, Ayar Manco should be called Manco Capac, the 'supreme rich one', and that they should go to Cuzco, where the ruler, Alcavicça, would welcome them. Uchu returned to his brothers and sisters, told them this news, and was transformed into stone, becoming a second *huaca*.

Below: A fanciful Spanish genealogy of Inca emperors, from Manco Capac onward.

Inca Cuzco (the plaza called Huanaypata), the remaining brother-ancestor, Ayar Auca, was turned into a stone pillar, which, like Mauqallaqta and Uchu, became a sacred *huaca*.

This left Manco Capac, his sisters and his son Sinchi Roca, a convenient outcome, which was in keeping with later Inca imperial practice of sister/wives, and a chosen descendant to the rulership. They began the building of Cuzco.

INCA AMBITIONS

This 'standard' version contains all the necessary elements of Inca legend, including in mythical form the wandering, conquering, alliances and divine intervention needed to telescope what must have been the folk memory of their long and complex history.

Left: A fanciful 18th-century Spanish colonial depiction of an Inca prince sporting a sun pendant, indicating his imperial status.

Below: Regarded as the 'sons of the sun', Inca emperors were carried about in stately fashion on a litter, shown here on a wooden kero cup.

THE FINAL ROAD TO CUZCO

However, the remaining ancestors did not proceed straight to Cuzco. They stopped first at nearby Matao, where they stayed for two years, and where another strange event occurred. Mama Huaco, an expert slinger, hurled a stone at a man in Matao and killed him. She split open his chest, removed his heart and lungs and blew into the lungs to inflate them. The watching people of the town fled in terror.

Finally, Manco Capac led the ancestors to Cuzco. They met Alcavicça and declared that they had been sent by their father, the sun, which convinced Alcavicça to allow them to take over. In return the ancestors 'domesticated' the inhabitants of the valley by teaching them to plant maize. (In one version it was Manco Capac who planted the first field; in another it was Mama Huaco.) At the place that would become the centre of

The Incas were ambitious, however. They felt a need to link their personal creation to world creation, and thus legitimize their right to rule through divine sanction. They vigorously promoted their own political agenda, and were particularly keen to establish their origins as special and to convince others that *their* place of origin was universal – that is, the same as that of the Incas. The 17th-century Jesuit priest Bernabé Cobo describes this official state line as 'caused by the ambition of the Incas. They were the first to worship [at] the cave of Pacaritambo as the [place of the] beginning of their lineage. They claimed that all people came from there, and that for this reason all people were their vassals and obliged to serve them'.

Above: The large oval eyes, feline grin, snake, trophy head and other symbols of this sheet-gold Inca sun disk seem to be a composite of sacred ancient Andean iconography.

VARIATIONS ON A THEME

In other variations of the story, the Incas were more devious – they rewrote and reshaped their story to justify their actions and to incorporate long-held beliefs of the peoples they subjugated. Thus, in one version the ancestors deliberately tricked the inhabitants of the Cuzco Valley into believing them to be the descendants of the sun, not just his ambassadors. Manco Capac made, or had made, two golden discs – one for his front, one for his back. He climbed Mt Huanacauri before dawn so that at sunrise he appeared to be a golden, god-like being. The populace of Cuzco was so awed that he had no trouble in assuming rulership.

Another version, given by four elderly *quipucamayoqs*, contains an undercurrent of the resentment that must have been harboured by local inhabitants at the outsiders' invasion. The story suggests that the whole fabric of Inca rule was illegitimate.

In this variation, Manco Capac was the son of a local *curaca* in Pacaritambo, whose mother had died giving birth to him. His father gave him the nickname 'son of the sun', but also died, when Manco Capac was 10 or 12, never having explained that it was just a nickname. What is more, the commoners of the town were convinced that Manco was actually the son of the sun, and the two old priests of his father's household gods encouraged this belief. As Manco Capac reached early manhood, the priests promoted Manco's conviction, telling him that it gave him the right to rule. Filled with this idea, he set off for Cuzco with several relatives and the priests, taking his father's idol, Huanacauri. He arrived on Mt Huanacauri at dawn, bedecked in gold, thus dazzling the people and convincing them of his divine descent

Yet another version of the state origin myth associates the ancestors with the Island of the Sun in Lake Titicaca, from which Manco Capac led them underground to Pacaritambo. This was a deception meant to justify Inca conquest. Being born on the Island of the Sun made Manco Capac 'son of the sun'. Local myth described a great deluge that destroyed the previous world and claimed that the sun of the present world first shone on the island. He placed his son and daughter on the island to teach the locals how to live civilized lives. The Incas believed that these were Manco Capac and Mama Ocllo, and that the creator, Viracocha, bestowed a special headdress and stone battle-axe upon Manco Capac, prophesying that the Incas would become great lords and conquer many other nations.

Below: In a 20th-century revival of the Inti Raymi (June/winter solstice festival) women are dressed to represent acllas *virgins.*

ISLANDS OF THE SUN AND MOON

The Island of the Sun and the Island of the Moon were sacred places in the southern half of Lake Titicaca, just offshore north of the Copacabana Peninsula. Sitting almost at the centre of the lake, the Island of the Sun was a dramatic location from which to observe the passage of the sun across the high, clear mountain sky. The Incas believed that the islands were the birthplaces of the sun and the moon, or that the sun, moon and stars were created and set in motion from the Island of the Sun by the god Con Tici Viracocha Pachayachachic – 'creator of all things'.

A MOST SACRED PLACE

The Incas identified and named the Island of the Sun and built a shrine there dedicated to Viracocha. The shrine was the focus of an annual pilgrimage by the Inca emperor and nobility. Alongside the sacred Coricancha in Cuzco, and the much more ancient shrine and oracle to Pachacamac in the central coastal city of the same name, this shrine was one of the most sacred sites in the Inca realm until sacked by the Spaniards in their lust for gold. A sacred stone – the Rock of the Sun, a partially modified natural boulder – set up in an open space, and from which the sun was believed to have risen, still stands on the island overlooking the lake.

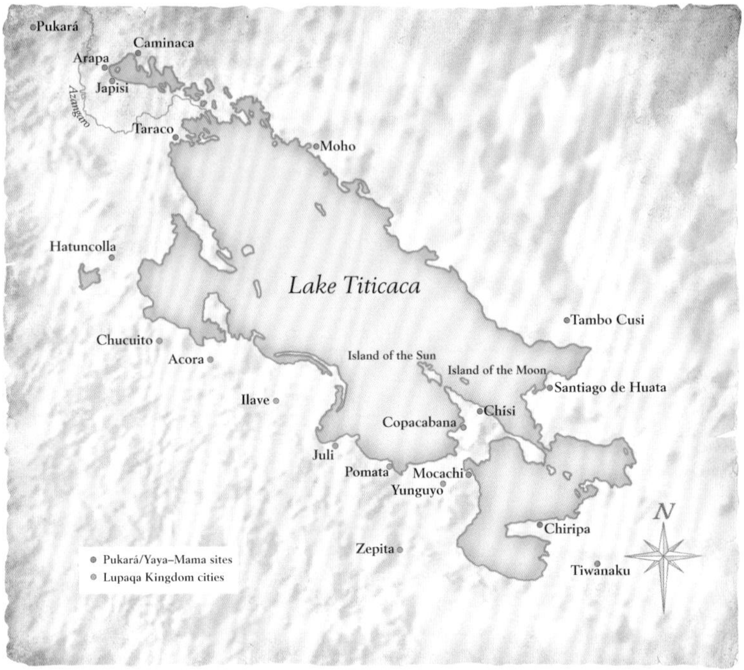

Above: This map shows Lake Titicaca, with the sacred Islands of the Sun and Moon, and ancient sites of religious importance.

Below: The sacred Island of the Sun, Lake Titicaca, rising steeply from the lake, where Viracocha created the sun and the moon.

In one version of the Inca state creation story Manco Capac and his sister/wife Mama Ocllo (and in some variations their siblings as well) were associated with the Island of the Sun in a deception meant to justify Inca conquest of the local peoples. They were said to have led their brothers and sisters from the Island of the Sun, either through the earth or overland to the caves at Pacaritambo.

A PRE-INCA CULT

When the Inca emperor Pachacuti subjugated the Titicaca Basin in the mid-15th century, part of his task was made easier by entering into alliances with some of

Above: The Incas revered the site of Tiwanaku on the southern lakeshore. They built temples to Viracocha and Inti on the Island of the Sun.

the city-states there, such as the Lupaca. The Incas no doubt played on local rivalries to conquer those who resisted their incursions. Pachacuti soon realized the ancient importance of the lake and islands in local religious belief, and with characteristic Inca policy, recognized and honoured the local ruins still visible at Tiwanaku on the southern lakeshore.

Hard evidence of the pre-Inca sacredness of both islands is given by archaeological finds. Hammered sheet-gold and silver objects in the forms of cut-out llamas and the image of Tiwanaku's principal deity – the god with large round eyes and a rounded square face depicted on the Gateway of the Sun, so-called for the sun-like rays surrounding the god's face – have been found on both islands and on the mainland at Tiwanaku itself. A gold disc depicting the god, along with a gold cup and ceramic vessels, were found in the lake off Koa Island, just off the north end of the Island of the Sun. The llama features frequently in Tiwanaku and later sacrificial ritual, and clearly these objects were sacred offerings to the sun by priests or pilgrims.

AN INCA PILGRIMAGE SITE

It was Pachacuti, the great builder, who began the Inca temple and shrine on the Island of the Sun. According to Inca records the temple was administered by 2,000 cult retainers. The temple complex included a *tambo* (a way-station to accommodate pilgrims) and an *acllahuasi* (a 'house of the chosen women' known as *acllas* – hand-picked Inca girls trained to serve the cult of Inti, the sun god, who was ultimately regarded as the Inca emperor himself). In addition to the *tambo* and *acllahuasi*, storehouses were built near Copacabana to provide provisions, clothes and other supplies to the temple attendants and pilgrims.

It seems likely that the Incas adopted a much older cult of the sun established by the people of Tiwanaku, or earlier peoples, on the island. The association of the island as the birthplace of the Inca ancestors would certainly have been an advantageous link in Inca efforts to justify their belief in the right to rule others. One Spanish chronicler, the Augustinian Alonso Ramos Gavilán, claims that the local inhabitants had sent a priest to Cuzco to seek patronage from Pachacuti.

Father Bernabé Cobo devotes an entire chapter of his book on Inca religion to 'the famous temple of Copacabana'. He calls the two islands Titicaca (Sun) and Coata (Moon) and says that there were in fact 'two magnificent temples', one on each island. It is Cobo who claims that the islands were regarded as sacred before the Incas arrived in the region and declares that 'they took charge of enhancing the shrine'. Cobo describes how Tupac Yupanqui, Pachacuti's successor, undertook to enhance the shrine, first by fasting there for several days to show his devotion, and then by establishing an annual pilgrimage to the temple. To reach the Rock of the Sun, pilgrims were obliged to undergo a long ritual route including many stops for observances and offerings, both at mainland *huacas* and on the island.

Below: The extensive ruins of an acllahuasi *on the Island of the Moon bear witness to the importance of these sites of annual pilgrimage.*

CHAPTER ELEVEN

LEAVING THIS EARTH

The Incas regarded life and death as two of many stages in the cycle of being in which all living things took part. From birth through life and into death, there was a rhythm and sense of renewal. In a sense, in Andean belief one never 'left' the earth, for it was from the earth that people came (as described in the creation myth, when Viracocha created humans from clay, and also when they emerged from the earth into which he had dispersed them) and to it that they returned, becoming part of it at burial or remaining on it as a mummy preserved for ritual occasions.

Death did not always occur naturally, of course, and there is wide evidence of ritual sacrifice in an endless attempt to placate the gods. Once dead, rich and powerful ancient Andeans could expect an elite burial with all the trappings, possibly including mummification. Their bodies might be stored in family *chullpas* (burial towers) or buried.

The Lower World (the earth), or Hurin Pacha, was intimately linked to the World Above (Honan Pacha) and the World Below (Uku Pacha), the worlds of the gods, supernatural beings and spirits. Trained individuals, the shamans, could leave Hurin Pacha temporarily through the use of hallucinogenic drugs. They could travel in their altered mental state to converse with and seek help from the gods on behalf of individuals and the nation in general. In order to do so they could also transform into another being, for example a jaguar or an owl, taking on that being's perceived supernatural powers.

Left: Inca agricultural terracing on the steeply rising slopes above Bahia Kona on the Island of the Sun, in Lake Titicaca.

THE CYCLE OF LIFE AND DEATH

Andean belief held that the cycle of being for all living things was a procession through states of being. It began as a general vegetative state, passed through a tender, juicy young state (babies, young shoots) into a progressively drier, firmer more resistant state (adulthood, mature plant), then became a desiccated, preserved state (mummies, dried and stored crops). But this was not the end. When a person died, his or her desiccated remains were like dried pods from which seeds dropped to begin the cycle anew, as their spirit proceeded to its final resting place.

Such basic concepts seem logical in societies that were ultimately reliant on agricultural and pastoral ways of life. Birth, growth and seeding were metaphors taken from the plant world; stages of life were like those observed so closely while tending herds of llamas. The origin of each new generation from the seeds of the last was essentially an exchange of the old for the new.

Below: This Moche painted ceramic piece depicting young maize cobs on the stalk reminded the Andeans of birth and growth.

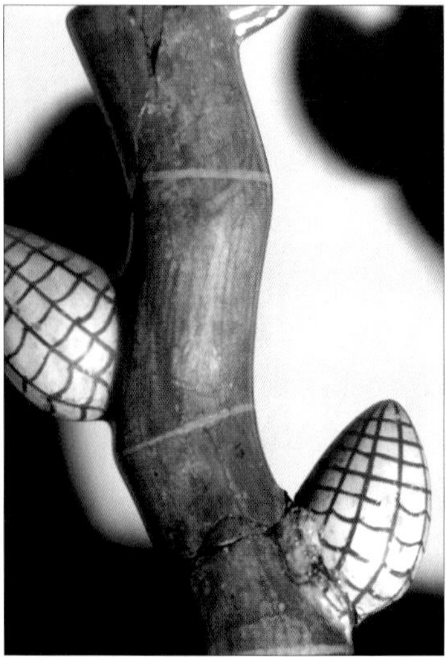

A CARING SOCIETY

During life on earth, the individual was bound into a web of mutual caring. Adults cared for babies and children just as the young cared for the aged. Each individual had their personal role in society and exchanged produce and commodities, depending on their occupation. Shamans cared for the people, while priests, who looked after the welfare of the state and were intermediaries to the gods, were supported by the people and made offerings and sacrifices to the gods on their behalf. Finally, rulers governed and redistributed the wealth of society according to each person's needs within fixed, accepted roles and stations. On a larger scale, different regions were engaged in exchange networks, both socially and for trade. Such networks of exchange were mimicked by the belief that death represented an exchange of old for new.

The Inca sources from which the Spaniards recorded these beliefs must be the culmination of beliefs from the earliest agriculturalists, refined and elaborated through millennia.

Above: Ancient Andeans were reminded of the cycle of life by objects around them, such as this effigy bottle representing old age.

METAPHORICAL IMAGES

The cult of the founding ancestors reflects these themes. The Quechua word *mallqui* (tree) can be glossed as 'ancestor'. The three caves or windows at Tambo Toco were depicted with a tree. From the middle window, Capac Toco, came Manco Capac and the other Inca brother/sister–husband/wife ancestors. In it was a golden tree whose branches and roots connected it to the left-hand window, Maras Toco, occupied by Manco Capac's paternal ancestors. Next to the golden tree was a silver tree, connected to the right-hand window, Sutic Toco, occupied by his maternal ancestors.

Above: Ancient Andeans learned to maximize crop production through the use of natural fertilizer, such as guano from off-shore islands.

Another metaphorical depiction of regeneration and reproduction showed the *mallqui* next to the *collca*, the storehouse in which the year's harvest was kept.

Reflecting an animal metaphor, the rotting of the dead body was conceived as a process that lasted a year after the living body ceased to breathe, during which time the bodily fluids and flesh became desiccated. As this happened, the spirit of the individual emerged, just as a living seed escapes from a dried plant pod, to go to its rest.

PACARINA: RETURN TO ORIGINS

The concept of *pacarina* incorporates rebirth or regeneration. *Pacarina* was the place of origin, the place from which one's ancestors (one's tribe, nation or *ayllu* kinship group) emerged. It could be a tree, rock, cave, spring or lake, and it was a magical shelter from the ravages of the world. Andean tradition held that, after death, the spirit returned to its *pacarina* – the essence of being finally returning to its birthplace.

THE DYING PROCESS: A JOURNEY

Ancient Andeans thought of death as a gradual process, one that continued beyond the time when the body actually ceased functioning on earth, and during which the dead continued to inhabit the living world. Temporary states of being during life were regarded as near-death conditions, such as deep sleep, fainting, drunkenness and drug-induced states.

The journey ultimately began at birth. However, with the cessation of breathing and earth-life functions, the body began its death journey towards fulfilling its purpose of reunion with its ancestors and regeneration. The human spirit was the 'vital force' (Quechua *upani* or *camaquen*; Aymara *amaya* or *ch'iwu*; and in Latin/Spanish translation *alma* and *anima*).

Different sources name the spirit's final destination. Inhabitants of Collasuyu and Cuntisuyu called it Puquina Pampa and Coropuna. Cajatsmbo documents name Uma Pacha, and documents of the Lima region name Upaymarca. Coastal peoples called the final resting place the Island of Guano. More generally, the final resting place was perceived to be a land of farms, where the dead sowed their seeds. The spirit continues to tend the fields and crops, and to experience thirst and hunger as the body does on Earth, and is fed by the living with offerings of food and drink.

The spirits of the deceased were regarded as dangerous, and it was necessary to help them reach the end of their journey, lest they wander among the living, causing violence, sickness and accidents. To reach the Island of Guano, the *anima* was carried by sea lions. To reach Upaymarca, the spirit had to cross a broad river on a narrow bridge made of human hair, known as Achachaca (Bridge of Hairs). In one variation of the cycle, the spirit must encounter a pack of black dogs. Thus, the link is maintained between 'living' and 'dead'.

Right: This Moche stirrup-spouted vessel is a portrait of a living, healthy, laughing man, enjoying life to the full.

BURIAL PRACTICES

Burials of the earliest periods are rare. Few are known from the Preceramic Period, suggesting that bodies were exposed to the elements or otherwise unceremoniously disposed of. Those burials that have been found within Preceramic cave sites were mostly in a flexed position, often on one side. Food, stone tools, beds and pigment fragments were the usual grave goods. As belief in an afterlife or life cycle developed, more care was taken of the deceased, leading to the elaborate preparation and burying of bodies.

Like Paracas, the long-lived pilgrimage and oracle site of Pachacamac was a prime burial place for both rich and poor. The desire was obviously to be buried at the sacred site, and Pachacamac served a large region for more than a millennium.

BODY PRESERVATION

The Chinchorros culture of northernmost Chile provides some of the earliest mixes of ordinary and distinguished burials. Between about 8,000 and 3,600 years ago, most bodies were buried without special treatment. On about 250 bodies, however, a tradition of deliberate preservation is evident: bodies were de-fleshed and disarticulated, then reassembled and buried inside cane or wooden shafts. About 6,000 years ago, at La Paloma on the central Peruvian coast, corpses were salted to arrest deterioration before being placed in burial pits. These two cultures introduced the long-held practice of preservation of at least chosen individuals, and the belief that the body must be intact in order to enter the afterlife.

Burials in the late Preceramic and Initial Period onward, whether especially elaborate or not, were commonly in the shape of some type of crypt. At Preceramic Kotosh, for example, stone-built chambers were used for ritual and then as burial crypts.

Below: Inca burials were accompanied by ceremonial drinking of chicha *beer from* kero *cups to help the deceased into the next life.*

SUBTERRANEAN CHAMBERS

The Early Horizon necropolis on the Paracas Peninsula has many more burials than would have been needed by the nearby surrounding settlements. It can, therefore, be concluded that it was a dedicated cemetery for communities within a large region stretching inland. The burial chambers are intermixed and show obvious social differentiation, indicated by the sizes of the burial bundles, the sizes of chambers, and the grave goods that accompanied the bodies on their final journey.

The burial chambers were large, subterranean, bottle-shaped tombs. They often contained multiple burials, indicating that they were reopened repeatedly through generations. One tomb contained 37 burial bundles. The bundles were piled on top of each other, and in some cases the largest bundle, of the most important person, was placed in the centre of the chambers and surrounded by 'his people'.

The nature of Paracas burial shows the early development of kin-group association in ancient Andean civilization. In life, kin-groups worked together within agreed reciprocal obligations; in death, the kin-groups were buried together in their group associations over generations.

Above: Mummification techniques, together with the extreme desiccation of the Atacama Desert, preserved both human bodies and other organic matter, such as these reed pipes.

BURIAL BUNDLES

All bundles were elaborately wrapped in layers of textiles. Commoner bodies were wrapped in plain and fewer layers of cotton textiles and accompanied by plain ceramics and perhaps a few 'special' pieces. The richest burials were wrapped in much more elaborate textiles and accompanied by the richest ceramics, metalwork and exotic products from afar. Low mounds inland from the cemetery were apparently stages for the preparation of the bodies into mummy bundles.

The association of burial and rich textiles established in the Paracas and succeeding Nazca cultures was an association that continued right through to Inca society. The importance of textiles is attested by industries that produced

Above: The dry Nazca desert preserves the remains of thousands of burials, but, when exposed, the elements soon destroyed any textiles and artefacts that were not looted.

cloth exclusively for burial wrappings – which was a substantial demand on the state economy and human labour.

SUPPLIES FOR THE JOURNEY

Burial rites among most Andean peoples included gifts of clothing, food and *chicha* beer for their journey in the cycle of being.

Middle Horizon Wari tombs were often equipped with a hole in the top or side of the crypt, plus a channel to facilitate offerings of food and drink long after the individual had been laid to rest. Such feeding maintained the vital link between a people and their deceased ancestors. In Inca society, mummies were brought out on ceremonial occasions and offered food and drink.

SPECIAL PRACTICES

Burial in the Middle Horizon, Late Intermediate Period and Late Horizon was commonly in a subterranean chamber in a seated position. Burials were often in shaft-like chambers, with later burials placed on top of earlier ones, maintaining the tradition of reopening kin-group mausoleums. Besides crypts and subterranean chambers of various sorts, several special types of burials have been discovered. For example, elongated hall-like rooms around the patios of Wari dwellings sometimes had human burials beneath their plastered floors, sometimes with small caches of valuables. The Akapana temple at Tiwanaku included ritual eating and burial, the primary burial being a man seated holding a puma effigy incense burner. In the Late Intermediate Period in the Titicaca Basin seated, subterranean chamber burials endured, but more important individuals developed the practice of burial in raised towers called *chullpas*.

One special Inca ritual practice was deliberate exposure to lightning, although it was recognized as potentially fatal.

Right: Inca funerary rites as depicted by Guaman Poma de Ayala c.1613. Note the mummified body in a chullpa *burial tower.*

A *qhaqha* (person or animals killed by lightning) was buried at the place where they were killed.

As the body was taken to its burial place, the Incas would make a mourning sound for the dead like the cooing of a dove. It was invented upon the death of the founder ancestor Ayar Uchu, according to the state creation myth.

ELITE BURIALS

Archaeological evidence from elite burials is abundant. Unfortunately, though, many rich tombs have long since been looted by treasure seekers.

Above: The Late Intermediate Period and Late Horizon Colla of the Titicaca Basin buried generations of mummified bodies in chullpas *– as at the Sillustani necropolis.*

ELITE INCA BURIALS

Father Bernabé Cobo, in his 17th-century *Historia del Nuevo Mundo*, describes Inca burial customs as he observed them. He declares that there was greater concern for one's place of burial than for one's dwelling when alive. Although graves and rituals varied, each province having their own practices, it was common for the elite dead to be buried lavishly. The body was dressed in all its finery – the deceased's best clothing and jewellry. Depending on the person being buried, the body would be accompanied by weapons or a person's tools of trade. Food and drink were placed on top of the dead body.

Important local men were often buried with servants and favourite wives, who would be ritually strangled before being placed in the grave, or made drunk before being buried alive with the corpse. The funeral was conducted by relatives and friends, who escorted the body to a cemetery with mourning and chanting, dancing and heavy drinking. The ceremony lasted for a longer or shorter time according to rank. Chants recalled the most memorable deeds of the dead person, told where he or she had lived, and good deeds done by the deceased to or for the chanter.

Extremely important, legendary Inca individuals were often not 'buried' but recognized as special sacred *huacas*.

Left: Elite members of society were wrapped in numerous rich textile mantles and other garments.

According to legend, Manco Capac was turned into stone when he died. The stone was located by the Polo de Ondegardo, a Spanish magistrate, in 1559 in Membilla, now a suburb of Cuzco. A *quipu* found in an Inca burial mound indicated that the individual was an important local leader or governor.

ELITE BURIAL PARACAS STYLE

Elaborate burial accompanied by rich grave goods began in the Early Horizon Paracas culture of the southern Peruvian coast. The status of the burials in the Cavernas Paracas cemetery is revealed by the number and sumptuousness of the accompanying burial goods, since the most important individuals were sent on their journey into the afterlife with splendid riches. Less wealthy individuals were buried in plain bundles, and some bundles contained more than one body.

Right: The elite were dressed in exotic feather headgear and bone, shell and sheet-gold jewellery, preserved by the desiccating desert conditions and careful tomb burial.

Some desiccated mummy bundles were 2m (6½ft) high. Offerings included gold, feathers, animal skins and imported goods, such as shells from distant shores. Paracas bodies were tightly flexed and held together with cords. Their skulls sometimes show trepanation: pieces of skull drilled and removed by incision with an instrument or by scraping.

PREPARING A MUMMY BUNDLE

Each elite Paracas mummy bundle is unique, but its preparation and basic configuration followed important shared 'rules' or procedures.

One representative bundle was 1.7m (5½ft) high and 1.4m (4½ft) across the base. The entire bundle comprises no fewer than 25 plain cotton wraps and 44 richly decorated wraps. The body was placed on a deerskin within a large basket. Offerings of maize, yuca tuber and peanuts, and of unspun llama fibre, a *Spondylus* shell from the distant northern coast, a cloth pouch probably containing body paint, and a human skull were grouped around the body.

This assemblage was wrapped within multiple layers of cloth. Most of the pieces were wound around the body, rather than 'dressing' it. First, there are 15 embroidered garment sets, many of them unfinished, indicating that they were burial 'gifts' prepared specifically for entombment. Their decorations include common symbolic images and themes: felines, serpents, sea creatures, birds and supernatural beings.

Around these, and including the basket, were several layers of plain cotton cloth, some pieces up to 10m (33ft) long. This made the person 'larger than life' and thus emphasized their importance, as it would have been emphasized in life by the wearing of layers of loincloths, skirts, tunics, shoulder mantles, ponchos, headbands and turban-like headgear. These outer bundles enclosed two staffs, a third staff with a feather top and an animal skeleton; six shoulder mantles; a leather cape; a bright yellow, tropical, Amazonian bird-feather tunic; and a headband. Finally, the entire mummy bundle was encased in a huge plain cloth sewn up with long stitches. It is estimated that the manufacture of the textiles and the preparation of such a bundle required anything from 5,000 to 29,000 hours.

Such elaborate ritual burial practices continued in the succeeding Nazca culture in the same region.

COLLA *CHULLPAS*

Special burials were accorded to important individuals in the Late Intermediate Period and Late Horizon Colla of the Titicaca Basin in unique *chullpa* tower stone burial chambers among the Collas people – as at the Sillustani necropolis. *Chullpas* are fitted stone volcanic masonry structures of one to three storeys, round or square in base plan. They were erected near towns or in separated groups, functioning as family mausoleums. Most *chullpas* contained generations of burials, with bodies wrapped in rich textiles, and they continued to be built into Inca times.

The richest elite burials ever found in the Americas were discovered in the Lambayeque Valley, where the Moche flourished in the Early Intermediate Period and early Middle Horizon, followed by the Lambayeque-Sicán culture of the later Middle Horizon and Early Intermediate Period. Neither used mummification.

ELITE BURIAL, MOCHE STYLE

The rich, unlooted tombs of the Moche Lords of Sipán were discovered by Walter Alva and Susana Meneses in the 1980s. The Sipán tombs reveal the riches and the exquisite craftsmanship of Moche metallurgy and ceramics. Yet Sipán was neither the capital nor the main focus of much Moche power during *c.*AD100–800. It is hard to imagine what riches have been lost that must have come from looted tombs, or that lie as yet undiscovered in unfound Moche tombs.

At Sipán, altogether twelve tombs were found in six levels of generations of burial. In the lowest level was the 'Old Lord of Sipán' and in the topmost level were the tombs of the 'Lord of Sipán' and of the Owl Priest. The levels of tombs contain burials, artefacts and depicted scenes that confirm the ritual scene images on the walls, ceramics, textiles and metalwork excavated at other Moche sites, especially the ritual sacrificial scenes painted on red-on-white ceramics and on murals. The Sipán tombs date from *c.*AD100–300. The offerings in the tombs and the costumes worn by the deceased are identical to those worn by the priests depicted in the sacrificial ceremonies.

Below: Ritual burials have been found beneath many Andean pyramid platforms, as here at Moche El Brujo.

Above: Early Intermediate Period Moche lords were elaborately buried in richly furnished tombs, only a few of which remain unlooted.

LORDS OF SIPÁN AND OWL PRIEST

The principal body in Tomb 1, of the 'Lord of Sipán' – undoubtedly that of a local noble or regional ruler of the Lambayeque Valley – personified the Warrior Priest. He wore a crescent-shaped back-flap and

Right: Moche elite deceased were richly dressed and their faces covered with sheet-gold masks. This example has copper inlaid eyes and traces of red paint.

rattles suspended from his belt. Both back-flap and rattles are decorated with the image of the Decapitator God, in this case a human-like spider with a characteristic Decapitator fanged mouth and double ear-ornaments, perched on a golden web. The spider imagery is thought to reflect the parallel of the blood-letting of sacrificial victims and the spider's sucking of the life juices of its prey.

Offerings consisted of three pairs of gold and turquoise ear-spools (one of which shows a Moche warrior in full armour); a gold, crescent-shaped headdress; a crescent-shaped nose-ornament; and one gold and one silver *tumi* knife. At the Warrior Priest's side lay a box-like sceptre of gold, embossed with combat scenes, with a spatula-like handle of silver studded with military trappings.

Near Tomb 1, Tomb 2 contained offerings not quite so rich, but significantly including the body of a noble with a gilded copper headdress decorated with an owl with outspread wings – clearly the Owl or Bird Priest of Moche friezes. Sealed rectangular rooms near the two tombs contained other rich offerings – ceramic vessels and miniature war gear, a headdress, copper goblets – and, even more tellingly, the skeletal remains of severed human hands and feet, probably those of sacrificed victims.

In the lowest levels, Tomb 3 contained the body of the 'Old Lord of Sipán', who lived about five generations earlier. His burial goods included two sceptres – one gold, one silver – and he wore six necklaces – three of gold and three of silver.

PRIESTESS FIGURES

Futher rich tombs confirming the accuracy of the Moche friezes and ceramic scenes come from San José de Moro in the Jequetepeque Valley. Here Christopher Donnan excavated the tombs of two women, which contained silver-alloyed copper headdresses with plume-like tassels, and other trappings of the priestess figure. These tombs have been dated to *c.*AD500–600.

Left: Repoussé-decorated sheet-gold kero *drinking cups from a rich Chimú burial. The one on the right shows warriors or possibly the ancient Chavín Staff Deity.*

ELITE BURIAL, SICÁN STYLE

The Sicán culture, which succeeded the Moche in the Lambayeque Valley, has produced equally rich tomb burials at Batán Grande, a few kilometres (miles) across the valley. Batán Grande was the largest Middle Horizon–Early Intermediate Period religious centre of the Sicán culture in the Lambayeque Valley. The ceremonial precinct comprised 17 adobe brick temple mounds, surrounded by shaft tombs and multi-roomed enclosures, with rich burials and rich furnishings reminiscent of the Moche Sipán lords' burial.

In the 1980s Izumi Shimada excavated the tomb of a Sicán lord at Huca Loro, one of the Batán Grande temple mounds, dated *c.*AD1000. The burial was of a man about 40–50 years old, accompanied by two young women and two children who had probably been sacrificed to accompany him. The lord was buried seated and his head was detached and turned 180 degrees, and tilted back to face upwards. He wore a gold mask and his body was painted with cinnabar. The grave contained vast numbers of objects – most of them gold, silver, or amalgamated precious metals (*tumbaga*) – arranged in caches and containers. The lord's mantle alone was sewn with nearly 2,000 gold foil squares. Other objects included a wooden staff with gold decoration, a gold ceremonial *tumi* knife, a gold headdress, gold shin covers, *tumbaga* gloves, gold ear-spools and a large pile of beads.

RITUAL SACRIFICE

Human and animal sacrifice was a common practice throughout ancient Andean civilization. It became a part of ritual from the Preceramic Period and continued into Inca times. Llama sacrifice was especially important in Tiwanaku, Wari and Inca ritual. The latter is an important scene in the Inca state creation myth. The founders sacrificed a llama to Pacha Mama before entering Cuzco. Mama Huaco sliced open the animal's chest, extracting and inflating the lungs with her breath, and carried them into the city alongside Manco Capac and the gold emblem of Inti.

SEVERED HEADS

These are perhaps the most powerful image of ancient Andean human sacrifice, and are a common theme in textile and pottery decoration, murals and architectural sculpture. Severed heads can be seen dangling from the waists of humans and supernatural beings in all ancient Andean cultures. As well as heads, other severed human body parts feature pictorially and in actuality in tombs.

The marching band of warriors on the monumental slabs at the ceremonial complex of Cerro Sechín is interspersed with dismembered bodies, severed heads – singly and in stacks – and naked captives. One warrior has trophy heads hanging from his waistband. One of the three adobe images at Moxeke is thought to represent a giant-sized severed head.

Severed heads form an important theme in the Chavín Cult, used both as trophy heads and as portrayals of shamanic transformation.

In Paracas and Nazca culture the Oculate Being has streaming trophy heads floating from its body at the ends of cords. Trophy heads feature frequently on Paracas and Nazca textiles and pottery. Real severed human heads were placed in Paracas and Nazca burials. There was a Nazca cult that collected caches of the severed and trepanned trophy skulls of sacrificial victims, and many human skulls have been modified to facilitate stringing them on to a cord.

Above: A Nazca warrior or priest displaying a fresh trophy head – an integral part of ancient Andean religion.

DECAPITATORS

Titicaca Basin Pukará imagery also featured disembodied human heads. Some were trophy heads carried by realistically depicted humans; others accompanied supernatural beings with feline or serpentine attributes, thought, as in the Chavín Cult, to represent shamans undergoing transformation. The Pukará Decapitator sculpture is a seated male figure holding an axe and severed head, and the Pukará ceramic theme known as 'feline man' depicts pairs of fanged men lunging or running, facing one another or one chasing the other, each carrying a

Left: Nazca cemeteries included caches of skulls, many of which show trepanation and perforations for threading on to a cord.

Above: The Moche Pañamarca mural (restoration drawing) depicts the sacrifice ceremony, presided over by a priestess.

severed head and a staff. A cache of human lower jawbones found at Pukará indicates ritual sacrifice and/or warfare, either in the real or mythological world.

Images of the Decapitator God dominated temple and tomb friezes and murals in the Moche capital and are found at Sipán in the Lambayeque Valley, where the tomb of the Lord of Sipán was found. The nearby tomb of the Owl Priest contained boxes of offerings that included the bones of severed human hands and feet. Similar to the Pukará Decapitator, the Moche god holds a crescent-shaped *tumi* ceremonial knife in one hand and a severed human head in the other.

Tiwanaku and Wari craftsmen continued the severed-head theme in all media. The Akapana Temple at Tiwanaku incorporated a buried cache of sacrificed llama bones. Most of the human skeletons found buried on the first terrace and under its foundations were headless, and at the base of the western staircase a black basalt image of a seated, puma-headed person (*chachapuma*) holding a severed head in his lap was found. Another Tiwanaku *chachapuma* sculpture is a standing figure holding a severed head.

The ultimate severed head is perhaps that of Atahualpa/Inkarrí, who was killed by the Spaniards. His body parts were buried in different parts of the kingdom, with his head in Lima. It is said that one day a new body will grow from his head, and the Inca emperor will return to revive the people's former glory.

SACRIFICIAL BURIALS

Human sacrifice became not only a part of religious ceremonies necessary to honour the gods, but also a ritual associated with elite burial, emphasizing the power and importance of the individual.

The earliest evidence indicative of human sacrifice comes from two burials at Late Preceramic Huaca de los Sacrificios at Aspero. The first was of an adult, tightly flexed with the joints cut to force the unnatural position and to fit the body into a small pit, wrapped only in plain cloth. The second was of a two-month-old infant placed on its right side. It wore a cloth cap and was wrapped in cotton textile. Accompanying it were a gourd bowl and 500 clay, shell and plant beads. This bundle was placed in a basket, the whole wrapped in another layer of cloth, then rolled in a cane mat and tied with white cotton strips, and finally laid on two cotton wads. The assemblage was covered with an inverted, finely sculptured stone basin. The pair appears to commemorate the premature death of an infant of important lineage and a sacrificial victim to accompany its burial.

The Paracas Cavernas and Nazca Cahuachi cemeteries show numerous signs of ritual human sacrifice. Caches of skulls and trepanning have been mentioned. At Cahuachi it is obvious that some individuals were sacrificial victims. While honoured burials were mummified and accompanied by exquisitely decorated, multicoloured woven burial coats and pottery, sometimes with animal sacrifices, the sacrificial victims – men, women and children – had excrement inserted into the mouth, their skull perforated for threading on to a cord, their eyes blocked, and their mouth pinned by cactus spines or the tongue removed and placed in a pouch.

COMMEMORATIVE SACRIFICES

The roughly contemporary Moche culture of the northern coastal valleys practised a ritual of elite burial through generations as the huge Huaca del Sol pyramid was built in the capital, Cerro Blanco. A burial oriented north–south, as was the pyramid platform, was made near the base of the first phase of construction. Later burials were incorporated in successive phases as the platform was enlarged. There were several burials with mats and textiles within the adobe brick layers of the third phase, some of them of adolescents. Lastly, on top of the final construction stage of the fourth phase was an interment of a man and a woman, extended on their backs, accompanied by 31 globular vessels. The exact meanings of such burials cannot be known, but their association within construction phases of the huge platform was probably as sacrificial offerings for the well-being of the Moche people and their rulers.

Such a conclusion is strengthened by what can only have been a mass sacrifice behind the twin pyramids of Huaca de la Luna, also at Cerro Blanco. An enclosure at the base of the platform contained the mass grave of 40 men, aged 15 to 30, many of them deliberately mutilated. They may have been sacrificed to the gods during a time of heavy rain caused by an El Niño event to solicit the return of good weather, for the sacrificial victims were covered in a thick layer of water-deposited sediments and the bones showed signs of cutting and of deliberate fracturing. As El Niño events occurred regularly in cycles, there may be other such mass sacrifices yet to be discovered.

Above: As well as human sacrifice, animal offerings to the gods were a regular ancient Andean religious practice, performed at designated times of the year.

The sacrificial scenes on Moche ceramics were actually performed by Moche lords such as the elite individuals known as the Lord of Sipán and the Owl Priest at Sipán. Judging by the frequency with which the scenes are shown on ceramics and murals, the ritual was a regular event, perhaps re-enacting a mythical story. The tradition of sacrifice appears to have survived the collapse of Moche power, even within the Lambayeque Valley, as illustrated in the sacrifice of two women and two children at later Lambayeque-Sicán Huaca Loro (Batán Grande).

CAPACOCHA SACRIFICE

The Incas associated red with conquest and blood. The chronicler Murúa says that each red woollen thread of the Inca

Left: Ritual sacrifice was performed by priests, perhaps impersonating gods or in shamanic 'transformation', as here, wearing a jaguar or puma mask.

state insignia, the Mascaypacha – a crimson tassel hung from a braid tied around the head – represented a conquered people and also the blood of an enemy's severed head.

The Inca practice of *capacocha* sacrifice was a ritual that continued these ancient traditions. As well as honouring the gods, it emphasized the power of the Inca rulers and maintained control over subjugated peoples. Specially selected individuals, usually children, from among the high-ranking *ayllu* kinship lineages of the provinces of the empire were brought to Cuzco to be prepared for the ritual. The selection was made annually and those chosen were destined to be sacrificial victims after ritual ceremonies in the capital. *Capacocha* sacrifices were offerings to either the sun god Inti or the creator god Viracocha, or to both of the gods. Momentous events such as war, pestilence, famine or other natural disasters could also provoke *capacocha* sacrifices.

Right: A Chimú ritual gold tumi *sacrificial knife, for slitting the throat of the victim, decorated with possibly feline heads.*

In Cuzco, the chosen ones were sanctified by the priests in the Coricancha precinct, who offered the victims to Viracocha, and then marched back to their home provinces along sacred *ceque* routes that linked the provinces to the capital. The victims were sacrificed by being clubbed to death, strangled with a cord, having the throat slit before burial, or by being buried alive in a specially constructed shaft-tomb.

Capacocha sacrifices renewed or reconfirmed the bond between the Inca state and the provincial peoples of the empire, reasserted Inca overlordship and reaffirmed the hierarchy between the Inca centre and the provincial *ayllus*.

CAPACOCHA CHILDREN

Children were sometimes drugged with *chicha* (maize beer) before being sacrificed. Votive offerings usually accompanied the victim in death, such as elaborate clothing, male or female figures of gold, silver, bronze or shell dressed in miniature garments, llama figurines and miniature sets of ceramic containers.

The victims were sometimes carried up and left on high mountaintops regarded as sacred *huacas*, where their bodies would sometimes become preserved in the cold dry conditions that prevailed at such high altitudes. Famous examples include those at Cerro el Plomo in the Chilean Andes, Mount Aconcagua on the Argentinian–Chilean border, Puná Island off the coast of Ecuador, the 'ice maiden' at Mount Ampato and the two girls and a boy sacrificed and buried on Mount Llullaillaco.

Left: A deer sacrifice performed by Death as a skeleton, displayed on a Moche ceramic stirrup-spouted ceremonial vessel.

MUMMIES AND MUMMIFICATION

This preservative treatment of the human body before burial, or even as a state precluding burial, was the ultimate ancient Andean expression of ancestor reverence. It was not an attempt to cheat death on Earth, nor a denial of the cycle of life, but rather an act of recognition of the next stage in the cycle. It was a preparation for the journey and a method of preservation that maintained the contact between those living in this world and those who had moved on to the next stage. In fact, mummification was not necessarily always achieved deliberately, but could also be the result of climatic conditions, since the desiccating conditions of the desert would preserve exposed bodies. In the same way, desiccation and freeze-drying methods used to preserve stored foodstuffs had been discovered by the ancient Andeans probably accidentally originally, and then deliberately applied.

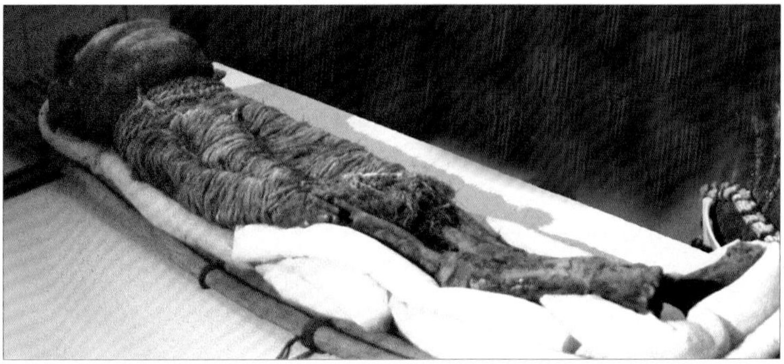

Above: Cinchorros mummifiction in northern coastal Chile predates Egyptian burials by some 500 years.

THE CHINCHORROS MUMMIES

The earliest mummification in the world was practised by the people of the Chinchorros culture in the Chilean Atacama Desert, starting about 5000BC. The Atacama is one of the bleakest places on Earth and officially recognized as the driest.

Mummification by the Chinchorros predates the earliest Egyptian mummification by about 500 years. It also demonstrates the beginnings of differentiation in burial practices within their community by the special treatment of chosen individuals. Most Chinchorros dead were buried in earthen graves without special treatment. About 250 individuals, however, had been preserved. Curiously these earliest mummies were not of revered elderly members of society; rather the majority of them are of newborns, children or adolescents.

Chinchorros 'morticians' perfected a high degree of skill. The deceased body was left exposed to decompose then completely de-fleshed. Cerebral and visceral matter were extracted and the

Left: Removal of the soft material, salting and careful wrapping helped to preserve organic materials in Paracas burials.

skin treated with salt to help preserve it. The bones were then reassembled as in life and secured in their positions with cords and cane supports. The form of the body was then replaced with fibre, feather and clay stuffing, held inside the skin, which was stitched in sections at the tops of the arms, wrists, torso, abdomen, groin, knees and shins as necessary. A clay death mask was applied to the skull, complete with sculpted and painted facial features, and a coating of clay applied to the body to delineate fingers and toes, with painted finger- and toenails. A wig of human hair was often attached as well. The result was a stiffened, statue-like form.

There is variation in treatment, presumably owing to individual skill and developments in preservation methods over generations.

The mummy was kept above ground as a continuing family member. Some mummies show surface damage, which in some cases was repaired. The preserved cadavers were clearly kept accessible for some time before finally being buried. Some burials were in family groups of adults and children. One such interment spanned three generations from infants and children to mature adults and a few very aged adults.

The inclusion of infants and children, especially separately or in group burials of the young, seems to rule out specific ancestor worship. However, the development of social hierarchy and perhaps lineage privilege is shown by the selection. Presumably special treatment and inclusion above ground within the community continued until the lineage no longer merited a distinct social position, at which time the mummy was then buried in an earthen grave.

LA PALOMA

The Chinchorros mummies were not the only ancient Andean attempts to preserve the body after death. The Preceramic site of La Paloma on the central Peruvian coast in the Mala Valley was short-lived, but comprised three superimposed settlements with some 4,000 to 5,000 circular huts in total. Abandoned huts later served as graves in which, from as early as about 4000BC, corpses were treated with salt to deter putrefaction. In combination with the dry coastal desert climate, the bodies were desiccated and stiffened as whole forms. At the time, such treatment contrasted sharply with the burial of disarticulated bodies in tropical and other areas.

THE ESSENCE OF PRESERVATION

Even these earliest methods of mummification seem to recognize the concept of essence. The methods do not attempt to halt decomposition of the flesh. Rather they preserve the essence of the earthly form, presumably in order to provide a 'vessel' for the journey of the spirit, or 'vital force', that ancient Andeans believed to be the next stage in the cycle of life. In Inca times, mummies were the preferred symbol of corporate identity and kinship solidarity. The Chinchorros and La Paloma peoples' early efforts at mummification reveal the antiquity of Andean belief that an intact body vessel was critical for the spirit to be able to enter the afterlife and join the world of the ancestors.

Above: A richly coloured Paracas woollen burial wrap, decorated with felines and perhaps the face of the Oculate Being, reveals the high status of a burial.

The elite burials of the north-coast Moche Sipán lords and later Sicán lords in the Lambayeque Valley were not deliberately mummified. The tradition of elaborate trappings certainly prevailed, but there was no deliberate mummification of the bodies. Their exquisite garments and tomb furniture did not, in the long term, preserve the bodies of the deceased lords, but their dress and grave goods certainly reveal a desire to prepare them and supply them for their journeys into the afterlife.

THE PARACAS/NAZCA MUMMIES

The traditions and concepts established at Chinchorros and La Paloma continued at Early Horizon Paracas and Early Intermediate Period Nazca, about halfway along the coast between the two Preceramic sites. The elaborate mummy bundles interred in the three Paracas cemeteries – Cavernas, Cabeza Larga and Necropolis – and the Nazca Cahuachi cemetery show a multi-layered established social hierarchy, clearly defined by the levels of treatment in burial. The dry desert climate was a significant element in preservation, while the elaborate treatment of Paracas and Nazca corpses in multiple layers of burial textiles protected the mummies from deterioration. Social position was indicated by the size and elaboration of the mummy bundle. Once again, the treatment was to provide a vessel for the journey into the afterlife.

The attention to detail in procedures and the multiple layers of textiles and other trappings in Paracas and Nazca burials have been described above. The importation of foreign objects and materials in Paracas and Nazca graves – including exotic shells and llama wool garments, as well as the native-grown cotton textiles – reveals the extent of contact and trade between the coast and other regions, both sierra and tropical. It is significant that with such long-distance communication must have come ideas as well as objects and commodities, and it is this factor that perpetuated the Andean concepts of mummification and concepts about the nature of the afterlife. The time and labour required to produce one Paracas elite mummy bundle demonstrates the depth and sincerity of these beliefs.

The Pre-Inca practice of mummification is emphasized by the discovery of a row of mummy bundles in the burial of the puma-headed priest (*chachapuma*) beneath the summit structures of the Akapana platform at Tiwanaku. The priestly mummy's importance was accentuated by a row of mummies facing him in the tomb.

Below: Richly dyed multiple layers of cotton and woollen burial textiles and a feathered headdress emphasize the importance of this Paracas individual.

Above: An Inca mummy bundle borne on a litter for deposit in a mausoleum, from which it could be brought out on ritual occasions.

CHIMÚ/INCA MUMMIFICATION

Late Intermediate Period Chimú and Late Horizon Inca mummification was the culmination of the long tradition of Andean preservation of the body for the afterlife. Chimú and Inca mummification was achieved in a manner essentially the same as the methods developed by the Paracas people, the critical elements being desiccation and an elaborate mummy bundle of textiles and elaborate garments and jewellery, including precious metals and exotic items. Embalming included the use of alcohol – *chicha* beer made from the maize cultivated in a field near Cuzco was produced expressly to embalm the body of the ancestor Mama Huaco and was used for the succeeding Inca Qoya empresses.

INCA *MALLQUIS* MUMMIES

Every Inca community would have had its special *mallqui* (as it was called in the central and northern Andes) or *munao* (as it was called along the central coast).

The *mallqui* mummy was the community-level founding ancestor, the protohuman descendant of the deities – the great *huacas* such as Inti (the sun) or Illapa (thunder and lightning). In time, the term was applied to more recent ancestors of the kin group. Alongside *mallquis*, ancestors could also be 'mummified' in a transformed state: ancestors who had been petrified and who stood in sacred locations around the landscape. These were known as *huancas*, *chacrayocs* and *marcayocs*. Like the *mallquis*, these stone ancestors represented the first occupation of the region and the first *ayllu* kinship group called out by Con Tici, Imaymana or Tocapo Viracocha at the time of creation.

Inca *mallquis* were commonly kept in caves or in special rooms near the community. Some caves were reported by Spanish priests to hold hundreds of mummified ancestors. The Inca royal mummies – both the Sapa Inca (Inti) and the empress Qoya (Quilla) – were housed in special rooms in the Coricancha Temple in Cuzco, to be brought out on auspicious occasions and festivals and included as 'living' members of the royal household. After the Spanish Conquest they survived, hidden by Incas reluctant to relinquish ancient beliefs, until the late 16th century, when Spanish priests and administrators finally tracked them down and burned them as heretical.

CHIMÚ ROYAL MUMMIES

The immense Chimú capital at Chan Chan in the Moche Valley had at its core the walled city of *ciudadellas*, which housed the living and dead royal households of the Chimú kings. Each *ciudadella* compound comprised a 'city within the city' to accommodate the mummified remains of the king and both dead and living retainers. They 'lived' in rooms on special platforms, including labyrinthine divisions and thousands of storerooms and niches, and even miniature U-shaped ceremonial structures harking back to the most ancient cultures of the north coast.

Above: A Middle Horizon Wari mummy bundle. They were preserved and brought out on special occasions by most Andean cultures from the Early Horizon onward.

FREEZE-DRIED MUMMIES

Another type of mummification occurred, perhaps intentionally, in the desiccated climatic condition of remote mountaintops. These were the *capacocha* child and young adult victims of the Inca ritual sacrifice of chosen representatives from the provinces of the empire. Cold storage of sierra agricultural production was a long-standing practice, complementing the hot, dry conditions used to dry foods by desert cultures. In the remote, dry, cold high-sierra locations of *capacocha* sacrifice and burial, the combination of elaborate bundling in textiles and the climatic conditions naturally preserved the bodies. The locations and the intent to revisit the *huacas* thus created by the sacrifice indicates that preservation through mummification was counted upon.

ANCESTOR WORSHIP

Reverence for one's *ayllu* kinship ancestors was integral in Inca society regardless of social rank. Special veneration was given to nobles and supreme respect to the royal pair. The enshrined mummies of the Incas and their Qoya wives were carefully tended. Even today the skull of an ancestor is kept in some Andean households to 'watch over' it and its occupants.

Signs of pre-Inca ancestor reverence are evident in the elaborate preparation and care of bodies in Paracas and Nazca cemeteries; especially revealing is the continued reopening of tombs to inter new family members or the maintenance of access to *chullpa* towers for the same purpose. Like so many practices in Andean civilization, the intensity of ancestor worship reached its most vivid and demonstrative phase among the Incas, who, with the Chimú, developed substantial industries around ancestor worship.

THE ROLE OF *MALLQUIS*

The mummified remains (*mallquis*) of Chimú and Inca rulers and their queens were cared for by dedicated cults. At Chan Chan they were housed in the *ciudadella* compounds. The cults of Inti and Quilla were housed in the Coricancha precinct in Cuzco. The *acllas* (chosen women) of Inti not only tended the *mallquis* of former Sapa Incas but were also the concubines of the reigning Sapa, thus forming a worldly link between the ancestors and the living Inti.

Every *ayllu* maintained mummified ancestor bundles and housed them carefully in special buildings or in nearby caves. *Mallquis* were believed to be the repositories of supernatural powers. As founding ancestors they were regarded as revered divinities, or representatives of the gods, and infused with *camaquen* – the vital force of all living things. They were able to transfer *camaquen* to crops to make them grow and to llama herds to make them multiply. Legendary exploits of *mallquis* were told about their ability to sustain agricultural production. They were responsible for the introduction of the different regional crops and for maintaining the fertility of the land. They had taught the people the different methods of agriculture such as irrigation and terracing to increase production.

Such beliefs maintained established land rights and the mutual obligations within and between *ayllu* kinship groups. They helped to co-ordinate labour between groups, communities and regions.

CONSULTING THE FOREBEARS

Inca ancestor mummies were consulted for numerous reasons, both for everyday concerns and on ceremonial occasions on issues of vital importance. They were consulted before undertaking a journey outside the community, for naming and marriage ceremonies in the life cycle, and on auspicious dates in the agricultural calendar such as sowing and harvesting.

On these occasions they were brought out to participate in the ceremony. They were dressed in fresh clothing, offered food and drink, and generally treated as living, active members of the community. Songs and dances were performed before them and the stories of their exploits told.

Left: An Inca carved wooden head with shell inlay eyes, dressed in dyed textiles – probably from a mummy bundle or more probably a huauque *double.*

Right: Ancestor worship began as early as the Nazca, who placed generations of the deceased in mausoleams and had kinship areas at ritual sites such as Cahuachi.

Spanish attempts to eradicate what they regarded as idolatrous beliefs were fiercely and secretively resisted. Local-level ancestors were considered crucial to community coherence, and most survived well into the 17th century.

HUAUQUES

The Quechua word *huauque* means 'brother'. The term was especially applied to man-made doubles – statues made in the images of the ruling Sapa Incas and other chiefs and nobles during their lifetimes. In his *Historia del Nuevo Mundo*, Bernabé Cobo describes these effigies as well dressed and of various sizes, and says that they were held equivalent to the imperial and noble *mallquis*. They included hollows wherein parts of the reigning emperor were placed when he was alive, such as trimmings from his hair or fingernails. Upon his death the ashes of his burned viscera were usually put into the hollow. Many such duplicates were hunted down by the Spaniards and destroyed along with the actual mummies.

Huauques were made of different materials and had more refined characteristics according to rank. The *huauque* of the upper division of an *ayllu* would have proper facial and other human-like features. That of the lower division would have amorphous or animal features. The *huauques* of earlier Sapa Incas were made of stone while those of the later rulers were made of gold.

After the Sapa Inca's death his royal *panaca* corporation undertook the care of his *mallqui* and *huauque*. During another emperor's lifetime such statues could be used as *mallqui* substitutes, especially on occasions when the real mummy might be at risk of damage, such as on a long journey or when the living emperor was on a campaign of conquest. The loss of such an idol would be less serious than the actual destruction of a *mallqui*, for loss of the latter would amount to a state disaster: it would mean the loss of the *panaca's* identity.

A *huauque* could also represent a mythical ancestor. In this case invented descent could be confirmed by the effigy for political expediency. Once again, Inca practice appears to follow ancient Andean traditions. The greenstone idol Yampallec of the Sicán ruler Naymlap accompanied him in his conquest of the Lambayeque Valley, and the attempt of his descendant Fempellec to remove the idol was fiercely and successfully resisted by the priests who constituted the royal *panaca*. Nevertheless, the dynasty ended with Fempellec when the priests disposed of him.

Below: As the Incas were so attached to their mummies and ancestor worship, here depicted by an ancestor mummy on a litter, it took the Spaniards over a century to stamp it out.

TRANCES AND TRANSFORMATION

The ancient Andean cycle of life included trances and transformations during which life on earth was left and other worlds or states of being were entered.

TRANSFORMATIONAL STATES

Some temporary states of being could be experienced by everyone: for example near-death conditions, deep sleep, fainting and drunkenness. More profound states, such as transformation in order to commune with the spirit world, however, were usually drug-induced and were the realm of the shamans and high priests.

Below: This Moche effigy vessel depicts a jaguar-attired shaman with a jaguar emerging from his head.

That such beliefs, like most Andean religious concepts, were ancient is shown in the series of transformation sculptures at Chavín de Huántar in the circular sunken court of the New Temple. These portray a classic trip – the transformation of a human shaman into a revered jaguar. During such a transformation the shaman acquired the powers and wisdom of the animal into which he or she was changed.

Other states of transformation included the conversion of animals and of human heroes or deities into stone, to become sacred regional *huacas*. The reverse could also happen: stones or other features of the landscape could temporarily transform into living beings. The classic example is the calling upon the gods by Pachacuti Inca Yupanqui for help against the Chanca assault on Cuzco, traditionally in 1438. The gods transformed the stones of Pururaucas field into warriors. After the defeat of the Chancas, Pachacuti ordered that the stones should be gathered and distributed among the capital's shrines.

The Moche mural known as the 'Revolt of the Objects' represents another transformational theme – that of everyday objects sprouting limbs and humans with animal heads. This mythical story of the world gone mad and then returned to order was still told in Inca times and recorded by the Spaniards.

SHAMANSIM

This is the term used to describe a person who has special powers, usually aided by hallucinatory plant drugs, to gain access to the spirit world. In ancient Andean cultures the role of the shaman was crucial in everyday life. Priests of the most important temples, including the retainers of the most important oracles and shrines, such as Chavín de Huántar, Pachacamac and the Island of the Sun, were supreme shamans, but every local community would have had their local shaman as well. While the high priests served as intermediaries between the community and the lofty world of the gods, local shamans were consulted for everyday issues such as sickness and fortune.

Above: On a stirrup-spouted vessel, a shaman wearing a jaguar headband and mushroom cap treats a woman with his healing touch.

Shamans in transformational states or in drug-induced states of being have been depicted in Andean cultures from the time of the building of the earliest dedicated ceremonial precincts. Such duality

*Above: The San Pedro cactus (*Trichocereus pachanoi*) was, and is, a rich source of vision-producing mescaline.*

in being is perhaps expressed in the symbolic crossed-hands friezes of the temple walls at Preceramic Period Kotosh. At the Initial Period coastal sites of Garagay, human–animal transformation is depicted in images of insects with human heads, and at Moxeke the earliest representation of shamanic trance may be represented by the adobe sculptures. Spiders with human heads, frequently depicted in the Moche and other cultures, were symbolic as predictors of the future, especially on climatic matters. Moche effigy pots even depict scenes of shamans at work, bent over their patients lying prone before them.

Below: A northern Moche ceramic figurine from the Vicus region shows a shaman clearly in a trance, sporting enhanced feline canines.

The role-taking of humans as deities in scenes of ritual is most famously depicted in the sacrificial scenes on Moche pottery and murals showing the Warrior Priest, Owl Priest and a priestess re-enacting the blood-letting ritual after symbolic combat.

HALLUCINOGENS

Shamanic transformation and trance for curative or special powers was normally induced through the use of hallucinatory plant drugs. The most common hallucinogens were coca leaves (*Erythroxylon coca*), coca incense, the San Pedro cactus (*Trichocereus pachanoi*) (the source of vision-producing mescaline), tobacco and various tropical mushrooms.

Classic characteristics of a hallucinogenic trance are shown in the adobe sculptures of Moxeke and Huaca de los Reyes: jawless lower mouth and/or fangs, flared nostrils and wide eyes with pendent irises. Such symbolic imagery is prolific in Chavín art and widely distributed in the northern and central Andean and coastal regions, and farther south at Karwa (Paracas). Drug-induced stares were woven into the faces of Paracas and Nazca fabrics and on pottery decoration. The faces of countless Moche ceramic effigy vessels and figures in ceramic and mural story scenes reveal otherworldly states of being.

In addition to depictions of various hallucinogenic states, there was a variety of drug paraphernalia, including snuff trays, tubes, pipes and small knives for chopping. Coca leaves were chewed in a complex, many-staged ritual connected to war and sacrifice. Coca was also frequently used, along with *chicha* beer, to drug sacrificial victims before dispatching them.

Drug paraphernalia has frequently been found among grave goods, but a unique cave burial of a local medicine man, herbalist or shaman of the Callahuaya people, dated to the latter half of the 5th century AD, was found near Huari. He was accompanied by the tools of his practice: a wooden snuff tablet decorated with a Tiwanaku 'attendant angel' figure with a trophy head on its chest; a basket with multi-coloured front-facing deity figures; and various herbal plants that would have been used in his trade.

Left: The Moche often displayed shamanic healing rituals in their ceramics. Here a shaman wearing a feline headband prays, probably to the gods, on behalf of a sick or dead person.

CHAPTER TWELVE

A NEW GOD

Conversion of the peoples of Mesoamerica and South America began shortly after Columbus landed on the islands of the Caribbean Sea. Once it was realized that he had not sailed west and reached the Orient, the Christian kings and queens of Spain and Portugal and their clergy saw a ripe new world for conversion to the path of Christ.

Many concepts in Christianity – in this case Spanish Catholicism – were ideas not unfamiliar, superficially, to ancient Andean beliefs. Similarly, Christian priests interpreted various elements in the mythical stories related to them by their converts as aspects of or vague references to Judeo-Christian truth.

Native Andeans were selective in their adoption of Spanish customs and tried to maintain as many of their cherished beliefs as they could. They were accustomed to having foreign gods forced upon them and to incorporating them into their pantheon, for the Incas had been as energetic as the Spaniards in this practice.

Andeans interpreted Christianity in their own way, blending it into their own beliefs, and adapting to incorporate the new 'faith'. The outcome was an 'Andean Catholicism' that persists to the present day. In this way Andeans are 'dual citizens' in the worlds of the past and the present.

Despite great changes in Andean culture during the 500 years after the Spanish Conquest, much of Andean life remains inspired by the ancient concepts of exchange, collectivity, transformation and essence.

Left: An eighteenth-century Spanish colonial Corpus Christi procession. The bearing of the figure on a litter may be a vestige of Inca ancestor worship.

THE MEETING OF TWO GREAT FAITHS

When the Incas were expanding their empire, they had insisted that the state cult of Inti become part of the religion of their subjects. However, ancient Andean religious belief had always had many gods, not just one: there was an overarching creator god (with several regional names), but also many local gods. Belief in the entire landscape as sacred could not deny the relevance of local gods in the development of pre-Inca cultures. So the Incas tried to incorporate all these gods into their cult rather than to exclude them, and to show that the ancient ways and legends were, in fact, part of their own inheritance, and that they were merely the final arbiters.

When their fortunes changed with the arrival of Francisco Pizarro, however, it was the turn of the Incas to be converted. Attempts to convert them and their subject peoples began with Father Valverde, the friar who accompanied Francisco Pizarro on his expedition against Atahualpa. Feigning peace, Pizarro had instructed Valverde to approach Atahualpa brandishing a crucifix and a Bible as they entered the main courtyard of Cajamarca on 15 November 1532. Valverde delivered a speech on Christianity. His words, translated by an interpreter, were said to be understood by Atahualpa, though we can never be sure. Atahualpa certainly understood what he was being asked to do – forsake his own god for another – for when Valverde handed him the Bible he threw it to the ground and replied, pointing at the sun, 'My god still lives.' This declaration refers to the cult of the Sapa Inca, who, as representative and son of Inti, the sun, was worshipped as a deity.

Above: Father Valverde, presumably appalled, had his Bible defiled when Atahualpa allegedly threw it to the ground.

THE CULT OF VIRACOCHA

Before the Inca state cult transferred its focus to the sun god Inti, Viracocha had been the centre of attention and worship. Yet the antiquity and history of the cult of Viracocha is open to debate. What seems clear is that the Inca Viracocha was a combination of elements. The legend of his wanderings gives him the full names of Con Tici (Ticci, Titi or Ticsi) Viracocha Pachayachachic, or Coniraya Viracocha, sometimes including Illya. *Con* was the name of a central coastal creator deity. *Tici* is foundation, beginning or cause. *Ticsi* refers to crystal, *illya* to light. *Pacha* is an element in another coastal creator god, Pachacamac, meaning the universe, time and space. Finally, *yachachic* means teacher.

Viracocha's temple in Cuzco was at Quishuarcancha. Father Bernabé Cobo records that it contained a golden statue of him in human form about the size of a 10-year-old boy. Another Viracocha image was made of textiles and kept in the Temple of the Sun in the Coricancha.

The rise to dominance of Inti over Viracocha occurred during the 15th century, when there was a power struggle in Cuzco. The dispute was between the Inca

Below: This engraving fancifully depicts an offering to Inti, the Inca sun god. The kneeling man may represent a Catholic priest.

Above: The Spaniards symbolically built the Church of Santo Domingo on the foundations of the Inca sacred Coricancha.

ruler Viracocha (and his chosen heir Inca Urco) and Inca Pachacuti, another of his sons. The history was about 100 years old when Pizarro arrived, and details were obscured by time and by the Incas' obsession with having an official version for the new ruler. However, it cannot be coincidental that Viracocha had the name of the deity ultimately to be displaced and that his supplanter's name was the Quechua word for the revolution of the cycle of time! It was Pachacuti Inca Yupanqui who initiated the installation of the sun cult of Inti and began the rebuilding of Cuzco, the Coricancha Temple and the great Sun Temple of Sacsahuaman.

Among ordinary people the cult of Viracocha was not nearly so prominent as the worship of local deities, especially mountain deities and the earth deity Pacha Mama. The original derivation of *vira* and *cocha* can be traced to Aymara in the Titicaca Basin. In fact, Viracocha became a term used to refer to Spaniards and Christians in general and today is an honorific name for Westerners.

JESUS THE SUN

The Andean equation of Jesus Christ with the sun began in the early colonial period, an association that conformed to their 'former' belief that the Sapa Inca was the son of the sun and their association of Viracocha, creator of the sun and the moon, with Inti. The Christian god and the sun were both celestial deities and their conceptualization was similar.

The sun cult was revived in the 20th century. Today the sun is addressed as Huayna Capac (Young Lord), Hesu Kristu (Jesus Christ), Inti Tayta (Father Sun) and Taytacha (also Jesus Christ), a perfect combination of celestial deity, sun, and father and son.

The equation of the Virgin Mary with Pacha Mama is also colonial. Mary is linked to the moon through the moon's intimate association with the earth and its annual cycles through the agricultural year. The association is most prominent in August, at crop planting. In September the ritual of Coya Raymi (the empress's feast) is held to celebrate its successful completion. The moon is addressed as Mama Quilla (Mother Moon). Women take the active role and issue invitations to men to participate. Women's interest in the crops continues to the December solstice, when young boys take over care of the growing crops and the festival of Capac Raymi is held in honour of the sun.

SHARED BELIEFS

Christian missionaries saw elements in Inca belief that convinced them that they were merely 'lost children' of Christ. Indeed, many Andean religious concepts and Christian beliefs are superficially similar. The Andean concept of dualism – oneness within two – is not unlike the Judeo-Christian trinitarian belief of one within three.

The ultimate creator god Viracocha was a rather remote, overarching deity whose omnipresence was similar to the concept of God the Father. Viracocha's pervading presence throughout the universe was an omnipresent force, not an idol (although, like Christ, he was represented on Earth). Inca stories of a flood and of a single man and woman as progenitors of the human race could be perceived as the essence of Christian truth, if slightly corrupted by the passage of time and errors in record.

The biblical story of creation, in which humans began on earth with a man and a woman created by the supreme deity, resembled Andean belief, which also included a flood that destroyed everything that went before. Plagues and divine retribution were familiar, and sacrifices and gifts to the gods – for example the mass sacrifice at Huaca de la Luna at

Below: In this version of Father Valverde's attempt to convert Atahualpa, Pizarro is depicted kneeling – an unlikely occurrence.

Cerro Blanco to alleviate the effects of an El Niño event – were familiar pleas to the supreme being for help in bearing life's daily burdens.

Similarly, the legend of the wandering beggar Viracocha – as Christ, Son of God, who walked upon the earth and taught the people – was reconciled and incorporated. The ability of Viracocha to walk on water convinced many that Jesus must have come to the New World, perhaps after his resurrection or in a second visitation.

Sacred places of worship were also a familiar idea, including wells, springs and the importance of water. The concept of pilgrimage to sacred sites had been an Andean practice from at least the Early Horizon Chavín Cult. Sacred places as repositories for relics were everywhere in the Andean countryside and in villages, towns and cities. Christian worship and attribution of miraculous powers to saints' bones and pieces of the cross was recognizable.

FAMILIAR BELIEFS

Saints' feast days are celebrated with dances, the performers wearing masks to impersonate saints, much as the ancient Moche blood-sacrifice figures wore deity masks. A stone statue of Viracocha made by the Canas peoples of Cacha in the image of a Spanish priest in long white robes, and Viracocha's calling out of the ancestors, were attributed to the Titicaca Basin deity Tunapa, whom the native chronicler Pachacuti Yamqui believed to be Saint Thomas. Another native chronicler, Guamon Poma, believed Viracocha was Saint Bartholomew.

SHARED SYMBOLS

Ancient Andeans were also comfortable with much of Christian symbolism. Worship involved sacred objects: the cross, the chalice, candles and sacred vestments. The creed was 'kept' and recorded in the Bible. God was the creator and his son was Jesus, who walked the earth and taught. Drugs were used: incense and wine in ceremony and sacred acts. And there was sacrifice, the crucifixion of Jesus Christ, a concept definitely familiar to ancient Andeans.

FINDING COMMON GROUND

Like the Incas, Christian preachers were willing to 'bend' a little in their efforts to convince themselves that their New World converts' beliefs proved that Christian religion had been witnessed throughout the world – that things were always as they were in their Christian world. However, the recorders were the Spaniards themselves, and they were inclined to alter the stories

Above: Ancient Andeans would have recognized the concept of human sacrifice but have had difficulty with the victim being described as the god himself.

they were told to fit preconceived ideas. For example, the three Viracochas (Con Tici, Imaymana and Tocapo) were a perfect triad that could be equated with the Holy Trinity, but what sixteenth-century Spanish priests did not know was that triadism is a concept in many cultures in the world.

In Andean triadism the kin-relationship of father and two sons, or three brothers, is less important than the structure of one principal and two helpers. This form is present in cult histories throughout the Andes. In some versions there is a fourth figure, Taguapaca, who disobeyed the father's instructions and was thrown into the River Desaguadero for his disobedience – the perfect foil of evil destroyed to leave the three principals of the narrative.

One of the ways in which Andean belief has survived is by being combined with Christianity. Some combinations were deliberate, as Spanish priests tried to ease the acceptance of Christianity. Much else was a natural blending of the Andeans' own beliefs with Christian ones: for example the sun is merged with Jesus, the Virgin Mary with Pacha Mama (the earth goddess) and Saint James of Santiago with Illapa.

Below: This puma devouring sinners was an attempt to seduce Native Americans into Christian belief using an Andean symbol.

Right: The Virgin Mary here remarkably resembles an Inca mummy bundle, and even has a staff-holding Inca depicted on her gown.

IMPORTANT DIFFERENCES

Belief in an afterlife is a universal religious concept, though the idea that one's conduct on Earth was partly responsible for the nature of the afterlife was less entrenched in Andean belief. The difference was the Andean concept of *pachacuti*: a great cycle that repeated endlessly through time. Suffering was here on Earth, and the final journey of the spirit after physical death was allied to the Andean concept of essence, and the idea that death was the ultimate stage in life's cycle, with no thought of rebirth.

The concept of a second coming was embraced in Inkarrí, but is fundamentally more concerned with the return of the Incas to their rightful place in the scheme of things, their ingrained belief in *pachacuti* and a destiny to rule, rather than the Christian concept of Christ's return.

Spanish priests were unable to suppress the Inca solar cult: it survived in the central highlands and to the coast at Pachacamac. The sun continued to be a principal deity superior to mountain protector-guardian deities, and two aspects were recognized as daytime-sun, in the sky, and night-time sun, which travelled through the earth overnight. Throughout the highlands, the cults of Inti and Punchao (daytime sun) survived into colonial times and were associated with maize and the potato. In the 1560s a messianic movement called Taqui Onqoy (dancing sickness) revived the ancient *huacas* of Titicaca, Pachacamac and others, perhaps eschewing the sun as associated with the Inca elite, who had been overpowered by the Spaniards.

Ultimately, ancient Andean beliefs could not be reconciled with Christian ones. The connections and parallels were too vague, and there were too many variations in Andean belief. Although there are undoubtedly similarities, they are merely superficial, for the concept of one god was fundamentally alien to ancient Andeans. However, Andeans were happy to keep their ancient religious ideas alongside Christianity, as long as they didn't have to give them up entirely. Thus, the Incas remained true to their belief in an established cycle of life in which they were at the cusp, destined to rule in the name of Inti. They were following the path that was ordained, fulfilling their destiny. Of course, the Spanish conquistadors held a similar belief, but they were conquering in the name of *their* god.

SACRED LOCATIONS

Reverence for sacred locations has never abated in Andean belief. From the powers of mountain gods and Pacha Mama to household deities such as Ekkeko, Andeans believe that offerings to such 'gods' can bring good fortune.

Spanish priests and administrators, focusing on conversion and on the elimination of ancestor cults, only slowly realized the tenacity with which Andean peoples stuck to their essential belief in the sacredness of the local landscape. Such beliefs go back to the foundations of the earliest cultures of the Andes and the first architectural ceremonial centres that mimicked the shapes of the landscape. The destruction of cult objects could not weaken such beliefs.

Andeans continue to regard identifiable stones or rock outcrops near their towns as characters from legendary scenes who have been turned to stone.

The ancient site of Pachacamac is perhaps the most ancient pilgrimage site in use. It persisted in colonial times as a sacred place. The Señor de los Milagros, or Crito Morado, here filled the place of the pre-Hispanic cult. Modern Peruvians visit Pachacamac to make offerings, especially to Pacha Mama.

Below: Tens of thousands of people participate annually in the El Calvario ritual, merging Christian belief and sacred places.

HOUSEHOLD DEITIES

Ekkeko is a case in point. An Aymara deity dating from the Middle Horizon Tiwanaku culture, he was incorporated into Inca religion. Ekkeko household deity figures persisted through colonial times and are kept in households today to bring good luck. They are offered everything from coca leaves to Coca Cola in asking them to bring the household good fortune. The presence of Ekkeko makes every household a 'sacred place'. The use of such deity figures spread in the 1970s to many countries well beyond the Bolivian Altiplano.

Similarly, Inca stone and metal sculptures of plants and animals were considered repositories of health and powers for well-being. They were placed at *huacas* throughout the land. Today, Andeans keep small stones that either resemble animals or plants or have been carved to do so. Known as *inqa*, *inqaychu*, *conopa* or *illa*, they are believed to be gifts from mountain *apus*. Some have been passed down through many generations. Modern versions can be miniature plastic trucks, rubber sandals, cans of drink, money or even passports, and they can be bought at pilgrimage sites before being offered to local deities or saints.

Above: Shrines remained sacred to the Inca. The seated-puma-shaped rock at Qenqo continued to remind the Incas of Viracocha.

Taking an object that belonged to a deceased important person in one's *ayllu* kinship group to that person's favourite place would invoke the person's memory among his descendants and also enhance the power of the sacred place. The act was not merely repetitious, but was meant to build the kin-group's history and link it through time to the present.

HUACA SHRINES

The royal *panaca* and sacred *huacas* of the Inca emperors were especially important to kin-group history. As part of the cult of the Sapa Inca as Inti's representative on earth, when Tupa Yupanqui died, his son Huana Capac visited the places

Above: The Qoyllur Rit'i ritual, begun after an alleged 18th-century miracle, revives the ancient Andean concept of ritual procession.

his father liked best, especially in Cajamarca, and built shrines at them. One tradition in the history of Inca origins describes Mount Huanacauri as the 'father' of the three founding ancestors, who were turned into stone around Cuzco. Even today, some Andeans regard local *huacas* in their region 'like parents'. Such places were believed to have given rise to their ancestors, and local caves were often where Andeans stored the mummified remains of ancestors until they were destroyed in colonial times by the Spaniards. Substantial evidence for provincial shrine systems like those around Cuzco – for example colonial records – is sparse, however, and probably awaits discovery by ethnohistorians.

Below: This Qoyllur Rit'i procession is to the sacred Mt Sinakara, where Mariano herded his llamas and met the mestizo boy.

QOYLLUR RIT'I

One of the most celebrated 'modern' festivals involving place is Qoyllur Rit'i in the southern Andes, attended annually by tens of thousands of people. Held during the three weeks leading to the feast of Corpus Christi, the ritual is focused on several sanctuaries around Ocongate. Costumed dancers perform in honour of 'El Señor'.

The ritual is a typical mixture of ancient and Christian beliefs. The object of devotion is an image of Christ that miraculously appeared on a rock: El Señor de Qoyllur Rit'i (Lord of the Snow Star). The ritual began in the late 18th century, when the Catholic authorities replaced an indigenous cult with a Christian shrine. The Catholic Church officially accepted the miraculous appearance of Christ's image.

The ancient cult associated Ocongate as a venue of worship at the transition and regeneration of the new year. The blending of Christian and ancient belief revolves around the miracle in which a young llama herder, Mariano, encountered a mestizo boy on Mount Sinakara. Mariano was cold and hungry and the other boy shared his food. Mariano's herd increased and his father offered him new clothes as a reward. Mariano asked for new clothes for his friend too. He took the mestizo boy's poncho to market to have it duplicated. The Bishop of Cuzco noted the old poncho's fine material and asked Mariano about the mestizo. Church officials sent to meet him encountered him wearing a white tunic, surrounded by a blinding radiance emanating from a silhouette When one official tried to touch it, he grasped a *tayanka* bush, above which, on a rock, appeared the image of Christ crucified. Mariano fell dead and was buried at the foot of the rock where the image appeared. A chapel was built to house the Tanyaka Cross and Mariano's sepulchre. Christ Tanyaka is believed to have been transformed into the rock, and the Catholic Church later had Christ's image painted on the rock-face.

Below: Husband and wife believers burn incense and make an offering to Pacha Mama in a ceremony in the La Paz Valley.

PROCESSIONS, FESTIVALS AND RITES

Architectural forms and sculptures in mud plaster and stone show that processions, ritual festivals and sacred rites were a part of ancient Andean culture.

Left: The Nazca even made clay models of ancient processions, including a central shaman.

ANCIENT PROCESSIONS

Ancient Andeans were intimately familiar with the concept of sacred routes. Cuzco alone had more than 300 sacred shrines along sacred *ceque* routes, ranging from monumental buildings to natural features. So important were processional routes to the Incas that archaeologists project their use to as far back as the Initial Period, suggesting that processions through U-shaped ceremonial precincts proceeded down into and through sunken courts, back out of them, and up on to temple platforms mimicking mountains, to honour earth and sky deities.

The established purpose of the famous Nazca desert lines – geoglyphs – was for ritual processions that followed the course of the lines. Geoglyphs of animals, birds or geometric patterns consist of a single line that never crosses itself. There are also nodes from which lines radiate.

The tradition of *ceque* routes made Christian processional routes, such as the Stations of the Cross, easy to comprehend.

Below: The 'festival' of Inti Raymi, the Inca June/winter solstice, attracts large crowds and is taken seriously to revive ancient Inca pageantry at the shrine of Sacsahuaman.

Pilgrimage to holy shrines was also a common ancient Andean practice. Similarly, ancient Andean sacrificial practices made recognition of the apparent ritual execution of Christ a familiar concept.

The Qoyllur Rit'i ritual involves processions by two groups representing the warm lands of the north-west (from Paucartambo town) and the colder pasture land of the south-east (from Quispicanchis town). The procession represents ancient Andean regional opposition and mutual exchange, and even linguistic dualism, for the Paucartambos are Quechua speakers while the Quispicanchis speak Aymara.

FEAST DAYS

Just as early Christians in a pagan Europe adapted and combined many feast days and ceremonies into the Christian calendar as their religion spread, so Christian Andeans have equated many ancient Andean ceremonial days to established Christian dates.

The recitation of the myth-histories of founding ancestors in provincial communities was made at annual high points such as planting (Pocoymita) and harvesting (Caruaymita), both of which became associated with Christian holy days. Ancient Andeans began to harvest their various crops in mid-April, and finished the collection and storage of produce by early June. These activities coincided with the disappearance of the Pleiades constellation in the night sky in April and its June reappearance above the horizon. The Pleiades were called *collca* ('storehouse') by the Incas, and ancient Andeans regarded it as the celestial container of the essence of all agricultural produce. With the arrival of Christianity, the movable feast of Corpus Christi soon became equated with the rising of the Pleiades at the same time as the rising of the sun.

Festivals mixing ancient Andean ritual with Christian practice and dates are those of Capac Raymi (December summer solstice) and Inti Raymi (June winter solstice), and the revival of the ritual re-enactment of the founding of Cuzco by Manco Capac, celebrated annually.

Such rituals can be regarded as a rejuvenation of ancient belief and power, which would have been understandable

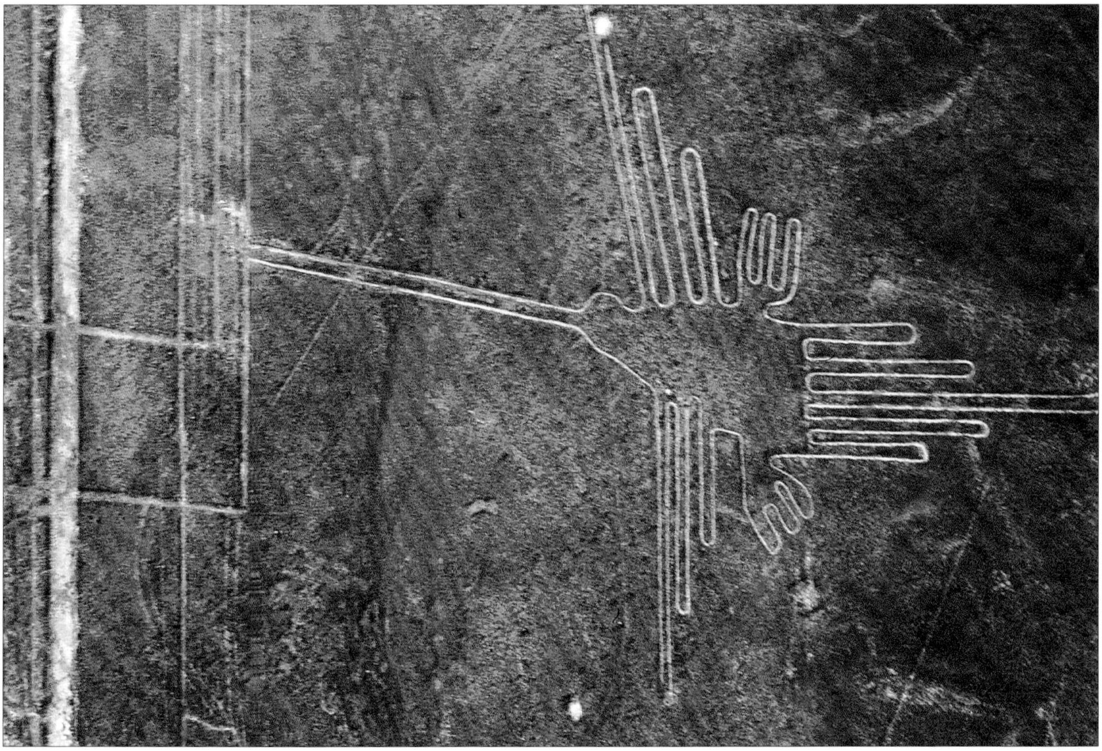

Above: Humming bird in the Nazca desert. Geoglyph lines were thought of as processional pathways, perhaps 'owned' by kin groups.

in an atmosphere and perception of powerlessness against hundreds of years of colonial oppression.

DEEDS OF THE ANCESTORS

When the first Spaniards entered Cuzco they witnessed the arrangement of the mummified Inca emperors in the main plaza. The keepers of Inca history, the *amautas* and *harahuicus*, were responsible for collating the histories and deeds of the emperors. On ritual occasions, it was their task to recite these histories in the forms of short stories by the former and poems by the latter, incorporating stylistic devices such as set speeches, repeated metaphor and refrains intentionally reshaped and elaborated from one performance to the next.

Occasions for such performances included the initiation rites of teenage boys as adults during the month leading up to Capac Raymi (late November–December), the summer solstice. The boys visited the peaks in the southern Cuzco Valley where the Inca ancestors stopped on their route to Cuzco. Other occasions were at the celebration of military victories, royal successions and, of course, royal funerals.

It was Inca Pahcacuti, religious reformer and initiator of the cult of Inti, who ordered that 'songs' (*cantares* in the Spanish chronicles) were sung by the attendants of the imperial 'statues' (ancestor mummies and *huauques*) at 'fiestas'. The performance began with the deeds of Manco Capac, the founder ancestor, and proceeded through the emperors up to the reigning Sapa Inca. Colonial records describe such performances of myth-histories in provincial centres as well.

STAMPING OUT IDOLATRY

Priests and Spanish administrators fought a continuing battle against what they regarded as idolatry, as manifested in the cults and virtual worship of the mummified remains of *ayllu* founders and ancestors. They ruthlessly hunted down and tried the perpetrators of ancestor cults and burned their mummified ancestors, until by the end of the 16th century all were destroyed.

In the eyes of the Incas, the Spaniards were equally wicked in their treatment of Inti. The great golden sun disc that hung in the Coricancha had been awarded to one of the conquistadors, who promptly gambled it away in a late-night card game – thus the Andean expression 'to gamble the sun before dawn'.

REVIVALS

Many Inca rites and processions have been revived, especially in the late 20th century. Based, as were their ancestors, primarily on an agricultural way of life, Native South American descendants and mestizos seek to alleviate the hardships of life by continuing to honour traditional belief in the sacredness of the land of their forefathers and to reconcile this with modern life.

ANIMISM AND COCA

Animism was fundamental in ancient Andean religion: the forces of nature were and are believed to be 'living beings' that affect life. Humans were only one group of beings among animals and plants. The images of supernatural beings based on living animals, such as the jaguar, snakes, predatory birds and spiders, and the depiction of transformation, reveal such belief. Animals were thought to possess powers and wisdom that could benefit humans, and certain humans, the shamans, were capable of shape-shifting to become, temporarily, the animal in question and take on the animal's nature.

Below: This Moche spouted vessel displays an intoxicated shaman, holding his wooden stick and coca container to make coca balls.

THE LIVING EARTH

Agriculture was fundamental to ancient Andean civilization and still forms the basis of most of Andean society. Agricultural fertility is therefore deeply ingrained in the Andean psyche, and with it worship of Pacha Mama – the living earth – and the natural elements. Ceremonial rites to Pacha Mama, the matrix for all life, continue to be performed regularly throughout the year, highlighted on important dates in agriculture, and also when visiting sacred places and at the start of a long journey. At harvest ceremonies, young women impersonate Pacha Mama Suyrumama by wearing long red dresses ('mother earth of the long dress that drags along the ground').

The field called Ayllipampa, near Cuzco, is dedicated to Pacha Mama. Bernabé Cobo described how farmers worshipped her at stone altars containing miniature women's clothing in the middle of the field. Other deities associated with Pachcmama are Mama Oca, Mama Coca and Mama Sara (Maize Mother). Central Andeans continue to maintain that the Inca ancestress Mama Huaco, who sowed the first maize field, and others sustain the agricultural well-being of the community. The field of Sausero outside Cuzco was dedicated to her.

Agricultural ferility is also believed to be affected by mountain *apu* deities and celestial gods, including Illapa (lightning and thunder), Cuichu (rainbow) and Ccoa (a supernatural feline who causes destructive hail).

THE POWER OF *CHICHA*

Today, rural *ayllus* continue to plough and plant communal fields at festivals. There are contests to see who can work fastest at ploughing and planting the largest amount of land. Festive meals are served, accompanied by plenty of *chicha* or maize beer. There are *chicha* libations and offerings of coca to Pacha Mama, the community ancestors and the local sacred places, alongside Christian prayers to the community's patron saints, who seem to have taken the place of the ancestors.

Above: Continuing ancient practice, a modern Peruvian makes an offering of coca leaves to a local deity or saint.

Llamas are ritually honoured in August. They are force-fed a *chicha*, barley and herbal mash to intoxicate them before being released on to the Altiplano, followed by their equally intoxicated herders singing and playing flutes. Such ritual drunkenness is believed to enhance fertility. Libations are poured to invite Pacha Mama and the *apus* to the celebrations. Intoxication also blurs the distinction between humans, animals and the landscape as they all 'dance together'.

SACRIFICE BEHIND THE ALTAR

Ancient sacrifices and offerings continued in secrecy well into Spanish colonial times. Although known as the 'sacrifice behind the altar' syndrome, this is not to be taken literally, as the sacrifices and offerings simply occurred in remote places away from churches. Animal sacrifices, together with offerings of agricultural produce and coca, and the burning of incense with prayers are still practised, often alongside offerings of modern 'western' products such as cigarettes and Coca Cola, and also often in connection with Christian ceremonies.

Above: Native South Americans and cholos *(people of Spanish descent) in a Christian-native ceremony at El Calvario, Bolivia.*

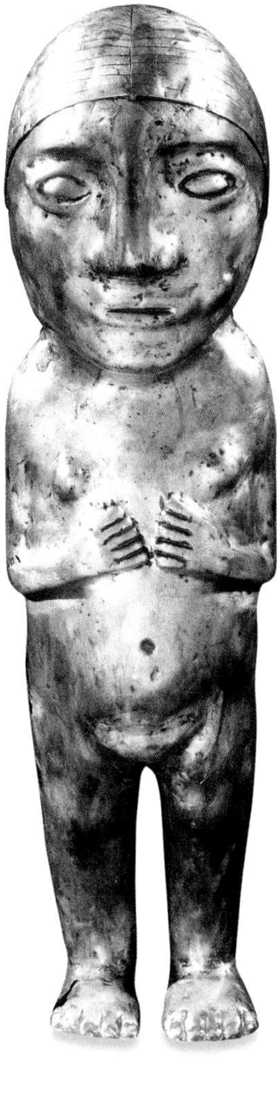

Left: A silver figurine depicts a woman with puffed cheeks, chewing a coca wad, which induces stamina and suppresses hunger.

Mountains (especially volcanoes), caves and springs remain particularly sacred. Mountains continue to be regarded as the dwelling places of the ancestral dead.

The fundamental Andean cosmological frame remains an anchor to Andean society: the sun rises over the sacred mountains in the east, brings life, and sets in the west, the final resting place of the dead.

SHAMANS

Local shamanism also still has an important place in local communities. For everyday illnesses, many Andeans consult their local *curandero*, a person skilled in the use of herbs and potions, harking back to the 5th-century AD Wari cave burial of a herbalist. Shaman-curers were frequently depicted in Moche and other effigy vessels.

Cures include the use of water and perfume exhaled over a (looted) skull from a pre-Hispanic burial, in the belief that the spirit of the deceased person will protect the afflicted as well as the curer from evil interventions. Potent hallucinogenic mescaline brews are still made from the San Pedro cactus. Chants and prayers used in such cures are a mixture of pre-Hispanic and Christian practices. Sticks, which represent swords, are used to fight with the spirits of 'the other world' and keep them from harming the patient. As in ancient times, the shaman acts as an intermediary between the human and spirit worlds.

COCA

The regular chewing of coca leaves continues as a stimulant and aid in coping with the harsh climate and high Andean altitudes. The Spaniards quickly learned its properties of keeping otherwise exhausted labourers and miners energized, and exploited its perceived sacred symbolic power as, once again, their Christian convictions were compromised by practical needs. Coca cultivation increased under Spanish rule. Coca leaves are a frequent offering to Pacha Mama especially, and there is irony in their 'integration' from ancient use to modern times, for the leaf is referred to as Hostia (the Host) and its ritual consumption compared to Holy Communion.

Coca remains a major part of the Andean indigenous economy and is, of course, exploited internationally in its refinement for the drug trade.

THE RETURN OF THE INCAS

Twentieth-century social studies of Andean culture have discovered an underlying theme that represents a source of post-Conquest cross-Andean unity: the theme of the dying and reviving Inca, as encapsulated in the legend of Inkarrí.

THE FIVE AGES

A late Inca cosmology comprised a five-age sequence of the creation of the Inca world. The First Age was ruled by Viracocha and the other gods, and death was unknown. The Second Age was that of the giants created by Viracocha, who worshipped him but who displeased him and were destroyed by a flood. The Third Age was inhabited by the first humans, again created by Viracocha, but they lived on a primitive level and lacked even the rudiments of civilization. The Fourth Age was that of the *Auca Runa* ('the warriors'), to whom Viracocha presumably imparted the arts of civilization, for these were the creators of the early civilizations such as the Moche and the Tiwanaku.

Below: After unsuccessful revolts against Spanish rule, the legend grew that the Incas retreated east into the rainforest to Paititi.

The Fifth Age was that of the Incas themselves, who spread civilization far and wide through conquest. The Fifth Age ended with the coming of the Spaniards and with the downfall of the Inca Empire, but upon their arrival the Spaniards were hailed as the returning emissaries of the creator and were referred to as *viracochas* – a term still used as one of respect.

THE STORY OF INKARRÍ

Inkarrí is the central character in a post-Spanish Conquest Inca millenarian belief in the 'dying and reviving Inca'. The derivation of the name itself is a combination of the Quechua word *Inca* and the Spanish word *rey*, both meaning 'king' or 'ruler'. The legend foretells a time when the current sufferings of the original peoples of the Andes will be ended in a cataclysmic transformation of the world, in which the Spanish overlords will be destroyed. The true Inca will be resurrected and reinstated in his rightful place as supreme ruler, and prosperity and justice will be returned to the world.

A typical example of one of the versions of the Inkarrí myth recounts how Inkarrí was the son of a savage woman

Above: A modern Peruvian impersonates the Sapa Inca at the festival of Inti Raymi. It is believed that the emperor will one day return.

and Father Sun. Inkarrí was powerful. He harnessed the sun, his father, and the very wind itself. He drove stones with a whip, ordered them around, and founded a city called K'ellk'ata, probably Cuzco. Then he threw a golden rod from a mountaintop, but found that the city did not fit on the plain where it landed, so he moved the city to its present location. When the Spaniards arrived, however, they imprisoned Inkarrí in a secret place, and his head is all that remains. However, Inkarrí is growing a new body and will return when he is whole again.

PACHACUTI

Belief in the return of Inkarrí is clearly in keeping with the Andean concept of *pachacuti*, the revolution or reversal of time and space. It arose from the native populations' sense that the Spaniards had created oppression and injustice. It may hark back to events of the first few

Right: Tupac Amaru, the 'last Inca emperor', was beheaded in Cuzco's central plaza. His head was spirited away and secretly buried.

decades after the Spanish Conquest, in which the last Inca emperor, Atahualpa, was believed to have been beheaded by Francisco Pizarro shortly after his defeat, and to the beheading of Tupac Amaru, a claimant to the Inca throne, who led an unsuccessful revolt against Spanish rule in the 1560s and 1570s. In different accounts, the two heads were taken to Lima or to Cuzco, but in both cases the belief is that, once buried in the ground, the head becomes a seed that rejoins its body in anticipation of return.

THE RETURN TO CUZCO

Another belief concerns the removal of Inca power to a hidden land. The legend records that upon being expelled from Cuzco the Incas travelled east through the mountains. They built bridges as they went, but they placed enchantments on their route so that no one could follow. If they did, the enchantment caused them to fall asleep on the spot for ever.

Below: The retreating Incas built enchanted bridges as they went, so that their route could not be followed.

The Incas travelled across the mountains into the jungle and established a hidden city called Paititi. Here they remain in hiding. 'Foreigners' who seek Paititi can never find it. One found a talking bridge; when he tried to cross it, he was chased away by huge felines and *amarus* (mythical serpent-dragons) guarding the bridge.

According to the legend, *pachacuti* will turn and the Inca will return, following the route they used when they left Cuzco. There will be tremendous hail and lightning, wind and earthquakes. *Amarus* will roar from mountains and mestizos will be chased away. When the Incas return they will recognize only their *runakuna* descendants, who wear traditional llama-wool clothing, and the Incas will assume their rightful place and rule again.

GLOSSARY

acllas chosen women, picked to serve in the state cult of Inti
acllahuasi special buildings where *acllas* were housed
amarus mythical serpent-dragons
amautas also *harahuicus* Inca record-keepers
andones hillside terraces
apacheta special type of *huaca* – a stone cairn on a mountain pass or at a crossroads
apu sacred deity who lives on a mountain top, or the mountain top itself
aridenes cultivation terraces
atl-atl spear thrower
auca treasonous enemy of the state
audiencias small divisions within Chan Chan *ciudadela*
ayar legendary ancestors of the Incas
ayllu a kinship group or division with mutual obligations to other *ayllus*
ayni the principle that governed cyclicity
capacocha specially selected sacrificial victim
ceque sighting line or sacred pathway leading from Cuzco

chachapuma puma-headed person
chicha beer made from maize
chullpa tower where the Colla people put mummified remains, and into which more could be added
ciudadela Chimú walled compound at Chan Chan
collca storehouse
curaca leader/official
curandero person skilled in the use of herbs and potions
hanan upper
huaca sacred place – a natural, man-made or modified natural feature
huaca adatorio sanctuary or temple
huaca sepultura burial place of the most important deceased individuals
huanca stone(s) regarded as the petrified ancestor of a people or *apu*
huauques man-made statues – doubles – made in the image of the ruling Sapa Incas and other chiefs and nobles during their lifetimes
hurin lower
idolatrías Spanish Colonial documents written as reports of the Spaniards' investigations of idolatrous practices among the native peoples
inqa (also *inqaychu, conopa* or *illa*) small stones that either resemble animals or plants or have been carved to do so, believed to be gifts from mountain *apus*
intihuatana a 'hitching post of the sun' – special *huaca* of Inti
kalanka rectangular hall used for public functions
kancha residential building
kero a drinking cup, especially for *chicha*, made from wood, pottery, gold or silver
mallquis mummified founding ancestor, Inca emperor or local leader
mama female
mit'a labour service/tax
mitamaes peoples redistributed within an empire
mitamaq the redistribution of people
montaña forested slopes of the Andes
moza commoner/outsider
napa miniature llama figurine
pacarina the place of origin, the place from which one's ancestors (one's tribe, nation or *ayllu* kinship group) emerged
pachacuti a turning over/revolution/a cycle of the world
pampa vast prairie in South America south of the Amazon
panaca kinship group; the royal panaca was the Inca *ayars*
plazas hundidas plazas or sunken courts
puna sierra basin or valley
qhaqha person or animal killed by lightning
quipu system of knotted bundles of string of different colours, used for recording information
quipucamayoqs knot-makers (i.e. makers and keepers of *quipus*)
runakuna Inca descendants who wear traditional llama-wool clothing
runaquipu-camayoc a census recorder
suyu quarter of the Inca Empire
tambo a way-station, which was used to accommodate pilgrims
tocoyrikoq provincial governor
topacusi golden cup or vessel
tumbaga amalgamated precious metals
tumi crescent-shaped knife used for ritual bloodletting or decapitation
wasi covered chamber
yanacona a selected court retainer
yaya male

INDEX

I would like to dedicate this book to my wife Anne, daughter Megan and son Sam.

This edition is published by Lorenz Books, an imprint of Anness Publishing Ltd, Blaby Road, Wigston, Leicestershire LE18 4SE; info@anness.com

www.lorenzbooks.com; www.annesspublishing.com

Anness Publishing has a new picture agency outlet for images for publishing, promotions or advertising. Please visit our website www.practicalpictures.com for more information.

A CIP catalogue record for this book is available from the British Library.

Publisher: Joanna Lorenz
Editor: Joy Wotton
Designers: Nigel Partridge and Adelle Morris
Illustrators: Anthony Duke, Rob Highton and Vanessa Card
Production Controller: Steve Lang

PUBLISHER'S NOTE

Although the advice and information in this book are believed to be accurate and true at the time of going to press, neither the authors nor the publisher can accept any legal responsibility or liability for any errors or omissions that may have been made.

PICTURE ACKNOWLEDGEMENTS

The Ancient Art and Architecture Collection: 5.5, 6bl, 8bl, 25tl, 25br, 37bl, 65bl, 81, 82bl, 90bl, 93bm, 111tl, 119tr, 153tr, 160bl, 161bl, 163tl, 191tr, 214-215, 216tr, 223bl, 228tr.

The Art Archive: /Album/J. Enrique Molina: 204, 219t, 224bl, 233tr, /Alcazar, Seville/Dagli Orti: 12tr, /Amano Museum, Lima/Album/J. Enrique Molina: 234bl, /Amano Museum, Lima/Dagli Orti: 5br, 145tm, /Amano Museum, Lima/Mireille Vautier: 141bl, 224tr, /Archaeological Museum, Lima/Album/J. Enrique Molina: 220bl, /Archaeological Museum, Lima/Dagli Orti: 25tm, 78, 84, 85tm, 126–7, 132bl, 136bl, 142bl, 142tr, 147bm, 154bl, 179tr, 179bm, 180, 188bl, 217br, 229, 230bl, 244tr, /Archaeological Museum, Lima/Mireille Vautier: 135bl, 159bl, 203tr, 234tr, 246bl, /Archbishops Palace Museum, Cuzco/ Mireille Vautier: 210tl, /Arteaga Collection, Peru/Mireille Vautier: 151br, 210br, /Biblioteca Nazionale Marciana, Venice/Dagli Orti: 39tl, /Bibliotheque des Arts Decoratifs, Paris/Dagli Orti: 238bl, /Stephanie Colasanti: 160tr, 165tr, 169t, 211tm, 211br, 239tl, 244bl, /Dagli Orti: 4.4, 4.5, 5.1, 26tr, 44tr, 60bl, 74–5, 80bl, 88, 94-95, 102bl, 105tr, 114bl, 128-129, 133bl, 134tr, 135tr, 144tr, 150, 162bl, 162br, 166bl, 166tr, 169br, 170bl, 171bl, 172tr, 176tr, 177t, 178bl, 190, 192bl, 193bl, 195t, 200tr, 213br, 220tr, 242tr, /Chavez Ballon Collection, Lima/Mireille Vautier: 194tr, /Gold Museum, Lima/ Mireille Vautier: 185, /La Gringa Collection/Mireille Vautier: 137br, /Money Museum, Potosi, Bolivia/Mireille Vautier: 241tr, /Musee du Chateau de Versailles/Dagli Orti: 13tr, /Museo Banco de Guayaquil, Ecuador/Dagli Orti: 5.3, 174–5, /Museo Ciudad, Mexico/Dagli Orti: 18tr, /Museo de Arte Colonial de Santa Catalina, Cuzco/Dagli Orti: 240, /Museo de Arte Municipal, Lima/Dagli Orti: 231, /Museo del Banco Central de Reserva, Lima/Dagli Orti: 235bl, /Museo del Oro, Lima/Dagli Orti: 113bm, 134bl, 141tr, 221, 227br, 228bl, /Museo Nacional de Historica, Lima/Mireille Vautier: 249tr, /Museo Nacional Tiahuanacu, La Paz, Bolivia/Dagli Orti: 24ml, 120tr, /Museo Pedro de Osma, Lima/Dagli Orti: 5.6, 236–7, /Museo Pedro de Osma, Lima/Mireille Vautier: 27tr, 35tr, 106tr, 208tr, 209bl, /Museo Regional de Ica, Peru/Dagli Orti: 183, /Museum Larco Herra, Lima/Album/J. Enrique Molina: 178tm, /Navy Historical Service, Vincennes, France/Dagli Orti: 18bl, /Science Academy, Lisbon/ Dagli Orti: 15, /University Museum, Cuzco/Mireille Vautier: 36tr, 121br, 158bl, 159tr, 176bl, /Mireille Vautier: 227tl, 238tr, 247bl.

Andrew McLeod: 6tr, 25bl, 26tm, 27bm, 27br, 140tm, 161tr, 250tm, 252bm, 253bm, 255br, 255tr, 256br, 256tl.

Sally Phillips: 7bl, 25bm, 26br, 102tr, 158tr, 253tl, 254bl.

Frances Reynolds: 25tr, 26bl, 27tm, 27bl, 46tr, 47tl, 68tr, 107tr, 125br, 250br, 251tr.

Nick Saunders: 21tr, 26bm, 27tl, 35bl, 38bl, 58bl, 61bl, 62tr, 65tr, 70tr, 89tr, 117tl, 121t, 147tr, 156tr, 162tr, 164bl, 171tr, 173br, 186, 194bl, 198bl, 208bl, 222t, 225, 235tl, 241bl, 245.

South American Pictures: 12bl, 13bl, 14bl, 16bl, 31bl, 34tr, 36bl, 37tr, 39br, 40bl, 40tr, 41tr, 69tl, 72tr, 93tr, 107bl, 122bl, 124tr, 137tl, 192tr, 198tr, 199bl, 205bl, 219br, 226tr, 230tr, 233bl, 239br, 250bl, 251br, 252tl, 253tr, 254tm /Danny Aeberhard: 53tr, /Ann Bailetti: 116tr, /Phillipa Bowles: 59t, /Hilary Bradt: 73, /Britt Dyer: 62bl, /Robert Francis: 48tr, 87bl, 91bm, 112tr, /Steve Harrison: 55bl, /Jason P. Howe: 248tr, /Kathy Jarvis: 4.2, 4.3, 20tr, 22–3, 26tl, 33, 42–3, 44bl, 45tl, 56–7, 63br, 82tm, 82br, 83tl, 83br, 105bl, 143tr, 145br, /Joseph Martin: 38tr, /Kimball Morrison: 177br, /Marion Morrison: 60tr, 101br, 200bl, /Tony Morrison: 1, 2, 4br, 4.1, 5.4, 8tr, 9tl, 10-11, 14tr, 19bl, 19tr, 20bl, 21bl, 28-29, 30bl, 30tr, 32bl, 32tr, 34bl, 41b, 46bl, 47br, 47tr, 48bl, 49bl, 49tr, 50tr, 51bl, 52bl, 52tr, 53bl, 54bl, 58tr, 59br, 61tr, 64bl, 66tr, 67tr, 71, 85bl, 85br, 86bl, 87tr, 89bl, 90tr, 91t, 92bl, 96, 98tr, 100tr, 101tl, 103br, 106b, 110tr, 111br, 113t, 114tr, 115br, 116bl, 117br, 118bl, 119bl, 123, 124bl, 130bl, 130tr, 131tr, 132tr, 138, 140b, 144bl, 146bl, 156bl, 157tl, 157br, 163br, 164tr, 165bl, 167tr, 167bl, 170tr, 173tl, 178br, 181b, 182bl, 184bl, 188tr, 191bl, 195bm, 196-197, 199tr, 201t, 202bl, 202tr, 203bl, 205tr, 206bl, 206tr, 207bl, 207tr, 212bl, 213tl, 216bl, 217tl, 222bm, 242bl, 243br, 246tr, 247tr, 248bl, 249bl, /Kim Richardson: 243t, 243bl, /Peter Ryley: 67bl, /Chris Sharp: 9br, 64tr, 77br, 99, 218tr, /Karen Ward: 55tr, 63tl.

Werner Forman Archive: 24tr, 122tr, 133tr, 139tl, /British Museum, London: 16tr, 68bl, 112bl, 139br, 154tr, / Dallas Museum of Art, Dallas: 3, 86tr, 87tl, 131bl, 223tr, /David Bernstein Collection, New York: 4.6, 108-109, 110bl, 118tr, 136tr, 146r, 152tr, 182tr, /Guggenheim Museum, New York: 54tr, /Maxwell Museum of Anthropology, Albuquerque, NM: 76bl, 77tl, /Museum fur Volkerkunde, Berlin: 17, 69br, 79tr, 100bl, 125tl, 153bl, 187bl, 189tl, 189br, 201bl, 218bl, 226bl, 232, 235br, /Private Collection: 5.2, 79bl, 148–9, 153br, 155bl, /Royal Museum of Art & History, Brussels: 184tr.

p.1 Carved Inca face. p. 2 Winay Wayna. p.3 Moche effigy jar Above: Sacsayhuaman. Left: Runkuaqay.